T0341739

THEORY *of the* LYRIC

THEORY
of the LYRIC

Jonathan Culler

Harvard University Press

Cambridge, Massachusetts

London, England

Copyright © 2015 by Jonathan Culler
All rights reserved
Printed in the United States of America
First Harvard University Press paperback edition, 2017
First printing

Library of Congress Cataloging-in-Publication Data

Culler, Jonathan D., author.
Theory of the lyric / Jonathan Culler.
pages cm
Includes bibliographical references and index.
ISBN 978-0-674-74426-4 (cloth : alk. paper)
ISBN 978-0-674-97970-3 (pbk.)
1. Lyric poetry—History and criticism. I. Title.
PN1356.C845 2015
809.1'4—dc23
2014039998

Contents

Preface

This project originated in my fascination with lyrics' strange way of addressing time, winds, urns, trees, or the dead and asking them to do something or to stop doing what they are doing. From the Greeks to the moderns, poets call on a universe they hope will prove responsive, and their demands often prove seductive. What is at issue here? What do such strange ways of speaking tell us about the investments and ambitions of lyric poetry and how we should approach it?

In 1975 I wrote an essay on the figure of apostrophe, in which I argued that this strange habit of address was central to the lyric tradition—the epitome of everything most daring and potentially embarrassing in lyric. That essay, the seed from which this project eventually developed, was a break with my own training in the New Criticism, where close attention to the language of literary works focused on elements that most contribute to a complex interpretation of the poem, and where, since questions of tone were extremely important—"What is the speaker's tone of voice here?"—apostrophes were neglected: they are so distinctly poetic, so unlike ordinary speech or meditation, that they do not help identify a tone recognizable from our usual experience. Apostrophes are set aside or, at best, treated as conventional marks of emotional intensity, but there they are, in the poems. What do they tell us?

Earlier that year I had published *Structuralist Poetics,* showing what recent French theory could contribute to the study of literature, and urging that literary study should be devoted not to developing new and more intricate interpretations of literary works but to exploring the underlying structures and conventions that enable literary works to have the meanings and effects they do for readers—in short, that poetics should take precedence over hermeneutics. My essay on apostrophe was a contribution to poetics, certainly, yet different from what I had undertaken in *Structuralist Poetics.* There, in a chapter called "Poetics of the Lyric," I was concerned above all with the moves by which readers generate interpretations when confronted with a poem. I saw poetics as an attempt to make explicit the moves of the interpretive process, to systematize the operations of literary criticism. My essay on apostrophe, on the other hand, though I did not realize it at the time, was no longer oriented by the New Critical assumption that poems exist to be interpreted. It sought, rather, to explore the most unsettling and intriguing aspects of lyric language and the different sorts of seductive effects that lyric may achieve.

My early work on lyric address provides the foundation for the broader, more comprehensive investigation that I undertake here, exploring other aspects of lyric that entice readers. But above all, I attempt to work out a general framework, a theory of the lyric, in which attention to these features of lyric is encouraged and not restricted by one of the narrow models of lyric that have in recent years organized most approaches to lyric poetry.

The study of literature has for some time championed the production of more intricate, more sophisticated, more complex interpretations of literary works. Much of the criticism that results is of great interest, but I have found it gratifying to turn aside from such aims. Here I do not aim to complicate but rather to focus on some of the most appealing poems of the Western lyric tradition without presuming to develop new interpretations: registering the sorts of pleasures they offer, highlighting the strangeness of their linguistic acts, identifying their distinctive rhetorical strategies, and trying to offer some account of the range of historical possibilities that they make available.

Since this project originated in work on apostrophe many years ago, I cannot thank all those who found this work interesting and offered further examples, comments, and criticism, but there are specific debts I can acknowledge. I owe special thanks to the various classicists who through the years have looked at my writing on the Greek and Latin lyric and, without warning me off their turf, offered suggestions and encouragement: Fred Ahl, Alessandro Barchiesi, Neil Bernstein, Gregson Davis, Michele Lowrie, Richard Neer, Sarah Nooter, Mark Payne, Hayden Pelliccia, and Pietro Pucci. They cannot, of course, be blamed for my errors, which Allison Boex has worked to prevent.

The library resources at Cornell University and at the Bibliothèque nationale de France have been crucial to this project, and I am indebted to the librarians at the American Academy in Rome and of the National Humanities Center. I am particularly grateful to Geoffrey Harpham and the staff at the National Humanities Center—the ideal place to work on a manuscript—and to the late Stephen Weiss, donor of its M. H. Abrams Fellowship, which I was privileged to hold. I am also indebted to Mike Abrams himself for his example and his friendship over the years.

Aspects of this project have spanned so many years and led to talks at so many universities and conferences that I cannot hope to thank all those who have made useful comments or objections that compelled me to reconsider my arguments. I wish to single out Michel Murat, who invited me to deliver some of this material in a series of seminars at the École normale supérieure in Paris; Paul Downes, Robert Gibbs and their colleagues at the University of Toronto, for inviting me to give the Alexander Lectures on this topic; and Ortwin de Graef, who brought me to the University of Leuven to teach an intensive course on theory of the lyric. Michael Sheringham's invitation to deliver the Zaharoff Lecture at Oxford was a special honor, since an earlier lecture in this series was Paul Valéry's "Poésie et pensée abstraite," which has been important to this project.

I am grateful to friends and colleagues who have read and generously responded to some of these materials in recent years, including Derek Attridge, Walter Cohen, Heather Dubrow, Paul Fleming, Roger Gilbert, Jennie Jackson, Richard Klein, Marjorie Levinson, Joannie Makowski, Clive Scott, and Lytle Shaw. I want particularly to thank Debra

Fried, with whom I have taught lyric poetry, and whose knowledge and standards of argument are difficult to live up to. Simon Jarvis and Jehan Ramazani offered useful advice in their review of the manuscript for the press. Cynthia Chase has enriched this project with almost forty years of conversation, discriminating judgments of poetry and criticism, and a careful reading of the manuscript. I offer thanks to the graduate students and research assistants with whom I have worked on the lyric through the years, especially Bob Baker, Sunjay Sharma, the late, much regretted Alan Young Bryant, and Klas Molde, whose dissertation on lyric enchantment and disenchantment came along just too late for me to benefit fully from it. For reading and commenting on drafts, I thank my former students Ben Glaser, Seth Perlow, and, above all, Avery Slater, who worked through multiple drafts. Avery's advice was crucial to the final execution of the project and I owe much to her assiduous questioning and her ability always to imagine that the book could be better—through which these pages have been greatly improved.

Portions of Chapter 5 appeared in "Apostrophe," Copyright © 1977 Cornell University. This article was first published in *diacritics* 7.4 (1977), 59–69. Reprinted with permission by Johns Hopkins University Press.

In Chapter 6 the diagram of Northrop Frye's mapping of the lyric is reprinted from Robert D. Denham, "Northrop Frye and Critical Method," figure 22, "Thematic Conventions of the Lyric," p. 123. Available at http://fryeblog.blog.lib.mcmaster.ca/critical-method/theory-of-genres .html. Reprinted by permission of Robert Denham.

THEORY *of the* LYRIC

Introduction

L yric poetry has a long history in the West but an uncertain generic status. The great comparatist Earl Miner concludes, "Lyric is the foundation genre for the poetics or systematic literary assumptions of cultures throughout the world. Only Western poetics differs. Even the major civilizations that have not shown a need to develop a systematic poetics (the Islamic, for instance) have demonstrably based their ideas of literature on lyric assumptions." And he adds, "The first thing to be said of lyric poetic systems is that they are not mimetic."[1] One might argue that it is for quite contingent reasons—the fact that Aristotle wrote a treatise on mimetic poetry, poetry as an imitation of action, and not on the other poetic forms that were central to Greek culture—that Western literary theory has neglected the lyric and, until the romantic era, treated it as a miscellaneous collection of minor forms, despite the flourishing of lyric in ancient Rome, the Middle Ages, and the Renaissance. Lyric was finally made one of three fundamental genres during the romantic period, when a more vigorous and highly developed conception of the individual subject made it possible to conceive of lyric as mimetic: an imitation of the experience of the subject. Distinguished by its mode of enunciation, where the poet

1

speaks *in propria persona,* lyric becomes the subjective form, with drama and epic as alternately the objective and the mixed forms, depending on the theorist. Hegel gives the fullest expression to the romantic theory of the lyric, whose distinguishing feature is the centrality of subjectivity coming to consciousness of itself through experience and reflection. The lyric poet absorbs into himself the external world and stamps it with inner consciousness, and the unity of the poem is provided by this subjectivity.

This conception of the lyric, as representation of subjective experience, while widely disseminated and influential, no longer has great currency in the academic world. It has been replaced by a variant which treats the lyric not as mimesis of the experience of the poet but as a representation of the action of a fictional speaker: in this account, the lyric is spoken by a persona, whose situation and motivation one needs to reconstruct. This has become the dominant model in the pedagogy of the lyric in the Anglo-American world, if not elsewhere. Students are asked, when confronting a poem, to work out who is speaking, in what circumstances, to what end, and to chart the drama of attitudes that the poem captures. In effect, the dramatic monologue, which puts on stage a character speaking to a defined audience or to him- or herself, has been made the model for lyric, which becomes the fictional imitation or representation of a real-world speech act. Of course, many great poems in the English tradition are dramatic monologues, and it is possible to read other lyrics in this way, but even in those cases this model deflects attention from what is most singular, most mind-blowing even, in those lyrics, and puts readers on a prosaic, novelizing track: the reader looks for a speaker who can be treated as a character in a novel, whose situation and motives one must reconstruct. This model gives students a clear task but it is extraordinarily limited and limiting. It leads to neglect of the most salient features of many lyrics, which are not to be found in ordinary speech acts—from rhythm and sound patterning to intertextual relations.

Lyric was once central to the experience of literature and to literary education, but it has been eclipsed by the novel, perhaps in part because we lack an adequate theory of the lyric. Even in the age of high theory, despite the interest in the linguistic analysis of poetic language, theoretical accounts of the lyric tended to be negative ones, designed to contrast with the real objects of theoretical interest. From Mikhail Bakhtin, who treated lyric as monological, in contrast with the rich dialogism of the novel, to Roland Barthes, for whom lyric sought to destroy language rather than engage with it in the potent experimental practices of the *nouveau roman* or other forms of prose, important theorists failed to develop a rich theoretical discourse about lyric, or of poetry in general, for that matter.[2] One result of the centrality of the novel to theoretical discourse as well as to literary experience and literary education has been the development of a novelizing account of the lyric that fails to respond to what is most extravagant and most distinctive about it.

The immediate impetus of this project, then, is critical: to investigate the inadequacies of current models and to explore alternatives by examining possibilities inherent in the Western lyric tradition. Current models falsify the long tradition of lyric and encourage students to think about lyrics in ways that neglect some of the central features of lyric poetry, both present and past. Since the goal is a more accurate and capacious account of the lyric, I do not attempt a broad survey of theories of the lyric but engage only those that seem particularly influential or promise to contribute to a better model. The latter range from ancient conceptions of lyric as a form of epideictic discourse (the rhetoric of praise or blame, focused on what is to be valued) to modern proposals to consider lyric as "thought-writing": writing thoughts for readers to articulate. An underlying question is what would be the criteria for an adequate theory of the lyric.

A major obstacle to the project of a theory of the lyric is the historicist presumption of much literary criticism today, especially criticism focused on the classical era, the Renaissance, or the nineteenth century. For such criticism, any broad claim is an illicit imposition that neglects the historical particularities of each era. The poet of ancient Greece singing or chanting with the accompaniment of a lyre to an audience on a specific occasion is very different from the Elizabethan courtier composing sonnets for circulation among aristocratic friends vying for patronage, and also from the modern poet composing verses for a volume to be published by a university press. How could there possibly be an account of lyric that encompassed these incompatible practices?

There are two answers to such a challenge. The first is that poets themselves, reading and responding to predecessors, have created a lyric tradition that persists across historical periods and radical changes in circumstances of production and transmission. Horace, adapting Greek meters for Latin verse, aspired to join the company of the *lyrici vates,* the nine canonical lyric poets of ancient Greece, even though the major Greek lyricist closest to him in time, Pindar, had died over 400 years earlier. Horace was as far removed from Sappho as we are from Petrarch and as far from Pindar as we are from Tasso. Horace himself was a model for poets from Petrarch to Auden, and Pindar inspired the lyric tradition of the ode in Western Europe. The vitality of the Petrarchan tradition right up to the twentieth century requires no comment, and Sappho became the model of the "poetess" in Victorian England. Ezra Pound's attempt to revive Troubadour poetry must be regarded as unsuccessful, but it testifies to the pertinence of an ongoing lyric tradition, despite great variation in the situations of aspiring and successful poets.

Moreover, a striking feature of the history of literary forms is that, unlike social and political history, it is reversible. We cannot return to earlier sociopolitical configurations, but poets can revive old forms, exploiting possibilities that have lain dormant for a while. "Poets can at any time resurrect them in their original form, a modernized version, or in a deeply intra-generic or intertextual manner: even extinct volcanoes are really only very dormant."[3] Who could have expected the villanelle and the sestina to resurface as they did in the twentieth century?[4] Lyric forms are not confined to one historical period but remain available as possibilities in different eras. A successful account of the lyric will highlight features that connect poems in the lyric tradition with one another and will also make possible descriptions of the evolution and transformation of the genre—not so easy with either the romantic model or the model of lyric as dramatic monologue. A theory of the lyric would, among other things, give us something of which to write the history.

A second, perhaps even more compelling response to the historicist critique of the possibility of a theory of the lyric is pedagogical. If students are not presented with an adequate model of lyric, they will read according to whatever inadequate models they have previously assimilated, whether from explicit accounts or halting surmise. A major goal of this project, then, is to develop a conception of lyric that is more adequate to the exploration of the most successful effects of lyrics of all periods. We need to provide students and other readers with a better model of the lyric in order to make possible a richer, more perceptive experience of lyrics. A different framework for thinking about lyric will prevent many poems from appearing to be failed examples of a dramatic monologue or a lyric of personal expression.

A further goal here is to combat what I take to be an unnecessary presumption of much lyric theory and pedagogy: that the goal of reading a lyric is to produce a new interpretation. This is a recent development in the history of poetry. In prior centuries readers expected poems to teach and delight; students were not asked to work out the sort of interpretations now deemed proof of serious study. They might parse, imitate, translate, memorize, evaluate, or identify allusions and rhetorical or prosodic strategies, but interpretation in the modern sense was not part of literary engagement until the twentieth century, and writers and readers may not have been greatly the worse for it. They could acquire knowledge of the tradition and develop considerable expertise and power of discrimination without assuming that the goal of engagement with poetry was producing interpretations. In sum, readers appreciated poems much as we do songs. We listen to songs without assuming that we should develop interpretations: we take them to illuminate the world, and we sing them to others or to ourselves, point out what we like about them, compare them to other songs by the same and different artists, and generally develop considerable connoisseurship about songs without engaging in interpretation. We might do well to ponder the fact that time has brought no falling off in love of song, while the presumption that poems exist to be interpreted has accompanied a diminution of interest in the lyric.

Of course, readers will still puzzle over poems and tease out their implications, much as I do in the chapters that follow. Since lyrics illuminate or interpret the world for us, we should be interested in what they mean, and this can demand careful attention, but it would be beneficial for literary studies and for the fortunes of poetry generally if all other ways of engaging with poems were not subordinated to interpretation.[5] Poetics and hermeneutics may be difficult to separate in practice, but in theory they are quite distinct: they come at literature from opposite directions. Given a text, hermeneutics wants to find the meaning. This may involve a wide range of activities, from biographical criticism, which seeks to discover what the author might have meant, to symptomatic readings which engage the work through an interpretive language, whether humanist, Marxist, psychoanalytic, mythic, sociopolitical, deconstructive, or historicist. The goal is to discover a meaning, and these are target languages into which lyrics can be translated. Poetics works in the opposite direction, asking what are the conventions that enable this work to have the sorts of meanings and effects it does for readers. It does not attempt to find a meaning but to understand the techniques that make meaning possible, techniques that belong to the generic tradition.

In practice, as I say, the two enterprises blend into each other, as the pages that follow will amply demonstrate. Although this is, above all, a project in poetics, reflecting on the nature of lyric and its range of possibilities, I do not resist offering interpretive remarks when I have a thought that seems worthwhile. Still, I am not attempting to develop new and ingenious interpretations so much as taking note of what this or that poem seems to accomplish and relating that to the techniques that I am exploring. At any rate, I believe that poetics' emphasis on the lyric tradition and the variety of its resources might help encourage more fruitful and pleasurable engagement with poetry.

I am not trying to develop a theory that treats all lyrics as instances of something in particular, whether a linguistic disposition or a deep psychic need. Nor am I trying to tell people how to decide whether something is a lyric or not; I start from a series of hypercanonical lyrics of the Western tradition and seek to identify their salient features.[6] What are the issues that arise from these poems? What are the parameters on which they differ? I take it as a working hypothesis that there is a lyric tradition and that an attempt to understand it and the central features of poems within it is not only crucial for the reading and appreciation of these poems themselves but crucial also to an understanding of revolts against the tradition and the consequent modifications and expansions of it. The features I identify in the lyrics I discuss do not constitute a checklist for deciding what is a lyric, but rather a system of possibilities that underlie the tradition and that ought to be borne in mind when reading poems that may have a relation to this tradition. And of course many features of lyrics are present also in other literary genres: none are restricted to lyric alone, even when they are especially characteristic of the lyric. Nor do I have firm views on how much modern poetry should count as lyric: many twentieth-century poets have denounced the idea of lyric and its fore-grounding of mellifluous voicing, and some have doubtless succeeded in producing work that needs to be read according to different principles; but reactions against the lyric tradition also gain meaning from that tradition. This is a topic that requires discussion rather than dogmatic claims about what counts as lyric and what does not.

Working from a selection of the most famous poems from different periods and language, the first chapter identifies important aspects of the lyric. The second takes up the notion of lyric as a genre and the history of thinking about this genre. Without indulging in lengthy discussion of genre theory, I sketch a conception of genre as a historical and critical construct that is both descriptive of affinities among texts and constitutive of critical understanding. I also consider more specific arguments that lyric is not a genre or a dubious one at best. Chapter 3 evaluates a number of theoretical accounts of the lyric in seeking to move toward a superior, more capacious theoretical framework. Hegel, as I mentioned, provides the most prominent theory of the lyric as a fundamentally subjective form, but his account has strengths that have often been neglected. In attempting to modernize Hegel's theory by recasting it in linguistic terms, Käte Hamburger distinguishes lyric utterance from fictional discourse. To claim that lyric is not, at bottom, a form of fiction seems a significant advance and in particular helps to identify the disadvantages of the most prominent current theory of lyric, which treats the poem as the speech act of a fictional persona: the fictional imitation of a real-world speech act. Possibilities for an alternative model that treats lyric as fundamentally nonmimetic, non-fictional, a distinctive linguistic event,can be drawn from classical conceptions of lyric as encomiastic or epideictic discourse—discourse of praise of blame, articulating values, not a species of fiction. Lyric, I conclude, involves a tension between ritualistic and fictional elements—between formal elements that provide meaning and structure and serve as instructions for performance and those that work to represent character or event.

Chapters 4 and 5 discuss two major aspects of this ritualistic dimension of lyric. Everyone recognizes the importance of rhythm to lyric, but the topic has been neglected, except in technical studies of prosody, because of criticism's overwhelming focus on interpretation. Unless rhythmical or metrical features directly affect the interpretation of a poem, they drop out of sight. This chapter seeks above all to highlight the importance of rhythm, repetition, and sound patterning as independent elements that need not be subordinated to meaning and whose significance may even lie in a resistance to semantic recuperation.

The other major contributor to the ritualistic aspect of lyric is lyric address, at its most spectacular and blatant in the invocation of absent or nonhuman addressees. My account of the lyric grants major importance to its characteristic indirection, which I call "triangulated address": addressing the audience of readers by addressing or pretending to address someone or something else, a lover, a god, natural forces, or personified abstractions. Such address is not confined to vatic or romantic verse but animates both classical and modern lyrics, and it can function in a range of ways. Disrupting narrative, invocation, or address makes the poem an event in the lyric present rather than the representation of a past event. The tension between the lyrical positing of an addressable and potentially responsive universe and skepticism about the efficacy of lyric discourse is a determining feature of a wide range of Western lyrics.

Starting with Northrop Frye's mapping of the domain of lyric, Chapter 6 examines the major oppositions that structure his account and my own, focusing on the relation between *melos* and *opsis* or "babble" and "doodle," sound patterning and visual patterning, then on the tension between song and story, the ritualistic and the fictional. What are some of the ways in which lyrics assimilate or deal with fictionality? The dramatic monologue, which is distinguished from other types of lyric, projects a fictional speaker. The other main strain of fictionality in lyric is narrative, which lyrics have ways of framing or subsuming, with distinctive temporal strategies. One of the major tasks of a poetics of the lyric is the identification of different structures deployed in addressing and illuminating the world.

The final chapter takes up the question of the relations of lyric to the sociopolitical world, where there is, of course, great historical variation, but also great indeterminacy, since the social efficacy of lyrics is difficult to estimate, even retrospectively, and depends to a considerable extent on the resourcefulness of critical discourse. Lyric can be a form of social action, which contributes to the construction of a world and works to resist other forms of world-making carried out by instrumental rationality and reified common sense, but the range of possibilities and the difficulty of determining what effects lyrics have is very great. I conclude with discussion of Theodor W. Adorno's famous claim that lyric has a utopian function that does not depend on overt social content, and with some examples in familiar lyrics of the subtle interplay of ideology and its deconstruction.

I begin, as I say, not with some attempt to deduce a model of the lyric from the nature of language or subjectivity or representation, but with a series of examples, in order to highlight some continuities and some of the most salient features of lyrics. My examples are among the most canonical lyrics of the Western tradition: from Sappho, Horace, Petrarch, Goethe, Leopardi, Baudelaire, Lorca, Williams, and Ashbery.[7] Though there are many circumstances in which enlarging the canon or attending to hitherto marginalized texts is the right strategy, when reflecting on the nature of the lyric there is a compelling argument for focusing on a series of texts that would be hard to exclude from lyric and that have played a role in the constitution of that tradition. What aspects of poems such as these does an account of lyric need to address?

In a project of this scope the writer can only acknowledge great unevenness, due to the accidents of my own linguistic competencies, acquaintance with poems and poets, and vagaries of attention. Since I have thought it important to offer concrete examples of each poetic phenomenon I discuss, I have tried to avoid obscure poems that might seem to have been tendentiously chosen and to stick with known works by very canonical poets, but the somewhat random character of these choices will doubtless strike readers. Though I cite poets from several European languages, the predominance of English has been unavoidable.

One of the most important functions of a theory of the lyric or a general model of lyric—a default model, shall we say—is to highlight aspects of lyric poetry that current conceptions have neglected, underlining connections between lyric practices of the past and lyrics of recent centuries. The goal of the theory of the lyric I am proposing is to displace inadequate models and replace them with a more pertinent and perspicacious account that does justice to the possibilities inherent in the tradition. In sum, the theory of the lyric is an enterprise of correction and rectification that offers resources for future engagement with lyric poetry.

ONE

An Inductive Approach

To identify and explore aspects of the lyric that are likely to be important for a theory of the lyric I begin not with definitions but with prototypes: celebrated poems in various languages and from different moments of the Western lyric tradition that can instantiate its proclivities and possibilities.

1. Nine Poems

A splendid, paradigmatic instance of lyric is the only complete poem by Sappho, who for the tradition functions as the lyric poet par excellence, as Homer is the epic poet. Her "Ode to Aphrodite" is a remarkable poem.

Ποικιλόφρον' ἀθανάτ' Ἀφρόδιτα,
παῖ Δίος δολόπλοκε, λίσσομαί σε,
μή μ' ἄσαισι μηδ' ὀνίαισι δάμνα,
        πότνια, θῦμον·

ἀλλὰ τυίδ' ἔλθ', αἴ ποτα κἀτέρωτα
τὰς ἔμας αὔδας ἀΐοισα πήλοι

ἔκλυες, πάτρος δὲ δόμον λίποισα
       χρύσιον ἦλθες

ἄρμ' ὑπασδεύξαισα· κάλοι δέ σ' ἄγον
ὤκεες στροῦθοι περὶ γᾶς μελαίνας
πύκνα δίννεντες πτέρ' ἀπ' ὠράνωΐθε-
       ρος διὰ μέσσω·

αἶψα δ' ἐξίκοντο· σὺ δ', ὦ μάκαιρα,
μειδιαίσαισ' ἀθανάτῳ προσώπῳ,
ἦρε' ὄττι δηὖτε πέπονθα κὤττι
       δηὖτε κάλημμι,

κὤττι μοι μάλιστα θέλω γένεσθαι
μαινόλᾳ θύμῳ· τίνα δηὖτε πείθω
ἄψ σ' ἄγην ἐς σὰν φιλότατα; τίς σ', ὦ
       Ψάπφ', ἀδικήει;

καὶ γὰρ αἰ φεύγει, ταχέως διώξει,
αἰ δὲ δῶρα μὴ δέκετ', ἀλλὰ δώσει,
αἰ δὲ μὴ φίλει, ταχέως φιλήσει
       κωὐκ ἐθέλοισα.

ἔλθε μοι καὶ νῦν, χαλέπαν δὲ λῦσον
ἐκ μερίμναν, ὄσσα δέ μοι τέλεσσαι
θῦμος ἰμέρρει, τέλεσον· σὺ δ' αὔτα
       σύμμαχος ἔσσο.

☞

Intricate, immortal Aphrodite,
snare-weaver, child of Zeus, I implore you,
do not tame my spirit, great lady,
with pain and sorrow.

But come to me now, if ever before you
heard my voice from afar and,
leaving your father's house,
yoked golden chariot and came.

Beautiful sparrows swiftly brought you
over the dark earth, with a quick flutter
of wings from the sky's height through the clean air.
They were quick in coming.

You, blessed goddess, a smile on your divine face,
asked what did I suffer, once again this time,
and why did I call, once again this time,

and what did I in my frenzied heart
most want to happen. Whom am I
to persuade, once again this time,
to lead to your affection.
Who, O Sappho, does you wrong?

For one who flees will soon pursue,
one who rejects gifts will soon be making
offers, and one who does not love will soon
be loving, even against her will.

Come to me even now,
release me from these mean anxieties,
and do what my heart wants done.
You yourself be my ally.[1]

Sappho's one complete poem is extraordinarily complex: an address to Aphrodite in which Aphrodite, in turn, is represented as addressing Sappho. With the proliferation, as in a fun-house mirror, of several Aphrodites (the present addressee, the past addressee, the figure descending, and the temporary speaker) and of Sapphos (the present petitioner, the past addressee of the goddess, and the petitioner at still earlier times mentioned in the goddess's past address), this poem "makes the rest of Greek lyric appear, by contrast, relatively single-minded."[2]

Invoking the goddess, the poem follows conventions of prayer in beginning with the attributes and parentage of the goddess and mentioning past occasions on which aid was forthcoming, but "the solemn conventions of prayer are set to the melodies of popular song, so that the meter itself seems to comment saucily on the matter. Worse yet, a final military

image (*symmakhos,* ally in battle) is marshaled in such a way as to make
the whole performance appear to poke fun at masculine battle-prayers."
In any event, it is not an ordinary prayer: with the extravagance often characteristic of lyric, it includes an account of Aphrodite's past visits that
strikes a surprising note: not just "you have helped me in the past," but
"a smile on your divine face, you asked what did I suffer this time [*dēute*],
and why did I call this time." The speaker's appeal represents past visits
as already involving Aphrodite's wry allusion to still previous appeals and
visits. Her smile accompanies the gentle mockery of the verses, signaling
amusement rather than anger or exasperation in its "what, you are calling
me again? what is it this time?" Anne Carson writes of this key term *dēute,*
"the particle *dē* marks a lively perception in the present moment: 'Look
at that now!' The adverb *aute* peers past the present moment to a pattern
of repeated actions stretching behind it: 'Not for the first time!' *Dē* places
you in time and emphasizes that placement: *now. Aute* intercepts 'now'
and binds it into a history of '*thens.*'"[3] We are thus engaged in a structure
of regress and repetition, where when called in the past Aphrodite already
responded, "what, not again!" "who is doing you wrong?" and offered
as consolation a law of repetition and reversal: "if she flees, she shall soon
pursue." Whether this invoking of what will happen to her who resists
love is something of a spell, an attempt to conjure this result by representing
the goddess as saying it, or whether the implication is that Aphrodite, responding to Sappho's request for aid, will, as she put it in the past, *persuade* the new beloved, once Sappho identifies her, or whether Aphrodite when she descends simply reminds Sappho of a law of desire, the result
is represented as ineluctable, so that Aphrodite seems to have answered
Sappho's appeal.

Especially powerful and seductive in the representation of Aphrodite's
response is the transition from reported speech to direct discourse (from
"You, blessed goddess, . . . asked / what did I suffer, once again this time,"
to "Whom am I to persuade, once again this time, / to lead to your affection. Who, O Sappho, does you wrong?"). The Greek does not use the
quotation marks that are inserted in modern editions, so the transition is
made by the play of pronouns, as Sappho passes from *I* to *you* and Aphrodite from *you* to *I,* and then back again at the end. This transition displays for us the stakes of apostrophic address—the wish, seldom realized

in the later lyric, that entities addressed might in their turn respond. It is especially effective to present such a delicate, amused response from the past—which carries more authority than would a response reported in the present ("and then you come and you say to me . . .").

The combination of the insistence on repetition—*deute*—and the sliding between reported speech and direct discourse creates the remarkable effect of an appearance by Aphrodite *in the present,* even though the poem claims to represent the appearance and the speech of past occasions. As the goddess shifts into the present and future of "Whom am I to persuade, once again this time? / . . . Who, O Sappho, does you wrong?" we seem to have Aphrodite present and speaking now in the moment of the poem's utterance. The speech event narrated happens not only then but also now—in every instance of "this time" as the poem is performed. Readers experience her speech as if she were already here, fulfilling the request.

This poem is not the product of a ritual occasion (though it alludes to such rituals of invocation). The double consciousness, the intricate-mindedness that inserts in the prayer to the goddess the amused chiding by that goddess is a great strength of the poem, and it illustrates that the institution of lyric composition already, in Sappho's day, allows a highly complex composition. Mikhail Bakhtin treats poetry as monological, reserving dialogism for the novel, but here at the beginning of the lyric tradition, we find dialogism. Marshall Brown writes of lyric, "dialogue is precisely what the lyric counterpoint of voices provides. Whether we call it music, suggestiveness, or haunting, the interior distance achieved by lyric is an opening onto a dynamic mental space whose power has often been felt, even if it is rarely formulated."[4]

This lyric is neither the direct expression of a subjectivity newly discovered nor the ritual expression of community values. Even at this early date, "the institution of lyric composition," John Winkler writes, "was strong enough to occasion her songs as songs."[5] And these songs were repeatedly performed by others as far away as Athens, where Solon was supposedly so enraptured by a song of hers sung by his nephew at a symposium that he expressed the desire to learn this song and die.[6] What makes a poem induce one to learn it by heart, as we say, and how does this relate to its character as event? How is the singularity of the poem's event-ness connected to the poem's provocation or the seduction that makes one want not only to repeat it but to be able to repeat it at will?

For us, it is striking that this originary lyric seems intricately performative. Literary theorists have welcomed the notion of performative language, language which accomplishes the act to which it refers, as in "I hereby call the meeting to order," because it transforms the linguistic terrain: literature becomes no longer a marginal and derivative linguistic practice, a set of pseudo-assertions, but can claim a place among creative and world-changing modes of language that bring into being that to which they refer or accomplish that of which they speak.[7] The notion of the performative poses important problems, which I discuss in Chapter 3, but it can help describe cases like this, as when a request to Aphrodite to appear is formulated so as to create the impression that she is doing so.

Whether or not this poem might be called performative in accomplishing what it describes, at the very least its management of time and voice is powerfully efficacious, suggesting that what it asks—attention to the tribulations of love—is at the moment being granted, as we experience the seductive force of Sappho's Aphroditean art. The address to Aphrodite is a remarkably intricate poetic speech act: a performance of poetic invocation of the spirit of love, which gives a face and voice to this powerful force and performatively accomplishes what it seeks, while persuading listeners to a more complex attitude toward love—more complex than the speaker represents herself as holding. The invocation of Aphrodite seems to succeed and offers us, even, a certain confidence in love, with the double perspective that the poem proposes: each new encounter with love is a different, possibly agonizing experience for the sufferer, but for the goddess each is the repetition of a pattern—the one who flees now will necessarily become a pursuer when she is older—a pattern the poem offers us as a law of the world. Encouraging the acquisition of this sort of intricate-mindedness, the poem brilliantly gives its readers the dual perspective of Aphrodite's amused but sympathetic declaration of repetition and "Sappho's" immersion in the intensity of the now. The essential mystery of the lyric, Brown writes, "is its way of being of two minds."[8]

This example gives us lyric as performance and event, as a public act of what I call "triangulated address"—speaking to listeners through an apostrophic address to an absent power. In its consummate success, it provides a model for lyric—albeit one that later lyrics will find it difficult to live up to.

We encounter, in this poem at the beginning of the Western lyric tradition, a number of features that are germane to a theory of the Western lyric. First, there is a complexity of the enunciative apparatus. Although articulated in the first person, this is anything but a straightforward statement by a speaker. Here we already find both the centrality of the act of addressing or invoking another and the self-reflexive putting-into-play of the status of that other, as often happens with apostrophe. Second, the hyperbolic or extravagant character of this invocation of the other, which here takes the form of the multiplication of discourse and perspectives of the other, makes the poem not the fictional representation of an experience or an event so much as an attempt to be itself an event. Third, the poem's allusions to a context of ritual foreground the question of the poem's own ritualistic character as spell or chant, confirmed by various forms of repetition, including metrical patterns, and what is called "ring structure," the return at the end to the request of the beginning. Fourth, the poem is optative; articulating desire, it allows itself to imagine a response to its call or address and works to constitute an active relationship to what might be resistant and other, even if that relation brings destruction, as happens in later lyrics. And finally, this poem, with its deictic apparatus of the here-and-now of enunciation and other rhetorical structures, presenting itself as an event in a time that repeats, creates for us effects of presence that will henceforth be one of the fundamental possibilities of lyric and links value to that mortal time that Jacques Derrida calls "living on," not to some kind of transcendence of mortality.[9]

When we move from Greece to Rome, we encounter Horace, who adapted Greek meters to Latin and aspired to be placed among the nine *lyrici vates,* the canonical Greek lyric poets, as he says in the first of his Odes. "No other lyricist has possessed the idea of his genre so completely," writes Ralph Johnson in *The Idea of Lyric.*[10] Although his poems are written for circulation in manuscript, he presents himself as a singer to the lyre, affirming a relation to the tradition. One of his most famous odes warns of the dangers of love.

Quis multa gracilis te puer in rosa
perfusus liquidis urget odoribus
    grato, Pyrrha, sub antro?
        cui flavam religas comam,

simplex munditiis? heu, quotiens fidem
mutatosque deos flebit, et aspera
    nigris aequora ventis
        emirabitur insolens,

qui nunc te fruitur credulus aurea;
qui semper vacuam, semper amabilem
    sperat, nescius aurae
        fallacis! miseri, quibus

intemptata nites! me tabula sacer
votiva paries indicat uvida
    suspendisse potenti
        vestimenta maris deo.

What slim youngster drenched in perfumes
is hugging you now, Pyrrha, on a bed of roses
    deep in your lovely cave? For whom
        are you tying up your blonde hair?
You're so elegant and simple. Many's the time
he'll weep at your faithlessness and the changing gods,
    and be amazed at seas
        roughened by black winds,
but now in all innocence he enjoys your golden beauty
and imagines you always available, always loveable,
    not knowing about treacherous breezes—
        I pity poor devils who have no experience of you
and are dazzled by your radiance. As for me,
the tablet on the temple wall announces
    that I have dedicated my dripping clothes
        to the god who rules the sea.

                    [*Odes* 1.5, trans. David West]

The ode's final lines allude to the custom that survivors of shipwrecks dedicate their clothes to Poseidon, as does this survivor of the storms of love.

This is a poem whose "now" evokes a present of enunciation or discourse, but also possibly a scene, a here and now. It is a poem that could be read as the fictional representation of a speech act, and indeed it has been so read, as critics speculate on the speaker's relation to Pyrrha, the circumstances of the utterance, and the motives in addressing her thus, as if we were dealing with characters in a novel. "We meet a speaker," writes William Anderson, "who watches with imprecise emotion an obvious courtesan named Pyrrha and an inexperienced young man whose name is unknown to the speaker."[11] But is this a scene of voyeurism? The speech event that the poem might fictionally represent is hard to reconstruct. Where does it take place, for instance? And why would the speaker say this to Pyrrha? Is the speaker supposed to have stumbled upon Pyrrha in a cave, being amorously pressed by a gracile youth unknown to him? Presumably not, but if we posit that he encounters Pyrrha elsewhere, in the street, for instance, it is hard to imagine the motivation for the question, "What slim youngster . . . / is hugging you now?" Or if we take this as a wittily hyperbolic version of "so who are you seeing these days?" then it is hard to imagine the circumstances or rationale for the comments that follow, which would be better addressed to a young man. This is especially true given the *order* of the comments about this young lover: one might imagine someone saying, "I'm sure he is dazzled by your radiance now, not realizing that the future will bring storms," but the converse— "Many's the time / he'll weep at your faithlessness" though he be "dazzled" now—seems much more like musing about the vicissitudes of love than an utterance to the woman on a specific occasion. The poem would seem to make more sense if we take it as an act of *poetic address:* writing which imagines the addressee as it imagines the gracile youth, with his present excitement and his future disappointments; an act of poetic address which produces in the lyric present a vivid reflection on the vicissitudes of love.

The poem has also been read by classicists as a public utterance, of the sort that would be recited at a dinner, a vivid and knowing commentary addressed to a male audience. The rhetorical intent of the poem, argues Gregson Davis, is "disapprobation, not of the beautiful *hetaira,* but rather of the immature lover." He is naïve and a slow learner, who will be disappointed many times.[12] Whom does the poem seek to persuade or warn? The slim youth? Since he is not addressed at all, but pitied, as one of many "miseri," perhaps it is aimed at all those "poor devils" who don't anticipate the storms that will come. They can be conceived as part of the audience which the poem would persuade to adopt the attitude that the speaking voice projects of knowledgeable wariness. Pyrrha is elegant and not to be shunned; the youth should enjoy himself now, but not get too involved, for reversals will occur, suffering will follow, as we should wisely know. Here lyric takes upon itself the task of vividly imagining a future that carries present lessons for its readers or hearers.

In our two examples so far the intricacy of the apostrophic gesture and, in Sappho's case, the embedded prosopopoeia (making the addressee speak) prevent the poems from being adequately read as a fictional imitation of a real-world speech act, but of course the first does produce a speaker-character named Sappho and the second gives us an "I" whose judgments are presented as wisdom. The production of first-person speakers has been central to the lyric tradition—so much so that one recent argument by Paul Allen Miller ties lyric and what it calls "lyric consciousness" to the lyric sequence, inaugurated by Catullus, and exemplified first by the Latin love elegy, where poems discontinuously project an internally conflicted first-person speaker.[13] Reading the sequence, we put together a speaker with a conflicted inner life and contradictory reflections on the experience of love.

It seems implausible to derive the lyric from the discontinuous subject emerging from lyric sequences, since Greek lyrics precede the sequence, most lyrics are not part of sequences, and the consumption of entire sequences is a form of academic study more than of lyric reading, which has always sampled sequences for favorite poems. But let us consider the opening poem of Petrarch's *Canzoniere*, his world-changing sequence:

Voi ch'ascoltate in rime sparse il suono
di quei sospiri ond'io nudriva 'l core
in sul mio primo giovenile errore
quand'era in parte altr'uom da quel ch'i' sono,

del vario stile in ch'io piango et ragiono
fra le vane speranze e 'l van dolore,
ove sia chi per prova intenda amore,
spero trovar pietà, non che perdono.
Ma ben veggio or sì come al popol tutto
favola fui gran tempo, onde sovente
di me mesdesmo meco mi vergogno;
et del mio vaneggiar vergogna è 'l frutto,
e 'l pentersi, e 'l conoscer chiaramente
che quanto piace al mondo è breve sogno.

You who hear within these scattered verses,
the sound of sighs on which I fed my heart,
in my first errant youthful days, when I
in part was not the man I am today;
For all the modes in which I weep and speak,
between vain hope and vain suffering,
I hope to find pity and forgiveness,
from those who know love through experience.
Yet I see clearly now I have become
for a long time the talk of people all around, so that
it often makes me ashamed of myself;
and the fruit of my vanities is shame,
and remorse, and the clear knowledge
that worldly joy is but a fleeting dream.

[Trans. Mark Musa, modified]

This sonnet addresses the reader, though address to the beloved or to love is more common in this collection, which establishes the convention of the absent beloved (and hence a certain complexity of address or invocation). In its address to the reader it evokes the temporality of lyric, linked to an unlocated present of discourse—"You who hear" and "the man I am"—the present of discourse dominates a past of anecdote.[14] Lyric here is figured, very accurately, as what the Petrarchan tradition in fact became,

a repertoire of discursive possibilities: complaint, praise, hope, and suffering, relating inner and outer worlds. While this poem declares the
singularity of an individual experience of love—vain hopes and vain
sorrows—and the shameful self-centered raving ("vaneggiar") it produced,
the multiplication of sonnets and other lyric forms in this collection that
ring the changes on these possibilities of complaint, praise, hope, and suffering creates something like a template for a modern experience. The Petrarchan oppositions provide a common idiom, "a technology of ideation
of feeling," or a particular organization of affective experience, in which
supposedly individual experience can be formulated and whole national
languages "illustrate themselves."[15]

Alluding to the varied style of the sound or music of such combinations, this poem emphasizes the self-consciousness of lyric, whose subject is not so much the affective states of joy, hope, despair, etc. but what
can be said about them. And self-reflexivity is not a condition so much as
a process, as the poem stresses in the hyperintense self-division of the extraordinary line 11, which has four first-person pronouns in the original:
"di me medesmo meco mi vergogno" (the English translation gives us only
two "me"s). This poem about poetic complaint signals a fact that will ex-
tend well beyond the Petrarchan tradition: poetry is frequently about poetry, about the subject's relation to this production of poetic figures, or
of *fragments du discours amoureux,* to use Roland Barthes's splendid title.
Finally, there is the vision of this poetic activity as worldly conduct. Even
if we don't take altogether seriously the claim that the speaker is ashamed
to have made a spectacle of himself, the production of poetic discourse is
presented as a form of worldly behavior, for which one may modestly claim
to ask forgiveness as one seeks fame. The concluding line of the poem,
"che quanto piace al mondo è breve sogno," a striking, rhythmic maxim,
is nonetheless ambiguous in its implications. While the poetic speaker
condemns earthly pleasure as fleeting, what is the status of the vain
sighs, hopes, and pains that have constituted not only the sounds but the
very being of this poet? On the one hand, there is perhaps the suggestion
that this suffering is a perverse mode of worldly pleasure. On the other,
since the emphasis has been on the vanity of hopes, this last line seems
to detach itself from the vicissitudes of the experience reported and

become not fictive representation but moral apothegm, in keeping with a traditional function of the lyric as *epideictic* discourse.[16]

Petrarchan lyric sequences project a complex speaker and, despite the sense of conventionality produced by the subsequent tradition of love poetry, could be used to support the romantic model of lyric as intense expression of the subject's inner experience. Such sequences are more often read according to the implicit model that has succeeded it and now dominates lyric pedagogy: the lyric as a fictional representation of a speech act by a persona, not the poet. But despite the presumptions of lyric theory of the past two centuries, many lyrics do not project a speaker-character; it is scarcely a requirement of the genre. Let us turn to a poem unquestionably lyric without a first-person speaker, one of Goethe's most famous poems:

HEIDENRÖSLEIN

Sah ein Knab' ein Röslein stehn,
Röslein auf der Heiden,
War so jung und morgenschön,
Lief er schnell es nah zu sehn,
Sah's mit vielen Freuden.
Röslein, Röslein, Röslein rot,
Röslein auf der Heiden.

Knabe sprach: ich breche dich,
Röslein auf der Heiden.
Röslein sprach: ich steche dich,
Daß du ewig denkst an mich,
Und ich will's nicht leiden.
Röslein, Röslein, Röslein rot,
Röslein auf der Heiden.

Und der wilde Knabe brach
's Röslein auf der Heiden;
Röslein wehrte sich und stach,
Half ihm doch kein Weh und Ach,
Mußt es eben leiden.

Röslein, Röslein, Röslein rot,
Röslein auf der Heiden.

⤔

HEATH ROSE

A youth saw a little rose standing;
Little rose on the heath,
Was so young and morning-lovely.
He ran quickly to see it close up,
Saw it with much joy.
Little rose, little rose, little rose red,
Little rose on the heath.

The youth said, "I'll break you,
Little rose on the heath."
Little rose spoke: "I'll prick you,
So that you'll forever think of me,
And I don't want to suffer it."
Little rose, little rose, little rose red,
Little rose on the heath.

And the wild youth broke
The little rose on the heath;
Little rose resisted and pricked,
But no "woe" and "oh" helped her,
She just had to suffer it.
Little rose, little rose, little rose red,
Little rose on the heath.

[Trans. David Wellbery]

Here, there is no first person or character whose attitudes we have to re-construct. If we take the evocation of the rose in the refrain as addressing it, that implies an act of enunciation but not a subject or a character. The poem is a brief anecdote recounted in the past, a very common lyric struc-ture, though the rose's response to the youth's address lifts us out of an anecdotal space to a distinctively poetic one. And the repetition of the refrain attaches this story to the present time of lyric discourse in which the rose is repeatedly invoked.

The temporal structure is quite complicated: the anecdote in the past recounts a threat and a prediction which projects a future—"you'll forever think of me"—which will be a repetition of the past. And the poem, which returns chantingly in each stanza to the rose, illustrates in a way we might call performative what this would involve.

Refrain is an important constituent of lyric: first an instance of the repetition that Roman Jakobson famously took to define the poetic function of language: "the projection of the principle of equivalence from the axis of selection onto the axis of combination" so that equivalence becomes the constitutive device of the sequence.[17] (The function of equivalence is here emphasized also by the consonance of "sprechen," "brechen," "stechen," and "sprach," "brach," "stach," the key words of the poem.) But above all, refrain disrupts narrative and brings it back to a present of discourse.

Though very different from Sappho's ode to Aphrodite, this poem also presents a complexity of structures of address, a ritual aspect, effects of presence, and a certain performativity, as the reader, invited to repeat the refrain, finds him- or herself in the position of the "Knabe" who addresses the rose, and the poem produces the result that the rose predicts: you will always think of me. In addition to this performative aspect, of accomplishing what it names, the poem positions the reader as the speaker, who repeats this ritualistic discourse. This is a lyric where it would be pointless to ask who is speaking or in what circumstances. The reader speaks the poem, articulates the discourse that the poem offers. And finally, the poem posits, through its rhetorical structures, an interpersonal relation between man and nature (which interpretation in this case is likely to render sexual, with a scenario of defloration and castration), and where nature is invested with agency, affect, and signification in extravagant fashion, though one scarcely realizes this, since the poem is delicate and modest in appearance.

Our next example, one of the most famous romantic lyrics, Leopardi's "L'infinito," approaches the natural world in quite a different fashion.

Sempre caro mi fu quest'ermo colle
E questa siepe che da tanta parte

De'll ultimo orrizonte il guarde esclude.
Ma sedendo e mirando interminati
Spazi di là da quella, e sovrumani
Silenzi, e profondissima quiete,
Io nel pensier mi fingo, ove per poco
Il cor non si spaura. E come il vento
Odo stormir tra queste piante, io quello
Infinito silenzio a questa voce
Vo comparando; e mi sovvien l'eterno,
E le morte stagioni, e la presente
E viva, e'l suon di lei. Così tra questa
Immensità s'annega il pensier mio:
E'l naufragar m'è dolce in questo mare.

☞

Always dear to me was this solitary hill
And this hedge, which cuts off from view
The far horizon on almost every side.
But sitting here and gazing, endless
Spaces beyond that, and superhuman
Silences and profoundest quiet,
I invent for myself, so that the heart
Is almost frightened. And as I listen to the wind
Storming through these branches, I find myself
Comparing that infinite silence to this voice,
And they recall to me the eternal
And the dead seasons, and the present
And living and its sound. So in the midst of this
Immensity my thought drowns itself,
And shipwreck in this sea is sweet to me.

The opening line leads readers to expect the description of a beloved natural setting, but the poet emphasizes that the hedge on this hill blocks the horizon, so that with perception impeded, it is his thought that invents ("mi fingo") the distant spaces, superhuman silence and deep quiet. Comparing the sound of the wind with this infinite silence provokes thoughts of eternity and of other seasons than the present—dead and living.

We might expect a classic scenario of the sublime, where in the process of imagining the infinite his thought is overwhelmed, but invention is controlled here: he imagines infinity but not so much that the heart takes fright. As the various infinites of time and space are resolved into a sea, thought drowns itself, and the sense of being overcome or submerged is sweet rather than tragic—a process that can be repeated over and over in this lyric present.

The poet speaks from a particular place—*this* hill and *this* hedge that were always dear to him—but the natural scene is ultimately not important, except as a site for musing on the infinite and as a point of comparison. Numerous deictics, beginning with *this* solitary hill (*quest'*ermo colle), insist on *this* place, *this* voice, *these* plants. Yet other demonstrative adjectives qualify the purely imagined entities, and what starts as *that* infinite silence (compared with *this* voice of the wind), ends up as *this* immensity and *this* sea, in a strange reversal of what is most proximate.[18] Moreover, the initial verb, "Sempre caro mi *fu*," is in the *passato remoto*, indicating a concluded action: always dear to me *was* this hill, not "this hill always has been dear to me." This separates the self that loved the hill from the poet who now invents and compares and who experiences the sublime drowning of his thought in the sea of the infinite, even though this experience of self-negating thought may be what made the hill dear. Hyperbolic in evoking the infinite from a spot behind a hedge, the poem becomes not the recollection or praise of a particular sublime view but a celebration of imaginative self-reflexivity, as the mind pleasures itself by thinking its own negation. This poem gives us a first-person speaker in a particular situation but that spot is quickly exceeded as the poem situates itself in a present tense of "I invent," "I find myself/ Comparing," and "my thought drowns itself."

For the modern lyric, we move from the hills to the city streets—nowhere better epitomized than in Baudelaire's famous sonnet "A une passante." The early twentieth-century critic, Albert Thibaudet, who anticipated Walter Benjamin's analysis of Baudelaire as the first poet for whom urban experience was the norm, waxes eloquent about this sonnet, as a distinctively modern poem from the alienated world of modern cities, "a poem which, possible only in a great capital where people live as strangers to one another," "irremediably marked those whose youth belonged to the life of a great capital." The final line, he claims—"O toi que j'eusse aimée, o toi qui le savais!"—has become one that Parisians recite to themselves as they stroll through the city and has thus become part of the urban social imaginary, "consubstantiel à la poussière dorée du bou-levard" ("part and parcel of the golden haze of the Parisian boulevard").[19] Thibaudet's account suggests one social function of lyric: the articula-tion, perhaps in detachable apothegms, of what become shared struc-tures of feeling, or the social imaginary. But though this is certainly an urban poem, beginning with an isolated first line evoking the noise of traffic, the poem also takes up a lyric tradition of the *innamoramento*, the transfiguring initial sight of the beloved, as in Dante or Petrarch, love at first sight, which, as Benjamin says, Baudelaire transforms to "love at last sight."[20]

A UNE PASSANTE

La rue assourdissante autour de moi hurlait.
Longue, mince, en grand deuil, douleur majestueuse,
Une femme passa, d'une main fastueuse
Soulevant, balançant le feston et l'ourlet;
Agile et noble, avec sa jambe de statue.
Moi, je buvais, crispé comme un extravagant,
Dans son oeil, ciel livide où germe l'ouragan,
La douceur qui fascine et le plaisir qui tue.
Un éclair . . . puis la nuit!—Fugitive beauté
Dont le regard m'a fait soudainement renaître,
Ne te verrai-je plus que dans l'éternité?
Ailleurs, bien loin d'ici! trop tard! *jamais* peut-être!
Car j'ignore où tu fuis, tu ne sais où je vais,
O toi que j'eusse aimée, ô toi qui le savais!

TO A WOMAN PASSING BY

Around me roared the nearly deafening street.
Tall, slim, in mourning, in majestic grief,

A woman passed me, with a splendid hand
Lifting and swinging her festoon and hem.
Nimble and stately, statuesque of leg.
I, shaking like an addict, from her eye,
Black sky, spawner of hurricanes, drank in
Sweetness that fascinates, pleasure that kills.
One lightning flash . . . then night! Sweet fugitive
Whose glance has made me suddenly reborn
Will we not meet again this side of death?
Far from this place! too late! *never* perhaps!
Neither one knowing where the other goes,
O you I might have loved, as well you know!

[Trans. James McGowan, modified]

This sonnet, whose syntactic divisions after line 1 and again after line 5 imply that modern urban experience does not fit itself to the traditional lyric structure of the sonnet, takes the form of an anecdote in the past, but that narrated event is transformed in various ways. First, it is rendered significant—no longer mere anecdote—by the conventions of the genre themselves. Second, the hyperbolic turn of describing the woman's eye as "ciel livide où germe l'ouragon," from which the speaker drinks "La douceur qui fascine et le plaisir qui tue," creates an excess that can be recuperated as a mark of unbridled subjectivity (reading in the eye of a woman in mourning overpowering erotic possibilities) or else as a diffuse affect, of intensified alienation. Third, the poem pulls itself out of the narrative temporality of past event and into the distinctive space of lyric present with the address to the "Fugitive beauté" and the question that she manifestly cannot answer, "Will we not meet again this side of death?"—a question that therefore insists on the optative and extraordinarily self-indulgent dimension of the final alexandrine, "O toi que j'eusse aimée, ô toi qui le savais!" The sonnet begins as a representation of a singular event in urban surroundings, "Une femme passa," but the transformation produced by the logic of the genre pulls us into the lyric present—"j'ignore où tu fuis"—and into a hyperbolic, ritualistic and melancholic celebration of lost possibility, as the poem becomes itself an event, helping to structure the fantasies that give urban existence its excitement.

A different sort of example is Lorca's "La luna asoma" (The Moon Comes Out):

Cuando sale la luna	When the moon rises
se pierden las campanas	The bells die away
y aparecen las sendas	And impenetrable
impenetrables.	Paths come to the fore.
Cuando sale la luna,	When the moon rises
el mar cubre la tierra	Water covers land
y el corazón se siente	And the heart feels itself
isla en el infinito.	An island in infinity.
Nadie come naranjas	No one eats oranges
bajo la luna llena.	Under the full moon.
Es preciso comer	It is right to eat
fruta verde y helada.	Green, chilled fruit.
Cuando sale la luna	When the moon rises
de cien rostros iguales,	With a hundred faces all the same,
la moneda de plata	Coins of silver
solloza en el bolsillo.	Start sobbing in the pocket.

[Trans. A. Z. Foreman, modified]

This mysterious, engaging poem offers no speaker: nothing is gained by trying to imagine that someone is speaking and asking who or why. It is manifestly lyric writing, offering first hyperbolic, melancholic images— impenetrable paths, the heart as an island in infinity—but then shifting from solitude in a natural setting to multiplication and monetization: in place of a solitary heart we are given anthropomorphized silver coins with a hundred faces all the same sobbing in the pocket. The structure of the poem, highly ritualistic with three stanzas beginning "Cuando sale la luna," makes the nonconforming third stanza stand out; but what this salient stanza gives us is not a thought that centers the poem but the quasi-authoritative enunciation of a hitherto-unknown social norm: no one eats oranges under the full moon. Although the poem invites speculation about why this could be appropriate (oranges go with the sun or with blood, not with the pallor of the moon, perhaps), it seems above all amusing, especially when followed by a maxim that seems to parody the epideictic functioning of earlier lyrics. Pindar tells us (in his first Olympian ode) that "Water is best," and Petrarch that "worldly joy is but a fleeting dream," but Lorca announces that by the full moon you must eat chilled, unripe fruit ("Es preciso" means "it is necessary," not just "correct"). But the poem ends not with the dubious social directive but with the sorrow of replicability: our moments, like a hundred coins with identical faces, sob in the pocket—not a resource to be spent but hyperbolic isolation in a multitude.

In poems considered up to now the images have seemed easily interpretable: love as a sea, potentially stormy, a rose that may prick, eyes that flash like lightning. Here we encounter images, such as the sobbing coins, that invite hermeneutic attention but whose main function may be to signal imaginative strangeness, resistance to ordinary lines of thought, if not exactly utopian possibility. The title gives us a mildly animated moon that "peeks out" (asoma), but the stanzas offer ritualistic repetition in the present tense of habitual action, as the rising of the moon reveals our strange and estranged isolation.

For twentieth-century poetry there is a question of how much should be considered lyric or read within the framework of the Western lyric tradition. On the one hand, many twentieth-century poets have explicitly denounced a lyric model with its foregrounding of effects of voice, presence, and address, even though critical analysis has made it clear that such effects depend on rhetorical strategies and hence poets' manipulation of language. As I discuss in Chapter 6, poets have certainly succeeded in producing works that demand to be approached differently, offering text that can scarcely be articulated, seeking visual rather than primarily aural effects.

Cases less radical such as William Carlos Williams's poem XII in *Spring and All*, frequently referred to as "The Red Wheelbarrow," make use of spatial arrangements to produce lyric effects.

so much depends
upon

a red wheel
barrow

glazed with rain
water

beside the white
chickens.

The spatial disposition is crucial here, revealing a structure that would not be detectable when heard, but the line and the stanza, rather than the page, are still the functional units: four two-line stanzas, the first line of each stanza consisting of three words, the second of one word (of two syllables). The poem raises the question of the relation between the visual form and sound sequence, as the reader seems invited to treat the lines as breath groups, pausing at line and stanza endings. Lineation seems to serve as instructions for voicing. The enjambment produced by the verse pattern separates "wheel" from "barrow" and "rain" from "water," contributing to the sense of basic constituents of a world. Without rhyme or a regular metrical scheme, the poem succeeds in producing memorable language, in an unorthodox, unfinished version of the poem of praise.

Here there seems no reason to imagine a speaker-character or to attempt novelistically to supply a context of utterance. Hugh Kenner writes, "Try to imagine an occasion for this sentence to be said: 'So much depends upon a red wheelbarrow glazed with rainwater beside the white chickens.' Try it over, in any voice you like: it is impossible. . . . And to go on with the dialogue? To whom might the sentence be spoken, for what purpose? . . . Not only is what the sentence says banal, if you heard someone say it you'd wince. But hammered on the typewriter into a *thing made,* and this without displacing a single word except typographically, the sixteen words exist in a different zone altogether, a zone remote from the world of sayers and sayings." He adds, "Yet you do say, you do go through the motions of saying. But art lifts the saying out of the zone of things said."[21]

You do say it, but the poem gives us not a voice but voicing. There seems resistance to both the romantic/expressive model of lyric and its modern successor, lyric as a drama of the attitudes of a character. The poem does not create a character making an assertion in a fictional world but makes a statement about our world. It seems a poem of notation, recording a minor epiphany. The assertion of value ("so much depends") places this poem in the epideictic tradition of lyrics of praise, but the poems seems to stop too soon or, rather, the specification of chickens and rainwater makes it mysterious what the claim might be, so we puzzle over it, but we remember it.

Despite contemporary poets' resistance to the idea of lyric, many contemporary poems achieve their effects by engaging the lyric tradition. Consider the very intriguing example of the opening poem of John Ashbery's 2000 collection, *Your Name Here*. The title of the collection alludes to the bureaucratic language practices of forms or publicity: each of us can become the *you* hailed by bureaucracy or advertising, the *you* who has just won a million dollars in a lottery or the *you* to which an iterable bureaucratic process applies, as we fill in the form. *Your Name Here* foregrounds the problem of singularization and iterability, which seems central to lyric and which also subtends "This Room":

> The room I entered was a dream of this room.
> Surely all those feet on the sofa were mine.
> The oval portrait
> of a dog was me at an early age.
> Something shimmers, something is hushed up.
>
> We had macaroni for lunch every day
> except Sunday, when a small quail was induced
> to be served to us. Why do I tell you these things?
> You are not even here.

The poem connects the problem of singularization and iterability with the striking deictic effects of lyric—this room, or, in Italian, this "stanza"—where the *you*, as in this poem, remains unlocated.[22] Here the structure of lyric returns the recital of past events to a present of discourse, as in other examples considered above, but Ashbery's poem is unusual both in the explicitness with which it foregrounds the relation of lyric address—"Why do I tell you these things? / You are not even here"—and in its hyperbolic version of the strangeness that lyric here treats as natural, as in "The oval portrait / of a dog was me at an early age." As so often with Ashbery, we are induced to cast around for points of reference among literary or nonliterary discourses: this portrait recalls Dylan Thomas's "Portrait of the Artist as a Young Dog," Poe's short story "The Oval Portrait," or the portraits by William Wegman of dogs as people, the cliché of identity tied up with the childhood pet, or the commonplace that after a certain time master and dog come to resemble one another.

But the *punctum* of this poem, to use Roland Barthes's term for what grabs us, holds us, is the involution of the formulation, "a small quail was induced to be served to us," whose function is difficult to imagine. Though above all a joke, this line poses questions of language and agency (how is the quail induced? does the quail have a say?); it thus foregrounds above all the strangeness of lyric language, even as evocation of the ordinary ("every day / except Sunday"!). However it works, this enigmatic example is hyperbolic in its strangeness, a condition it relates to dream. Its conclusion is exemplary, with its joking yet ultimately serious foregrounding of the structure of song and ode, as well as the tradition of the love sonnet. The final lines—". . . Why do I tell you these things? / You are not even here"—could be taken to sum up the tradition of the lover's complaint, implicitly commenting, as poems so often do, on the lyric tradition as they perform it. One could even say that studying lyric is working to answer this question: "Why do I tell you these things? / You are not even here."

2. Four Parameters

These examples, among the most canonical lyrics from different periods, yield a number of resemblances that help sketch the parameters of a vital generic tradition and identify a series of issues to be investigated further. Eva Müller-Zettelmann, a German theorist describing the domain of the lyric, lists several "tendencies" that distinguish it from other genres: (1) brevity, (2) a reduction of the fictional element, (3) more intense formal structuring, (4) greater aesthetic self-reference, (5) greater linguistic deviance, and (6) greater epistemological subjectivity.[23] These are certainly plausible characteristics, which help above all to distinguish lyrics from narrative poetry, but the examples considered here offer some more specific and salient parameters of variation; and they might also lead us to question, at least provisionally, the presumption of greater linguistic deviance, which is not particularly manifest in the poems discussed.

We can organize these parameters according to four broad topics. These are, as will be evident, closely intertwined, but they need to be approached more schematically, whence a preliminary separation.

(1) First, I have highlighted the question of the enunciative apparatus of lyric in these examples, which provide a range of possibilities of indirection. The least indirect is Petrarch's first-person address to readers or listeners: "You who hear . . ." But this address to readers—anomalous among the examples—only highlights the indirection of the sonnet sequence generally, where readers are indirectly addressed through apostrophes to the absent beloved or to other posited addressees: flowers, water, love itself. Ashbery, foregrounding the complications of lyric structure, concludes with an address to an absent "you," whether the reader or a personal "you," the beloved, or both. Horace's ode gives us a characteristic version of indirection, imparting a more vivid, dramatic cast to a reflection on love which is addressed, via triangulation, to readers, then and now, through the address to Pyrrha. This more complex version is in play in Baudelaire's sonnet, where the woman described in the octet is addressed as absent in the sestet, and in Sappho, where the address to the goddess is complicated by its rehearsal of previous occasions when she addressed Sappho, which melds into direct address to the supposed speaker—all of which is implicitly addressed to listeners and readers. The poems by Goethe, Leopardi, Lorca, and Williams are not explicitly addressed, and while Leopardi's could be interpreted as musing overheard, the other three poems pose the question of how to think about and describe lyrics that avoid the fiction of a speaker and explicit address, offering instead writing for readers to enunciate.

The enunciative apparatus also poses the question of the lyric's relation to voice and voicing. Ever since the Greeks, lyrics have generally been encountered as writing that readers articulate, silently or orally, but the importance of sound for lyric has made the notion of voice loom large, both in poems themselves and in the critical tradition. The fact that written lyrics persist in alluding to lyres and presenting themselves as sung long after they take the form of writing emphasizes the importance of their aural dimension for their characteristic effects. "The principle of intelligibility, in lyric poetry, depends on the phenomenalization of the poetic voice," declares Paul de Man.[24] That is to say, to read something as lyric is allegedly to lend phenomenal form to something like a voice, to convince ourselves that we are hearing a voice. This is a potent conception in the critical tradition, and there are certainly lyrics that attempt to sound like someone speaking, but as the examples considered here suggest, there are many other lyrics where the text does not encourage readers to imagine the voice of a speaker or reward them for trying to do so: the poems by Goethe, Lorca, Williams, and Ashbery are good examples. Rather than imagine that lyrics embody voices, we do better to say that they create effects of voicing, of aurality. Certainly a theory of the lyric must consider whether effects of voicing rather than voice—as in the echoing of rhyme, assonance, or alliteration, and rhythmic patterning—are not the more fundamental dimension of lyric, on which the impression of the distinctive voice of a speaker is sometimes imposed. To what extent is the notion of lyric necessarily tied up with voicing and only occasionally with images of voice?

(2) Next we have what I have called lyric's attempt to be itself an event rather than the representation of an event. Here we encounter a basic issue in Western theories of literature: *mimesis.* For Aristotle, poetry (meaning what we call "literature") is an imitation of character and action, classified according to the status of actions and characters, a conception which leads him to focus on tragedy, comedy, and epic and to leave lyric aside, since it was considered a speech event, epideixis, rather than a representation of action. This is not to say that lyrics do not frequently present minimal action or characters—think of Sappho's Aphrodite, Horace's Pyrrha, Goethe's "Knabe," and Baudelaire's "passante"—but they are enlisted in nonmimetic enterprises.

The most striking of these is the presentation of assertions or judgments that are not relativized to a particular speaker or fictional situation but offered as truths about the world, as in Sappho's "one who flees will soon pursue," Horace's "Many's the time / he'll weep at your faithlessness and the changing gods," Petrarch's "worldly joy is but a fleeting dream,"

Lorca's "It is right to eat / Green, chilled fruit," Williams's "so much depends / upon / a red wheel / barrow." Modern readers have learned to scorn the idea that a poem might "have a message," for fear that otherwise everything save this meaning would become ancillary (why doesn't the poet just say what she means, then?); but many poems are messages that speak of the world and ask us to consider it in a particular light. While poems are more than statements about the world, they frequently offer praise or blame, urging us what to value, not via a character made to adopt a value, but in memorable apothegms offered for readers to repeat and remember.

"I think that this feeling . . . of an action taking place in real time, the time it takes to read the poem, is what we crave from poetry," writes James Longenbach, "even if a poem spends most of its time recounting an event that has already happened."[25] Most of the above examples do not involve mimesis of action, but several do contain minimal narrative sequences (Sappho, Goethe, Baudelaire) and thus representations of action. In narrative fiction the question of the relation between *story* and *discourse* or between what is enunciated and the enunciation is generally theorized as one of perspective—from what point of view are events reported (in fiction the priority of event to narration is presumed). How does lyric differ? In our examples, the present of discourse or articulation cannot be reduced to the narrating of past events; on the contrary, the narrated events seem to be subsumed by, trumped by, the present of lyric enunciation (narrating is no longer the right word). This can take different forms. In Sappho's poem, perhaps the most spectacular, the narration of past actions is formulated in a prayer, as part of an invocation, and then converted, as we have seen, into an event that seems to be occurring in the present, as if what we encounter is not a story about Aphrodite's appearance in the past but an instance of Aphrodite's present intervention. In Baudelaire's sonnet the narration of a past incident is interrupted and subsumed by an address to the "fugitive beauté," and the rest of the poem takes the form of virtual engagement with her in the present of discourse. Goethe's song offers a fictional representation, a minimal narrative, although the strange events of the exchange between youth and flower, and the compressed narrative without circumstantial detail, periodically interrupted by the refrain invoking the rose, seem to pull us out of a space of narrative into a ritualistic space of lyric discourse. Even these three poems, then, subsume representations of past events to an occurrence in the lyric present.

A distinctive feature of lyric seems to be this attempt to create the impression of something happening now, in the present time of discourse. Whether, as in Sappho's, the poem works brilliantly to produce a version of the event it describes or, as in Leopardi's, it tautologically performs the thinking that it evokes, putting us through a sweet drowning of thought, the lyric works to create effects of presence. Emphasis on the present of discourse—as in Petrarch's "You who hear" or Ashbery's "Why do I tell you these things?"—seems fundamental to the functioning of lyric. The question of how effects of presence are produced and their role in lyric is a major topic to be explored.

(3) Insofar as lyrics offer not representations of speeches by fictional characters but memorable writing to be received, reactivated, and repeated by readers, they partake of what I have broadly called the ritualistic, a concept that will become fleshed out as we proceed. I have in passing noted some ritualistic dimensions of lyric, whether allusions to ritual context, as in Sappho's ode, love poems as ritualistic complaint, or the centrality of the ritualistic refrain in Goethe's "Heidenröslein." I have so far scarcely emphasized the forms of linguistic patterning or stanzaic structure that seem to be central to the identity and the functioning of lyric, and especially to its hold on readers. The formal dimensions of lyrics—the patterning of rhythm and rhyme, the repetition of stanza forms, and generally everything that recalls song or lacks a mimetic or representational function—contribute to their ritualistic as opposed to fictional aspect, making them texts composed for *re*performance. For many of these lyrics it seems important that the reader be not just a listener or an audience but also a performer of the lines—that he or she come to occupy, at least temporarily, the position of speaker and audibly or inaudibly voice the language of the poem, which can expand the possibilities of his or her discourse. How should one conceive of this ritualistic dimension of lyric and how does it relate to thematic and other generic qualities?

(4) Finally, most of these lyrics have an explicitly hyperbolic quality, which is especially striking because they are brief. This takes different forms, from the arrival of a goddess to the prosopopoeia of speaking roses, to the self-annihilation in the imagining of the infinite, to the elevation

of the glimpse of a passing stranger into a moment of apocalypse, or the evocation of radical effects of the rising of the moon. Baudelaire himself writes that "hyperbole and apostrophe are the two forms of language which are not only most necessary but most pleasing in lyric."[26] Sometimes the hyperbole is blatant, as when a lyric claims that the prick of a rose will make you "forever" think of that rose; sometimes it seems the product of the generic convention that makes homely observation of a garden accessory into an epiphany. Is the hyperbolic character of lyric a fundamental constituent of the genre or simply a major possibility, a frequent version of poetic pretension? It is doubtless related to the optative character of poems, which often seek transformations of experience, the favor of the goddess, amorous success, acceptance by the world, the possibility that things might go better. Lyrics hyperbolically risk animating the world, investing mundane objects or occurrence with meaning. "Doch dichterisch wohnet der Mensch auf dieser Erde," writes Friedrich Hölderlin: "yet poetically, man dwells on the earth."[27] Lyrics seek to remake the universe as a world, giving a spiritual dimension to matter. This aspect of lyric should not be neglected, since it often provides the motive for readers' finding lyric words memorable and letting them inform experience.

These lyrics from different periods and languages identify a range of issues or parameters of variation that need to be incorporated in any account of the genre. They do not constitute a set of necessary features or invariants or a definition of the lyric, but they have, I believe, the virtue of being more central to the functioning and the power of lyrics than elements likely to be cited in any attempt at definition. But the question of what the lyric is or has been still awaits.

TWO

Lyric as Genre

Creatures of language, we encounter a wide range of discourses every day and sort them into genres, more or less automatically, so as to process them and determine how to respond: this is an advertisement; this is a friendly message; this is a news story. A society is in part constituted by its discourses; to be a functioning adult is to be able to recognize swiftly what sort of discourse we are dealing with. Though advertisers may try to trick us into paying attention by making their ads seem like something else, recognition quickly dawns. Turning on the television, we recognize a sportscast, a news report, a contest, a soap opera, a crime serial. Most of these genres of discourse are not the subject of intense theoretical debate: we don't argue about whether there are "really" such things as sportscasts or whether this is just a name we have abusively applied to a wide range of empirical discursive events. We could spend time wondering whether "criminal procedural drama" is an appropriate category or whether we need to sort all these programs with detectives, crimes, and lawyers in other ways. Someone might argue that we should distinguish between programs that center on the lawyers and those that center on detectives or police, but such choices do not seem to be of great moment.

The question would doubtless be not whether these are the "right" categories but what purposes a different classification might serve.

Why, then, is there more intense debate about literary genres, as if these were matters of great ontological import, since these too are classifications that bring together discourses under a general heading, on the basis of similarities deemed to be relevant to their functioning? One reason is that, since Aristotle, to identify the major types of literature has been tantamount to defining literature itself: literature, or previously "poetry," consists of these major types, as if genres constituted the logical divisions of the literary sphere. "Genre is the point of intersection of general poetics and literary history," writes Tzvetan Todorov; "in this sense it is a privileged object, which is enough to make it the principal subject of literary studies."[1] Insofar as literature has a history, it is at the level of genres that this history is best described.

Another reason for the importance genre takes on in literary studies is that in European literature up until the late eighteenth century, generic categories were essential to literary evaluation as well as to literary creation: Does this work succeed in doing what works of this sort are supposed to do? What Jacques Rancière calls a "representational regime" (as opposed to a literary regime centered on expression) governed literary production in the West. Generic notions were central to any reflection on literature. Horace begins the *Art of Poetry* by comparing the poet whose work cannot be "assigned to a single shape" to a painter who puts a human head on the neck of a horse or makes "what at top is a lovely woman end below in a black and ugly fish."[2]

1. Notions of Genre

Generic categories have been fundamental not only to the institution of literature but, as I mentioned above, to the production and reception of discourses of all sorts, but in *The Political Unconscious* Fredric Jameson maintains that genre criticism has been "thoroughly discredited by modern literary theory and practice."[3] While one might contest the idea that a compelling case has been made against the notion of genre, it is certainly true that the concept of genre has not fared well in literary studies of late, doubtless a sign that it is time to revisit it. Discussions of genre often cite a passage from Maurice Blanchot's *Le Livre à venir* (The Book to Come), which articulates an extreme version of what has become a common view:

> The book is all that matters [Seul importe le livre], just as it is, far from genres, outside of the rubrics, prose, poetry, novel, testimony, under which it refuses to place itself and to which it denies the power to fix its place and to determine its form. A book no longer belongs to a genre; every book stems from literature alone, as if literature possessed in advance, in all their generality, the secrets and the formulas that alone make it possible to give to what is written the reality of the book. It would thus be as if [Tout se passerait donc comme si], genres having faded away, literature alone were affirming itself, shining alone in the mysterious clarity that it propagates and that each literary creation sends back to it, multiplied—as if there were therefore an "essence" of literature.[4]

This passage is frequently quoted because it does represent a certain modern attitude. What we value in literature is the singularity of a literary work, and to expect it to conform to the conventions of a genre or to approach it through the lens of genre is to aim at something other than its distinctive literariness. But the two "as if" clauses and the conditional in the last sentence ought to alert those who cite this passage to the fact that there is something complicated going on here: to say "Tout se passerait donc comme si . . ."—"It would thus be as if" or "Things allegedly happen as if "—is to indicate that while this is the story told about genre it is not what actually happens. Far from affirming a notion of literature based on the book and separate from genres, Blanchot entitles this section of his essay "la non-littérature" and affirms that what has been at stake since Mallarmé is an impossible quest: "It is non-literature that each book pursues." Though Blanchot writes of a conception of literature since Mallarmé in which only the work counts—the work, which is seen as beyond what Blanchot in this essay calls "the reality of genres"—he is not so much affirming a positive concept of literature that could replace the reality of genres as sketching a negative one; he is describing a modern attitude, in which generic categories are deemed to have disappeared, more than he is challenging "the reality of genres." In this, his thought is considerably more complex than that of the early twentieth-century critic Benedetto Croce, for example, who affirmed the singularity of the work and notoriously maintained that everything relating to genres and to the classification of the arts could be burned without loss.[5] His opposition to the notion of genre was based on the concept of genre as rule—where obeying the rules of genres, as in neoclassicism, violates the creative spirit of literature. Genres oppress and stifle creativity. If it is true, as Jameson claims, that genre criticism has been discredited, what has been discredited is, first, the notion of a genre as a set of rules that a literary work ought to follow and, second, the idea that the purpose of generic categories is to classify works: to tell us whether this piece of literature is in fact a novel or an anti-novel, for example.

Though skepticism about the idea of genre has remained powerful in literary studies, there are signs of a growing recognition of the importance of genre categories.[6] If today what we are inclined to value in a literary work is its singularity, that singularity nonetheless emerges against the background of conventions of genres. The conventions, in fact, emerge most clearly in their violation or disruption. As readers of Michel Foucault, we know that norms are productive as well as constraining, necessary to the functioning of social and cultural meaning, and there is now a long and varied tradition, running from Ernst Gombrich's *Art and Illusion* through such works as Erving Goffman's *Frame Analysis* to recent cognitive science, demonstrating how essential various sorts of schemas or frames are to perception and creation.

There are two broad ways of approaching questions of genre. One can make generic categories the object of study or one can attempt to use them as instruments of study.[7] The first approach might undertake to determine, for example, what genres are functional for readers and viewers. What are the categories into which people are accustomed to sort the discourses or the narratives that they encounter? If people are inclined to say things such as "I find reality shows boring" or "I like police procedurals," that is evidence for the functionality of these categories for present-day subjects in their organization of experience. One can ask these questions about a particular historical period—what are the categories into which people sorted literary works?—with evidence coming from critical commentaries, publishing labels, organization of anthologies, and so on. Of course, what one discovers for the past is what we would also discover today: that there is no simple set of generic categories to which an "age" subscribes. People classify differently for different purposes, and in fact published discussions of categories are not firm indications of what is truly functional but, very often, arguments about how one ought to conceive of the literary field.

The fact that one cannot simply empirically ascertain what are the genres of a given moment vitiates attempts to treat genre categories simply as objects of analysis and indicates that they are also, ineluctably, reflective instruments of analysis that we use to identify traditions and which affect the domain they portray. Genres change as new works are created that either modify the categories or, eventually, delimit them differently in creating new categories. Fundamental to the nature of genre is the way in which new works allow us to see how earlier works were functioning, displaying already, perhaps in different form, features that are brought out more clearly by later instances. Analyzing the complexity of our reflection on generic categories, which themselves undergo change through our and others' deployment of them, Ralph Cohen writes, "Genre study is more than another approach to literature or to social institutions or scientific practices, it analyzes our procedures for acquiring and accumulating knowledge, including the changes that knowledge undergoes."[8]

There are a number of factors that influence the positing of a genre. A category may be functional for writers, who aim to produce a certain sort of work, writing with a general model in mind, as when Horace aims to adapt Greek meters and join the *lyrici vates;* a category can be functional for readers, who may read a narrative as autobiography; and categories may be posited by critics, as they seek to identify a tradition, highlight common features of works, or focus on contrasts between them. The more important the generic category, the more it may raise questions about its subspecies. Especially complicated in discussions of genre are questions of scale, since distinctions can be made at various levels: within the category *novel,* we can distinguish multiple possibilities, such as science fiction, romance, horror, crime fiction. Though we might think of these as subspecies of the genre *novel,* they are frequently referred to as types of *genre* fiction, as if the novel itself were above genre and only "lower" types of fiction had genres. This may be a sign of the anti-genre prejudices of our age; it is certainly evidence that these categories function as genres for writers, readers, and critics.

It is worth noting here a nagging problem: genre study is most interesting when most specific. It is less engaging to talk about the detective story in general than about the specific types of detective story that one might want to distinguish: the English country house mystery, the police procedural, noir detective fiction, and so on. There are fine discriminations to be made, arguments about the vitality of this or that tradition, and so on. By comparison, attempts to talk about the detective story in general are likely to court banality. But this does not mean that one can somehow abandon the category of detective fiction and keep only the subcategories, or that one can do without the genre of the novel itself. Within the system of literary possibilities, *detective story* and *novel* have both played a significant role in a capacious tradition. When we leave prose for poetry, we find narrowly defined categories, such as *aubade* or *epithalamion*, as well as broader categories such as *lyric* or *epic*, and categories of the middle range, such as *dramatic monologue*, or *ode*. The range of lyric subgenres is considerable (I take up this topic in Chapter 6) but they scarcely cover the domain of nonnarrative poetry. For genre-oriented critics, the temptation to concentrate on narrowly defined genres is always strong but needs to be accompanied by a broader focus if one is to give an adequate account of literature. The question of genre is largely a question of which categories are most useful, most likely to provide insight into the history of the literary tradition and the functioning of literature.

Essentialist concepts of genre posit a set of qualities that every instance of a genre must possess: identifiable distinguishing marks. Requirements of exactitude make such concepts difficult to formulate or sustain and pose obstacles for reflecting on generic change. Perhaps for that reason, theorists often deploy biological metaphors for discussing genres: a genre is like a species, whose members give birth to future members.[9] But whereas for biology individuals manifest the species, in literary genres new members can alter the genre. More popular in recent decades for reflection on genre is the notion of family resemblance: though there may not be distinguishing features that all works of a certain genre share, they resemble other members of the genre in various ways. Wittgenstein's use of the concept of family resemblance to discuss the category of *game* gives it respectability, but insofar as the idea of family resemblance does more than register an appropriately loose array of similarities, it begs the question of generic identity: if members of a family share a number of features (though not all of them the same features) it is *because* they genetically descend from common ancestors, and it is this biological link that ultimately distinguishes them from members of other families who might resemble them (two people who look a lot alike may belong to different families). With literary genres, where descent cannot be determined independently of features, the idea of family resemblance obscures rather than clarifies the situation and is best avoided, since it takes for granted without acknowledging it the genetic filiation that may be at issue. The notion of tradition, crucial to major genres, is different from biological descent, in that new members alter the tradition, bringing out salient aspects of its earlier members.

Genres can also be treated as social institutions, created by constitutive conventions, though the absence of clear evidence about what is acceptable or unacceptable makes it difficult to work convincingly with this otherwise quite appropriate notion. A superior version of the institutional model that works for many concepts is the "prototype model," which seems in fact to capture how we actually treat generic concepts. Color categories—blue, red, green—"do not have any obviously analyzable criterial attributes, formal structure, or definite boundaries, and they have an internal structure graded in terms of how exemplary of its category people judge a color to be."[10] Thus, red hair is not as good an example of *red* as a red fire engine. Similarly, a dining room chair is, for us, a better example of a chair than a dentist's chair. We even judge 7 a better example of an odd number than 8421, though in fact they are equally odd. For a wide range of concepts, people comprehend them less in terms defining criteria or boundary conditions (when something stops being red or stops being a chair) than in terms of central examples or prototypes: chairs are things like *this* or *this*. Given the role of tradition and imitation in the functioning of genres, genres may be best understood in terms of prototypes.

Traditionally theorists say there are two sorts of theories of genres, empirical and theoretical, the latter based on some claim about elementary possibilities of thought, representation, or discourse: Aristotle distinguishes literary types according to the possible modes and objects of representation. Northrop Frye bases genre categories on "radicals [root forms] of presentation": "words may be acted in front of a spectator, they may be spoken in front of a listener, they may be sung or chanted, and they may be written for a reader"—fundamental possibilities, which for him yield drama, epic, lyric, and narrative fiction.[11] Goethe spoke of the "drei echte Naturformen der Dichtung" ("three pure natural forms of poetry"): epic, dramatic, and lyric, which he distinguished from the variety of "Dichtarten," which one might translate as "empirical genres": ballad, drama, epistle, fable, ode, novel, parody, romance, etc.[12] The alternative to theories of genres based on logical divisions of a sphere of possibilities would be such empirical genres, groupings that are observed or practiced, based on principles other than theoretical. Empirical genres would be lists of whatever genres people believe exist, some based on form, others on content—classifications that do not seem very logical—like the categories we find in bookstores.

These do seem to be two different conceptions of genre, which we could call theoretical and historical, but in separating the two conceptions one obscures fundamental aspects of genre and creates the sort of confusion that contributes to the tendency to dismiss genres. On the one hand, theories of genre have indeed usually attempted to find a logical basis for taxonomies, but they use these to situate historically attested genres. They do not derive categories that correspond to no historically attested forms of literary practice. The attempt to posit genres based on fundamental features of language or communication always draws on historically existing genres, even if, as in the case of the nineteenth-century division into the subjective, objective, and mixed genres, theorists disagree about whether it is epic that is objective and drama that is mixed or vice versa. Insofar as genres are literary categories, the projection of naturalness onto them is fallacious, Gérard Genette argues: "in the classification of genres no position is essentially more natural or more ideal than any other."[13] They are all historical categories.

The distinction between theoretical and empirical conceptions of genre is a displaced version of an important distinction that is often ignored. On the one hand, from a rhetorical point of view, actually existing works are contingent manifestations of discursive possibilities. Rhetoric seeks to identify and classify discursive procedures that can be used to produce effective discourse; discourses are combinations of sentences, and there are many possible ways of combining sentences, in different sorts of speech acts. Crucial to discursive effects is an account of possible kinds of discourse. From this point of view, existing literary works could have been different—and one way of approaching literature is to imagine variations.[14] For rhetoric, the strategies a work might have adopted are significant. From the point of view of literary criticism, however, the existing works of literature are a given, not mere contingencies. They have established traditions that literary studies seeks to elucidate, and genres are the names of categories in these historical traditions. Because of the traditional association of genre theory with rhetoric, it has been easy to confuse the two perspectives and to take accounts of genre as bearing on general rhetorical and discursive possibilities; but what Blanchot calls the reality of genres is a historical one.

This is important because our historicist age has tended to be suspicious of generic categories that previous theorists have claimed to base on some fundamental aspect of language, communication, or representation, as if these were eternal, atemporal categories, which of course they are not (though they can be translated into rhetorical terms, as discursive possibilities). But on the other hand, genres are not merely contingent empirical groupings, categories that people have for various reasons found it convenient at one time or another for dealing with literature, as on the shelves of a bookstore. As historical categories, genres have a dual orientation, diachronic and synchronic, toward a historical tradition and toward a function in the cultural system of a particular historical period. As a genre, *detective fiction* is both a historical tradition (though always being reconceived or reconstructed) and at certain times a functional, constitutive category for writers, who set out to write a detective story (albeit one that may tweak or parody the conventions of the genre), and for readers, who read a text as a detective story and may be gratified or disappointed by the way in which a given text relates to the genre. The fact that one may read a given text as an autobiography or as a novel indicates that there are historical traditions with which the work may be allied and categories that are constitutive for reading and writing within a given cultural situation.

The dual aspect of generic categories is critical—since what is dismissed in critiques of genre is a simplified, one-dimensional version, purely historical and retrospective, or else purely a matter of current ideological practice. Because genres have a historical dimension and involve links with prior literary practices, which may be unknown to readers and writers of a particular moment, the analysis of genre cannot be restricted to what people of a particular linguistic moment might judge the operative generic categories to be. The models they are imitating might in fact be part of a longer tradition, which hindsight enables us to see clearly. Genre study analyzes our procedures for acquiring and accumulating knowledge and cannot simply accept as empirical fact every ascription and description of genre; we need to evaluate such claims, and to do that we need to pose the question of the relation of the groupings posited by later critics, including ourselves, to those posited by critics of an earlier era.

Given the particular historicizing inclinations of criticism these days, it is important to repeat that conceptions of genres are not just accounts of what people of a particular period thought: it is crucial to the notion of genre as model that people might have been wrong about them—unaware of affinities or ignoring continuities in favor of more striking novelties, or recognizing only an attenuated version of a larger tradition. Genre study cannot be just a matter, for instance, of looking at what Renaissance critics say about genres and using only those categories for thinking about Renaissance literature—though of course one should try them out, while keeping in mind the possibility that more capacious and historically informed categories may be useful.

It seems a condition of working on the topic of the lyric, for example, that one be able to argue that both critics and poets in their statements about poetry may have had erroneous conceptions of the lyric, which are undermined by the functioning of the poems themselves, when they are viewed in the context of a longer or broader lyric tradition. The desire to correct, which drives much academic research on subjects like this, presumes that lyric is more than a construction of the moment, that the weight of tradition helps make there be something to be right or wrong about. A given historical notion of the lyric or lyric genres can neglect or obscure crucial aspects of the nature and function even of the poems to which the idea supposedly applies. The theory of a genre is an abstract model, an account of a set of norms or structural possibilities that historically underlie and enable the production and reception of literature. A claim about a generic model is not, then, an assertion about some property that all works that might be attached to this genre possess. It is a claim about fundamental structures that may be at work even when not manifest, a claim that directs attention to certain aspects of a work, which mark a tradition and an evolution, its dimensions of transformation. A test of generic categories is how far they help activate aspects of works that make them rich and interesting, though it is crucial to stress that interpretation of individual works is not the goal of poetics, which seeks to understand how the system of literary discourse works and has worked.

2. Lyric History

What about lyric, then? Discussion of canonical lyrics in Chapter 1 identified some major parameters—not necessary features, but sufficient to indicate the continuity of the tradition. "Lyric is the most continuously practiced of all poetic kinds in the history of Western representation," writes Allen Grossman.[15] But what sort of continuity is this? A sketch of the history of thinking about the Western lyric, from the Greeks to the nineteenth century, will provide further material for reflection on the character of the genre.

Archaic lyric belongs to a ritualized, performative speech, sometimes deemed of divine origin (the seer, the poet, and the king are the "masters of truth"), oracular speech that produces truth. The difficulties besetting the category *lyric* begin with the ancient Greeks, whose distinctions among types of poetry involved both thematic circumstances and meters, which are correlated with mode of performance. *Lyric* or melic verse was poetry created to be chanted or sung with accompaniment by the lyre on various sorts of occasions. To cite some of the categories used by the Alexandrian scholars to categorize Pindar's lyrics, *epinikia* are victory odes, *paeans* are hymns to the gods, *dithyrambs* celebrations of Dionysius, *parthenia* are sung by choruses of virgins, *threnoi* are death laments and *enkomia* praise mortal heroes. Scholars also stress, though, that "in general one is more struck by the shared features than by the divergences between these types."[16]

Other lyric categories are songs sung at a wedding *(hymenaia, epithalamia),* popular songs sung at banquets and symposia *(skolia),* processional songs of thanksgiving *(prosodia)* and, increasingly specialized, the poem of farewell on someone's departure *(propemptikon),* or the song the excluded lover sings to the door that bars entrance to the beloved *(paraklasi-thyron)*. Lyric poetry as then conceived included a range of meters, primarily strophic, with Sappho, Alcaeus, Anacreon, and Pindar as major lyric poets. The nonnarrative poems of Archilochus and Theognis, in iambic or elegiac meters—iambic verse was recited and elegiacs were mainly composed for accompaniment by the flute—were not deemed lyric, though today many classical scholars treat these as lyric also, considering that other similarities should take precedence over distinctions of meter.[17]

Even after the development of writing, melic or lyric verse was performed—monody generally before small groups of like-minded persons, and choral lyric before larger groups on more ceremonious occasions. Children were taught to sing poetry—discussion of how this training should be conducted and precisely what should be sung is a topic on which Plato expatiates—and though we know practically nothing of the music that accompanied such singing and chanting, singing poems at banquets and other gatherings was a major cultural activity and choral lyrics were featured in civic gatherings. The fact that we possess only random fragments of what in Hellenistic times was still a huge corpus of verse—of Sappho's nine books there remains only one complete poem—means that any conclusions are highly speculative. We know that there existed archaic poetic practices of which we have no remnants at all, but lyric was a major strain of archaic Greek poetry. Critics such as Gregory Nagy and Jeffrey Walker argue that epic evolved out of archaic lyric, which not only precedes and generates particular literary genres, including epic and drama, but also epideictic and panegyric rhetoric in general.[18] In the *Poetics,* Aristotle himself offers a speculative genealogy, deriving all poetic genres from lyric encomia, hymns, and invectives. Questions of origin are notoriously difficult to adjudicate, but whether or not lyric precedes epic, as seems likely, it is clear that the link between lyric and discourse that aims to praise or persuade—epideictic discourse—is strong in archaic Greece and persists through the Renaissance. The central figure of the ancient lyric is Pindar, whom Harold Bloom has called "the truest paradigm for the Western lyric";[19] but all that has been preserved of his considerable lyric corpus are poems of one type, victory odes, which certainly complicates the understanding of ancient lyric.

"The appearance of a sudden profusion of lyric voices starting ca 700 BCE," writes Leslie Kurke, "is a historical accident, resulting from the development of a new technology—the reintroduction of writing into the Greek world around 750–10 BCE. There had always been songs sung and verses recited, but now, for the first time, writing provided the means to fix poetry and song as text and thereby preserve them." By the fifth century BCE singers became makers, and craft metaphors begin to emerge, though poems still frequently claimed divine inspiration.[20] In fact, the figure of poet as singer persists through the nineteenth century, even though few poems were sung.

The problem of lyric's uncertain generic status seems above all the result of the fact that Aristotle did not treat it as a major species in his discussion of mimetic poetry, although he was well versed in Greek lyric forms and cites many lyric examples in his *Rhetoric*. He himself composed a poem which may even have led to his leaving Athens, because of controversy about its genre: was it a paean, a species of hymn which should only be composed for gods, or an encomium, appropriate for celebration of a mortal hero?[21] (High stakes in genre disputes!) Lyric had in his day been eclipsed as a contemporary poetic practice by drama, especially tragedy, which deployed lyric meters in choral songs, but lyric was still of great cultural significance, as the citation of lyric examples by Plato and Aristotle himself amply testifies. In Plato's *Protagoras,* where the protagonists discuss the arguments of a poem by Simonides in order to reach conclusions about the world, everyone takes it for granted that, as Protagoras says, the most important part of a man's education *(paideia)* is to be capable of judging which sayings of poets are just and worthy, and to give reasons when questioned.

Defining literature (poetry) as mimesis, Aristotle lists on the opening page of his *Poetics* dithyramb, a type of choral lyric honoring Dionysus, along with epic, tragedy, and comedy as "all, taken as a whole, kinds of mimesis."[22] In the eighteenth century this mention would give critics an opening for claiming as Aristotelian the tripartite division of drama, epic, and lyric, but in the *Poetics* itself lyric poetry figures only under the heading of *melopoeia,* as a minor component of tragedy (the sung parts of tragedy), and not as a genre in its own right: *lexis* and *melopoeia,* diction and song, are two media in which mimesis is rendered in tragedy.

Plato's dialogues contain many remarks about poetry of the lyrical kind, including praise of Simonides and above all Pindar, but the varied remarks in the dialogues, many of which occur in disputations, do not constitute a systematic account of lyric. The famous passage in book 3 of the *Republic* which distinguishes poetry by mode of enunciation calls *dithyramb* a poem in which the poet speaks in his own person only (contrasted with *drama,* which is mimesis of the speech of characters, and with *epic,* which is a mixture of narration and speeches); but another passage speaks of composing in "epic, melic, or tragic verse," apparently recognizing a broader category into which dithyramb would fit.[23]

In other passages Plato treats poetry as a form of music, much as we might treat opera today, but throughout the dialogues he does not hesitate to quote lines of poetry without remarking on the music that accompanies them and to stage discussions of whether statements of poems are true or worthy of assent.[24] By the fifth century BCE, although lyric is still conceived as a musical performance it is in fact treated as text to be repeated and evaluated. Unlike epic and drama, which are forms of mimesis, lyric utterance is taken as a statement to be judged for its conformity to ethical and political values.

Neither Plato nor Aristotle is concerned with the characterization of lyric, a matter left to the librarians of Alexandria, who in the late third century and second century BCE worked assiduously on the elaboration of rhetorical and literary concepts and developed the category of lyric, or *melike poiesis.* Aristophanes of Byzantium of the second century BCE, the scholar thought most responsible for collecting and editing the work of Greek poets, promoted a canon of nine *ennea lyrikoi* who became the Latin *lyrici vates:* Pindar, Alcaeus, Sappho, Alcman, Anacreon, Simonides, and others less well known today. In a grouping that was preserved in Rome during subsequent centuries, lyric poets took their place in the canon alongside epic, tragic, and comic poets and two further classes of poets, iambic and elegiac. What we know of the Alexandrian compilations does not provide a theory of lyric or a principle of organization: no doubt the loss of the music and the distance from the performance practices created considerable uncertainty. Plato's complaint more than 150 years earlier, that poets had become lawless and were intermingling the old genres and types of music, indicates the difficulties that would have confronted Hellenistic scholars, who grouped the poems sometimes by meter, sometimes by thematic type, or the kind of occasion for which they were written.[25] But the work of the Alexandrian scholars of this era, for which most sources are lost, was a crucial stage in the development of a framework for discussions of discourse (rhetoric and poetics) in the West.

Understanding the nature of ancient lyric from what remains is difficult and speculative, especially since from Pindar, the most eminent lyric poet of ancient Greece, we have only the victory odes. The shortest of these is the eleventh Olympian, praising the victor in a boxing match:

ἔστιν ἀνθρώποις ἀνέμων ὅτε πλεῖστα
χρῆσις, ἔστιν δ᾽ οὐρανίων ὑδάτων,
ὀμβρίων παίδων νεφέλας.
εἰ δὲ σὺν πόνῳ τις εὖ πράσσοι, μελιγάρυες ὕμνοι
ὑστέρων ἀρχὰ λόγων
τέλλεται καὶ πιστὸν ὅρκιον μεγάλαις ἀρεταῖς.
ἀφθόνητος δ᾽ αἶνος Ὀλυμπιονίκαις
οὗτος ἄγκειται. τὰ μὲν ἀμετέρα
γλῶσσα ποιμαίνειν ἐθέλει:
ἐκ θεοῦ δ᾽ ἀνὴρ σοφαῖς ἀνθεῖ πραπίδεσσιν ὁμοίως.
ἴσθι νῦν, Ἀρχεστράτου
παῖ, τεᾶς, Ἁγησίδαμε, πυγμαχίας ἕνεκεν
κόσμον ἐπὶ στεφάνῳ χρυσέας ἐλαίας
ἁδυμελῆ κελαδήσω,
Ζεφυρίων, Λοκρῶν γενεὰν ἀλέγων.
ἔνθα συγκωμάξατ᾽: ἐγγυάσομαι
ὔμ μιν, ὦ Μοῖσαι, φυγόξενον στρατὸν
μηδ᾽ ἀπείρατον καλῶν,
ἀκρόσοφόν τε καὶ αἰχματὰν ἀφίξε-
σθαι. τὸ γὰρ ἐμφυὲς οὔτ᾽ αἴθων ἀλώπηξ
οὔτ᾽ ἐρίβρομοι λέοντες διαλλάξαιντο ἦθος.

☙

There is a time when men's need for winds is the greatest,
and a time for waters from the sky,
the rainy offspring of clouds.
But when anyone is victorious through his toil, then honey-voiced
    odes

become the foundation for future fame,

and a faithful pledge for great deeds of excellence.

This praise is dedicated to Olympian victors, without stint.

My tongue wants to foster such themes;

but it is by the gift of a god that a man flourishes with a skillful mind,
    as with anything else.

For the present rest assured, Hagesidamus son of Archestratus:

for the sake of your boxing victory, I shall loudly sing a sweet song,

an adornment for your garland of golden olive,

while I honor the race of the Western Locrians.

There, Muses, join in the victory-song;

I shall pledge my word to you that we will find there a race

that does not repel the stranger,

or is inexperienced in fine deeds,

but one that is wise and warlike too.

For neither the fiery fox nor loud-roaring lions change their nature.

[Trans. Diane Svarlien]

The celebration of a minor event—a boxing victory!—provides occasion
for praise of a community but foregrounds a manifest and assertive "I,"
although it was sung by a chorus. "This 'I' is prominent," writes Kurke,
"precisely because it does the work of mediating and finessing the divergent interests and claims of individual and community, elitist and
middling values, and for this reason there is no more mercurial and un-
stable 'I' than that of the epinikia." The lyric "I" of antiquity does give
rise to possibilities of individual singularity, as in Sappho or Archilocus,
and Bruno Snell argues that here, in a "lyric age," we witness the birth of
the modern mind, as poets came to know themselves as individuals with
an inner life. But such individuation comes primarily through the articulation to an audience of values or judgments that deviate from a social
norm, rather than allusion to inner states.[26] Despite the cases that to
modern ears seem expressions of individuality, the first person in ancient
lyric seems to be principally the site of a role—one which, as in Pindar,
often involves epideictic assertions of what should be valued. The "I"
works above all to unify a series of disparate remarks. These public,

ceremonious odes of Pindar, full of explicit claims about what is best or worthy and what we owe to the gods, inspired later poets such as Dryden, Hölderlin, or Wordsworth, whose orientations were quite different—a striking mark of the historical persistence of the genre.

This ode also highlights the performative quality of public lyric, which accomplishes the act of praise that it spends time describing. In general we can say that in Greece the lyric is a form for public or private performance and reperformance, with a strong ethical dimension and a variety of conventionally prescribed roles through which meaning and value can be negotiated, as singers perform lyrics created at particular moments.

The lyric is reinvented in Rome by Horace, who models himself on the Greeks and, extraordinarily, aims to join the canonical nine Greek lyric poets, to be placed among the *lyrici vates*—as he says in the first poem of his *Odes*. The Hellenistic scholars and grammarians who collected and organized the Greek canon, and who were Horace's conduit to the Greeks, had an intense sense of their belatedness—the last of the great Greek lyricists, Pindar, had died 400 years earlier—but Horace sought "to recreate the spirit of the Greek lyric in its entirety."[27] In the *Odes* he repeatedly identifies his achievement as one of creating in Latin songs not sung before: "I was the first to bring Aeolian song to Italian measures" ("princeps Aeolium carmen ad Italos / deduxisse modos" [3.30.13–14]). And his advice to other poets is to have always the Greek texts to hand—"handle the Greek models by night, handle them by day" (vos exemplaria Graeca / nocturna versate manu, versate diurna).[28] Although his poems are composed for circulation in written form, he presents himself as a singer to the lyre, beginning the first book of *Odes* with the hope that he may join the *lyrici vates,* if the muse Polyhymnia does not withhold the lyre of Lesbos (1.1), and continuing by invoking the lyre—"Come, my Greek lyre, / and sound a Latin song" (1.32)—and identifying with it: "People as they pass point to me as the player of the Roman lyre" (4.3). Figures of singing are scattered throughout the *Odes:* "What we sing of is drinking parties, of battles fought / by fierce virgins . . ." (1.6); "priest of the muses, I sing songs not heard before to boys and girls" (3.1); "Phoebus has given me the art of song and the name of poet" (4.6). Only in book 4, published ten years after the first three, does he speak of his poetry as writing.

A major theme of the Horatian ode is the distinction between the lyric and epic. Ode 3.3 consists mostly of a long speech by Juno about the Trojan war, but then closes,

> Non hoc iocosae conveniet lyrae:
> quo, Musa, tendis? Desine pervicax
>   referre sermones deorum et
>   magna modis tenuare parvis.

☞

> This will not suit my playful lyre.
> Where are you going, obstinate Muse? Stop
>   retailing talk of the gods and
>   reducing great matters to your tiny measures.

[Trans. David West]

An ode addressed to his lyre (1.32) defines the genre in relation to Alcaeus of Lesbos and the Greek lyric:

> . . . age dic Latinum,
>   barbite, carmen,
> Lesbio primum modulate civi,
> qui ferox bello tamen inter arma,
> sive iactatam religarat udo
>   litore navim,
> liberum et Musas Veneremque et illi
> semper haerentem puerum canebat,
> et Lycum nigris oculis nigroque
>   crine decorum.

☞

> . . . come my Greek lyre,
>   and sound a Latin song.
> You were first tuned by a citizen of Lesbos,
> fierce in war, who, whether he was where the steel
> was flying or had tied up his battered ship
>   on the spray-soaked shore,

would still sing of Bacchus and the Muses,
of Venus and the boy who is always at her side,
and of Lycus and his jet-black eyes
          and jet-black hair.

                              [Trans. David West]

The complex relation between war and lyric emerges here in the insistence on Alcaeus as a soldier, and the inclusion in the lyric of such matter, while maintaining that the subject of lyric is love. In 2.13, however, the subjects of love and war are divided between the two poets of Lesbos: Sappho is said to sing complaints about her girls and Alcaeus to sing the woes of a seaman's life, of exile, and of war. Ultimately, Horace's intricate gesture defines lyric against epic but reserves the right to include all manner of references to war, the gods, and politics in the poems presented as lyric.

As lyric poet, Horace engages in complex negotiations with the figure of Pindar. He eschews Pindar's sublime grandiloquence and public performance of epic myth in the famous Ode 4.2 which describes Pindar's poetry and which has been in quoted in practically every edition of Pindar's odes since the sixteenth century:

Monte decurrens velut amnis, imbres
quem super notas aluere ripas,
fervet inmensusque ruit profundo
          Pindarus ore.

                    ☞

Like a rain-fed river running down
From the mountains and bursting its banks—
Seething, immeasurable, deep-mouthed,
          Pindar races along in spate.

                              [Trans. David West]

But book 4 is full of political praise and myth, and the "Carmen Saeculare," commissioned by Augustus to celebrate the end of a century and which received a public performance and political centrality of which

Pindar could only have dreamed, is composed in the same Sapphic strophes as the ode to Pindar and is Pindaric in conception.[29] While Horace's
various *recusatio* poems provide an image of lyric as he conceives it—that
it "deals not with the great unrepeatable moments of historical time but
with the iterable time of the banquet; not with far-off mythic material of
epic or tragedy but with the quotidian non-events of the individual's life
at home"—the antithesis is drawn in such hyperbolic terms that the synthesis of his practice becomes all the more impressive. Pindar permits the
establishment of two poles between which Horace can oscillate, making
his version of lyric "the generic space wherein the serious and the amatory may coexist without falling to either extreme."[30]

Horace re-creates many Greek lyric types—thus 1.1 is a *priamel*, listing
the different choices of life—of soldiers, farmers, sailors, etc.—while noting
his preference for that of poet. He has versions of hymns, both *paean* and
dithyramb, enkomia, and *skolia,* banquet poems, and a *paraklausithyron*
(door poem). The first nine odes of book 1, called the Parade Odes because they parade this lyric program and virtuosity, are in nine different
Greek meters. One might note several salient features of the lyric as practiced by Horace: the poems are quite independent of one another—not
parts of a series, though they do lead readers to posit a speaker; they are
addressed to something or someone, though addressees may be fictional;
and deictics including temporal adverbs and the present tense promote
the fiction of utterance on an occasion. The poems about love are not poems
of seduction or of amorous anguish but reflective and monitory. They are
not introspective, though they question, warn, and comment as they address questions of how to live.[31] Satiric ventures he keeps for hexameter
verse, while remaking the tradition of the lyric, with a wide range of
discursive postures and topics of disquisition, from political issues to
amorous entanglement. Quintilian declares, "Of the lyric poets Horace
is almost the only one worth reading; he can be lofty sometimes and yet
he is also full of charm and grace, versatile in his figures and felicitously
daring in his choice of words."[32]

Catullus, born twenty years before Horace, is the author of the first book
of ancient monody that has reached us (almost) intact and is nearly as
influential as Horace for the later lyric tradition. The poems of the first half

of the collection, the so-called polymetrics, in different lyric meters, are usually contrasted with the poems in elegiac couplets that form the second half.[33] Not only does Catullus write some poems in traditional Greek lyric meters, but he adapts the famous fragment of Sappho's, "phainetai moi," discussed later in this chapter, that Longinus would later relay to European modernity as the very model of the sublime. The polymetrics, though, include much invective and obscenity as well as love poetry. Catullus, as far as we know, is the first poet in Greek or Latin who appears to write about a particular love affair in depth in a related collection of poems. Despite the fact that the target of ardor, Lesbia (whose name is another connection to the Greek lyric tradition), is mentioned in only a small number of Catullus's poems, the subsequent tradition has made his affair with Lesbia the center of the collection, taking as many poems as possible to concern Lesbia. Only those explicitly addressed to male lovers or to other named women escape. The most famous is a carpe diem poem:

Vivamus, mea Lesbia, atque amemus,
rumoresque senum severiorum
omnes unius aestimemus assis.
soles occidere et redire possunt:
nobis, cum semel occidit brevis lux,
nox est perpetua una dormienda.
da mi basia mille, deinde centum,
dein mille altera, dein secunda centum,
deinde usque altera mille, deinde centum,
dein, cum milia multa fecerimus,
conturbabimus illa, ne sciamus,
aut ne quis malus invidere possit,
cum tantum sciat esse basiorum.

꠩

Let us live, my Lesbia, and love,
And value all the talk of stricter
Old men at a single penny.
Suns can set and rise again;

For us, once our brief light has set,
There's one unending night for sleeping.
Give me a thousand kisses, then a hundred,
Then another thousand, then a second hundred,
Then still another thousand, then a hundred;
Then, when we've made many thousands,
We'll muddle them so as not to know
Or lest some villain overlook us
Knowing the total of our kisses.

[Trans. Guy Lee, modified]

The opposition between the loving couple and the censorious old men, between life and death, structures the poem, but the second part of the poem, instead of calling for a night of love before it is too late, multiplies kisses in a count that at first bespeaks haste but then promises to go on and on, as if the multiplication of kisses could install the lovers in the special temporality of the poem. But the ostensible reason for the multiplication of kisses is to baffle the count and deprive the censorious of knowledge with which the evil eye could harm them.[34]

The extravagant multiplication of kisses is provocation of the audience, though, because being carried away with passion, especially a passion for kisses, was a violation of norms of masculine behavior—unmanly. Catullus 16 virulently attacks Furius and Aurelius, who are said to register this: "because you've read of my many thousand kisses / you doubt my virility" ("vos, quod milia multa basiorum / legistis, male me marem putatis").[35] Is there a presumption that readers, like the grumpy old men of the present poem, will be put off, and is it perhaps readers who need to be seduced, for readers that the rhetoric is designed? This poem's relations with other poems in the collection suggest that Lesbia is scarcely the main focus. The startling census of kisses, the flouting of behavioural norms, and the clever turning of the language of accounting against the attempt to hold lovers accountable suggest a focus on readers rather than on relations with a beloved.

Nonetheless, Catullus's poems about love were taken to form a series. After him innumerable other poets found that they were irresistibly committed to loving a figure like Lesbia and recounting the ecstasy and the suffering of devotion to one dominating mistress. His collection sets the stage for a coherent genre, the Latin love lyric, often called the Latin love elegy because of the use of elegiac meter, in which Propertius loves Cynthia, Tibullus loves Delia, and Ovid loves Corinna. And after Dante and Petrarch established the genre in a European vernacular, we have a continuing international tradition. Since the poems about or to Lesbia, and those which there is no obstacle to linking with her, range from expressions of undying love to vicious vituperation, there is potential for a dramatic story here; and the reader's relation to this text may come to be based on this desire to know the story. We are teased and titillated, as "the text solicits the reader's desire for narrative closure and completeness—a desire ultimately doomed to frustration: the details within the text will support any number of . . . 'plots', none clearly predominant."[36] Paul Allen Miller, who idiosyncratically defines the lyric as a collection of poems in which we seek a narrative, deems Catullus the first lyric poet.

Roman lyric "is perhaps the most difficult genre to generalize about, both because of the complex historical continuities between Greek, Latin, and post-classical lyric, and because the two primary practitioners at Rome—Horace in his *Odes* and Catullus—have very little in common." But four general features of lyric are "variation within the corpus, relative independence of each poem, self-conscious reflection on one's status as late-comer in the poetic tradition, and (to differing degrees), a preference for the performative quality of early Greek poetry."[37] Though writing and the book have become the medium of lyrics, they retain a reference to the poem as event or performance.

Horace remains a dominant lyric presence in late antiquity, a school author, and the object of commentaries and references by other poets.[38] Under the Empire there was a shift in the conception of rhetoric from techniques for efficacious discourse to techniques for eloquence, and lyric poetry, especially in its epideictic dimensions, as poetry of praise, became more closely associated with rhetoric and cited by rhetoricians. One of these rhetorical treatises, remarkable both for its preservation of Sappho's most famous lyric and its resourcefulness in exploring how effects of sublimity depend upon both great conceptions and skillful rhetorical techniques, is *On the Sublime (Peri hupsous),* of the late first century CE or thereafter. Longinus does not speak of the lyric as such and cites a variety of literary and nonliterary works, but he presents Sappho's poem as an example of the power of combining selected elements into an organic whole. Sappho "never fails to take the emotions incident to the passion of love from its attendant symptoms and from real life. And wherein does she show her excellence? In the skill with which she selects and combines the most striking and intense of these symptoms." "Is it not wonderful," Longinus continues, "how she summons at the same time, soul, body, hearing, tongue, sight, skin, as though they had wandered off from herself? She feels contradictory sensations, freezes, burns, raves, reasons, so that she displays not a single emotion but whole congeries of emotion." The "supreme merit of her art" is "the skill with which she takes the most striking and combines them into a single whole."[39]

This poem has long served as the prime example of the sublime achievement of the lyric, with its representation of a speaker (and supposedly the author) powerfully proclaiming the passion by which she is felt to be carried away even as she describes it.

φάινεταί μοι κῆνος ἴσος θέοισιν
ἔμμεν' ὤνερ ὄττις ἐνάντίος τοι
ἰσδάνει καὶ πλάσιον ἄδυ φωνεί-
    σας ὐπακούει

καὶ γελαίσας ἰμέροεν τό μ' ἦ μὰν
καρδίαν ἐν στήθεσιν ἐπτόαισεν,
ὠς γὰρ ἔς σ' ἴδω βρόχε' ὤς με φώναι-
    σ' οὐδ' ἔν ἔτ' εἴκει,

ἀλλ' ἄκαν μὲν γλῶσσα †ἔαγε, λέπτον
δ' αὔτικα χρῷ πῦρ ὐπαδεδρόμηκεν,
ὀππάτεσσι δ' οὐδ' ἔν ὄρημμ', ἐπιρρόμ-
    βεισι δ' ἄκουαι.

ἀ δέ μ' ἴδρως κακχέεται, τρόμος δὲ
παῖσαν ἄγρει χλωροτέρα δὲ ποίας

ἔμμι, τεθνάκην δ' ὀλίγω 'πιδεύης
  φαίνομ' ἔμ' αὔτᾳ.

ἀλλὰ πὰν τόλματον ἐπεὶ †καὶ πένητα†

He seems to me equal to the gods that man
whosoever who opposite you
sits and listens close
            to your sweet speaking

and lovely laughing—oh it
puts the heart in my chest on wings
for when I look at you, even a moment, no speaking
            is left in me

no: tongue breaks and thin
fire is racing under the skin
and in eyes no sight and drumming
            fills ears

and cold sweat holds me and shaking
grips me all, greener than grass
I am and dead—or almost
            I seem to me.

But all is to be dared, because even a person of poverty . . .

                    [Trans. Anne Carson, modified]

The poem tantalizingly breaks off, perhaps because Longinus quoted what was relevant to his argument and presumed people knew how it concluded. The force of the poem comes in part from the description of physical symptoms: not "this is what I feel" but "this is what happens to me when I see you." The articulation of what dramatically happens whenever I catch a glimpse of you produces a striking effect: cast in the present tense, an account of what happens repeatedly, it nonetheless impresses us as something happening now, in the performative temporality of the lyric.[40]

This poem presents not only the paradox of the speechless state of one who elegantly narrates what happens but also a powerful declaration of helplessness which, as Neil Hertz writes, "bring the motifs of violence and risk of death into touch with the rhetorician's theory that an effective poem is an organic unity. For Sappho is introduced as an example of the poet selecting and composing elements so as to 'organize them into a single body'—only the elements she organizes into the body of her poem are precisely the names of the fragments of her natural body, seen as the debris of a shattering erotic experience." Hertz posits that what fascinates Longinus is "the point where the near-fatal stress of passion can be thought of as turning into—as indistinguishable from—the energy that is constituting the poem."[41] That sense of energy is crucial to the fortunes of both Sappho and Longinus: when translated in seventeenth-century France and England, this treatise became influential for conceptions of the sublime and of lyric possibility, presenting a poetry of passion—with sufferer as speaker—embodying a turn where the suffering becomes a source of poetic power.[42]

Late Latinity is not a great era for literature or lyric, though by the fifth century CE, "Proclus's *Chrestomathy* could list 28 genres of lyric poetry, broken down into four main categories: songs to the gods, songs for humans, songs to both, and occasional songs addressing neither gods nor mortals particularly."[43] In general, though, the category "lyric" itself makes only a minor appearance in late Latin and medieval texts, despite a proliferation of short, nonnarrative poems, both secular and devotional. Several developments at this point are crucial for the history of the Western lyric, though. First, with changes in the Latin language, especially the loss of the distinction between long and short syllables, there is a replacement of quantitative by accentual meters in Latin from the second century onward. This change also facilitated the development of rhyme, first in Christian Latin hymns and then in secular Latin lyrics and in vernaculars. Bishop Ambrose in the fourth century is credited with inaugurating the Ambrosian stanza of four four-beat lines, which became the basis for the later hymn tradition and much vernacular lyric in European languages. The first stanza of one of his most famous hymns illustrates the form:

Deus creator omnium
polique rector, vestiens

diem decoro lumine,
noctem soporis gratia

⁊

God that all things didst create
and the heavens doth regulate,
Who doth clothe the day with light,
and with gracious sleep the night

[Trans. F. A. Wright]

The medieval church greatly stimulated the production of hymns (monastic rules required the chanting of hymns at the eight canonical hours), which increasingly were rhymed, in shorter lines than classical hexameters, which made them easier to recall and to sing or chant. The celebrated "Dies irae" of the twelfth century is typical:

Dies iræ, dies illa,
solvet sæclum in favílla,
teste David cum Sibýlla!

Quantus tremor est futúrus,
quando judex est ventúrus,
cuncta stricte discussúrus!

⁊

Day of wrath and doom impending,
David's word with Sibyl's blending,
Heaven and earth in ashes ending!

Oh, what fear man's bosom rendeth,
When from heaven the Judge descendeth,
On whose sentence all dependeth.

[*The English Missal*]

As the Christian religious lyric developed out of Roman practices, there was also a rich tradition of popular songs associated with many aspects of everyday life, which we know about partly from the condemnations of ecclesiastics, though secular song was sometimes adapted to Christian purposes. There is short poetry in at least two Celtic languages (Irish, Welsh) and three Germanic ones (English, German, Old Norse), such as Caedmon's "Hymn" (c. 670) and Bede's "Death Song" (735), that precedes the Romance lyric, although these earlier traditions are ultimately peripheral to the main line of European poetry.[44] But by the year 1000, writes Peter Dronke, "the lyrical repertoire that was largely shared by all medieval Europe . . . is the product of ancient and scarcely separable traditions of courtly, clerical, and popular song. We can only infer the richness and many-sidedness of these traditions from the fragmentary written evidence that survives." The manuscript known as the *Cambridge Songs* (mid-eleventh century), a collection of some eighty medieval Latin poems from Germany, France, and Italy, shows the range of medieval Latin lyric, from love poetry to ecclesiastical satire, which had penetrated far beyond the Mediterranean basin. *Carmina Burana,* a twelfth-century manuscript, includes a vast range of Latin poems, love songs, and drinking songs, as well as sacred lyrics. The twelfth century sees the flowering of the love lyric in Latin, with songs celebrating love, spring, and joy in a wide range of stanzaic forms.[45]

Meanwhile, the medieval vernacular lyric was developing throughout the Mediterranean region. There are lively debates about priority: is the Arabic poetry of Muslim Spain, which may have been the earliest, the precursor of Hebrew and Provencal lyric? Is it primarily an inflection of earlier Arabic poetry or was it influenced by troubadour lyric, which must have existed before Guillaume de Poitiers (William of Aquitaine)? How important in this European medieval mix are Arabic lyric forms such at the *qasida,* a monorhymed panegyric poem focused on love? Maria Menocal maintains that the *muwasshahāt,* a complex strophic form usually written in colloquial Arabic but sometimes in Mozarabic, the Romance dialect of Christians in Muslim Spain, "invents new Romance and Arabic and Hebrew poetics in one swoop, all in the same poems: strophes both defined and differentiated by rhyme schemes." By the late tenth and eleventh centuries the Hebrew lyric in Spain had arguably inherited from Arabic poetry distinct lyric genres of praise and blame and songs of love *(ghazal).*[46] Other critics are skeptical, for the Arabic influence on other forms of writing is far more evident, and questions of origin and influence in these centuries of linguistic heterogeneity are far from settled. What is clear is the trend toward a wider array of complex stanza forms, shorter lines, and swifter tempos.[47]

Whatever the directions of influence, the Mediterranean region of the Middle Ages is the birthplace of the Romance vernacular lyric, whose most striking and influential practice was the troubadour lyric. Guillaume de Poitiers of the late eleventh and early twelfth century is the first troubadour whose work is preserved, though the ironies of a poem such as his famous "Farai un vers de dreit nien" ("I'll write a poem about nothing at all"), suggest all too clearly that there is already an established tradition to play off against:

> Amigu' ai ieu, non sai qui s'es,
> C'anc no la vi, si m'aiut fes,
>
> ⁀
>
> I have a mistress but I don't know who she is,
> because I never saw her, in faith.[48]

This is not just "Amor de lonh" (love from afar), as troubadour Jaufré Raudel called it, but love that is by definition hopeless. The troubadour lyric, in Occitan, celebrated love for an inaccessible mistress in stanzaic forms with fixed rhyme schemes and lines of specific numbers of syllables. Arnaud Daniel, the most accomplished technician, lover of intricate forms, produced one poem with a 17-line stanza, "L'Aura amara" ("The bitter breeze"), with lines of 6, 5, 4, 3, 2, and 1 syllables in a pattern that recurs, along with fixed rhyme scheme, in each of six stanzas and a truncated concluding stanza known as a *tornada*. The themes of the courtly love (fin'amor), the combination of sexual desire and its spiritualization, the power of the lady and the suffering of the lover, become staples of the Western lyric. At first, there appear to have been no distinctions among types of troubadour lyrics, but then the *cansó*, or love song, came to be distinguished from the *sirventes*, or satirical song, and the isolated stanza, *cobla*. Eventually other types of lyric were identified, including the *planh* (complaint), the *alba* (dawn song), *tenso* (debate), and *pastourela*. The earliest treatise of troubadour poetics, Raimon Vidal's *Razos de trobar* of the beginning of the thirteenth century, does not stress different types of song, but later works, such as the anonymous Catalan *Doctrina de compondre dictats,* codify by instructing how to write different types, and in the early fourteenth century, when Occitan lyric is threatened by the growing dominance of French, the *Sobregaya companhia del Gay Saber,* or "Exceedingly Merry Company of the Merry Wisdom" was founded in Toulouse to preserve the troubadour tradition, and Guilhem Molinier was commissioned to draw up a *Leys d'amors,* which stipulates the features of eleven "principal" lyric types, for which prizes could be awarded at poetic competitions in Floral Games in Toulouse.[49] Although the term *lyric* is not used by the troubadours, the progressive proliferation of categories of song and the lack of agreement about what the subcategories should be suggests that for purposes of describing the tradition a broad general category, such as lyric, is at least as useful as any particular array of specialized terms.

The troubadour lyric spread rapidly through Europe—the troubadours, and their northern counterparts, the *trouvères* of northern France and the Minnesingers of Germany, were often wandering minstrels. Latin, Provencal, and other vernacular poems were collected in *chansonniers* or song-books, which often included *vidas* or fictional biographies of troubadours and contributed to the notion of lyric as a poetry of the subject. Though lyric retains the idea of connection to music, the *chansonniers* contain little information about musical accompaniment, and much lyric is no longer musical: Curtis Jirsa notes, "A significant portion of the extant corpus of medieval lyric poetry, including the considerable body of Middle English meditative and penitential poetry from the 13th and 14th centuries, lacked musical accompaniment."[50] There is a growing tradition of lyrics not meant to be sung but used, for example, for private meditation. Lyrics offer "the position of a definite but unspecified ego whose position the audience is invited to occupy"; the first- and second-person pronouns invite each reader "to perfect or universalize himself by occupying that language as his own."[51]

Petrarch, who lived half of his life in Provence, pursued troubadour themes but in a sequence featuring the sonnet, which was not a troubadour form but was first developed in the Sicilian court of Frederick II (early thirteenth century). A closed form, contrasting with medieval lyrics in stanzas open to multiple iterations, the sonnet from the outset is written only. The sonnets of Dante's *Vita nuova* (1295) punctuate an autobiographical prose narrative with praise of Beatrice, amorous complaint, and the celebration of courtly love itself as a progression toward divine love through the lady's influence. Petrarch's *Canzoniere* established a grammar for the European love lyric: a set of tropes, images, oppositions (fire and ice), and typical scenarios that permitted generations of poets throughout Europe to exercise their ingenuity in the construction of love sonnets. The technical challenge of the form gives it a material, public dimension: writing sonnets became an activity by which in the sixteenth century especially, courtiers could display their wit and others could compete with them—although the poems claim to explore the affective predicament of an individual.

Petrarch, who still held Latin to be the best vehicle for poetry, praised Horace, in a Latin poem adopting the meter of Horace's first ode, as "You whom the Italian land celebrates as the king of lyric poetry" ("Regem te lirici carminis italus / orbis quem memorat"), reviving the term *lyric* which had been little used in the Middle Ages.[52] But only in the late fifteenth and sixteenth centuries does Horace become truly the archetype of a lyric poet. In France by the late fourteenth century there was a rich lyric tradition built on vernacular medieval verse, in which forms such as the *rondeau* and *ballade* had become standardized. The *rondeau* in particular was regularized as a thirteen-line poem in octosyllables or decasyllables, with two rhymes, one masculine and one feminine, and what is called a *rentrement,* whereby the opening word or phrase of the poem is repeated as a refrain after the second and third stanzas. Here is a sixteenth-century example from Clément Marot:

> Dedans Paris, ville jolie,
> Un jour, passant mélancolie,
> Je pris alliance nouvelle
> À la plus gaie demoiselle
> Qui soit d'ici en Italie.
>
> D'honnêteté elle est saisie,
> Et crois (selon ma fantaisie)

Qu'il n'en est guère de plus belle
Dedans Paris.

Je ne la vous nommerai mie,
Sinon que c'est ma grande amie;
Car l'alliance se fit telle
Par un doux baiser que j'eus d'elle,
Sans penser aucune infamie,
Dedans Paris.

☞

In Paris, that lovely city
one day, somewhat melancholy
I got a new alliance
with the most joyful girl,
between here and Italy.

She was affected by honorability
and I believe—at least in my phantasy
that there is hardly anyone more beautiful
in Paris.

I would not label her mine to you,
if she were not my great love
because our alliance became such
through a sweet kiss, that I received from her
without ever thinking anything infamous
in Paris.

[Trans. Dick Wursten]

The terrain we now call lyric became a contested domain in the six-teenth century, when in France, for example, the stanzaic lyric forms of Guillaume de Machaut, François Villon, Charles d'Orléans and the Grands Rhétoriqueurs were set against those with a classical pedigree such as the ode and, oddly, the sonnet, which through Petrarch acquired classic status. In 1550, listing the major genres of poetry as "l'Héroique, la Satyrique, la Tragique, la Comique, and la Lyrique," Ronsard proclaimed himself the first French lyric poet, 'le premier auteur Lyrique français," as he wrote

odes and sonnets, placing himself in the lineage of Pindar and Horace.[53]
His conception of the ode is as broad as Horace's—one of his most famous
is a lyric of three stanzas in octosyllabic lines beginning:

Mignonne, allons voir si la rose	Sweetheart, let us see if the rose
Qui ce matin avoit desclose	that only this morning unfolded
Sa robe de pourpre au Soleil,	its scarlet dress in the sun
A point perdu ceste vesprée	has lost, at vesper-time,
Les plis de sa robe pourprée,	the folds of its scarlet dress
Et son teint au vostre pareil.	and its colour, so like yours.

[Trans. Faith Cormier]

This carpe diem poem, working to establish the perennial comparison,
uses the fading of the rose to urge the lady to pluck her youth ("Cueillez,
cueillez, vostre jeunesse"). His fellow member of the Pléiade group of poets,
Joachim Du Bellay, also looks to odes and sonnets to defend and illustrate
the French language as properly literary. Echoing Horace's advice, he urges
the French poet to read and "handle day and night Greek and Latin texts"
and to abandon all those Romance forms crowned in the Floral Games in
Toulouse, such as "rondeaux, ballades, virelais, chants royal, songs and
such other spicy trivia [*épiceries*], which corrupt taste in our language and
serve only to testify to our ignorance." The French poet is told, "Sing me
these odes, still unknown to the French muse, with a lute tuned to the
sound of the Greek and Roman lyre, and let there be no verse that does not
bear the trace of some rare and ancient erudition. What will provide you
matter for this is praise of the gods and virtuous men, the fatal discourse of
worldly things, and the concerns of young men, such as love, freely flowing
wine, and fine eating" [*toute bonne chère*]. Epigrams and elegies, and eclogues are also desirable, as are sonnets, which he defines as a kind of ode:
"Sound me those handsome sonnets, an Italian invention no less learned
than pleasant, corresponding to the ode, and differing from it only in that
the sonnet has verses limited by rule, while the ode can run freely with
every sort of verse and even invent them at will, in the manner of Horace,
who sang in nineteen different sorts of verse, as the grammarians say."[54]

At the same time in Italy the theorist Antonio Minturno, writing in 1563,
made "lyric" not a term for miscellaneous minor forms, as it had been in

most Renaissance poetic treatises which followed Aristotle, or even in Sca-
liger, whose seven books of poetics devoted a great deal of space to what
he called numerous lyric genres. Miturno is the first to treat lyric as a genre
on a par with the epic and the dramatic: "How many, then are the divisions of poetry? Three: one is called Epic, the next Dramatic, and the third
Melic or Lyric." Minturno presents this scheme as if it were the classical
division and preserves the notion of imitation but broadens it, to include
discursive action as the basis for the lyric genre: lyric exhorts, celebrates,
prays, praises, blames; it teaches and delights, and Petrarch becomes a
model for the lyric. In response to the question of whether the lyric poet,
in speaking of himself, can be said to imitate at all, he affirms that "depicting the form of the body and the feelings [*affetti*] of the soul," as in
Horace and Petrarch, cannot be said not to imitate. Minturno is the first
to use the *Poetics* to give lyric a legitimacy that Aristotle refused it and,
as Gustavo Guerrero observes, in the best study of the concept of lyric
from medieval to modern times, "to project it back on antiquity, giving
it a clear and sufficient profile." In the sixteenth century the Italians and
the Spanish make lyric an encompassing category, whereas the French
with some notable exceptions do not, listing miscellaneous lyric forms.[55]

   In England also lyric was one of several kinds of nonepic or dramatic
verse, though Sir Philip Sidney singled it out in his *Defense of Poesy:* "Is
it the lyric that most displeaseth, who with his tuned lyre, and well-
accorded voice, giveth praise, the reward of virtue, to virtuous acts? who
giveth moral precepts, and natural problems? who sometimes raiseth up
his voice to the height of the heavens, in singing the lauds of the immortal
God?" Unlike Du Bellay, Sidney praises the "rude old songs" as well as
"the gorgeous eloquence of Pindar."[56]

   To modern eyes, as Roland Greene observes, "the disparity between
the available terms of lyric theory and the actual productions of the genre
becomes arrestingly evident" in the Renaissance. A major problem in discussions of lyric in this period is the lack of a place for lyric in the newly
authoritative Aristotelian framework: since the notion of mimesis is once
again foundational for accounts of literature, it is difficult to grant lyric a
major role. Sidney, for instance, still gestures toward mimesis—the poet,
he notoriously says, represents a golden world—but he also retains, as the
passage cited above indicates, the classical and medieval model of lyric

as a rhetorical practice—epideictic discourse—with the centrality of praise or blame, which makes it easier to treats lyrics as significant poetic productions. French theorists—Boileau and Rapin produce major poetic treatises in 1674—continue to list miscellaneous lyric forms without an overarching category. But Milton in his treatise "Of Education" speaks of the importance of learning "what the laws are of a true epic poem, what of a dramatic, what of a lyric"; and Italian theorists, confronted with the inescapable fact of Petrarch's literary eminence, follow Minturno in finding ways to admit lyric alongside epic and drama.[57]

M. H. Abrams, whose *The Mirror and the Lamp* is still the classic account of the shift from a mimetic to an expressive theory of literature in England and Germany, suggests that "the soaring fortunes of the lyric may be dated to 1651, the year that Cowley's Pindaric 'imitations' burst over the literary horizon and inaugurated the immense vogue of the 'greater Ode' in England." As early as 1704 John Dennis anticipated later English theorists in deeming epic, tragedy, and the greater lyric the major poetic genres.[58] Lyric becomes identified with the ode especially and set against epic, didactic, and narrative poetry.

The key moment in this history comes in the Abbé Batteux's *Principes de la littérature* of 1747, which simultaneously reinserts the lyric within the Aristotelian framework of literature as mimesis and yet lays the groundwork for the romantic elevation of lyric to the very type of literature. While seizing on Aristotle's reference to dithyramb as providing an opening for lyric, Batteux tackles head on the problem of mimesis: "When one examines lyric poetry only superficially, it seems to lend itself less than other types to the general principle that brings everything back to imitation. What! one cries out; 'the songs of the prophets, the psalms of David, the odes of Pindar and of Horace are allegedly not true poems? . . . Is not poetry a song, a cry of the heart? . . . I see no painting, no depiction.' Thus two things are true: first, that lyric poems are true poems; second that they do not have the character of imitation." But he concludes that lyric is in fact imitation after all, though it differs in what is imitated: "The other sorts of Poetry have actions as their principal object; lyric poetry is wholly devoted to feelings [aux sentiments], this is its matter, its essential object." Genette describes this as the last gasp of classical aesthetics: a final attempt to construct the literary field around the concept of imitation. But it is one that, in positing the centrality of lyric, ultimately undercuts the doctrine of imitation.[59]

Though Minturno and Batteux make lyric one of three major genres, a variety of other forces prepare the way for the consolidation of the romantic conception of lyric as expressive. The diffusion of Longinus's *On the Sublime,* especially after its translation by Boileau in 1674, contributed to the growing sense that the expression of passion is a major function of poetry. Ever since the Middle Ages, the psalms of David had been cited as a major example of lyric poetry, but Bishop Lowth's 1753 *Lectures on the Sacred Poetry of the Hebrews* promoted the sublimity of this poetry, which he presented as an imitation of the passions: "Since the human intellect is naturally delighted with every species of imitation, that species in particular which exhibits its own image, which displays and depicts those impulses, inflections, perturbations, and secret emotions, which it perceives and knows in itself, can scarcely fail to astonish and to delight above every other."[60] Eighteenth-century reflections which link poetry to the origin of language, of which Vico's *Scienza nuova* (1725), Rousseau's *Essai sur l'origine des langues* (1781), and Herder's *Treatise on the Origin of Languages* (1772) are only the most famous, contributed to the idea that poetry is more natural and elemental than prose, originally expressive rather than rhetorical. Such writings paved the way for an expressive theory of the lyric, directly formulated by Sir William Jones, who explicitly rejects the theory of poetry as imitation in his essay "On the Arts, Commonly Called Imitative" attached to his translations of "Asiatick" poetry.

Jones begins with a disdainful rejection of the Aristotelian "maxim": "It is the fate of those maxims, which have been thrown out by very eminent writers, to be received implicitly by most of their followers, and to be repeated a thousand times, for no other reason, than because they once dropped from the pen of a superior genius: one of these is the assertion of Aristotle, that all poetry consists in imitation, which has been so frequently echoed from author to author, that it would seem a kind of arrogance to controvert it." Explicitly contradicting Batteux, Jones claims that poetry and music have other origins, that cultures which do not value imitation have poets, and that in Mohammedan nations, where sculpture and painting are forbidden by law and dramatic poetry is unknown, yet "the pleasing arts of expressing the passions in verse, and of enforcing that expression by melody, are cultivated to a degree of enthusiasm." Jones appeals to a lyric tradition of epideictic poems that express praise, joy, love, or grief. While it is possible for poetry to imitate, "we may define the original and native poetry to be the language of the violent passions, expressed in exact measure, with strong accents and significant words"; and in defining what true poetry ought to be, he continues, "we have described what it really was among the Hebrews, the Greeks and Romans, the Arabs and Persians. . . . What did David or Solomon imitate in their divine poems? . . . The lyrick verses of Alcaeus, Alcman and Ibycus, the hymns of Callimachus, the elegy of Mochus on the death of Bion" are none of them imitations. "Aristotle himself wrote a very poetic elegy, . . . but it would be difficult to say what he imitated in it." And Petrarch was "too deeply affected with real grief to imitate the passion of others."[61]

The German aesthetician J. G. Sulzer articulated a similar and similarly influential view: the principle of imitation may apply to some of the arts, but poetry and music have their source in feeling, and the lyric is thus the epitome of poetry. As long as imitation was the lynchpin of the system of literature, it was extremely difficult to make a central place for lyric, however important lyrical forms might be in literary practice, but the eighteenth-century interest in origins, which encouraged the notion that poetry was an elemental practice, made it easier to break with imitation as the basis for reflections on literature and to imagine alternatives. By 1810 Madame de Staël could declare, for example, "Lyric poetry is expressed in the name of the author himself; no longer is it borne by a character . . . Lyric poetry recounts nothing, is not confined by the succession of time, nor by the limits of place . . . It gives duration to that sublime moment in which man raises himself above the pleasures and pains of life."[62]

German theorists quickly promoted the tripartite division of literature into epic, drama, and lyric, and Goethe's stipulation that these are the three pure natural forms of poetry becomes normative in the nineteenth century, though, as in other eras, many specific lyric genres are recognized by poets and critics. In Chapter 3, I take up modern theories of the lyric, including Hegel's highly refined version of the expressive theory, but first some very schematic remarks about the fortunes of the concept of lyric in nineteenth century England and France.

The shift from a mimetic to an expressive theory, charted by Abrams, makes it possible for lyric to become the model for poetry in general or "the poetic norm." "Lyric poetry," wrote John Stuart Mill, "as it was the earliest kind, is also, if the view we are now taking of poetry be correct, more eminently and peculiarly poetry than any other."[63] One reason for lyric's ascendency in the realm of poetry is the abdication of epic and drama: epic has become novel and drama has migrated from verse to prose. Narrative and didactic functions that nonlyrical poetry had previously performed were increasingly taken over by prose also. The Victorian critic A. J. Symonds explains that the novel now satisfies readers' thirst for both drama and epical narration, leaving for poetry only the lyric, on the one hand, and narrative and descriptive poetry on the other, which Symonds calls "idyll": "The genius of our century, debarred from epic, debarred from drama, falls back upon idyllic and lyrical expression. In the idyll it satisfies its objective craving after art. In the lyric it pours fourth personality." Even Robert Browning, whose dissatisfaction with the subjective, expressive model of lyric led to the development of the dramatic monologue, admits the priority of the lyric: "Lyric is the oldest, most natural, most *poetical* of poetry, and I would always get it if I could: but I find in these latter days that one has a great deal to say, and try and get attended to, which is out of the lyrical element and capability—and I am forced to take the nearest way to it: and then it is undeniable that the common reader is susceptible to plot, story, and the simplest form of putting a matter 'said I,' 'said he' & so on."[64]

In France, lyric also becomes the dominant form, despite the epic ventures of Victor Hugo in *La Légende des siècles.* The term *poésie lyrique* is at first applied to poetry of strong affective character, especially the ode, much practiced by Alphonse de Lamartine and Hugo, on a wide range of topics, from the personal to the political. Hugo's immense body of lyric work takes a very public stance even when, as in *Les Contemplations,* it claims to be "les mémoires d'une âme" ("the memoirs of a soul"): no question of lyric as simply "feeling confessing itself to itself in moments of solitude," in Mill's famous phrase.[65] The vatic poet can see the world in a grain of sand and address questions of human destiny and our place in the natural order, as well as responding to political injustice and personal tragedy. In mid-century a reaction against the Hugolian lyric by Théophile Gautier and others involved a conception of lyric as craft rather than vatic utterance, seeking force in elegance. With the poetry of Baudelaire, and then Mallarmé, Verlaine, and Rimbaud, the lyric became the ground for wide-ranging poetic experimentation, both thematic, as in Baudelaire, and formal in the others.

As lyric becomes the poetic norm in England, resistance to it becomes an impetus to poetic experimentation, from Browning's desire for more "objective" forms, which led to the dramatic monologue, to modernism's fragmentation of the lyric subject and imagist experiments. In the twentieth-century resistance to the lyric becomes very much a part of poetic practice. But this model of lyric as the passionate expression of the poet remained well-installed, especially in pedagogical contexts, until the mid-twentieth century: "Lyric poetry arouses emotion because it expresses the author's feeling." Or, "First, and most important, is the impression gained that the lines are spoken by the poet himself, giving expression to his personal feelings, aspirations, or attitudes."[66] Anglo-American New Criticism, eager for students to interpret poems rather than just appreciate them, succeeded in shifting attention from the poet to the text by the strategy of treating lyrics as spoken by a persona, not the poet (I return to this theory in Chapter 3), but poets have continued to conceive their work in relation to the expressive model, though most often in resistance to it, constructing poems that frustrate attempts to locate a coherent voice.

3. Lyric Genre

The rise of an expressive theory, which makes possible both the recognition of lyric as a fundamental genre and its promotion to the norm for poetry, also brings the beginning of a modern resistance to genre theory, as genres come to be seen as sets of rules that constrain creativity rather than modes of literary possibility. There is a shift, in Rancière's terms, from the representational regime, where literature is conceived as a set of generic categories based on mimesis—on what is represented—to an "aesthetic" expressive regime, where genre has little place and where literature can become self-expression or even a sublime vocation, a matter of devotion to a literary Absolute.[67] Expressive theory brings resistance to the hierarchy of literary subjects as well as the hierarchy of genres, as writers enjoy the revolutionary role of contesting the distinction between noble and ignoble, high and low. Any subject can be tackled in any literary mode. But above all, with this shift no longer is writing necessarily conceived as choosing a genre and working in relation to it.

A fascinating instance of anti-generic thinking, which is also bears directly on the expressive theory of the lyric, is Paul de Man's essay "Anthropomorphism and Trope in the Lyric." Juxtaposing "Correspondances" and "Obsession," two sonnets by Baudelaire, de Man interprets "Obsession" as a lyrical reading of "Correspondances"; that is, "Obsession" translates "Correspondances" so as to make it intelligible according to the protocols of interpretation and conventions of the lyric, conceived as the expression of a subject. "Correspondances," which lacks a first-person speaker, gives us a series of declarations, in the epideictic tradition, about relations between the natural world and spiritual meanings.

CORRESPONDANCES

La Nature est un temple où de vivants piliers
Laissent parfois sortir de confuses paroles;
L'homme y passe à travers des forêts de symboles
Qui l'observent avec des regards familiers.
Comme de longs échos qui de loin se confondent
Dans une ténébreuse et profonde unité,
Vaste comme la nuit et comme la clarté,
Les parfums, les couleurs et les sons se répondent.
Il est des parfums frais comme des chairs d'enfants,
Doux comme les hautbois, verts comme les prairies,
—Et d'autres, corrompus, riches et triomphants,
Ayant l'expansion des choses infinies,
Comme l'ambre, le musc, le benjoin et l'encens,
Qui chantent les transports de l'esprit et des sens.

☞

Nature is a temple in which living pillars
Sometimes give voice to confused words;
Man passes there through forests of symbols
Which look at him with understanding eyes.

Like prolonged echoes mingling in the distance
In a deep and tenebrous unity,
Vast as the dark of night and as the light of day,
Perfumes, sounds, and colors correspond.
There are perfumes as cool as the flesh of children,
Sweet as oboes, green as meadows
—And others are corrupt, and rich, triumphant,
With power to expand into infinity,
Like amber and incense, musk, benzoin,
That sing the ecstasy of the soul and senses.

[Trans. William Aggeler]

"Obsession" treats the subject of echoes and correspondences in a different way, transforming the impersonal "Correspondances" into the obsession of a speaker/subject and offering a paradigm of the romantic conception of the lyric.

OBSESSION

Grands bois, vous m'effrayez comme des cathédrales,
Vous hurlez comme l'orgue; et dans nos cœurs maudits,
Chambres d'éternel deuil où vibrent de vieux râles,
Répondent les échos de vos *De profundis*
Je te hais, Océan! tes bonds et tes tumultes,
Mon esprit les retrouve en lui; ce rire amer
De l'homme vaincu, plein de sanglots et d'insultes,
Je l'entends dans le rire énorme de la mer.
Comme tu me plairais, ô nuit! sans ces étoiles
Dont la lumière parle un langage connu!
Car je cherche le vide, et le noir, et le nu!
Mais les ténèbres sont elles-mêmes des toiles
Où vivent, jaillissant de mon œil par milliers,
Des êtres disparus aux regards familiers.

☞

You scare me, forests, as cathedrals do!
You howl like organs, and in our damned heart

Those mourning chambers where old death-rales ring,
Your *De Profundis* echoes in response.
Ocean, I hate you! Your waves and tumult,
I find them in my soul; the conquered man's
Mad laughter, full of insults and sobs,
I hear it in the roaring of the sea.
But how you'd please me, night! without those stars
Whose light speaks in a language that I know!
For I seek the black, the blank, the bare!
Ah, but the darkness is itself a screen
Where thousands are projected from my eyes—
Those vanished beings whom I recognize.

[Trans. James McGowan]

The mysterious declaratives of "Correspondances," such as "Nature is a temple," give way to address to the woods, to the ocean, and to night, setting up a specular relationship between subject and object, man and nature. The series of apostrophes in the latter posit a relationship between speaking subject and the natural world such that qualities, like echoes, can be passed back and forth, and the poem poses the question of whether patterns are projected from outside to inside (the mind finds in itself the stormy tumult of the sea) or vice versa (but the darkness is a screen onto which thousands of dead are projected from my eyes). "The canon of romantic and post-romantic lyric poetry," writes de Man, "offers innumerable versions and variations of this inside/outside pattern of exchange that founds the metaphor of lyrical voice as subject."[68]

This self-reflexive sonnet thematizes in ironic fashion the poetic imagination's tendency to find itself in nature, as it energetically exercises this capacity. The declaration that nature is a temple is psychologized into affect—the woods frighten me as cathedrals do—and the surrealistic speech of living columns in "Correspondances" is naturalized in "Obsession" into the frightening but natural roar of wind in the trees. When nature is animated by lyric invocation, the stars, like Goethe's rose in "Heidenröslein" (discussed in Chapter 1), can speak "un langage connu" and even the black of night becomes a screen for projection. "Obsession" brings out specular relations between the subject and nature that are left in shadow in "Correspondances" and installs us, in part through the impression of a voice, in a hyperbolic lyric regime. "Obsession" can be read as an internalization of "Correspondances," but also as an exteriorization, a making evident of the subject that is absent from "Correspondances" but presupposed by the expressive model of the lyric.

De Man puckishly writes that these two sonnets were "obligingly provided by Baudelaire for the benefit, no doubt, of future teachers invited to speak on the nature of the lyric." "Obsession" beautifully fulfills the romantic model of the lyric, as it performs a lyrical reading or translation of "Correspondances." "What we call the lyric, the instance of represented voice," de Man writes, involves various rhetorical and thematic characteristics, including "the tropological transformation of analogy into apostrophe," "the grammatical transformation of the declarative into the vocative modes of question, exclamation, address, hypothesis, etc.," and "specular symmetry along an axis of assertion and negation (to which correspond the mirror images of the ode, as celebration, and the elegy, as mourning)." So far, so good. "Obsession" illustrates some of the major possibilities of the lyric. But what of "Correspondances"? De Man writes, "all we know is that it is, emphatically, *not* a lyric. Yet it and it alone contains, implies, produces, generates, permits (or whatever aberrant verbal metaphor one wishes to choose) the entire possibility of lyric."[69] The mysterious "Correspondances" seems to serve as a kind of "ur-text" that implies or provokes the rhetorical strategies of the genre. It thus works indirectly to explicate the nature of the lyric, as exemplified by "Obsession." But de Man goes on to declare, "The lyric is not a genre but one name among several to designate the defensive motion of understanding, the possibility of a future hermeneutics. From this point of view there is no significant difference between one generic term and another: all have the same apparently intentional and temporal function." That is to say, genre terms promise the possibility of eventually making sense of this text according to conventions of a genre. But de Man proceeds to an even more sweeping conclusion: "Generic terms such as 'lyric' (or its various subspecies, 'ode,' 'idyll,' or 'elegy') as well as pseudo-historical period terms such a 'romanticism' or 'classicism' are always terms of resistance and nostalgia, at the furthest remove from the materiality of actual history."[70]

This sounds like a classic rejection of the reality of genres and of periodization. Generic terms, such as *lyric,* like period terms, are only names for ways of contingently ordering things so as to defend against the disorderly play of language and history and make sense of the world.

Now it is certainly possible to think of genres merely as names for strategies of reading, not types of text, but this is not de Man's account. The conception of the lyric that enables us to understand a poem's language by imagining that we are hearing the voice of a speaking subject is, for him, not a contingent strategy but a potent reality of our engagement with the world. As a poem that admirably fulfills these expectations, "Obsession" is indeed a lyric. If "Correspondances" is not, it is because it works to help expose as tropological operations all those lyrical strategies—"the entire possibility of lyric"—that make "Obsession" a lyric. De Man is not denying that "Obsession" is a lyric; rather, he is, in effect, singling out "Correspondances" as an anti-lyric—a demystification of the lyric—that helps us to observe the play of apostrophe and proposopoeia and the production of an image of voice in the other exemplary lyric.

The implications of de Man's essay are two-fold. First, the claim that genres, like period terms, are categories that we use to make sense of linguistic productions, is certainly true—this is one reason we need such terms. Note, though, that these categories also function for writers themselves, enabling Baudelaire to produce the lyric "Obsession" according to this model of the lyric. But second and most important, de Man's essay stands as a critique of a certain expressive model of the lyric, instantiated in "Obsession": lyric as centered on the subject, producing the effect of hearing a voice, and structured by an opposition between man and the world and tropological exchanges between inside and outside. His analysis of the figurative operations through which this sort of lyric functions and the demonstration that "Correspondances" is not a lyric according to this model constitute a demystification of this particular conception of the lyric.[71] They lead to the conclusion, though this is not de Man's aim, that we need a more capacious notion of lyric to counter the modern notions of lyric intelligibility linked to the voice of the subject. "Correspondances," as epideictic discourse attempting to tell truths about the world, where we have impersonal voicing but not "a voice," does not fit the romantic lyric model but does indeed instantiate this broader lyric tradition.

In a curious twist, a modern historicist critique of the category of lyric, often known as "the new lyric studies," has adopted de Man's notion of "lyrical reading" to argue that the category of lyric is an illicit imposition of modern criticism on various poems that we have, willy-nilly, made into lyrics through lyrical reading. But, strangely, this critique gets de Man's actual argument backward: for de Man, Virginia Jackson and Yopie Prins write, "Baudelaire's 'canonical and programmatic sonnet 'Correspondances' fits the bill as a lyric *par excellence*," and he seeks "to salvage Baudelaire's poem from the versions of lyric reading to which it has proven so susceptible. He looks for that alternative in one of Baudelaire's prose poems, 'Obsession,' written at least five years after 'Correspondances,'" where he finds "a prose undoing of the supremely lyrical 'Correspondances.'"[72] "Obsession," however, is not a prose poem but a sonnet. It does not undo a lyrical "Correspondances" but performs a lyrical reading of a poem that, for de Man, far from being "supremely lyrical," is not itself a lyric at all. (He is quite firm on this point!) Historicists should try harder to get their facts straight.

Taking from de Man the notion of *lyrical reading* that transforms texts into lyrics, Jackson and Prins maintain that criticism has made a vast range of poems into lyrics. As "poetic subgenres collapsed into the expressive romantic lyrics of the 19th century, the various modes of poetic circulation—scrolls, manuscript books, song cycles, miscellanies, broadsides, hornbooks, libretti, quartos, chapbooks, recitation manuals, annuals, gift books, newspapers, anthologies—tended to disappear behind an idealized scene of reading progressively identified with an idealized mode of expression."[73] Jackson's principal example comes in her book *Dickinson's Misery*: for Emily Dickinson, writing verse was continuous with other mundane activities such as writing letters to friends, reflecting on daily affairs, exchanging keepsakes, and so forth, but critics have transformed her writings into lyrics, studying them as the expression of a poet directed at an audience of readers ready to interpret them.

Dickinson is a particularly interesting case for evaluating the importance of lyric as a generic category. Jackson and Prins list a rich array of nineteenth-century verse genres that the imposition of the lyric supposedly suppressed—"elegy, ode, hymn, eclogue, ballad, drinking song, and verse epistle"—but was Dickinson writing in any of these genres? That would be a difficult argument to sustain: Dickinson wrote in hymn meters but did not write hymns. Some of her poems might be interpreted as elegies, but even that is something of a stretch. In fact, Jackson does not attempt to show that Dickinson's poems "really" belong to any such genres. What was Dickinson writing, then? Having studied Dickinson's schoolbooks and other readers and manuals of the period, Cristanne Miller concludes, "In the early and mid-19th century United States, 'lyric' described any poetry that was not distinctly dramatic, epic, or narrative, that was harmonic or musical in its language, or that was conceived as song. Dickinson's poetry fits this model." Dickinson would have learned that lyrics—short-lined and relatively brief poems—allow for the sort of fertile formal innovation and experiments of thought that she came to practice; compared to her predecessors, she "is a better *lyric* poet, as she would have understood the term."[74]

The historicist critique apparently seeks to dissolve the category of lyric to return us to a variety of particular historical practices, or at least to insist that the texts Dickinson wrote are not in themselves lyrics; but in order to produce a sweeping indictment of a century and a half of lyrical reading or "lyricization," Jackson conflates two quite different historical operations. First, there is the process in the nineteenth century where the expressive lyric—lyric as the intense expression of the poet—becomes the norm. This is an operation Abrams describes in *The Mirror and the Lamp* and is what Jackson alludes to in speaking of the "idealized mode of expression" of "expressive romantic lyrics." Quite different is the critical operation by which Anglo-American New Criticism, after the 1940s, takes the poem away from the historical author and treats it as the *speech* of a persona. New Critical readings, Jackson writes, "created an abstract personification in place of the historical person and consequently created an abstract genre accessible to all persons educated to read lyrically, in place of the verse exchanged by people with varying degrees of access to one another who may have read according to their historical referents."[75]

This is certainly true, but there are at least three points to be made here. (1) The two models of lyric—lyric as expression of the feelings of the poet and lyric as the representation of a fictional poetic speaker or persona—arise at different historical moments and have quite discrete functions. To lump them together as "lyricization" seems historically irresponsible. It is the first that produces the historical reduction of the importance of various lyric subgenres in the nineteenth and early twentieth centuries and the second that establishes in the mid-twentieth century a distinctive mode of reading poems as the utterance of a fictional persona. (2) In the case of Dickinson, one might observe that whether or not it is illicit to treat her as a poet writing for posterity rather than as a spinster scribbling lines for friends and acquaintances, twentieth-century criticism has been more than eager to attempt to reconstruct her very specific conditions of production and preservation of texts and has come to value every mark or dash in the manuscripts. The author Dickinson has scarcely been made "an abstract personification." (3) Finally, the question of whether lyrics should be read as the expression of the author or the speech of a constructed persona or whether we need a better model than either is an issue I take up in Chapter 3, when discussing theories of the lyric, but it should be separated from the question of whether it is more appropriate to treat poems as in principle accessible to all readers or as "verse exchanged by people with varying degrees of access to one another who may have read according to their historical referents," as Jackson puts it. Poems have generally circulated in a variety of ways, and poets have often hoped to be read by people they do not know, perhaps even after their death, so the charge of ignoring concrete historical modes of circulation is scarcely a potent critique of the concept of lyric as iterable discourse, open to being reperformed in a variety of contexts. Jackson herself cites cases where Dickinson sent the same lines to different correspondents, in effect treating the text as a replicable poem.

What I have been calling the romantic model of the lyric as expression of the poet has remained very much on the horizon for poets in the twentieth century—if only as a model to be resisted or rejected. One major strain of twentieth-century North American poetics, from Louis Zukofsky and Gertrude Stein through Jack Spicer, Charles Olson, and Robert Creeley to the Language writers and subsequent Conceptualists, has worked in opposition to a notion of the lyric. In particular, the idea of lyric tied to what de Man calls "the phenomenalization of the poetic voice"—the concept of the poem we understand by convincing ourselves we are hearing a voice—has been for many a model to avoid. What do we make, asks

Marjorie Perloff, of poems like Lyn Hejinian's or Charles Bernstein's, "whose appropriation of found objects—snippets of advertising slogans, newspaper headlines, media clichés, textbook writing, or citation from other poets—works precisely to deconstruct the possibility of the formation of a coherent or consistent lyric voice?"[76] What we say is that they have produced texts that require to be read by other models, but there is a range of possibilities here.

Many twentieth-century poems, like John Ashbery's "This Room," still require sounding or voicing and may juxtapose phrases that evoke various voices, even as they undercut the possibility of making sense of the poem by hearing a coherent voice. Poems like this ask to be read in relation to the lyric tradition, to which they frequently allude. On the one hand, a wide range of poems go further in resisting a model which presumes the centrality of aurality, the rhythmical and sonorous effects of voicing. These range from shaped poems and concrete poems that can scarcely be read, only seen or described, to poems that refuse in other ways a relation to voice and an enunciating subject. Bernstein's poem entitled "this poem intentionally left blank," consists of an otherwise blank page, with this inscription and with margins that are marked to make sure that the "poem" is seen as the reproduction of a page.[77] Playing against the model of pages of legal documents that are blank except for the sentence that proclaims their intentional blankness, Bernstein raises the question of whether the poem is a blank page or this inscription announcing blankness. Whatever we conclude, we no doubt ought to allow him to have succeeded in escaping lyric. The question, though, is not so much whether particular poems count as lyric, but rather to what extent reference to the parameters of that tradition are presupposed—as something to be cited, parodied, deployed, denounced, or worked against—though whether or not we want to call it "presupposed" may beg the question, since the issue really is whether approaching a given poem or poetic corpus in relation the lyric tradition enriches the experience of and reflection on the poems in question.

In a notorious article, René Wellek concludes that the idea of lyric, at least in the conception inherited from the poetic theory of German romanticism as expression of intense subjective experience, does not work. "These terms cannot take care of the enormous variety, in history and different literatures, of lyrical forms and constantly lead into an insoluble psychological *cul de sac:* the supposed intensity, inwardness and immediacy of an experience that can never be demonstrated as certain and can never be shown to be relevant to the quality of art." "The way out is obvious," he concludes, "One must abandon attempts to define the general nature of the lyric or the lyrical. Nothing beyond generalities of the tritest kind can result from it."[78] Wellek proposes that we focus instead on describing particular genres, such as the ode, elegy, and song, their conventions and traditions—a not very promising strategy for nineteenth- and twentieth-century poetry, certainly, where many of the most interesting lyrics do not seem to belong to those particular genres or subgenres. Such a step would entail a major theoretical and practical failure, ignoring a vast group of poems that do depend upon a conceptual frame for their effects.

In fact, a compelling argument for lyric as a genre is that we have no better alternatives. The broader category, *poetry,* has a long history but is too broad to be of much use: it immediately demands subdividing. If, then, we were to attempt to eschew *lyric* as an imposition of modern criticism and focus on the narrower lyric genres, such as the ode, the ballad, the song, the elegy, and genres defined by form such as sonnet, villanelle, and sestina, we would find, first, that there is no established array of lyric genres. In any period, the more developed a quasi-academic poetics, the greater the proliferation of named lyric genres or subgenres, whether by Alexandrian librarians, or late Latin rhetoricians, or officials of troubadour contests, or scholars who specialize in the Renaissance. And, of course, even the more popular and persistent categories do not remain stable. The complaint about the term *lyric*—that it means different things in different times and places—can be lodged against *elegy, ballad,* and even *ode,* which is rather different in the hands of Pindar, Horace, Ronsard, Collins, Keats, Neruda, and Robert Lowell The historical disparities that appear to motivate the desire to abandon the category *lyric* reappear in the case of more narrowly defined genres, and do so more insidiously, one might imagine, since while it is blatantly obvious that the lyric changes, it is less obvious that *ode* might be a slippery, even dubious category. Moreover—this is the second disadvantage of any attempt to focus on narrower categories and avoid *lyric*—there has never been a comprehensive set of subcategories. If we scrap *lyric* we would always need a further category, such as *miscellaneous short poems,* to accommodate all those lyrics that do not fall under one of the other generic headings—even if we try to include them by multiplying genres defined by content, adding to *aubade* or dawn poem, and *ekphrasis* or poem about a work of art, the genres of pastoral, praise poem, nocturne, lover's complaint, valediction, hymn, epithalamion, and so on to our list of possibilities.

In her historicist objection to idea of the lyric, Jackson complains that *lyric* erases the subgenres. Of troubadour poetry she writes, "the elaborate medieval distinctions between the many genres of such verse (e.g., *chanson, tenso, descort, partimen, alba, pastourelle, dansa, sirventes, cobla*) are lost when we describe troubadour poems as consistently or essentially lyric."[79] But such distinctions are not lost: to grant that these poems count as lyric, belong to a lyric tradition, does not prevent scholars from discussing whatever distinctions seem to them significant (as I mentioned above, many of the troubadour categories arise rather late). With modern poems too the category of lyric does not prevent us from recognizing an elegy or an epithalamion, or even an aubade.

In fact, critics characteristically operate with different scales and distinctions, depending upon the orientation of their projects. Roland Greene, a scholar of the Renaissance, edits the *Princeton Encyclopedia of Poetry and Poetics,* which is dedicated to detailing and preserving more poetic categories than anyone could ever hold in mind. Writing of the Renaissance, he notes that the category of lyric is not widely seen as applying to the many genres of short verse, and he even appears to be skeptical of the value of the category.[80] But in his ambitious and wide-ranging *Post-Petrarchism,* which discusses the history of the lyric sequence since Petrarch, he does firmly treat lyric as a genre, describing his project in these terms: "Within a general theory of the lyric's properties as discourse, how can we account for the prevalence over five centuries in many literary cultures of the old and new worlds, of the lyric sequence?" He defines lyric as involving a dialectical play of ritual and fictional phenomena (an account I take up in Chapter 3); and he makes lyric a continuous tradition within which the distinctive Petrarchan lyric sequence arises. He needs the lyric as a long-standing genre so that he can "recover the lyric sequence within the genre at large," identifying a particular lyric practice that arises with Petrarch (Catullus and Propertius are said to write lyrics but not yet lyric sequences) and continues to our own day. The immense variation in the lyric sequences he discusses—by Petrarch, Edward Taylor, Whitman, Neruda, and many others—"merely confirms the need for a theoretical argument pitched as widely as possible to include lyric sequences from the Renaissance to the present."[81] In order to write the history and chart the differences, he needs to treat the lyric sequence as a subspecies of the genre *lyric*.

Such generic concepts remain a resource crucial for literary history, perhaps even the major site of literary history: if literature is more than a succession of individual works, it is at the level of genre that it has a history: the modifications of genres, the rise of new genres, and the eclipse of the old. Critics' treatment of genre thus can vary according to the project: treating the troubadours as initiators of the tradition of the Western love lyric or stressing the differences between different species of troubadour lyrics. Yet in order for these differences to become salient, there must be a broader common ground of comparison. In particular, broad concepts are necessary for there to be something that has a history. The notion of lyric as a genre, then, at bottom embodies a claim that *poetry* as a whole (which includes long narrative poems of various sorts) is in various ways a less useful category for thinking about poems than is *lyric;* that there is a Western tradition of short, nonnarrative, highly rhythmical productions, often stanzaic, whose aural dimension is crucial; that thinking such productions in relation to one another both highlights features that might otherwise be neglected or obscured and brings out similarities and differences that are crucial both for poets and for readers.

Historicist arguments about changing circumstances of production and reception are often powerful—I have stressed that genres are indeed historical rather than transcendental categories—but in one important sense genres resist the logic of historical determination: they have the singular property of being potentially resistant to unidirectional historical evolution, in that generic possibilities once exploited remain possible, potentially available, while political, social, and economic systems have moved on in ways we think of as irreversible. We cannot return to the ancient

Greek polis or the Renaissance city-state, but poets can revive the lyric practices of those times, as Horace revived Greek meters, eighteenth-century Englishmen revived the Pindaric ode, Pound took up the troubadours, Eliot promoted the metaphysical lyric, and mid-twentieth-century poets resurrected the long-dormant sestina. A genre is not just a historical evolution but a historically evolving set of possibilities with potential to surprise.

The claim is, then, that a broad conception of lyric as genre is helpful for thinking about short, nonnarrative poetry, permitting exploration of its historical tradition, making salient its discursive strategies and possibilities in a range of periods and languages. In an afterword to an issue of *PMLA* on genre, Bruce Robbins argues that the case for genre is its capacity to encourage historical comparison. Genre is a crucial instrument combatting the professional inclination to focus on a particular literary period—which he calls a "norm that has been adopted for a long time out of laziness. It is one level of magnification among others, no less valid than any other but also no less arbitrary." Genre, he insists, offers us "versions of history that take us beyond the period-by-period agenda of our ordinary studies." "Why," he concludes, "would criticism voluntarily deprive itself of the additional scale of transperiodic vision and the aggregations it brings into view?"[82] Why indeed, especially, if a capacious generic concept can also enlarge possibilities of reading and engagement?

THREE

Theories of the Lyric

Despite the proliferation of theory in literary studies since the 1960s, little attention has been paid to the theory of lyric. We could even say that since the 1930s theoretical discourses that focus on poetry have had in view something other than the lyric. Julia Kristeva's account in *La Révolution du langage poétique* (Revolution in Poetic Language) treats literary production and indeed linguistic production in general as a dialectic of *le semiotique* and *le symbolique,* two modalities of discourse which are inseparable in the process of "signifiance," but her analysis gives as much weight to the prose of Lautréamont as to the poetry of Mallarmé and does not lead to a theory of the lyric. Heidegger offers an eloquent philosophical account of poetry, focused especially on lyric examples—primarily the poetry of Hölderlin—but while taking poetry as the privileged site for the unconcealment or presencing of Being and the happening of Truth, Heidegger is disdainful of poetics, of attention to prosody, image, and other features of the language of poems, and indeed distinguishes *Dichtung,* true poetry attuned to Being, from *Poesie,* which one might translate as "poetizing." Heidegger's lack of interest in genre or in features of genre and his conception of poetry as a condition of ontology make his thought an unpromising starting point for a theory of the lyric.[1] We do better to turn to Hegel, whose detailed account of the lyric can prove very useful.

1. Hegel

Hegel provides an explicit theory of the lyric in the context of his *Aesthetics,* a systematic account of the arts that is internally coherent and follows a developmental logic. Although his theory is of interest in itself, it compels attention above all as the fullest expression of the romantic theory of the lyric—articulated also in various forms and less systematically by others—which has exercised vast influence, even among those who have never read a word of Hegel. For him, as for others, lyric is the subjective genre of poetry, as opposed to epic, which is objective, and drama, which is mixed. In the lyric the "content is not the object but the subject, the inner world, the mind that considers and feels, that instead of proceeding to action, remains alone with itself as inwardness and that therefore can take as its sole form and final aim the self-expression of subjective life" (1038).[2] Poetry is an expressive form, and even what is most substantive is communicated as "the passion, mood or reflection" of the individual. Its distinguishing feature is the centrality of subjectivity coming to consciousness of itself through experience and reflection (974, 1113).

Before entering into detail, it is worth noting the place of lyric in the overall scheme of Hegel's aesthetics, for the account of lyric is determined less by observation of the features of particular poems (which often do not fit the model particularly well) than by the logic and architectonic of the whole system. Art forms are a material realization of spirit—man has the impulse to produce himself and recognize himself in whatever is external to him—and they follow a developmental logic of progressive idealization. Thus, architecture is the beginning of art, in which heavy matter predominates and spirit has not yet realized itself; spiritual life only "glints in it," aspirationally; there is merely an external or symbolic relation between content and form. Sculpture still uses "heavy matter" but achieves an expression of spirit, which is given a corporeal shape: embodied spirituality becomes the content of the work and there is a realized unity of material form and spiritual content. Then come three arts that give expression to spirit as spirit, as spirit frees itself and dominates external matter. Painting no longer uses heavy matter in its three spatial dimensions but a mere surface to achieve a first "inwardizing" or spiritualizing of the external, transforming real sensuous appearance into semblance, while still employing a physical medium of representation. Music cancels spatial objectivity and uses the medium of sound alone for the expression of "explicitly shapeless feeling which cannot manifest itself in the outer world and its reality but only through an external medium that vanishes and is cancelled at the very moment of its expression." It is thus a more advanced stage of spiritualization than painting, but it still relies on the sensuous form of sound. Finally, poetry is "the absolute and true art of the spirit and its expression as spirit, since everything that consciousness conceives and shapes spiritually within its own inner being speech alone can adopt, express, and bring before our imagination." Poetry is more spiritualized or idealized since it does not rely on the senses: language is not, for Hegel, "a sensuous existent in which the spiritual content can find a corresponding reality," though he does in other ways allow for the importance of the organization of the signifier in lyric (as I discuss below and in Chapter 4). Poetry "tries to present to the spiritual imagination and contemplation the spiritual meanings which it has shaped within its own soul" (626).

Art in general thus manifests for Hegel the progressive self-realization of spirit—in this case, increasing spiritualization or idealization, as the material means become less important. The theoretical relations among the arts recapitulate an historical development: symbolic art of the archaic period is best represented by architecture (e.g., the Pyramids), whereas sculpture is the acme of classical art, and the three arts he calls "romantic" (painting, music, and poetry) find their fullest development in the era of dawning individualism. "Romantic" art, for Hegel, means essentially art of the Christian era, hence medieval and postmedieval art, and its distinctive moments include Christian piety, chivalry, Shakespearean individualism, and the art of nations. Although the development of art involves a progressively more intense manifestation of spirit, this should not be conceived as progress in all respects, since for Hegel classical art is "the consummation of the realm of beauty. Nothing can be or become more beautiful," because the spirit is completely realized in external appearance. Yet, he adds, "there is something higher than the beautiful appearance of spirit in its immediate sensuous shape"—whence the transcending of the sensuous material in romantic art, where spirit is "pushed back into itself out of its reconciliation in the corporeal into a reconciliation of itself with itself" (517–518). The classical world could achieve the harmonious fusion of spirit and world, but the later era suffers a split between spirit and sensuous world (this will be important for lyric). The inadequacy of the external world for the fullest display of the depth and complexity of spirit means that for romantic art, beauty becomes something subordinate to the spirit's reconciliation with itself.

When we turn to poetry within this conceptual framework, we find that lyric best exemplifies the process of spiritualization, the reflexive action of consciousness: "For romantic art the lyric is as it were the elementary fundamental characteristic" (528). Lyric becomes the poetic norm, for the external world enters only insofar as the spirit finds in it a stimulus for its activity (972). Hegel distinguishes two operations that characterize lyric: on the one hand, the lyric poet "absorbs into *himself* the entire world of objects and circumstances and stamps them with his own inner consciousness"; on the other the poet "discloses his self-concentrated heart, . . . raises purely dull feeling into vision and ideas, and gives words and language to this rich inner life" (1111). In both cases lyric differs from epic, whose unity derives from action: in lyric, though "episodes" are not forbidden, the unity of the poem is provided by the poet's inner movement of soul (1119).

Although the essence of lyric for Hegel is subjectivity attaining consciousness of itself through self-expression, he stresses that the lyric process is one of purification and universalization: "Poetry does deliver the heart from the slavery to passion by making it see itself, but does not stop at merely extricating this felt passion from its immediate unity with the heart, but makes of it an object purified from all accidental moods." But it is not liberation *from* feeling so much as liberation *in* feeling: "this emergence from the self means only liberation from that immediate, dumb, void-of-ideas concentration of the heart which now opens out to self-expression and therefore grasps and expresses in the form of self-consciousness what formerly was only felt." The lyric is not a cri de coeur. It becomes "the language of the *poetic* inner life, and therefore however intimately the insights and feelings which the poet describes as his own belong to him as a single individual, they must nevertheless possess a universal validity" (1111–1112).

Thus, despite the centrality of subjectivity to his account of the essential nature of the lyric, subjectivity functions as a principle of unity rather than a principle of individuation: what is essential in this theory is not that the formulations of a lyric reflect the particular experience of an individual but that they be attributed to a subject, which brings them together. While for Hegel the point of unity must be the inner life of the poet, this life may be "fragmented and dispersed into the most diversified particularization and most variegated multiplicity of ideas, feelings, impressions, insights, etc.; and their linkage consists solely in the fact that one and the same self carries them, so to say, as their mere vessel." To provide this linkage the poet "must identify himself with this particularization of himself . . . so that in it he feels and envisages himself" (1133). The tension between conceiving the poetic subjectivity as a mere vessel and requiring that the poet identify himself with this particularization of himself illustrates the tension between the demands of Hegel's formal system of poetic possibilities and the logic of the progressive realization of the spirit, in which the goal is for the subject to realize itself as itself (whence Hegel's inclination at certain moments to deploy notions of genuineness or authenticity as a standard of poetic value). Differentiating lyric from the narrative style of epic, Hegel sketches a series of lyric types, from hymns or dithyrambs and psalms, in which the poetic subjectivity is subordinated to the divine subject, to odes, where the subjectivity of the poet becomes "the most important thing of all," to the song, where "the whole endless variety of lyric moods and reflections is spread out" (1141–1142).

While declaring that the poet must recognize himself as himself in the particularization that his lyric offers, Hegel notes that despite the details a poet presents, "we have no inclination at all to get to know his particular fancies, his amours, his domestic affairs, . . . we want to have in front of us something universally human so that we can feel in poetic sympathy with it." He evinces particular admiration for lyrics of Goethe which "may be called convivial" in that a man in society "does not communicate his *self*" but, putting "his particular individuality in the background," amuses the company with his anecdotes and reflections, "and yet, whatever he may portray, there is always vividly interwoven with it his own artistic inner life, his feelings and experiences." Hegel thus allows for such performances as Goethe's "Heidenröslein" (discussed in Chapter 1) and at this point explicitly countenances a wide range of lyric possibilities, from "wholly senseless gibberish, tra-la-la, singing purely for the sake of singing," which can offer a "purely lyric satisfaction of the heart," to poems of Schiller which articulate "a mind which has as its highest interests the ideals of life and beauty and the imperishable rights and thoughts of mankind" (1121–1122).

Hegel devotes twenty pages to versification, where he describes a great division in the history of lyric, based on prosody and its epistemological implications. What he calls the "rhythmical versification" of the classical lyric, with a prosody based on vowel quantity rather than on accent, leads to very flexible melodic possibilities, whereas the stress meters of modern, noninflected languages highlight the most meaningful syllables, especially with the "thumping" of rhyme (1028). In rhythmical versification "the spiritual meaning is not yet independently emphasized and does not determine the length of syllables or the accent; on the contrary the sense of words is entirely fused with the sensuous element of sound and temporal duration, so that this external element can be given its full rights in serenity and joy, and ideal form and movement can be made the sole concern" (1022). In the modern, Christian era, there is a fall from the unalienated harmonies of classical verse and the experience of time that it affords: in modern languages the power of a more independent rhythm is "damped down" and stress on the meaningful syllables highlights the spiritual meaning, separating it from sound, while rhyme draws attention more forcefully to the sounds themselves. Rhyme thus brings new emphasis both to the coincidence of material form of the two rhyme words and to the difference of meaning that separates them. The result is "alienated time, the time of unhappy consciousness, the experience of modernity."[3]

Prosody contributes to the role of subjectivity in the lyric. Consciousness recognizes itself in the organization of sensuous material in classical prosody, but in postclassical prosody accent falls especially on the meaningful words, giving consciousness the experience of the spiritualization of matter in the concept. Rhyme, bringing like-sounding words together, highlights the separation of sound from meaning, generating an experience of interiority, and bringing memory centrally into play, contributing to subjectivity's self-recognition. Compared with the rhythmical versification of classical poetry, rhyme "is on the one hand more material but, on the other hand, within this material existence more abstract in itself"; it draws "the mind's and ear's memory to a recurrence of the same or associated sounds and meaning, a recurrence in which the percipient is made conscious of himself and in which he recognizes himself as the activity of creation and apprehension and is satisfied" (1028–1029). The self-recognition afforded by lyric is thus, through the functioning of modern prosody, that of the reader as much as that of the author. Formal patterning and rhyme in particular have the effect of marking the presence of subjective order in the sensuous and creating that possibility of self-recognition for the reader as well as the author.

Hegel's theory of the lyric is more complicated than is often allowed. Three points are particularly salient: the question of subjectivity, the role of language, and the theory's relation to major lyric prototypes.

(1) Subjectivity. Despite his commitment to an organic logic of the historical development of the fine arts, Hegel is cognizant of the range of lyric possibilities and eager for differentiation, especially differentiation that can be historically charted while maintaining distinctions between the lyric and the narrative mode of epic. Though he makes lyric the subjective form, his stress on the purification or universalization of the poetic subjectivity, which functions above all as a unifying principle, and on the lyric poet's identification with a partial subjectivity articulated in the poem allows the model to adjust to lyrics that do not foreground a personal subjectivity. Moreover, as the account of prosody makes clear, the subjectivity that recognizes itself in lyric, and that experiences the event of rhyme, is the subjectivity of the reader as well as the author. As we shall see under (3) below, a conception of subjectivity and of its centrality seems to determine his treatment of prototypical examples.

(2) Language. For reasons of contrast with other arts, Hegel stresses that the poet works on imagination rather than on language, though lyric is distinguished by its remodeling of language. Early poetry did not confront a world organized by systematic thought, but once prose has taken

dominion, in a world where "the mere accuracy of the prosaic way of putting things has become the ordinary rule," separating "feeling and vision
from . . . intellectual thinking," lyric "has to undertake the work of completely recasting and remodeling," transforming "the prosaic consciousness's ordinary mode of expression into a poetic one," while nonetheless
preserving "the appearance of that lack of deliberation and that original
freedom which art requires" (1006, 976–977). Embodying the freedom
of the spirit and working "its way out of the mind's habitual abstractness
into a concrete liveliness [*Lebendigkeit*]," poetic language brings an estrangement from the prosaic perception of the world (1006). In proposing
the two terms of a comparison, simile (unlike metaphor, which Hegel dismisses as mere ornament) encourages a lingering or absorption in the object that foregrounds the freedom of the mind in generating and exploring
this externality (lyric loves "to tarry in the particular"). But Hegel also
notes that lyric's need to "make its mark with new invention" can lead to
"artificiality, over-elegance, manufactured piquancy, and preciosity"
(1006). Like many before and after him, he distinguishes rhetoric from
true feeling and imagination: a poet "deficient in original genius tries to
find in the sphere of linguistic skill and rhetorical effects a substitute for
what he lacks in real forcefulness and effectiveness of invention and achievement" (1010). Such cases involve a descent back into the objective heterogeneity and particularity of the medium of language.

(3) Prototypes. The complaint about deficiency in original genius
comes in a comment on Virgil and Horace, in whom "we feel at once that
the art is something artificial, deliberately manufactured; we are aware
of a prosaic subject matter, with external decoration added" (1010). The
question of how Hegel's theory of the lyric allows him to situate lyric
examples is certainly pertinent to an evaluation of the theory, though
Hegel rightly insists that a properly philosophical aesthetics seeks to
grasp the logic of art and does not derive its conceptions of art from particular examples. But for a theory of the lyric, one cannot avoid consideration of how it deals with major examples. Horace, mentioned frequently
in the *Aesthetics*, is said to be more original in his satires and epistles, but
even there "exquisite and cultivated but certainly not poetic" (515). He is
artful and aims to please, and in the odes often "uses his calculated ingenuity" to make lyrical leaps (1135). Compared to Pindar, "Horace is very
jejune and lacking in warmth, and he has an imitative artistry which seeks

in vain to conceal the more or less calculated finesse of his composition" (1142). Pindar, on the other hand, is extravagantly praised ("attains the summit of perfection") as one who, while celebrating, on commission, a victor in games, "easily turns from the external stimuli given him to profound utterances on the general nature of mortality and religion, and then, along with this theme, on heroes, heroic deeds, the foundations of states, etc., and he has in his power not only their plastic illustration but also the subjective soaring of his own imagination. Consequently, it is not the thing which goes ahead, as it does in epic, but subjective inspiration, captivated by its object, so that this object seems . . . to be borne and produced by the poet's mind" (1151).

Horace is condemned for making poetry out of mundane occurrences, such as preparations for a dinner; he is seen as the calculating man of letters—"as a cultured and famous man I will write a poem about this"—whereas the Greek professional poet who is handsomely paid for his tributes to victorious aristocrats is treated rather as an inspired bard because of the nobility of mind, the enthusiasm of the expression, and the drama of cultural myth displayed in his odes (1118). For Hegel, there is in Pindar an exciting struggle: "the poet's own subjective freedom flashes out in the struggle against the topic which is trying to master it. It is mainly the pressure of this opposition which necessitates the swing and boldness of language and images. . . . the loftiness of the poet's genius is preserved by the mastery displayed in his continual ability to resolve this discord by perfect art and to produce a whole completely united in itself, which, by being his work, raises him above the greatness of his subject matter" (1112).

The evaluation of Pindar and Horace depends in part on a historical narrative, according to which Rome represents a fall into the prosaic which only the coming of Christian spirituality redeems, making possible a romantic art in which, eventually, the mundane can become legitimate subject of lyric. Horace is denigrated for deciding to make poems out of minor events of his life. Yet Hegel immediately continues, "But Goethe above all in recent times has an affection for this kind of poetry because in fact every occurrence in life became a poem for him" (1118). Goethe is praised for achieving a kind of "objective humor" which Hegel sees as one of the promising possibilities of the modern lyric. (I return to this topic below.)

One could argue that Hegel's theory of the lyric as the objective brought into universal focus through the subjective leads him astray in the characterization of Pindar. How plausible is it to praise the victory odes, one of which we glanced at in Chapter 2, as the triumph of subjective expression? Pindar, Hegel writes, "so mastered his topic that his work was not a poem about a *victor* at all, but was sung out of the depths of his own heart" (1119). One answer would be that in fact Hegel's account of a purified subjectivity as a formal unifying factor could properly describe Pindar's odes, since there is no unity of action and the unity is given only by the act of first-person celebratory and epideictic utterance, whether the first person is conceived as the poet himself, the chorus performing the ode, or another performer on some other occasion. If this is so, then the theory might be criticized for failing to discriminate between different versions of what it calls subjective expression. That is to say, if it is indeed appropriate to describe Pindar's lyrics as "sung out of the depth of his own heart," this alerts us to the inappropriateness of assuming that Hegel's theory is an expressive theory in the modern sense of the term, in which the poem is an expression of the distinctively individual imaginative experience of the poet. Is it right to assume, as a model for the whole genre, that the poetic process begins with a "full" individualized subjectivity of which the poet first becomes conscious and then "purifies" in the process of poetic expression? Since for Hegel the telos of subjectivity is pure thought, there is good reason to resist identifying it with the modern notion of subjectivity as personal affectively colored experience—as opposed to the objectivity of uncontaminated thought. As for the judgment of Horace, who is frequently faulted for deviating from Hegel's expectations, Hegel's model of the lyric prior to the modern age seems to foreclose the possibility of the Horatian lyric, in its combination of measured reflection and public utterance, which for many readers through the centuries has been extremely attractive as well as successful. Hegel's conception of the historical evolution of the spirit does not square with our own sense of the diverse historical possibilities of lyric, which vary within a given age and do not seem determined by a teleological progress of mind or spirit.

Hegel's conception of history as the progressive manifestation of the spirit—a process of increased spiritualization—is in tension with his perception of the Greek lyric, and especially Pindar, as the apogee of lyric achievement, so that its later story is one of a fall into the prosaic and a struggle to escape. Especially interesting, therefore, are his remarks on the lyric of the present, where the German lyric alone draws his attention. He does not mention his classmate Hölderlin, another fervent admirer of the Greek lyric whose poems were scarcely known until after Hegel's death, but Klopstock, Schiller, and Goethe are highly praised at different points in his exposition and for different reasons. As culmination of his account of the history of the lyric, he devotes three pages to Klopstock, "a great figure" who has "helped start a new artistic epoch amongst us," enabling "the German muse to measure itself against the Greeks, the Romans, and the English." Praised for his patriotic fervor, "his enthusiasm for the honor and dignity of the German language and for historical figures in our early history," Klopstock embodies a national lyric enamored of freedom, even though he also composed "many frigid Odes" (1154–1156).

Schiller, as I have already mentioned, is praised for "the grand fundamental thought" of his bardic verse. He is contrasted with Goethe, who "sings quietly to himself or in a convivial coterie." But describing the tendency of romantic art at to dissolve into either the imitation of external objectivity or the liberation of subjectivity, Hegel evokes a synthesis, which he calls *objective humor,* in which "the heart, with its depth of feeling, and the spirit and rich consciousness shall be entirely absorbed in the circumstances, etc., tarry there, and so make out of the object something new, beautiful, and intrinsically valuable" (610). He cites, as "a brilliant example of this, Persian poetry, which deals with its objects entirely contemplatively," and Petrarch, where "we admire the freedom of the inherently ennobled feeling which, however much it expresses desire for the beloved, is still satisfied in itself . . . imagination here removes the object altogether from the scope of practical desire; it has an interest only in this imaginative occupation, which is satisfied in the freest way with its hundreds of changing turns of phrase and conceits, and plays in the most ingenious manner with joy and sorrow alike" (610). He has identified what is ultimately a self-reflexive tendency of the lyric, as it becomes poetry about its own poetic exploration.

Here the achievement of lyric is its performance of tropological possibilities, the play of the linguistic imagination, which exemplifies the spirit's progressive quest of freedom. Hegel's culminating instance is Goethe's combination of "this ingenious freedom of imagination but also of its subjectively more heartfelt depth" in the late poems of the *West-östliche Divan,* particularly "Wiederfinden" ("Reunion"). In this lyric, which he finds superior to Goethe's early verse, "love is transferred wholly into the imagination, its movement, happiness, and bliss. In general, in similar productions of this kind we have before us no subjective longing, no being in love, no desire, but a pure delight in the topics, an inexhaustible self-yielding of the imagination, a harmless play, a freedom in toying alike with rhyme and ingenious meters—and with this all a depth of feeling and a cheerfulness of the inwardly self-moving heart which through the serenity of the outward shape lift the soul high above all painful entanglements in the restriction of the real world" (610–611).

This paean to the subjective freedom of the lyric imagination, which concludes the discussion of particular art forms and historical modes, as if this were the acme of modern art, celebrates an unusual lyric. It begins as a love poem, with conventional images ("star of stars") and conventional rhymes *(Herz/Schmerz),* celebrating a reunion with a former lover:

> Ist es möglich! Stern der Sterne,
> Drück ich wieder dich ans Herz!
> Ach, was ist die Nacht der Ferne
> Für ein Abgrund, für ein Schmerz.
> Ja, du bist es! meiner Freuden
> Süßer, lieber Widerpart;
> Eingedenk vergangner Leiden,
> Schaudr ich vor der Gegenwart.

☞

> Star of stars, O can it be,
> I press you to my heart again!
> What a chasm is the night,
> Of being far apart, what pain!
> Yes, it is you, of all my joys
> The dearest image, sweetest rhyme.

Bygone suffering I recall
And shudder at the present time.

[Trans. Christopher Middleton]

There follow three stanzas of a creation myth, in which God's creative "Let there be . . . !" ("Es werde!") evokes a cry of anguish, as the universe is divided into separate realities; light and darkness flee each other and all is dumb, silent, and desolate. Then God was lonely and created the dawn, which allowed the separated elements to come together again in love. The last two stanzas return to the reuniting lovers, with a general injunction:

Sei's Ergreifen, sei es Raffen,
Wenn es nur sich faßt und hält!
Allah braucht nicht mehr zu schaffen,
Wir erschaffen seine Welt.

So, mit morgenroten Flügeln,
Riß es mich an deinen Mund,
Und die Nacht mit tausend Siegeln
Kräftigt sternenhell den Bund.
Beide sind wir auf der Erde
Musterhaft in Freud und Qual,
Und ein zweites Wort: Es werde!
Trennt uns nicht zum zweitenmal.

Grasp or snatch, no matter how,
Take hold they must, if they're to be:
Allah's work for now is done,
Creators of his world are we.

Thus, on wings of rosy dawn
To your lips I flew and fly,
Starbright with a thousand seals
Night our bond will ratify.

Together on the earth we stand,
Paragons in joy and pain,
And a second "Let there be!"
Shall not tear us apart again.

The retelling of the creation myth transforms the lovers' attempt to reunite into a broader and more elevated imaginative operation—not the contingent matter of why this man needs this particular woman, as Hegel puts it elsewhere—and suggests that "the freedom we struggle to realize in our romantic partnerships is a species of that greater freedom—human freedom in general—that we moderns claim for ourselves."[4] Distanced from subjective longing and immediate feeling, this poem transfers the anguished energy of more conventional love poetry "wholly into the imagination," as Hegel puts it, and both exemplifies the reflexivity of consciousness recognizing itself, which is held to be exemplary of lyric, and achieves a freedom in feeling also said to characterize the lyrics of Petrarch.

Hegel's account of what makes Klopstock, Schiller, and Goethe—three quite different poets—exemplary of the modern lyric suggests that while Hegel defines lyric as the subjective form, the expression of subjectivity in the modern sense is certainly not the model of lyric: "Wiederfinden" is specifically not an expression of subjective experience. What Hegel especially values are, first, the expression of *national* feeling (in Hegel the endpoint of the spirit in freedom): lyric is linked to folksong which embodies the national spirit; and, along with Klopstock's patriotic fervor, Goethe's songs are praised as "the most excellent, profound, and effective things given to German in recent times because they belong entirely to him and his nation, and since they have emerged on our own soil they also completely strike the note of our spirit" (1157). Second, while Pindar is said to write from the depths of his heart, it is the elegant and energetic articulation of noble thought, its epideictic functioning, that emerges as the clearest value, as in Schiller's poetry, and indeed also in "Wiederfinden," where the witty and speculative use of the creation myth generates a claim about moderns' exercise of freedom. Finally, Hegel especially values in lyric the "objective humor" that seems to represent the culmination of romantic art, in which, through an imaginative "toying" with poetic language, spirit or subjectivity so suffuses the object or circumstance evoked as to "make out of the object something new, beautiful, and intrinsically valuable." Though the Hegelian framework requires that lyric be subjectivity encountering itself, subjectivity is not the expression of personal affect nor the articulation of individual experience, but above all a formal unifying function for lyric, which, as the treatment of prosody suggests, is also manifested in the experience of the reader.

An important but controversial attempt to salvage Hegel and redefine the romantic conception of the lyric comes in Käte Hamburger's discussion of "The Lyrical Genre" in *Die Logik der Dichtung*. Claiming to offer an analysis based on linguistic features, she distinguishes two logical possibilities: a linguistic sequence can be the statement of a real subject about an object or a function that creates fictive subjects and thus mimetic forms. The latter function does not belong to the statement-system of language: the author uses language to create a fictional representation of reality, in the form of fictional characters who may speak. Mimesis of enunciation is distinguished from real enunciation, and lyric belongs to real enunciation or statement, nonmimetic and nonfictive. Our experience of a novel, she writes, is very different from our experience of a poem, which is the statement of a subject and not the representation of a fictional utterance or statement. "The much disputed lyric I is a statement-subject" (or "subject of enunciation"—*ein Aussagesubjekt*), and its statements are real propositions of the experience of an object, *Wirklichkeitsaussage*.[5]

Hamburger notes that she seems to be confirming the conception of Hegel and the German tradition that in lyric it is the poet who states directly, but she emphasizes that this is not a return to the notion of the *Erlebnislyrik*, or "lyric of experience," in which the subject is the person of the poet. The statement-subject is not a personal "I" but a linguistic function. Since the statement-subject is a subject of enunciation and not a person, "the concept of subjectivity will be eliminated from the theory of the lyric, and it will be possible to categorize even the most modern forms and theories of lyric poetry—such as text and text theory, within this generic concept."

She then makes a further fundamental distinction: while the majority of real statements are communicative (historical, theoretical, or pragmatic, in her scheme), lyric statement (unlike fictional discourse), though situated within the statement-system of language, lies "beyond the frontiers" of communicative statement: "The lyrical genre becomes constituted through the so to speak 'announced' intention of the statement-subject to posit itself as a lyric 'I.'" The principal evidence of such positing of a lyrical "I" is the context in which it appears, and the effect of the positing of a lyric "I" is a focus on what she calls the *sense-nexus* rather than the *object-nexus*. "The lyric statement does not aim at having any function in an object- or reality-nexus." It "is a reality statement even though this statement has no function in a context of reality," but "the statement is loosed from a real context and recoiled into itself, i.e. onto the subject pole." Or again, "we experience the lyric statement as a reality statement, the statement of a genuine statement subject, which can be referred to nothing but the subject itself. And precisely what distinguishes the experience of lyric poetry from that of a novel or a drama is that we do not experience a poem's statements as semblance, as fiction or illusion."[6] The thrust of her argument is thus to distinguish the mediating function of fictional assertions, which posit a fictional narrator and fictional world, from lyric assertions which we receive directly, as statements of a lyric subject.

Hamburger then turns to the question of the relation between the lyric "I" (the statement-subject) and the author or biographical subject, and argues that it would be an error to assert either that they are the same or that they are by definition not the same. There is a logical identity between poet and the lyric "I," but this does not mean that the experience reported is that of the biographical person. She cites Goethe's "Mit einem gemalten Band" ("With a Painted Ribbon"), which concludes:

Fühle, was dies Herz empfindet,	Feel what the heart is feeling,
Reiche frei mir deine Hand,	Freely give to me your hand,
Und das Band, das uns verbindet,	Let the tie that binds us together
Sei kein schwaches Rosenband!	Be no fragile ribbon of roses!

Hamburger claims that "it is just as inadmissible a biographism to say that this *I* is not Goethe and this *Thou* not Friederike, as to maintain that they are. This means that there is no exact criterion, neither logical nor aesthetic, neither intrinsic nor extrinsic, that would tell us whether we could identify the statement-subject of a lyric poem with the poet or not." Although we experience the statements as belonging to what she calls "the experience-field of the statement-subject," which is what makes it possible for us to experience the poem as a reality statement, this has no bearing on whether it corresponds with the experience of the author. In fact, whereas the fictive reality of a novel can be compared to the nonfictive reality of an author's life, "the lyrical reality statement cannot be compared with any reality . . . We are dealing only with that reality which the lyric I signifies as being *its,* that subjective, existential reality which cannot be compared with any objective reality which might form the semantic nucleus of its statements."[7] The relation between the lyric "I" and the poet is indeterminate because of this incommensurability.

This could be seen as a different version of Hegel's account of the lyric subject as divesting itself of contingencies so as to give expression to the universal, making the subject of lyric enunciation, which provides the unity needed for lyric, something other than an individualized human subject. Treating the lyric "I" as positional—the subject of the articulated experience, something like the purely positional or functional grammatical subject of a sentence—Hamburger thus seeks to maintain the essential orientation of Hegel's theory—lyric as the subjective form—while giving it a modern, perhaps structuralist twist by making it a theory about types of language and removing from it the question of the lyric subject's relation to the subjectivity of the author. Her theory, though, has often been misunderstood or neglected. One reason, I think, is that her conception of the indeterminacy of the relation between the lyric "I" and the biographical subject may seem hard to differentiate from the claims of critics who insist on the *fictional* character of the speaking subject of lyric. Why insist that the lyric subject is a real subject of enunciation within the statement-system of language if one then turns around and says that the content of the experience really affirmed by this subject may have no relation to that of the author-subject? The reason is simple: there is a crucial difference between treating the lyric as projecting a fictional world, with a fictional speaker-persona, and maintaining that the lyric makes real statements about this world, even though the relation of these statements to the experience of the author is indeterminate.

The translation of Hamburger's work into French in 1986 gave rise to lively debates about the nature of "le sujet lyrique," as theorists sought formulations that would escape from the biographism that had reigned in the French critical tradition without falling into the fictional: what sort of impersonal subject—a "subject of enunciation"—is the best general model for reflection on lyrics?[8] Certainly the historical range of lyrics suggests that the relation between the subject of lyric sentences and the poet as biographical individual is indeterminate, and any model of the lyric that attempts to fix or prescribe that relationship will be inadequate.

Hamburger's insistence that lyric is not a fictional mode, that lyrics do not project a fictional world but make reality statements about this world, has the implication, very significant for a theory of the lyric, that lyrics can tell truths and can also lie. That poets lie is a long-standing accusation, which critics and theorists have too often sought to rebut by treating lyric as fiction, but the risk that alleged truths might be lies is a cost of trying to speak of the world and make it intelligible. Without the possibility of lies, there is no truth.

There are two other points to emphasize in pursuing Hamburger's insights, which put the theory of the lyric on a promising track. First, the terms *fiction* and *fictional* bring confusion to reflection on lyric. In English *fiction* means novels and short stories—you don't find poetry in the fiction section of a bookstore or library. But we consider all literature fictional in the sense that it is a creation of the imagination: poems may recount experiences that did not or do not occur, and the subject of enunciation implied by first-person statements of a poem can appear just as fictional as the narrator of a novel or short story, in the sense that both are invented. But to speak of a fictional speaker or fictional speech act risks deploying for lyric a model based on fiction and thus implicitly assimilating poetry to fictional narrative and fictional worlds, with disadvantages I discuss below.

Second, while lyric is not fiction, it may contain fictional elements, as we shall see. And in fact, we have a well-established term for poems that contain representations of the linguistic act of a fictional speaker: the dramatic monologue (*Rollengedicht* in German) combines features of the lyric and of fiction. In distinguishing lyric from dramatic monologue, Hamburger's theory has the great virtue of resisting the dominant tendency of twentieth-century lyric pedagogy, to which I now turn: treating lyric as a mimetic form and reading poems as if there were mini-fictions. Her work is valuable in taking the essential first step of treating lyric enunciation not as the fictional imitation of an ordinary speech act but as a linguistic event of another type, an act of poetic enunciation which one can attribute—why not?—to the poet, but a poet who remains in a biographically indeterminate relation to the claims of the poem itself.

2. Imitation Speech Acts or Epideixis?

The major alternative to the romantic theory of the lyric has been an adaptation of it that subordinates expression, especially self-expression, to mimesis. I noted in Chapter 2 that it was a more robust conception of the individual subject (political, economic, affective) that enabled theorists in the eighteenth century, such as Abbé Batteux, to install lyric as a major genre in a neo-Aristotelian framework by treating it as an imitation: an imitation of the experience of the subject. Once lyric was established as the subjective form, romantic theorists, such as Sir William Jones and then Hegel, could jettison mimesis for expression: the lyric is fundamentally expressive of the experience of the poet. Modern criticism, increasingly cognizant of the problems of treating lyric as the direct and sincere expression of the experience and affect of the poet, has moved toward something of a compromise position, treating lyric as expression of a persona rather than of the poet and thus as mimesis of the thought or speech of such a persona created by the poet. If the speaker is a persona, then interpretation of the poem becomes a matter of reconstructing the characteristics of this persona, especially the motives and circumstances of this act of speech—as if the speaker were a character in a novel.

This is the conception of lyric promoted by the New Criticism: with the insistence that interpretation focus on the words on the page rather than the intentions of the author, it became a point of doctrine that the speaker of a lyric is to be treated as a *persona,* not as the poet him- or herself, and the focus becomes the drama of attitudes expressed by this speaker-character. W. K. Wimsatt and Cleanth Brooks write, "Once we have dissociated the speaker of the lyric from the personality of the poet, even the tiniest lyric reveals itself as drama." In the Anglo-American world, this principle has become the foundation of pedagogy of the lyric.

The classic textbook *Sound and Sense* tells students, "To aid us in understanding a poem we may ask ourselves a number of questions about it. Two of the most important are *Who is the speaker?* and *What is the occasion?*" After reminding students that "Poems, like short stories, novels, and plays, belong to the world of fiction" and advising them to "assume always that the speaker is someone other than the poet," the textbook concludes: "We may well think of every poem, therefore, as in some degree dramatic—that is the utterance not of the person who wrote it but of a fictional character in a particular situation that may be inferred." Helen Vendler, who usually emphasizes quite vigorously that "A lyric poem is a script for performance by its reader," and who in her own critical writing does not generally pursue fictional speakers, nonetheless in her influential twenty-first-century textbook *Poems, Poets, Poetry* presumes a fictional speaker: "Given that each poem is a fictive speech by an imagined speaker," students should work out the circumstances, goals, and motives of this fictional speech act, and attempt to make themselves into the speaker.[9] Confronted with a lyric, we interpret it by asking what is the situation of the speaker and attempt to make explicit what would lead someone to speak thus and feel thus.

Though dominant in the Anglo-American world (but not in France or Germany), this model is seldom defended as a theory of the lyric. The most explicitly theorized version is offered by Barbara Herrnstein Smith, who takes literary works in general as fictional imitations of real-world speech acts: the novel is fictional history or fictional biography; a play is an imitation of conversation; a poem is a fictional imitation or representation of an utterance; and thus "lyric poems typically represent personal utterances." It is, she writes, as if every poem began, "For example, I or someone might say . . ." The poet is not saying these things but representing them being said by someone. Revising the Aristotelian tradition of literature as mimesis, Smith insists that poetry is a representational art and each poem represents a fictional speech. "Everything a poet says may be true, but his saying of it is not. It is as an utterance that a poem is a fiction, a pretense." The most obvious example of this, she notes, is dramatic monologue, and citing it as paradigmatic, she emphasizes that "what is central to the concept of the poem as fictive utterance is not that the 'character' or 'persona' is distinct from the poet, or that the audience purportedly addressed, the emotions expressed, and the events alluded to are fictional, but that the *speaking, addressing, expressing,* and *alluding* are themselves fictive verbal acts." So "Keats's ode 'To Autumn' and Shakespeare's sonnets are precisely as fictive as 'The Bishop Orders His Tomb' or Tennyson's 'Ulysses,'" two well-known dramatic monologues.[10] This theory, now very widespread even though Smith is seldom recognized as its theoretician, urges students to treat every poem as a dramatic monologue, a fictional act of speech by a speaker whose situation and motives must be reconstructed.

This model makes the lyric into a mini-novel with a character whose motives are to be analyzed. It is often pedagogically efficacious, since gives students a task that is familiar from their dealings with novels and their narrators, but it does not work for large numbers of lyrics. Why, then, does so astute a theorist as Smith adopt it? There are three reasons, I believe. First, she wants to emphasize, correctly, that lyric poems (and other literary works) are not historical utterances. They are composed or created at particular historical moments, and thus are fundamentally historical productions, but as utterances they have a special character: they are not said by someone on a particular occasion. Whether the notion of *fictive utterance* is the best way to capture this aspect of lyrics, however, is certainly open to question. Second, Smith wants to resist attempts, especially common in the 1960s, to distinguish the actual language of poetry—poetic language—from everyday language, since an important principle of her method for describing poetic structure is that poetic effects are achieved by the ways in which the language of poems is tied to the uses of discourse in other contexts, for other purposes. But the fact that poetic effects depend upon "our experience with an incalculable number of verbal experiences, acts and scenes" does NOT mean that the poem is a fictional representation of a real-world utterance.[11] We can perfectly well maintain that the meaning of words and phrases is a function of their use in everyday as well as literary contexts without imagining that in the poem they are represented as spoken by a fictional character. Third, she wants a simple formal solution to the problem that often bedevils the theory and pedagogy of the lyric, the relationship between the "I" of the lyric and the poet. The premise of the imitation speech act enables her to say simply that the "I" is by definition fictional since the poetic utterance is a fictional imitation of personal utterance—rather than warn against linking the "I" with the poet, as if this were a matter of tact or critical strategy, or a possibility to be adjudicated on a case-by-case basis.

What is surprising, and for me confirmation of the dubiousness of Smith's premise that lyric is a fictional representation of a possible real-world speech act, is that despite the care with which she explains this conception of the lyric, it plays almost no role in her actual accounts of poems, for many of which it would be extremely difficult to say what possible utterance or speech act they are representing. Thus, the very first example in *Poetic Closure,* introduced to help define terms, is Emily Dickinson's "The Heart asks Pleasure—first":

> The Heart asks Pleasure—first—
> And then—Excuse from Pain—
> And then—those little Anodynes
> That deaden suffering—
> And then—to go to sleep—
> And then—if it should be
> The will of its Inquisitor
> The privilege to die—

What is the real-world speech act being represented here? It is scarcely obvious—we would have to invent one and trying to imagine a speaker would be a diversion from appreciating the poem. What we have is a poetic reflection on the propensities of the human heart, with a real kicker in the tail, when "Inquisitor" and "privilege" give us a judgment not easy to attribute either to a speaker or to the heart. Smith's discussion of stanza forms concludes with another poem, George Herbert's "Virtue," for which nothing is gained by trying to conceive it as a representation of a speech act of "personal discourse":

> Sweet day, so cool, so calm, so bright,
> The bridall of the earth and skie:
> The dew shall weep thy fall to night;
>   For thou must die.

Sweet rose, whose hue angrie and brave
Bids the rash gazer wipe his eye:
Thy root is ever in its grave

                And thou must die.

Sweet spring, full of sweet dayes and roses,
A box where sweets compacted lie;
My musick shows ye have your closes,

                And all must die.

Onely a sweet and vertuous soul,
Like season'd timber, never gives;
But though the whole world turn to coal,

                Then chiefly lives.

Her discussion of this poem's formal structure—the effects of closure achieved in the third stanza, which are then countered by the revelation of the fourth—rightly make no attempt to work out what sort of usual speech event is being imitated or what is the situation and motive of an alleged speaker who addresses the day, the rose, and the spring.

One instance where Smith does take up the question of lyric as imitation speech act is a discussion of a distinctive present tense: not the present tense of general, typifying assertions, such as "The Heart *asks* Pleasure First," but that of present-tense narration: "I walk through the long school-room questioning," or "My heart aches, and a drowsy numbness pains my sense . . ." She calls this "simultaneous composition," which represents "more or less interior speech," though the speech act she adduces to explain the structure of such lyrics is sports-casting, where the announcer reports the events of a game in the present tense. Is Keats's "Ode to a Nightingale" a fictional representation of a real-world speech act such as a sportscast? It is possible to think of it in this way—as fictional play-by-play—despite the incongruity of the comparison. But Smith's term *simultaneous composition* actually takes us in another, ultimately more productive, direction. She writes, "the poem is generated in accordance with the passage of time *during which* it is presumably being composed."[12] But by her theory, the time of actual composition by the poet should not have anything to do with the speech act represented in the poem: the poet is supposed to construct, at his or her leisure, a fictional representation of a speech act by a persona; that speech act might then be simultaneous with actions being performed by this character, but that would not be "simultaneous composition." Smith's formulation seems to admit that this poem is presenting a special poetic speech act, not a fictional imitation of a nonpoetic speech act. That is, she has not identified a real-world speech act which Keats is supposedly imitating. What we are responding to is not a real-world speech act that is represented in fiction but to a poetic speech act.

On several other occasions Smith also admits that readers respond not to the representation of a real-world speech act by a fictional speaker but to a poetic construction: "although a lyric may imitate logical discourse, that is not what it is, and the reader's experience of its conclusion will be determined by the fact that he ultimately responds to the poem as something other than a piece of reasoning."[13] The point really should be a broader one: that we respond to something more than an imitation speech act: we respond to all those elements in the poem that distinguish it from nonliterary discourse. For instance, she discusses Robert Frost's "Nothing Gold Can Stay":

> Nature's first green is gold,
> Her hardest hue to hold.
> Her early leaf's a flower;
> But only so an hour.
> Then leaf subsides to leaf.
> So Eden sank to grief,
> So dawn goes down to day.
> Nothing gold can stay.

"The appropriateness of the conclusion," she writes, "is experienced without regard for the speaker's particular motives or circumstances."[14] This is important. One can go further and say that here, as often, there is no point in trying to imagine a speaker, motives, and circumstances. We can analyze the progression by which the gold of the first line becomes the gold of the last line—the symbol of enduring value becomes ultimately transitory—without imagining a speaker who revises his observations and comes to a realization. That would be unnecessary novelizing.[15]

These last three lyric examples—from Dickinson, Herbert, and Frost—do not fit Smith's theory. They demonstrate the need for a broader conception of lyric, one not centered on a fictional speaker. This need is the more obvious if you think of poems discussed in Chapter 1, such as Goethe's "Heidenröslein," Lorca's "La luna asoma," and Williams's "Red Wheelbarrow," or Baudelaire's "Correspondances," from Chapter 2. These poems are versions of what I have called *epideictic* discourse: public poetic discourse about values in this world rather than a fictional world.

I return to this broader model in a moment, but why should the model of lyric as dramatic monologue, which takes a particular case as a general model, have come to dominate lyric pedagogy and much literary criticism in the Anglo-American world? There are several possible reasons. First, given the increasing priority of prose fiction in literary education, this model offers the line of least resistance, especially since the English canon contains many engaging dramatic monologues. Students are accustomed to the idea that every narrative has a narrator, whose point of view is central to its effects; when they are faced with the strangeness of a poem, the task of identifying a speaker, a situation, and a motive has the virtue of familiarity. And it works: many lyrics can be read in this way, as the act of a speaker on whose situation and motives we can fruitfully speculate. Second, the cultural weight of claims (first by modernists and then New Critics) about the impersonality of art objects leads to emphasis on the poem as artifact rather than effusion of the poet. The dramatic monologue model cleverly adopts such a view, while allowing subjectivity its place as what is represented in the fictional representation of speech acts.

Finally, this model of the lyric, which takes all language in the poem as emanating from a represented subject, may answer a need that Herbert Tucker detects in asking why, after all, the dogma that the speaker of a lyric is a persona and not the poet was so readily accepted. ("The old king of self-expressive lyricism is dead: Long live the Speaker king!") The fiction of the lyric speaker, he argues, has for us several seductive features. It "brackets the larger problem of context . . . and puts us in compensatory contact with the myth of unconditioned subjectivity we have inherited. . . . We modern readers have abolished the poet and set up the fictive speaker; and we have done so in order to boost the higher gains of an intersubjective recognition for which, in an increasingly mechanical age that can make Mill's look positively idyllic, we seem to suffer an insatiable cultural thirst." That is to say, we want to believe that our subjectivity is free and independent of contexts to which we might belong, and imagining the language of a poem as coming from a fictive, nearly contextless speaker, reflects back to us an image of the subject we imagine ourselves to be. It is this thirst for "the intersubjective confirmation of the self," suggests Tucker, that "has made the overhearing of a persona our principal means of understanding a poem."[16] By presuming that the language before us originates in a speaker-subject and that reading the text is overhearing a speaker, we confirm in a mirroring operation our own status as subjects and originators of language rather than its products. With the presumption of a persona, we can convince ourselves that everything happens between speakers and defend against the impersonal force of language.

Though such considerations may explain readers' acceptance of this model, they do nothing to make up for its failure to capture much of what is distinctive and historically important in the lyric tradition. And, as Tucker points out, even for poems that do invite us to imagine a speaker, "to assume in advance that a poetic text proceeds from a dramatically situated speaker is to risk missing the play of verbal implication whereby character is engendered in the first place, through colliding modes of signification. It is to read so belatedly as to arrive only when the party is already over."[17]

One way to explore the implications and limitations of this model is to consider how it affects one's way of attending to a poem that *can* be read as a fictional imitation of a nonpoetic speech act. What difference does it make whether we adopt this model or not? Consider Robert Frost's "Spring Pools":

These pools that, though in forests, still reflect
The total sky almost without defect,
And like the flowers beside them, chill and shiver,
Will like the flowers beside them soon be gone,

And yet not out by any brook or river,
But up by roots to bring dark foliage on.
The trees that have it in their pent up buds
To darken nature and be summer woods—
Let them think twice before they use their powers
To blot out and drink up and sweep away
These flowery waters and these watery flowers
From snow that melted only yesterday.

According to our current model, to read this as a lyric is to focus on a speaker and see the poem as a drama of attitudes. The deictic of "*These pools*" gives us a situation—a speaker in the presence of pools (this model inclines us to ignore the plural of "in *forests*" which does precisely the opposite, taking us away from a singular situation toward a general condition of pools in forests). Imagining the speaker as a man standing before *these* pools, we can construct a little narrative: he notices that they still reflect the sky almost perfectly because there are as yet no leaves, but this mirroring which brings heaven and earth together is threatened. The pools reflecting the sky, like the flowers there beside them, which live briefly in the sunlight, will vanish; and so he links them with the flowers: the pools and flowers both shiver and will soon be gone. Realizing that the water of these pools will not just evaporate or flow into a brook but will be sucked up by the trees to create the leaves that will blot out the sky, he bursts out in indignation at what the trees "have it in them" to do: destroy the short-lived presences of this scene through their power "to blot out and drink up and sweep away." "Let them think twice," with its tone of colloquial bluster, usually signals a threat: "you'd better think twice about doing that, otherwise I'll . . ." Since there is no achievable threat here, the phrase becomes a figure of intensity and contributes to a more vivid image of a voice.

The piquancy of this poem lies in its departure from usual attitudes to nature and the spring, a poetic speaker's defense of the underdog, as it were. Instead of celebrating the budding of trees, the forest's coming to life, the poem presents the burgeoning of the leaves as trees exploiting their power to "darken nature," to devastate not just the early flowers but also the pools that enabled the trees to leave.

Reading this as something overheard, we project a character and a narrative, which includes a reaction that is comical in the realistic frame: the muttering "let them think twice" about the trees, which proceed in their natural operation without any sort of thinking. What this approach has trouble dealing with are those elements that do not make much sense in an empirical frame, such as the flowery chiasmus of "these flowery waters and these watery flowers," which melds the two elements as part of a process, or the ritualistic note of repetition of

> And like the flowers beside them, chill and shiver,
> Will like the flowers beside them soon be gone.

But especially foreign to the model of the dramatic monologue is the literary allusion of the final line, which has to be attributed to the poet addressing readers rather than to the character looking at the pools. Answering François Villon's famous question—"Mais où sont les neiges d'antan?" ("Where are the snows of yesteryear?")—the poet tells us where they are: melted into pools that the trees drink to bring on summer foliage. The refrain of Villon's poem about human transience is here taken literally and made the basis of a poem about the transience of nature which surprises by showing the possibility of appreciating any moment in an ongoing process: the very beginnings of spring which would usually be valued for their role in bringing on the spring in its lushness. From this perspective, the bluster of "Let them think twice" functions much as do bardic requests to time, seasons, and natural forces to hasten or to slow their operation. The desire for a responsive nature, manifested here in a poem by a generally down-to-earth poet, evokes that tradition of poems that call in order to be calling, to mark both their poetic calling and the optative relation to language, which does not merely represent but strives to be an event. These are features of the poem that do not fit the model of the imitation speech act.

There are numerous reasons to resist the model of lyric as dramatic monologue. It pushes lyric in the direction of the novel by adopting a mimetic model and focusing on the speaker as character, but it is deadly to try to compete with narrative on terrain where narrative has obvious advantages. This model ignores or reduces, with its normalizing novelizing, the characteristic extravagance of lyric on the one hand and its intertextual echoes on the other; and it neglects all those elements of lyric—including rhyme, meter, refrain—not imitated from ordinary speech acts. It implicitly denies three dimensions of lyric: the effects of presentness of lyric utterance, the materiality of lyric language that makes itself felt as something other than signs of a character and plot, and the rich texture of intertextual relations that relates it to other poems rather than to worldly events.[18] Any aspiring theory of the lyric must keep these squarely in view.

One unusual twist on the idea of lyric as utterance—though not the speech of a character—is proposed by the aesthetician Kendall Walton in "Thoughtwriting—in Poetry and Music." Walton's main aim is to argue against the claim by philosophical aestheticians that if music conveys emotion this requires the positing of a person or *persona* whose emotion the music is imitating. To make this argument he takes a detour through poetry. Although Walton is known for his conception of art as mimesis and make-believe, he here acknowledges that poetry does not warrant being treated as a world-projecting fiction, and he proposes the concept *thoughtwriting,* on the model of *speechwriting.* Speechwriters produce language for others to use. They themselves do not assert what they write but offer formulations that others can employ to make assertions or express feelings: "It is not unlikely that poets sometimes have, as at least part of their purpose in composing a poem, the objective of making words available for use by their readers . . . The poet might expect the reader merely to recognize her invitation to use the words himself, to recognize her role as thoughtwriter." He continues: "Poets needn't mean what they say, any more than speechwriters must, although they often do." According to this model, the poem isn't a work of fiction any more than a speech written by a speechwriter is: "the text doesn't make anything fictional." There is no need to posit a narrator or a speaker of the poem; there is no fictional world. "The reader alone uses the words." Walton does admit that appropriating the words of a poem, lightly or seriously, is not incompatible with recognizing a poetic speaker, "but it seems to me that the thoughtwriting function of a poem is sometimes by far the most important one." In "'Twas the Night before Christmas," to cite one of his examples, we don't pay attention to the fictional character who narrates an encounter with Santa Claus; we make use of the words ourselves. Of course often in reciting a poem, deploying the words the poet has generously offered for our use, we are trying on a thought as much as expressing it, projecting and perhaps above all intensifying a mood—"I fall upon the thorns of life! I bleed!" or "I have heard the mermaids singing each to each / I do not think that they will sing to me!" It is not so much that the poet has written lines with which I can express my thought more elegantly or forcefully than I could in my own words but that the poet makes available memorable words, expanding my linguistic possibilities, offering formulations with which to attempt an intensification of mood. Poems provide formulations that may explain for you a situation you had found incomprehensible. Although lovers may use love poems to communicate their feelings to each other, poems are also recited to try out or intensify an affective possibility, to invoke, excite, or celebrate love.[19] C. S. Lewis writes of the Elizabethan love sonnet that a good sonnet, like a good song, "was like a good public prayer: the test was whether the congregation can 'join' and make it their own . . . It does not matter who is speaking in 'Since there's no helpe' any more than in 'Oh mistress mine' . . . The whole body of sonnet sequences is more like an erotic liturgy than a series of erotic confidences."[20]

Thoughtwriting is not an adequate model for lyric, for our interest and pleasure in lyrics come from more than thoughts, but it is a useful reminder that lyrics do not require fictional speakers and are written for readers to repeat. Lyrics are made for repetition. Alessandro Barchiesi, an expert on the classical lyric, writes, "Lyric can be tentatively (transhistorically) defined as a first person utterance whose performative conditions are reconstructed by a re-performing reader, who typically positions himself somewhere in a continuum whose extremes are a generic voice and some individual idea of the author."[21] We could say as much of the three poems discussed by Barbara Herrnstein Smith—by Dickinson, Herbert, and Frost—that do not fit the model of dramatic monologue. They are poems readers perform while placing them somewhere on a continuum between anonymous wisdom and the thought of an author. The "authoredness" of lyrics is important—they are not found language but composed for us by an author—but readers have considerable scope in choosing whether to treat them as the thought of a particular author or as general wisdom.

These three poems embody a version of lyric that has a long history: public discourse about what is important. One reason why lyric poetry has no place in Aristotle's *Poetics* is that for him the poet is an imitator of actions, the creator of a fictional world, whereas lyric poets of archaic Greece mostly make assertions about gods and men of *this* world. Pindar's odes celebrate victors and articulate the cosmological framework and social values within which men are to be praised, as in "The race of men and gods is one; we both draw our breath from a single mother," or "Of things done in justice and against justice, not even Time, the father of all things, could make the outcome of the actions undone. But with a fortunate allotment, oblivion may occur."[22] In this tradition, Mark Payne writes, "the poem is a forum for direct truth claims about the world on the part of the poet, regardless of the particular status of the 'I' that speaks the poem. Even if this 'I' is the chorus or a 'professional' rather than a 'personal' 'I,' it does not produce the kind of fictional speech that Aristotle had in mind as the telos of narrative poetry, in which the truth claims are to be evaluated in only with respect to the fictional speaker and the world he or she inhabits." While Aristotle's *Poetics* "offers a theory of fiction and makes impressive claims for its value; it has nothing to say about what we think of as poetry, namely, lyric."[23]

Whether we actually want to say that Pindar's odes written for choral performance are thoughtwriting, this tradition supports Hamburger's claim that lyric is not fictional utterance but the real utterance of a subject of enunciation. Today as well many lyrics are statements with real illocutionary force, seeking to persuade listeners to take a particular view of an issue or problem, as in Philip Larkin's most famous poem, "This Be the Verse":

> They fuck you up, your mum and dad.
> They may not mean to, but they do.
> They fill you with the faults they had
> And add some extra, just for you.
>
> But they were fucked up in their turn
> By fools in old-style hats and coats,
> Who half the time were soppy-stern
> And half at one another's throats.
>
> Man hands on misery to man.
> It deepens like a coastal shelf.

> Get out as early as you can,
> And don't have any kids yourself.

Accounts of lyric as imitation speech act make little allowance for such poems, which appear throughout the history of the genre; they claim to offer truths, to cast values in a new light, to ostentively disclose aspects of the world and praise what should be noted and remembered, but they claim especially to offer thought in memorable form.[24] Quoting Paul Celan, who maintains that the obscurity of poetry "has been bestowed upon it for the sake of an encounter," to enable readers to open themselves to unexpected formulations, Payne writes, "I do not think that we yet have a good way of naming the conceptual resources of the lyric in this regard. None of the available terms—*gnome, sententia,* maxim, and so on—seem to me to capture what is distinctively lyric, namely the sense of the sudden emergence of new conceptual possibilities. The terms we have equate universality with the preconceived, the proverbial, the commonplace, whereas what we have here is, by contrast, the novel, the unexpected, the unthinkable."[25]

One term for acts of language that are both iterable and inaugural, that live by repetition but seek innovating effects, is the *performative*—a term that has prospered in literary criticism of late. But the notion of the performative is tied to a specific theory of language and can easily mislead. At the end of this chapter I take up the question of the performative and performance and the particular functions that a notion of the performative might most usefully serve in a theory of the lyric. What we require, though, is a broader framework that recognizes the role of fictional elements, such as plot and character—fictional speakers and representation of events—while maintaining the primacy of all those other aspects of lyric not reducible to story, starting with lyric's availability for reiteration, repetition. The positing of a fictional speaker-character is an inappropriate general strategy, and the crucial step is to reject this as a general model for the lyric and treat it as one possibility among others: a particular determination of lyric rather than the default model. But since it is a pertinent response to some poems, we need a model that allows for it by acknowledging the tension in lyric between story and character, on the one hand, and song on the other, but the ultimate dominance of song as distinctive of lyric. Roland Greene's concept of the *ritualistic* dimension of lyric seems especially promising, for while it alludes to anthropological and religious domains that may or may not be relevant, it captures first of all the principle of iterability—lyrics are constructed for repetition—along with a certain ceremoniousness, and the possibility of making something happen in the world (practitioners of rituals hope they will be efficacious). The concept of ritual encourages concentration on the formal properties of lyric utterance, from rhythm and rhyme to other sorts of linguistic patterning.[26]

Discussing the lyric sequence—a series of related poems in which a broad narrative is discernable—Greene maintains that "lyric discourse is defined by the dialectical play of ritual and fictional phenomena, or cor-relative modes of apprehension that are nearly always available in every lyric, though particular specimens, collections, and schools may try to protect one at the expense of the other." For him, the ritual element is first everything that can be construed as "directions for a performance." "In the full play of its ritual mode, which goes well beyond prosodic elements to include rhetorical, semantic, and symbolic features, lyric is utterance uniquely disposed to be re-uttered," and it offers "a performative unity into which readers and auditors may enter at will." On the other hand, there is the fictional element, "where the poem's voice is posited not as the reader-auditor but as character" and "where the history evoked by the work is not merely coextensive with its performance" but involves a plot and circumstances that suggest a fictional world.[27] The fictional is what we produce when we attempt to imagine a fictional speaker and a situa-tion of utterance, as in the dramatic monologue, but also the past events that are evoked in the act of lyric enunciation and subordinated in var-ious ways to present meaning (a topic I discuss in Chapter 6).

Greene is studying not the lyric per se but the lyric sequence, from Pe-trarch to Neruda, where a series of lyrics from one author creates an im-petus to posit a fictional world, a plot of some kind, and a speaker-character with divergent moods. In his account of the lyric sequence—significantly, he speaks of "lyric discourse" rather than lyric—he is rightly inclined to grant equivalence to these two elements or modes, the ritualistic and the fictional:

These modes of apprehension are theoretically available in every spec-imen of lyric, and give onto each other easily and often. They are the factors in a dialectical operation that produces many of the outcomes that we recognize as belonging to lyric discourse, as well as most of the responses we call its criticism: each of the modes, hardly impervious to the other, recapitulates and contains the dialectical movement. . . . A poem that seems to embody one of these phenomena will nearly always see the alternative mode break forth, suddenly and incontestably, to interrogate it, and the critic who reads by passing over these interrogations will discover that certain of lyric's resources, and much of its appeal, must remain unaccountable.[28]

It is certainly true that focus on the fictional element alone, which the model of lyric as dramatic monologue promotes, leaves unaccountable many other elements, as we have seen, and especially the appeal of lyric that depends on its ritualistic aspects. These require that we right the balance. Whether a neglect of the fictional, in the case of individual lyrics that do not have speakers, has unhappy consequences is less certain. In a lyric sequence such as Petrarch's *Canzoniere* or Shakespeare's *Sonnets,* the tension between the ritualistic and the fictional is clearly central, but in individual lyrics the fictional may not make itself felt, except if imposed by our critical model of lyric. Moreover, lyrical sequences with reconstructable plots are relatively rare. Many sonnet sequences can be seen as erotic liturgies rather than stories, as C. S. Lewis notes. Most lyrics are encountered either in isolation or in a collection where there may be little plot to reconstruct and where attention naturally falls on the range of affects, the characteristic verbal and rhythmical techniques, and the general ethos of the poems. In Baudelaire's *Les Fleurs du Mal,* for instance, there is no real plot, despite efforts of critics to find one, nor a consistent fictional speaker, despite the ubiquity of the first person. The collection's attraction lies especially in the range of attitudes brilliantly made available, as readers accede to a distinctive vision of the world—not a fictional universe but our world, in all its grim and nefariousness seductiveness. In some lyric sequences and in dramatic monologues the fictional may trump the ritualistic, but the opposite is far more common, though seldom explicitly acknowledged.

The history of both lyric and criticism has involved, Greene claims, shifting relations between the fictional and ritualistic. Poetic movements and critical approaches will privilege now one, now the other, subsuming the second to help establish the other's primacy, but "neither alternative can prevail, though the dicta of movements will always try to give one or the other finality."[29] This is doubtless true for the lyric sequence, where the question of plot, character, and fictional world usually arise, but for the lyric in general criticism must resist the dominance of the fictional, lest the distinctiveness of lyric be lost. Just to redress the effects of this dominant model, we must focus on the ritualistic elements of lyric. There are three especially important strains: one is what Northrop Frye calls the roots of lyric, *melos* and *opsis,* which he translates as *babble* and *doodle,* the foregrounding of linguistic patterning, which will be discussed in Chapter 4 on rhythm and repetition. The second, the ritualistic dimension of lyric address, is the subject of Chapter 5. The third, which I take up here, is what has been loosely called the performative character of lyric: ritual that seeks to make something happen.

3. Performative and Performance

J. L. Austin distinguished *performative* utterances, which accomplish the action to which they refer, from *constative* utterances, which make true or false statements. "I promise to pay you tomorrow" does not report on an act of promising but is itself the act. Many performatives have an explicitly ritualistic character: "I hereby call this meeting to order." "I now pronounce you man and wife."[30] Poems clearly do contain some true performatives: from Horace's "We sing of of drinking parties, of battles fought / by fierce virgins with nails cut sharp to wound young men" and Herrick's "I sing of brooks, and blossoms, birds and bowers . . . ," to Baudelaire's "Andromaque, je pense à vous" ("Andromaque, I think of you"), which perform the acts to which they refer. But the appeal of the notion of the performative for literary critics goes far beyond that of such explicit formulae. Austin introduces the notion as a critique of the tendency of his colleagues, analytical philosophers, to assume that the business of language is to describe a state of affairs or to state a fact, and that other sorts of utterances should be regarded as emotive, or pseudo-statements. It is natural to go on to ask, Austin writes, whether many apparently pseudo-statements really set out to be statements at all, and he proposes the distinction between constative utterances, which make a statement and are true or false, and another class of utterances which are not true or false and which actually perform the action to which they refer: performatives. To say "I warn you not to eat that" is not to describe a state of affairs but to perform the act of warning.

In "Signature Event Context" and other articles, Jacques Derrida's engagement with Austin makes explicit what is scarcely evident in Austin's more narrowly drawn specification of the performative: the link of the concept of performative language to the creative power of language and to the problem of origination in general.[31] Austin's title is *How to Do Things with Words,* but his account could be taken to imply that we do things with words when we gather ourselves to perform a public, authorized act, according to socially stipulated rules, whereas in fact we act through language in singular yet iterable ways all the time. Performative acts may originate or inaugurate, create something new.

Although Austin excludes literature from the domain of analysis as fundamentally nonserious, literary theorists have welcomed the notion of performative language because it describes a particular kind of linguistic practice into which literature might fit. Against the traditional model, which sees language as essentially making statements about what is the case and makes literary discourse marginal and derivative, a set of pseudo-assertions only, Austin's account provides an alternative for the active, creative functioning of language: language as act rather than representation. Literary discourse can take its place among performative linguistic practices that bring into being that to which they refer or accomplish that of which they speak—creative and world-changing modes of language. The theory of performative language acknowledges this linguistic mode, so central to literary value.

Since literary criticism involves attending to what literary language does as much as to what it says, critics have found the idea of performative language valuable for characterizing literary discourse, especially that of fiction.[32] The fictional sentence does not refer to a prior state of affairs and is not true or false. Just as an act of appointing—"I appoint you three as a committee to consider this problem"—brings into being the entity, the committee, to which it refers, so a novel performatively brings into being what it purports to describe. The beginning of Joyce's *Ulysses,* "Stately plump Buck Mulligan came from the stairhead bearing a bowl of lather on which a mirror and a razor lay crossed," does not refer to some prior state of affairs but creates this character and this situation.

This sort of performative power is important for literary studies, but Austin's theory raises more problems than it solves and requires modification if it is to be truly useful, especially for a theory of the lyric. If the notion of the performative is seen as a solution to the status of literary discourse rather than as a problem requiring further investigation, it risks distracting critics' attention from more important concerns.

First, if all literary discourse is performative by convention, because it is literature and not a set of propositions, then the notion of the performative becomes less useful for talking about particular works or parts of works which, by virtue of especially artful construction, seem successfully to enact what they delineate. Although the potential self-reflexivity of all literature has become something of a credo since the days of the New Criticism, critics still feel that it counts as an accomplishment for the literary work to enact or bring about what it purports to describe, and especially that it counts as an accomplishment for the critic to explain how this happens. We have an interest in distinguishing, therefore, between a an alleged general performativity of literature and its special achievements, such as that of Sappho's "Ode to Aphrodite," discussed in Chapter 1, where a request to Aphrodite to appear is formulated so as to create the impression that she is doing so. Though it is indeed tempting to conceive of literature as fundamentally performative and, therefore, to make the goal of critical analysis the elucidation of literary performativity (showing how the poem does what it says), we should bracket the notion of a general performativity of literature, in order to retain some distinctiveness for genuinely performative effects.

Second, if the general performativity of literature is best illustrated by its creation of fictional characters and events—the bringing into being for literary purposes of characters and situations that did not previously exist—then this performativity is closely linked to fictionality, as my example of the opening of *Ulysses* suggests. While treatises on poetics often cite Sir Philip Sidney's dictum that the poet "nothing affirmeth and therefore never lyeth," a poetics of the lyric should resist such blanket claims. As I have stressed, fictionality does have a restricted place in lyric, in tension with its ritual character, but fiction is not the general mode of being of lyric. Many poems make claims about the world—claims which readers and even their authors may judge to be false.[33] Käte Hamburger rightly treats lyric not as world-creating fiction but as real-world utterance, albeit of a special kind. It would therefore be wrong to embrace for lyric a notion of performativity correlated with fictionality. The epideictic element of lyric, which certainly involves language as action but not of a fictionalizing kind, is central to the lyric tradition: it includes not just praise or blame but the many statements of value, statements about the world that suffuse lyric of the past and the present, from Sappho's claim that what is most important is what one loves, to Larkin's "They fuck you up, your mum and dad . . ." Lyrics do not in general performatively create a fictional universe, as novels are said to do, but make claims (quite possibly figurative ones) about our world. Keats's "Ode to a Nightingale" does not posit a fictional universe in which people talk to birds but articulates desires in our world.

A further problem is what counts as success for the performative. In Austin's account, performatives are not true or false but felicitous or infelicitous. If I order you to open the window you are likely to say to me, "You can't order me about"; or if I promise you that the United Nations will take possession of chemical weapons, you will point out that I am not in a position to make any such promise. These are both causes of infelicity. Are there comparable causes of infelicity in a poem? Austin's account of the performative would lead one to ask of an alleged literary performative whether it is felicitous or infelicitous, and here lies a difficult question. Could a poem be infelicitous because I have no authority as a poet, just as I lack the authority to command you? Or is the felicity of a poetic element a matter of successfully fitting into the work, enabling the poem to establish itself and live and function as a poem? If so it is related to the sort of literary functionality that critics have long sought to elucidate. In that case, the notion of performativity would not contribute a great deal to literary criticism, which already has effective ways of discussing an element's contribution to the effect of the whole. But Austin's concept of the performative seeks to put language back into a social context of use, as opposed to a decontextualized analysis of truth or falsity of propositions. Perhaps, then, one should say that literary discourse achieves felicity only insofar as it is published, received as literature, disseminated, inscribed in memory, and repeated by others in acts of reading.

The fact that we have difficulty deciding what would make a literary work felicitous or infelicitous indicates that Austin's theory of performative utterance may create more problems than it solves and does not provide the best framework for thinking about the nature of the lyric. It seems preferable to reserve the term *performative* for more particular level of success, for the special cases whereby a poem succeeds in bringing about what it describes. Some poetic statements, as I have noted, do this. Let us, therefore, save the notion performative language for the special structural efficacy or successful formulation in a work, as in Sappho or Goethe, where without an explicit performative construction, the poem seems to accomplish what it names.

In *How to Do Things with Words*, as Austin explores the opposition between performative and constative utterances, he recognizes the difficulties of identifying two separate classes of utterance: sentences with a constative form and without performative verbs, such as "There is a bull in this field," may accomplish the act of warning, and uttering a true or false statement ("The cat is on the mat") is to perform the act of stating (it could be rephrased as "I hereby state that the cat is on the mat," which accomplishes the act in question). Consequently, he modifies his account and instead of two classes of utterances he distinguishes three aspects of any speech act: the *locutionary* act (of producing a given utterance), the *illocutionary* act (the act I perform *in* speaking this utterance in particular circumstances), and *perlocutionary* act (acts that I may accomplish *as a result* of the illocutionary act). In uttering the sentence "I promise to come tomorrow," I perform the illocutionary act of promising (a performative) and may perform the perlocutionary act of reassuring you, or in some circumstances, threatening you, and so on. The illocutionary acts (the domain of the performative) depend upon social conventions and do not require special ingenuity: it is not difficult to promise or to warn or to state. But "perlocutionary acts," writes Stanley Cavell, "make room for, and reward, imagination and virtuosity . . . Illocutionary acts do not in general make such room. I do not in general wonder how I might make a promise, or a gift, or apologize or render a verdict. But to persuade you may take considerable thought, to insinuate as much as console may require tact, to seduce or confuse you may take talent."[34] One disadvantage of the notion of the performative is that if it leads us to celebrate the performative character of literature, as a simple consequence of the conventions of literary discourse, we risk neglecting the more important perlocutionary effects that poets are seeking to achieve by virtue of producing a text that performatively establishes itself as a poem: effects such as moving readers, provoking reflection, leading them to act differently—all perlocutionary consequences that cannot be predicted. The most important acts a poem performs are likely to be those not entailed by it.

In a discussion of rhetoric and philosophy, ancient and modern, Barbara Cassin, seeking the appropriate modern translation for *epideixis,* praises Austin's move from the performative/constative distinction to the categories of the illocutionary and the perlocutionary: "this is where we pass beyond the performative, *stricto sensu,* to a performativity broadened out to performance" and where we see the importance of considering speech as performance rather than strictly performative. Despite the plurivocity of the term *performance* in both English and French, "performance" is doubtless the best translation of *epideixis:* discourse conceived as an act, aiming to persuade, to move, to innovate.[35]

Restricting the notion of the performative to illocutionary effects, effects achieved *in* saying something in particular, we can discuss directly what Austin calls perlocutionary effects, without worrying about "felicity" or the general structure of Austin's theory of language. What sorts of effects do poems have? I glancingly referred to one sort of effect in citing Thibaudet's claim about Baudelaire's "A une passante" (Chapter 1): that the final line has entered the social imaginary and is repeated by strolling Parisians, helping them imagine the erotic and melancholic potential of anonymous metropolitan encounters. In "Che cos'è la poesia," Derrida approaches poetry in these terms, as what strives to be memorable, to live in memory: "'Apprends moi par coeur,' dit le poème" ("Learn me by heart," says the poem). "The poetic," Derrida writes, "would be what you desire to learn but from the other, thanks to the other, and under dictation from the other, by heart, *imparare a memoria.*" The poem addresses you— "learn me by heart, copy out, watch over and preserve me." The lyric, by its formal patterning and mode of address, asks to be learned by heart, even if that seldom happens; its efficacy depends upon its success in making its words memorable, having them remembered. And Derrida's text calls "poem" not just that which asks to be learned by heart but "that which learns or teaches us the heart, which invents the heart."[36] Sometimes this happens; poems can do this; but often it does not: at this level the poem's efficacy is not be given by virtue of the poem's formulations but depends on the ways in which its performance is received. It is far better—certainly more accurate—to think of the poem as performance, which may or may not be efficacious, rather than as a performative, which is supposed to bring about, by convention, that of which it speaks.

The notion of the performative has the great virtue for a theory of literature of foregrounding language as act rather than representation, but, beyond that, the performative is the name of a problem, not a solution to the question of the status of literary discourse. We seem, in sum, to have four different cases. First, there is a general performativity linked to the conventional character of literary discourse, which could be said to bring into being that which it describes. This applies especially to fictional discourse. The basic performativity of the lyric is different, and so a second case: not the creation of a fictional world but the simple event of establishing itself, constituting itself as a lyric. At this level—which is of little interest because it applies so broadly—the performativity of individual elements of the poem consists in their contribution to the overall effect of the poem. The third case, to which I propose to restrict the notion of the performative, is the poem's success in bringing about what it describes, as when Sappho's superb lyric craftsmanship creates the effect of making Aphrodite respond. The fourth case, which we do better to call "performance" rather than the performative, is the lyric action or lyric event, the poem's functioning in the world. The lyric performance succeeds as it acts iterably through repeated readings, makes itself memorable. The consummate success is, ironically, to become a commonplace, to enter the language and the social imaginary, to help give us a world to inhabit: "Créer un poncif, c'est le génie. Je dois créer un poncif," wrote Baudelaire ("To create a cliché is genius. I must create a cliché").[37] The poet's ultimate success would be for an original formulation to become a cliché, which is the mark of Shakespeare's preeminence. While I believe it is valuable to preserve the notion of the performative character of lyric for the third case, it is more crucial to explore the performance or perlocutionary efficacies of lyric discourse, its epideictic function as articulator of memorable formulations. Much of its success depends, as I have suggested, on the ritualistic aspects of lyric, to which I now turn, with discussions of rhythm and sound patterns and then of lyric address.

FOUR

Rhythm and Repetition

Roman Jakobson defines the poetic function of language as "the projection of the principle of equivalence from the axis of selection onto the axis of combination," so that "equivalence becomes the constitutive device of the sequence." That is, items are chosen for combination in sequence because they are in various respects equivalent and thus produce a rhythm of repetition with variation. The poetic function, of course, is not confined to poetry: Jakobson's most striking example is the political slogan "I like Ike," where the same vowel is repeated three times, two of the three words rhyme, and *I* is included in both *Ike* and *like,* "a paronomastic image of the loving subject enveloped by the beloved object."[1] Set off as a slogan, its three stressed vowels give it a chant-like rhythm that makes it enviably compelling.

Poetry, for Jakobson, is where this poetic function becomes the "dominant, determining function." In the *Anatomy of Criticism,* Northrop Frye introduces the discussion of lyric by citing a line of verse from Shakespeare's *Measure for Measure:*

Ay, but to die, and go we know not where:

We can hear of course the metrical rhythm, an iambic pentameter spoken as a four-stress line. We can hear the semantic or prose
rhythm, and we hear what we may call the rhythm of decorum, the
verbal representation of a man facing the horror of death. But we can
also, if we listen to the line very attentively, hear another rhythm in it,
an oracular, meditative, irregular, unpredictable, and essentially discontinuous rhythm, emerging from the coincidences of the sound
pattern:

Ay:
But to die . . .

        and go
        we know

                not where . . .

Just as the semantic rhythm is the initiative of prose, and the metrical rhythm is the initiative of *epos,* so this oracular rhythm seems to
be the predominating rhythm of lyric.[2]

Frye's procedure here highlights the difficulties of discussing lyric
rhythm. In order to distinguish the rhythm of lyric from that of epic or
narrative poetry, he takes a verse from a play (though he says he is taking
a line of poetry "at random"), breaks up the ten-syllable metrical line, and
arranges the fragments as a kind of free verse, with shorter lines that highlight rhymes—this to create a lyric rhythm, which he calls "associative"
and "oracular." Since he knows full well that many lyrics use a regular
meter of long lines, and that internal rhymes and other kinds of sound
patterning are found in narrative and epic verse as well, Frye's formulations suggest that thinking about lyric rhythms involves hearing differently, attending to sorts of patterning that might not compel attention in
narrative poetry. The associative rhythm involves "paranomasia, sound-
links, ambiguous sense-links, and memory-links."[3] He notes that poets
undertaking long poems develop the skill of thinking in the meter they
have adopted, which frees them to tell stories and develop ideas, whereas
in lyric greater importance falls on the various kinds of equivalence, of

brief metrical units, lines, and stanzas, but also of the sound patterning of rhyme, alliteration, and assonance and the possible semantic relationships such patterning brings.

Such pattering is highly seductive, which is in part to say that a given sequence of sounds does not have some fixed, necessary effect, but invites readers to an experience. Virtuoso performances of verse prosody, writes Simon Jarvis, "entice answeringly virtuosic performances of fantasy from their readers," when they draw us in, and make themselves, as Paul Valery says, "not just noticed and respected but desired and thus repeated," as we want to hear again a seductive line or stanza that "creates the need to be heard again." "Language that has been made to sing may be presumed to have just authority," writes Robert von Hallberg. "Musicality authenticates poetry."[4] Nietzsche observes that "even the wisest among us occasionally becomes a fool for rhythm—if only insofar as we feel a thought to be *truer* if simply because it has a metrical form and presents itself with a divine hop, skip, and jump."[5] Sound patterning gives lyric utterances authority that is neither justified nor justifiable—always open to question, yet a starting point to lure readers into the poem.

But let us start with an example of a lyric using a meter often deployed for narrative poetry, so as to identify some of the salient issues. Valéry's sonnet "La Dormeuse" ("The Sleeping Woman") like Frye's example, uses a meter in which narrative poetry and lyrics are often written, the twelve-syllable French alexandrine, but its rich sound patterning gives it what Frye calls an associative rhythm, a sonorous intensity unlikely to be found in narrative poems. It projects a personal situation—a lover watching his beloved sleep—but the intense phonological patterning pulls the language away from a situation of personal expression into a mode of impersonal sensuousness.[6] The sonnet begins:

Quels secrets dans son cœur brûle ma jeune amie,
Âme par le doux masque aspirant une fleur?
De quels vains aliments sa naïve chaleur
Fait ce rayonnement d'une femme endormie ?
Souffles, songes, silence, invincible accalmie,
Tu triomphes, ô paix plus puissante qu'un pleur,

Quand de ce plein sommeil l'onde grave et l'ampleur
Conspirent sur le sein d'une telle ennemie.

☞

To what secrets in her heart does my young friend set fire,
Soul breathing in through its sweet mask a flower?
From what vain nourishments does her innocent warmth
Draw this radiance of a sleeping woman.
Breath, dreams, silence, O invincible calm,
You triumph, o peace more potent than a tear,
When the heavy wave and fullness of this deep sleep,
Conspire on the breast of such an enemy.

[Trans. Geoffrey Hartman, modified][7]

The repetition of sounds—*ma, amie, âme, masque, aspirant* in the opening lines, then *souffles, songes, silence, invincible* of line 5, and *paix, plus, puissante, pleur* of line 6—reaches its climax in lines 9 and 10 (intensified as a couplet by the unusual rhyme scheme):

Dormeuse, amas doré d'ombres et d'abandons,
Ton repos redoutable est chargé de tels dons,
Ô biche avec langueur longue auprès d'une grappe,
Que malgré l'âme absente, occupée aux enfers,
Ta forme au ventre pur qu'un bras fluide drape,
Veille; ta forme veille, et mes yeux sont ouverts.

☞

Sleeping girl, golden mass of shadows and yieldings,
Your impressive repose is charged with such gifts,
O doe, long and languorous beside a grape cluster,
That though your soul be absent, even busy in hell,
Your form, pure torso draped by a fluid arm,
Watches, your form watches and my eyes are open.

The fantastic line "Dormeuse, amas doré d'ombres et d'abandons," where words for sleep, gold, shadows, and gifts echo each other, creates a seductive, sensuous event, as the sonnet distinguishes the form of the sleeping woman, a mass of golden shadows and yieldings, from her soul, absent and possibly demonic, the enemy of this gorgeous surface. The poem engages this surface, addressing not the girl but the peace that here triumphs, and animating the form—*ta forme veille*—which is made the subject and not just object of the gaze. The living girl is absent but the form is awake and watches. The unusual rhythm of the last line, where the syntax requires stress on the opening syllable, *veille,* and a pause following (as I discuss later, this is anomalous in the alexandrine), gives this line a disruptive force: the action of the poem is that the form, abstracted from the human, watches.

The autonomy of the associative rhythm of the sound patterning and of the rhythm of stresses is, in this case, part of the poem's theme—that the beauty of forms is independent of our sense of the human; the girl has an *âme* but is celebrated as an *amas,* a mass rather than a soul, albeit a gilded mass. In principle, though, this structure is separate from any particular semantic content or consequence. Lyrics often foreground the sense of language at play, shaped as if by forces of its own, independent of any author—by its own phonological and rhythmical structures. Valéry writes, "I was suddenly *seized* by a rhythm that imposed itself on me, and that soon gave me the impression of an outside force [*un fonctionnement étranger*], as if someone else were using my living machine" [*machine à vivre*]—as though this living authorial self were in fact a machine being operated by someone or something else, as if the poem gave us not a personal subject but a general subject.[8] This sense of rhythm in the broad sense as something independent of writer or reader may be very strong in lyrics, where language seems to be echoing itself, with words generated by their phonological resemblance to other words, as in "Dormeuse, amas doré d'ombres et d'abandons." That sense of independence is especially marked in stanzas with short rhyming lines or in minor forms of lyric—jingles, limericks, nursery rhymes, counting rhymes, where sound and rhythm rather than meaning are the source of attraction:

One, two,
Buckle my shoe.
Three, four,
Shut the door . . .

If, despite Frye's suggestion, we cannot identify lyric rhythms as such—rhythms to be found in lyrics exclusively and not in narrative poetry—still there are rhythmic effects, patterns of sound events, that become a focus of attention in lyrics and are experienced as particularly central to the working of these poems. Though this chapter will focus on lyric examples, much of what I say can apply to other forms of poetry as well.

There seems widespread agreement among poets and theorists about the centrality of rhythm to lyric. Valéry, like other poets, evokes rhythm as the key element in the genesis of a poem: "it was born, like most of my poems, from the unexpected presence in my mind of a certain rhythm." T. S. Eliot concurs, observing that "a poem may tend to realize itself first as a particular rhythm before it reaches expression in words, and that this rhythm may bring to life the idea and the image." "We know poetry is rhythm," writes Yeats, distinguishing the rhythms that pick up and spectrally convey a tradition from the mechanistic cadences of music hall verse: "it is the rhythm of a poem that is the principal part of the art." Statements about the foundational character of rhythm, such as Nicolas Abrahams's claim that "rhythm produces in the reader the fundamental affect of the entire poem," come from poets, critics, and theorists of all stripes.[9]

If poetry were to be defined as mimesis, as Aristotle supposed, then we could not consider rhythm foundational, but if lyric, unlike *epos* and drama, is not fundamentally a form of mimesis, and Aristotle, who actually wrote lyrics, may be held to concede as much in excluding it from consideration in his treatise on mimetic poetry, then one should start elsewhere. I have said that lyric aims to be an event, not a representation of an event, and sound is what happens in lyric: sound becoming patterned, even when lyrics are entirely written. "Sound arrives as an event," writes Jean-Luc Nancy, "while the visual is there before and after."[10] For Hegel, it is the arrival of the nonsemantic echo or repetition that creates for the subject a distinctive poetic experience. Quite apart from the historical link of lyric to chanted recitation and the modern usage that by calling the words of songs "lyrics" emphasizes the connection with rhythm, one can argue that it is rhythm above all that makes lyrics attractive, seductive, and memorable. If lyric is pleasurable language, language that gives pleasure, its rhythms and sound patterning may be largely responsible. If lyric is memorable language—language that asks to be learned by heart and repeated, recited—it is largely because of its rhythms. Many of us have in our heads an entire array of trivial rhymes—limericks, nursery rhymes, advertising jingles, and even poems that mean little to us but have seduced by their associative rhythms. Isobel Armstrong reports the experience of being obsessed by a rhythm but not recalling the poem: "de de dum, de de dum, de dum de; de dum, de de dum, de dum." She calls it a "pulse, halfway between a sound and a pressure." Not a sign, notation, or code, but something else: "a somatic pressure encouraged by the sound system of the poem's language"; "it asked for words but was independent of them." And when the lines did come into her head (lines 3 and 4 of Tennyson's "Break, Break, Break," discussed below) she got some of the words wrong, as she later discovered.[11]

Rhythm gives lyric a somatic quality that novels and other extended forms lack—the experience of rhythm linking it to the body and, perhaps, to the rhythms of various natural processes—and thus contributes both to a different sort of pleasure from those promoted by novels and to a sense of a special otherness: lyrics are language, but language shaped in other ways, as if from elsewhere. Although our body has its own rhythms, of breathing and of heartbeats, our rhythmic competence most often responds to rhythm as something exterior which nonetheless engages us, draws us to beat in time with it, finding or sensing a pattern, in noises, movements, action in the world. With complex rhythms we may move our hands, hips, and feet to different beats. Rhythm is an event without representation. When we find rhythm in language, it enlists us in a process in ways that other texts do not, which is one reason why rhythm may be what is most salient in lyrics.

A reader of verse, attentive to the rhythms and verbal patterning, produces or articulates the text as he or she hears it, occupying, however temporarily, the position of speaker. Many of the well-attested effects of lyrics, including the "hearing" of rhymes that are rhymes only for the ear and not the eye *(here/near/bier/queer),* imply a subvocalization, placing the reader in the position of virtual speaker. "The reader of verse," Clive Scott claims, "is poised between the will to read and the will to 'hear,' the will to speak and the will to be spoken, the will to control language (utter it) and the will to submit to language (assimilate it.) . . . rhythm is the mediating force between text and reader, reader and self, the place where these conflicting impulses of will play out their drama." And again, "The reading of verse is most properly described as a dialogue between a reading self and a listening self, where the listener speaks."[12]

Frye writes that the core of poetry is not descriptive meaning and not the poet's cri de coeur but "a subtle and elusive verbal pattern"; that the root of lyric is *melos* and *opsis,* which in English are related to the associative processes of "babble" and "doodle," two kinds of verbal patterning. *Opsis,* or verbal design, whose root form for Frye is *riddle,* starts with the playful association of images, meanings, and structures and can lead to visual patterns in poetry. Of *melos,* the sound patterning of poetry, he writes, "The radical of *melos* is *charm:* the hypnotic incantation that, through its pulsing dance rhythm, appeals to involuntary physical response." Elsewhere he continues, "The rhetoric of charm is dissociative and incantatory: it sets up a pattern of sound so complex and repetitive that the ordinary processes of response are short-circuited. Refrain, rhyme, alliteration, assonance, pun, antithesis: every repetitive device known to rhetoric is called into play. Such repetitive formulae break down and confuse the conscious will, hypnotize and compel to certain courses of action."[13]

The capacious category of charms, including work songs, drinking songs and lullabies, recalls what in "Che cos'è la poesia?" Jacques Derrida describes as the lyric's demand to be learnt by heart, its appeal to *Gedächtnis* rather than *Erinnerung,* to rote memory, the by-heart, rather than the memory of understanding. With novels we characteristically recall plots and characters rather than phrases, but to remember a lyric is to remember at least some of its words. In this it is linked to other melic forms, such as song lyrics, which we can recall without understanding: they do not need to be comprehended to be appreciated, and indeed may even be treasured for the impenetrability that makes them tokens to be repeated—charms, in effect. Responding to notions in literary theory of the "ideal reader" or "super-reader" that readers might aspire to be—the reader of novels who notices every detail, carefully constructs characters and makes every connection—Scott urges that in the case of poetry "what we need as readers is a reason for reading the same thing over and over again," which may, of course come from thematic subtlety or intricacy, but is perhaps more likely to come from the seductiveness of rhythms that create charms we would ideally know by heart.[14] Rhythm is one of the major forces through which poems haunt us, just as poems themselves are haunted by rhythms of other poems.

If rhythm is fundamental to the appeal of lyric, it is largely neglected by criticism, in part because criticism is interpretive and looks for textual features that not only contribute to meaning but may suggest new meanings or hitherto unknown nuances of meaning. Though critics do, in their interpretive quest, sometimes focus on aspects of the metrical movement of lines, seeking to find through the metrical analysis patterns or features that can somehow be enlisted in an interpretation, the strategies for recuperating metrical structures are limited—speeding up, slowing down, and emphasis are the most common effects. These are scarcely exciting, and those where a more precise contribution may be claimed, as in cases of mimetic suggestiveness, are rather dubious. And rhythm is still more difficult to grasp than meter.

"Rhythm is surely the vaguest term in criticism," writes T. V. F. Brogan in his encyclopedia article on the subject, offering discouragement where one hoped for inspiration.[15] The study of rhythm is especially difficult because rhythm is something as utterly familiar as tapping our foot in time to music or as the regular strides with which we walk most comfortably. It is near to hand yet a phenomenon observed throughout nature, wherever there is periodicity. It appears to be a property of systems yet it is above all an experience, dependent upon the frames and expectations with which we approach phenomena (as we make the ticking of a clock into a duple rhythm: *tick, tock*). And the notion of rhythm encompasses both the regularity of a musical beat or higher-level forms of symmetry and various forms of irregularity—from the syncopation that is tied in with beats to higher-level asymmetrical structures where different forms of prominence (phonological, prosodic, syntactical) create differing temporal experiences.

This chapter considers approaches to rhythm and repetition that highlight the centrality of rhythm to the construction of the lyric and the experience of lyric, though they are also more diffusely at work in other kinds of poetry as well. We might start with Blake's "The Tyger":

Tyger! Tyger! burning bright
In the forests of the night,

What immortal hand or eye
Could frame thy fearful symmetry?

In what distant deeps or skies
Burnt the fire of thine eyes?
On what wings dare he aspire?
What the hand dare seize the fire?

And what shoulder, & what art.
Could twist the sinews of thy heart?
And when thy heart began to beat,
What dread hand? & what dread feet?

What the hammer? what the chain?
In what furnace was thy brain?
What the anvil? what dread grasp
Dare its deadly terrors clasp?

When the stars threw down their spears,
And watered heaven with their tears,
Did he smile his work to see?
Did he who made the Lamb make thee?

Tyger! Tyger! burning bright
In the forests of the night,
What immortal hand or eye
Dare frame thy fearful symmetry?

This is a lyric that has generated a vast literature of interpretation, most of which passes over its rhythmic structure, but what is most striking about it, what makes it a compelling poem, rather than a prose reflection on the power of creation, or on the threat of the French Revolution, or anything else, is its rhythm: the four-beat rhythm, with strong initial stress in all but five lines, the rhythm of nursery rhymes and counting songs. "It is the rhythm of song-verse," writes Andrew Welsh, "in which the one-two-three-four of the steady beat is far more important in determining the movement of the language than the consistently repeated patterns and counted sylla-bles of foot-prosody." Accompanying this steady beat of the song-rhythm is the rhythm of the syntax, with short questions contrasting with undivided lines, and other rhythmical movements set up by repeated sounds: the alliterations, assonances, rhymes, and other sound echoes woven through "The Tyger." Along with **b**urning **b**right, Tyger **b**right, and **fr**ame **f**earful, we have the hammering repetition of the twelve "what"s. This is a charm-rhythm, the language of incantation, invocation. In addition to the meter, Welsh writes, "we also hear in it the questioning of the rhythms of speech-*melos* and the sound echoes of charm-*melos* caught up and carried along on the steady beats of a children's song. And in such songs the deeper powers of this old rhythm persist."[16]

This rhythm is the most arresting aspect of the poem; what we make of it when we apply interpretive pressure, place it in one or another thematic or mythic or historical context in order to derive a meaning, is of interest, certainly, but one might wonder whether these interpretive efforts are not in some measure the product of a desire to justify the hold that such strange rhythmic sequences have on us. They have a power to inscribe themselves in mechanical memory independently of any attempt to remember them, and rather than consider ourselves victims of some jejune susceptibility to rhythm independent of meaning, we devote ourselves to intricate explorations of theme.

But since the most striking feature of Blake's poem is the four-beat meter of his quatrains, we should begin with meter, which is the focus of most discussions of rhythm.

1. Meter

The problem of the relation between rhythm and meter is a venerable one: among the Greeks there was already a division between the *rhythmikoi* and the *metrikoi;* the former saw poetic rhythm as related to music, a temporal art, and the latter treated it as a metrical structure. But the vast body of work on the movement of verse focuses on meter, and for most of the history of lyric, poems were written in relation to particular metrical frames, specific patterns of syllables of particular types. Metrics has been a contentious field, with different systems of notation and conceptions of meter and vigorous struggle between the proponents of different approaches; and in recent decades it has been to a considerable extent captured by linguists, whose generative metrics sets itself the task of writing rules that would distinguish metrically well-formed lines from those that experienced readers would deem not well formed, which is a different goal from that of rhythmical analysis, in that the descriptions assigned by the generative apparatus may be irrelevant to rhythmic effects. For such reasons, it is very tempting for critics to avoid the topic altogether in their discussions of poetry. Even the experts recognize this problem. Brogan concludes the *Princeton Encyclopedia*'s article on *Prosody* by noting:

> Over the past century there has been a general perception that prosody is a desiccated subject, a stony little patch of ground frequented only by eccentrics, fanatics, and pedants. The indictments are easy to finger: verse theory took nearly two millennia to free itself from the detritus of Classical prosody; it has never been able to give even an adequate theory of meter; it has been unable to agree on not merely concepts and terms but underlying assumptions about the nature of poetry itself (text, performance, experience). . . . It has been too willing to base theory on whatever versions of linguistics have been current; it has too often failed to distinguish linguistic processes from artistic conventions. . . . Yet the failure to give final answers is not proof that the questions are trivial; quite the contrary. . . . verse structure lies at the very core of our understanding of poetry.[17]

What to do, then? An account of lyric predicated on the centrality of rhythm to the distinctiveness and the attractions of the form needs at least to identify problems to be avoided and offer some indications of ways of thinking about the contribution of meter to verse structure that might be especially relevant to lyric.

A striking feature of poetic meters is that from a wide range of features of natural languages, they select a very small number and organize them into a limited set of rather restricted patterns which, used in a wide range of cases, from nursery rhymes to the most sophisticated poems, come to have special potency.[18] Meters select from the phonological features of the language and segment the sound continuum into units that are set in a relation of equivalence, with marked positions in each unit filled by some kind of prominence, usually called the *ictus*. A meter consists of regular patterns of contrastive structures. In general the poetic line is the major unit of meter, with a meter defining a line as a certain combination of contrasts, generally duple or ternary, and lines sometimes combining into larger metrical units, such as couplets or stanzas, though the focus on the metrical line has led to a relative neglect of the unit of the stanza, important for lyric.[19]

Classical meters were based on patterns of alternation between "long" and "short" syllables, but "quantity" in syllables, as a phonologically functional element of the language, disappeared from Latin around the fourth century, and syllable length was replaced in European vernaculars by stress or accent. Latin church poets transformed quantitative meters into meters based on a certain number of syllables, but Western metrical theory tenaciously sought to preserve the apparatus of classical prosodic analysis, allowing ideas about the hierarchy of cultures to trump fidelity to the features of language.[20] Thus the notion of the metrical foot was imported into English and other modern languages, even though the prosody of modern languages works differently. Languages have successfully adopted meters from other languages whose phonological and prosodic apparatus is unlike their own: Catullus, Horace, and Hölderlin, for example, adopted Greek meters; English adopted forms from Romance; and Russian adopted Polish and German verse forms. But languages differ in the phonological features that are available to fill the marked positions in verse structures, so such adaptation cannot be taken for granted. And the varying metrical practices of particular languages complicate any attempt to discuss meter in general.

While meter never accounts for rhythm as experienced (I return to this problem below), it certainly contributes to rhythm, establishing norms for the repetition of elements and making possible also the violation of the norms that it establishes. In French, for example, the principal meter since the sixteenth century has been the alexandrine, defined as a line of twelve syllables with a medial caesura, a formal division sometimes realized as a pause. Since French lacks the distinction between long and short vowels that was central to classical meters, the alexandrine could be based purely on syllable count with rules about its division into two hemistiches and about the one feature of French most similar to vowel length in classical languages, the so-called *e caduc*, an unstressed *e* in a syllable not followed by a consonant, in word-final position, which can be mute or pronounced according to its environment.[21] For the classical alexandrine, the sixth syllable must be word-final and ideally the end of a phrase, a significant syntactic break, and must be able to take a tonic accent, so not an *e caduc*.[22] In fact, though the alexandrine is a syllabic and not a syllabic-accentual meter, it often lends itself to a four-beat rhythm, with stresses falling not only on the sixth and twelfth syllables, as the meter itself prescribes, but on one other syllable within each hemistich (here separated by a //; the stressed syllables are underlined and in bold type):

> La sot**tise**, l'er**reur,** // le pé**ché,** la lé**sine,**
> Oc**cup**ent nos es**prits** // et tra**vaill**ent nos **corps.**

☞

> Folly and error, stinginess and sin,
> Possess our spirits and fatigue our flesh.

In these opening lines of Baudelaire's "Au lecteur," the meter prescribes a caesura after *l'erreur* and *esprits,* and the verse falls into a four-beat rhythm, with stress on second syllable of the four nouns in the first line, the two verbs and the first noun in the second line, and on the monosyllabic *córps*.[23] But such a rhythm, if continued, would swiftly become monotonous, and stress outside the sixth and twelfth positions is rhythmical rather than metrical. In French stress is determined more by phrase structure than by the prosodic contours of individual words: stress falls on the terminal syllable of a phonemic group. Hence, "Regar**dez!**" ("Look!") takes stress on the final syllable, but in "Regardez-**moi**" ("Look at me!") no syllable of the verb would be stressed. Thus in the next two lines of Baudelaire's poem, the meter is the same but the rhythm is different because of the phrase structure:

> Et nous alimen**tons** // nos ai**mabl**es re**mords,**
> Comme les mendi**ants** // nour**riss**ent leur ver**min**e.

☞

> And we feed the feelings of remorse we like,
> as beggars take to nourishing their lice.

The first hemistich of each line has even, rising rhythm with a stress only on the sixth syllable. Even within regular alexandrines, it is important to the success of the verse that the phrasal organization insure some rhythmical variety.

The convention of the alexandrine with its customs about the placement of the caesura (treated as "rules") makes it possible for poets to achieve rhythmic effects by violating those rules. Victor Hugo proudly proclaimed "J'ai disloqué ce grand niais d'alexandrin" ("I dislocated that great fool, the alexandrine"), in a verse of twelve syllables that phrasally falls into three rhythmic measures of four syllables each: *J'ai disloqué//ce grand niais//d'alexandrin;* the required caesura after the sixth syllable is thus overrun or swallowed up in the phrase "ce grand niais," which it would divide. This structure, which soon came to count as a metrical variation on the alexandrine ("the romantic trimeter"), is just one form of rhythmic disruption that the rules of the alexandrine made possible. The conclusion of Baudelaire's "Sonnet d'automne" illustrates the rhythmical variety that is possible.

> 9. Aimons-nous douce**ment.** // L'Am**our** dans sa gué**rit**e,
> 10. Téné**breux,** embus**qué,** //**band**e son arc fa**tal.**
> 11. Je con**nais** les en**gins**// de son vieil arse**nal:**
> 12. Crime, hor**reur** et fo**lie!** //—Ô p**â**le margue**rit**e!
> 13. Comme **moi** n'es-tu **pas** //un so**leil** autom**nal,**
> 14. Ô ma si **blan**che, ô ma// si **froid**e Margue**rit**e?

Let us love gently. Cupid in his den,
Hiding in somber ambush, bends his bow.
I know his arsenal, his worn-out bolts,
Crime, madness, horror—oh pale marguerite,
Are we not both like the autumnal sun,
O my so white, my so cool Marguerite.

[Trans. James McGowan, modified]

Contrasting with the two smooth-running alexandrines of lines 11 and 13 are lines 9, 10, 12, and 14: in 9 and 12 the caesura comes at a serious syntactic break, requiring a real pause in recitation; in line 10 the verb ***bande*** requires an expressive stress; and most strikingly, in line 14 the syntax, dividing the alexandrine into a sequence of $4 + (5 + 3)$ syllables, produces an unexpected and emphatic pause on ***blanche,*** preventing any kind of pause at the normal point of caesura, and producing an extra-long final sequence with closural weight. Contrast this line with a regular alexandrine Baudelaire might have written, such as "O ma **blan**che, ma **froi**de, // o jo**lie** Marguer**ite**," where the first two adjectives seem attenuated and the final phrase much less weighty.

Because the rules for the French alexandrine were quite firm and explicit, they made possible a range of rhythmic effects but left aside much of what contributes to rhythm: except for accents on the sixth or twelfth syllable, group terminal accents are not metrical but rhythmic. "French is an accentable language but not an accented one," writes Clive Scott, and given the importance to rhythm of accents that are not metrically determined, "French metrical analysis is left to nurse a profound unease with its rhythm-generating, non-rhythmic syllabism."[24] This is especially true for the French octosyllable, a verse line with no prescribed caesura, where a line-terminal accent falls on the rhyme words, but where internal rhythm is variable and uncertain: a reader seeks to structure the line in reading and hesitates between two, three, and four accents. Théophile Gautier's "Symphonie en blanc majeur" illustrates the problem.

> Le marbre blanc, chair froide et pâle,
> Où vivent les divinités ;
> L'argent mat, la laiteuse opale
> Qu'irisent de vagues clartés . . .

> The white marble, cold and pale flesh,
> Where the divinities live
> Matte silver, the milky opal,
> That vague light makes iridescent . . .

The fourth line seems to call for three accents, especially because the pre-posed adjective *vagues* with the pronounced *e caduc* calls for emphasis.

The third line gives us two noun-adjective pairings that can be treated as rhythmically equivalent, despite the disequilibrium in syllables, or else the preposed adjective, *laiteuse,* can attract emphasis. "The octosyllable is, and almost inherently so, rhythmically ambivalent," so that the reader is compelled to enter the poem, "to create its rhythmic shapes," within the context of the rhymes which provide the dominant shaping force. In French, in sum, meter specifies an arrangement of syllables, within which stress patterns appropriate for phrasal groupings can produce a rhythm. "Rhythm and meter actualize two completely different principles, which should never be confused," writes Scott. "Crudely put, meter is linguistic, objective, quantitative, mono-dimensional, repeatable / discontinuous; rhythm, on the other hand, is paralinguistic, subjective, heterogeneous, qualitative multi-dimensional, and irreversible."[25] This view is perhaps more easily defended for French than for English.

In the case of English, the problem is different because, unlike French, English is an accented language, with stress assigned to particular syllables in English words, and especially because English prosodists of the Renaissance, after attempting to write rules for English verse strictly following the classical model (quantitative metrics), abandoned this but kept the classical feet, with stressed syllables occupying the place of long vowels and unstressed that of short vowels, thus establishing a tradition of inappropriate analysis that persists to this day. "Traditional metrics, taken over wholesale from classical prosody as once understood, did not work," concludes Brogan in the *Princeton Encyclopedia.*[26] It is often an obstacle to the study and appreciation of poetry rather than a means of entry. Assessment of traditional foot metrics is far beyond the scope of this discussion, but it is perhaps worth illustrating problems it needlessly creates, since a different approach will then appear all the more attractive.

Foot-prosody describes English meters in terms of the number of feet and the dominant type of foot, where the foot is a particular combination of stressed and unstressed syllables (iambic pentameter, dactylic hexameter, etc.). Analysts then attempt to describe metrical practices through what is called foot substitution, where another kind of foot is substituted for the foot stipulated as "normal" for the meter. (The most common substitutions, e.g., a trochaic for an iambic foot in first position in iambic pentameter, are then deemed regular.) But foot-substitution encounters serious difficulties which are not in fact difficulties in the experiencing of poetic rhythm. Thus a line such as Auden's "Eárth recéive an hónored gúest" poses no rhythmical problem for English speakers: there are four stresses (marked ´), including the initial and final syllables of the line, alternating with unstressed syllables. But if one attempts to scan this in foot-prosody, there is uncertainty about whether to call it a trochaic line with a "catalectic" final foot (a foot in which the final syllable has been dropped, indicated by bracketing: ´-/´-/´-/ ´[-]) or an iambic line with a truncated initial foot ([-] ´/-´/-´/-´). (The best solution is doubtless to take the line as trochaic, since the virtual final unstressed syllable can manifest itself as a slight pause before the stressed onset of the next line, but this does not mitigate the system's inappropriate implication of rhythmic uncertainty.) Foot-scansion contributes nothing here except confusion, by suggesting that the line is somehow rhythmically anomalous, whereas in fact this four stress line, with strong initial and final stress, is a frequent pattern for solemn verse, as well as for nursery rhymes: *Jáck and Jíll went úp the híll.*

A different sort of example of the irrelevant implications of foot-scansion might be the beginning of Shakespeare's Sonnet 29. Though the poem is written in the meter supposedly most amenable to foot-prosody, iambic pentameter, foot-substitution scansion gives us the following pattern for lines 1 and 3, where the backslash separates feet and bold type indicates feet substituted for iambic feet:

> ***Whén in*/**/disgráce/with fórt/**une and**/**mén's éyes**
> *I all alone beweep my outcast state,*
> *And tróu/ble déaf/**heáv'n with**/my bóot/less críes,*
> *And look upon myself, and curse my fate,*

Derek Attridge notes that the implication of this analysis should be that line 1 is more irregular than line 3, since it has three substitutions—feet one, four, and five—while the latter only has one, foot three. This is the result of foot-scansion's different ways of treating the juxtaposition of two stressed syllables: because of the artifice of feet, the sequence in line 1 of two unstressed and then two stressed syllables - - ´ ´ *(une and/**mén's éyes**)* is treated as a more radical substitution of two feet than the combination in line 3 of two stressed and two unstressed syllables ´ ´ - - *(**déaf/heáv'n*** *with/my*). For a reader, however, line 3 involves a greater sense of rhythmic tension, because in line 1 the shift of a stress from the *and* to *men's,* which is analyzed as substitution of one pyrrhic foot and one spondee for two iambs, is in fact only a mild rhythmical displacement, giving us slightly greater stress on the penultimate word of the line, *men's,* as is expected when one-syllable adjectives modify a noun whose first syllable is stressed; whereas in line 3 the stress on *heav'n* (required by the syntax), represented in foot-scansion by a simple inversion of an iamb into a trochee, comes at a point in the line where a beat would not be expected. The juxtaposition of two stresses, *déaf héav'n,* "slows down the movement over both words and creates a point of rhythmic emphasis," followed by a release and compensatory speeding up.[27] Foot-scansion implies that the meter of line 1 is more complicated and disruptive than that of line 3, whereas the opposite is true.

A final example might be Tennyson's famous

Break, break, break,
On thy cold gray stones, O sea!
And I would that my tongue could utter
The thoughts that arise in me.

Readers have little difficulty grasping the rhythm of this opening stanza, despite the initial puzzle of the first line. There are three pronounced beats per line with a fourth, silent beat, expressed as a pause. (One can read the lines omitting the pause, but they will feel rushed). It has a clear rhythm, which no doubt helps account for its popularity, but for foot-prosodists, it poses a conundrum. Dana Gioia asks, "What is the meter of Tennyson's poem? A traditionalist might label it anapestic, but that scansion does not adequately account for the opening line, which can only be explained as stress meter. The lines range from three to nine syllables in length, and, if one divides them into accentual-syllabic feet, one discovers as many iambs as anapests (not to mention the recurring monosyllabic feet). To label this poem as iambic or anapestic, therefore, is misleading, since almost every line would then, to some degree, be irregular. Yet the poem is tangibly metrical—one hears a steady beat common to both the three-syllable and nine-syllable line."[28] The fact that it poses such a problem for foot-scansion when its rhythm is easily graspable for readers indicates that a different conceptual framework is desirable.

What is the alternative? A widely accepted recent approach to English verse comes in the work of Derek Attridge, who has produced a series of books on the rhythms of English poetry that abandon foot-scansion, as masking the fundamental operations of English verse, which is based in stress. Attridge argues for the centrality to the English tradition of four-beat verse, especially the four-beat quatrain. Accounts of the English poetic tradition frequently focus on iambic pentameter, for good reasons—it is the principal meter of Shakespeare, Milton, and Wordsworth, and especially important for narrative verse. Instead of taking pentameter as the norm, Attridge suggests that the basic distinction for English is between four-beat verse and nonfour-beat verse (of which five-beat verse is the most common instance), which makes iambic pentameter above all a way of resisting the ballad stanza or hymn stanza and bringing more speech-like rhythms into poetry, through a verse line with no fixed internal division and a relatively flexible accentual pattern. But even with iambic pentameter we often make a line a four-stress line if we can: "To bé or nót to be, thát is the quéstion" or "Is thís a dágger that I sée befóre me?"

Beginning not with prosodic theory but with the most basic rhythmic abilities, Attridge notes how quickly a rhythm imposes itself when someone reads a poem such as A. A. Milne's "Disobedience":

James James
Morrison Morrison
Weatherby George Dupree
Took great
Care of his Mother,
Though he was only three.
James James
Said to his Mother,
"Mother," he said, said he;
"You must never go down to the end of the town, if you don't go
down with me."

"Simply a string of names," writes Attridge, but the fact that people so quickly give it the same rhythmical organization indicates that "the brain, and the muscles of the vocal organs, have already been programmed to give a distinctive rhythmic shape to the material," namely the structure of four beats repeated four times that occurs everywhere in popular verse and song as well as in much literary verse. Arranging the poem to bring out this structure, Attridge places a B beneath the beats.[29]

James James Morrison Morrison
  B   B   B   B

Weatherby George Dupree
  B   B   B   [B]

Took great care of his Mother,
  B   B   B   B

Though he was only three.
  B   B   B   [B]

James James said to his Mother-
  B   B   B   B

"Mother," he said, said he;
  B   B   B   [B]

"You must never go down to the end of the town,
        B   B   B   B

if you don't go down with me."
  B   B   B   [B]

Striking here are the virtual beats marked [B] that occur at the end of alternate lines, where speakers pause before continuing with the next line. This pattern, of a four-by-four form with virtual beats after every seventh beat, is the 4.3.4.3 stanza familiar from hymn tunes (called "common measure") and ballads, as well as many lyrics. The silent or virtual beats "function as highly effective rhythmic articulators; they mark the mid-point and the end of the group, and augment whatever structuring is effected by the poem's rhymes and by its syntactic and semantic segmentation. A virtual beat of this kind gives a strong sense of finality to the previous beat, which is the one on which the rhyme regularly falls."[30] Emily Dickinson's poem that begins

Because I could not stop for Death—
He kindly stopped for me—
The Carriage held but just Ourselves—
And Immortality . . .

like many of her other works is written in this "common measure," into
which we automatically cast Milne's rhyme.

Attridge's example illustrates an uncanny rhythmic ability. Even very
young children, who can barely pronounce the words, can recite a nursery
rhyme like the one below, even though this requires "knowing"—I put
the word in quotation marks—that each word in the first line takes a stress,
whereas in the third line only every second word is stressed.

Star light star bright,
The first star I see tonight,
I wish I may, I wish I might,
Have the wish I wish tonight.

Upon this edifice of shared ability, Attridge argues, is built the entire English poetic tradition. The four-by-four formation, four groups of four
beats, "is the basis of most modern popular music, including rock and
rap, of most folk, broadside, and industrial ballads from the middle ages
to the 20th century, of most hymns, most nursery rhymes, and a great deal
of printed poetry."[31] Attridge's approach describes meter as a regular pattern of beats, generally realized as stressed syllables, alternating with one
or more off-beats. Both beats and off-beats may be virtual, and syllables
that would be stressed for syntactic or other reasons may be demoted to
the status of off-beats, taking only secondary stress. Tennyson's "Break,
Break, Break" would be scanned as follows, with beats marked as *B*, off-
beats as *o* or -*o*- for double off-beats, and virtual beats or off-beats, usually realized as pauses, placed in brackets:

Break, break, break,
  B   [o]   B   [o]   B   [o B]

On thy cold gray stones, O sea!
  -o-   B   o   B   o   B   [o B]

And I would that my tongue could utter
-o-   B   -o-   B   o   B   o   [B]

The thoughts that arise in me.
o   B   -o-   B   o   B   [o B]

This analysis captures the same regularities and the same stress patterns as foot prosody without the artificial confusion of foot substitution.[32]

Poems that seem to use other meters may have the underlying rhythmical structure of the four-by-four stanza. Notoriously, limericks, which are printed in five-line stanzas, have three four-beat lines, each with a virtual (silent) beat at the end, and two short lines which add up to a four-beat line with internal rhyme, so they are a version of the fundamental four-by-four form, often called "short meter":

A **gentle**man **din**ing at **Crewe** [beat]
Found a **rat**her large **mouse** in his **stew.** [beat]
Said the **wai**ter, "don't **shout** and **wave** it a**bout,**
Or the **rest** will be **want**ing one **too.**" [beat]

One could even argue that the four-by-four form underlies one of the most powerful metrical creations of that great poetic inventor Gerard Manley Hopkins. His "Spelt from Sibyl's Leaves," which he called the longest sonnet ever written, relies on a strong metrical pattern of eight stresses per line, but along with unusual stresses ('), he marks a caesura in each line, no doubt recognizing that readers need this division in order to keep track of the four stresses on each side of the caesura. The caesuras help, but the meter of the sonnet would have been less difficult to grasp if the poem had been printed in tetrameter quatrains, as here:

EARNEST, earthless, equal, attuneable,
vaulty, voluminous, . . . stupendous,
Evening strains to be tíme's vást,
womb-of-all, home-of-all, hearse-of-all night.

This poem is written in "sprung rhythm," an invention of Hopkins's which closely resembles a purely accentual meter, where there can be many unstressed syllables between accented syllables. This sonnet was "made for performance," Hopkins wrote; and "its performance is not reading with the eye, but loud, leisurely, poetical (not rhetorical) recitation. It should," he concludes, "be almost sung."[33] (I take it that poetical recitation would give full allegiance to sound patterning, while rhetorical recitation would emphasize meaning.) Here, many of the desired stresses need to be marked because a reader could not imagine this organization of stress patterns, which run against the syntactical grain. In the text below, the accent marks are those provided by Hopkins. I put stressed syllables in bold to facilitate the leisurely, poetical reading (caesuras are marked with a backslash /).

EARNEST, **earth**less, equal, at**tune**able, / **vaul**ty, vo**lu**minous, . . .
    [beat] . . . stu**pen**dous

Evening **strains** to be **tíme's vást,** / **womb**-of-all, **home**-of-all,
    hearse-of-all **night.**

Her **fond** yellow **horn**light **wound** to the **west,** / her **wild** hollow
    hoarlight **hung** to the **height**

Waste; her **earliest stars, earl**-stars, / **stárs prin**cipal, over**bend** us,

Fíre-féaturing **heaven.** For **earth** / her **being** has un**bound,** her
    dapple is at an **end,** as-

tray or a**swarm,** all **through**ther, in **throngs;** / self **ín** self **steep**èd
    and **pásh**ed—**qúite**

Dis**remem**bering, **dísmém**bering / **áll** now. **Heart,** you **round** me
    right

With: **Óur** évening is over us; **óur** night / **whélms, whélms, ánd**
    will **end** us.

Only the **beak**-leaved **boughs dra**gonish / **da**mask the **tool**-smooth
    bleak light; **black,**

Ever so **black** on it. **Óur** tale, O **óur** oracle! ' **Lét** life, **wán**ed, ah **lét**
    life **wind**

Off **hér** once **skéined** stained **véined** variety / upon, **áll** on **twó**
    spools; **párt,** pen, **páck**

Now her **áll** in **twó** flocks, **twó** folds—**black,** white; / **right,** wrong;
    reckon but, **reck** but, **mind**

But **thése** two; **wáre** of a **wórld** where **bút** these / **twó** tell, **eac**h off
    the **óth**er; of a **rack**

Where, **self**wrung, **self**strung, **sheathe**- and **shel**terless, / **thóughts** agaínst thoughts ín groans grínd.[34]

This is a remarkable example of a poem where the meter of an eight-beat line, with beats separated by an equal time intervals (*isochronous* is the technical term) provides much of the rhythm, as in nursery rhymes, counting rhymes, or chants, yet without the feeling that other sorts of potential expressivity are sacrificed. The rhythmical effect Hopkins seems to seek is quite different from reading an accentual-syllabic meter such as iambic pentameter in a singsong fashion while beating time, overcoming word stress and phrasal prosody by stressing alternate syllables, as one would in chanting "The **quálitý** of **mér**cy **ís** not **straíned**." In the final hemistich of Hopkins' distended sonnet, for instance, a continuous isochronic beat would be fully compatible with both the prosody of English speech and the verbal parallelism of the line, which would lead one to read *thóughts against thóughts in gróans grínd,* stressing the four content words and leaving unstressed the two prepositions. But Hopkins calls for the strongly counterintuitive yet expressive pattern stressing the two prepositions—*thóughts agaínst thoughts ín groans grínd*—which grates against the grammar. The power of this metrical rhythm combines with alliteration, which characteristically goes with the metrical pulse, in a sort of blind force that destroys identities, even as it marshals the distinctive resources of linguistic creativity to articulate this bleak vision of a world that is dissolving in blackness. In this poem, with its neologisms and unusual lexical collocations, the repetition of sounds seems the generative force: meaning is produced by running the changes on distinctive sounds, even as what is announced is the disappearance of all distinctions, except good versus evil, though that distinction seems overwhelmed by the driving amoral sonic energy of the poem. Made for oral performance, as Hopkins declared, it illustrates the paradox that the more astonishing the vocal acrobatics of a poem, the less it evokes a human voice. This is a poem without a speaker but where voicing and sound events are extremely prominent: a vocalic tour de force without a speaking voice.

A metrical form related to Hopkins's sprung rhythm, but which escapes the tension in his practice between the metrical frame and the regular stress patterns of the language, is sometimes called strict stress meter or *dolnik,* the Russian term for this form: the dolnik line, which usually feels strongly regular as it moves forward without faltering, with both binary and ternary patterns, has a fixed number of stresses but the number of unstressed syllables between stressed syllables can be either one or two and the number of unstressed syllables before the first stress in the line can be zero, one or two.[35] Thus, Heine's *Lyrisches Intermezzo* no. 21 has pairs of unstressed syllables in every line after the first.

So **hast** du **ganz** und **gar** vergessen,
Daß ich so **lang** dein **Herz** besessen,
Dein **Herz**chen so **süß** und so **falsch** und so **klein,**
Es kann **nir**gend was **Süß**res und **Fals**cheres **sein.**

So **hast** du die **Lieb'** und das **Leid** vergessen,
Die das **Herz** mir **tä**ten zu**sam**men**pressen.**
Ich **weiß** nicht, war **Lie**be **grö**ßer als **Leid?**
Ich **weiß** nur, sie **wa**ren **groß** alle **beid'**!

⌐

So much have you forgotten wholly
That I possessed your heart entirely,
Your heartling so sweet and so false and so small
There can nowhere be smaller or falser at all.

So far from your mind have gone love and suffering
That had once constricted my heart so tightly.
I wonder, did love surpass torture's sense?
I know this: together, both were immense!

[Trans. Avery Slater]

Dolniks may be composed in three-, four-, or five-beat lines, but the four-beat form is most frequent. Marina Tarlinskaja claims that the strict stress four-beat meter typically accompanies English poems dealing with simple rather than sophisticated subjects, no doubt because of the form's association with the ballad tradition. But Tennyson's elegiac "Break, Break, Break" is a dolnik, as are many other poems on subjects not especially simple. What they share is an easy rhythm, which often makes them especially memorable, even when the language is complex or unfamiliar. A fine example is Hopkins's "Inversnaid." Here is the opening stanza:

> This darksome burn, horseback brown,
> His rollrock highroad roaring down,
> In coop and in comb the fleece of his foam
> Flutes and low to the lake falls home.

The variation between single and double off-beats in lines with four beats generates a swinging rhythm in lines that vary between seven and ten syllables but are experienced as metrically regular.

Metrical forms, as Tarlinskaja suggests, may carry implicit allusions to their most common themes (this is especially true of stanza forms). In Dickinson, the use of "common measure" and other hymn meters sets up thematic expectations—that poems about death will imagine life everlasting, for instance—which the poems frequently frustrate, achieving a special ironic slyness as they deviate from the paths of hymns. But generally it is not easy to tie particular meters to specific effects. In *Poetry as Discourse* Anthony Easthope explores the social meaning of meters: the four-stress meter of ballads and nursery rhymes is collective, popular, and, in Easthope's view, natural, whereas iambic pentameter is a bourgeois imposition—abstract, linear, essentializing. It conceals the process of its production and the position of the subject of enunciation; its greater flexibility enables it to seem natural, an imitation of speech, and its cultural prestige makes the more popular form seem vulgar and crude.[36] In iambic pentameter there is the idea of an abstract metrical norm with individual variation—hence a reinforcement of individualism—unlike the four-beat meters where there is communal chanting, no gap between group norm and individual realization.

Now it is easy to dismiss such broad-brush characterization of a major English meter that has served a vast range of purposes in the hands of immensely skilled practitioners of varied political persuasions, but much of what he says is defensible, at a very general level. Even if the reading of social meanings is rather too simplistically enlisted in a story of class struggle and the triumph of the bourgeoisie, Easthope is right to link iambic pentameter to the idea of representing the speaking subject as individual—to hearing a voice—and to associate tetrameter with a position of enunciation not marked as that of an individual subject. Four-stress popular meters make available a collective subject position, and one joins that position as one chants or repeats: "Jack and Jill went up the hill." We are not inclined to ask who is speaking here or to try to posit a person from the image of voice, and much of the pleasure comes from participating in that implicitly collective position. The same is arguably true of "Tyger, Tyger, burning bright, / In the forests of the night," but not of "When in disgrace with fortune and men's eyes." Certainly four-stress meter can impose a certain impersonality, as in Goethe's "Heidenröslein." The five-beat line, as Attridge notes, is "a much weaker rhythmic Gestalt than a four-beat line, and is the simplest way of avoiding the much stronger rhythmic drive of four-beat verse." Four-beat falling and triple meters are furthest from spoken English, while the line closest to the rhythms of speech is "five-beat rising duple verse or iambic pentameter."[37]

Such associational effects of meters and social meanings of rhythms vary from language to language. Comparative studies of rhythm should help illuminate the rhythmical repertoire of particular languages, identifying what we tend to think of as natural and inevitable as, in fact, a cultural construction or convention. Thus, Tarlinskaja notes that

in different literatures the same general meter, . . . influenced by the language's phonology and poetic traditions, assumes dissimilar forms. The topical associations and thematic preferences of the same general meter may also change, and even become opposite when adopted in different literatures. For example, the so-called ternary meters, as in "My dear Lady Bab, you'll be shocked, I'm afraid, / When you hear the sad rumpus your ponies have made" (Thomas Moore), seem suitable to English poets for descriptions of fast motion and light, joyful subjects, and to Russian poets for slow motion and grave, melancholy subjects. The possible reasons are as follows. In the modern English poetic tradition, disyllabic meters (particularly the iamb) strongly predominated, and the infrequent ternary meters were perceived against the background of the prevailing binary meters. Disyllabic intervals between adjacent stresses in ternary meters were hurried through in the same span of time as monosyllabic intervals in the iamb. This phenomenon causes the English ternary meters to be subconsciously associated with speed and lightness and thus, metaphorically, with lightness of subject matter. In the Russian poetic tradition, ternary meters are relatively frequent and stand on their own; they have never been perceived against the background of binary meters. Disyllabic intervals between stresses in the ternaries were assumed to be longer and therefore "slower" than the monosyllabic meters of the iamb.[38]

Tarlinskaja's account illustrates the possibility of engaging in comparative study of rhythm to illuminate the power of rhythms in individual languages and their history. An English poet attempting to treat a solemn theme in triple meter seems thwarted by the meter. Thus William Cowper's "The Poplar Field" uses the felling of poplars to lament mortality itself.

> My fugitive years are all hasting away,
> And I must ere long lie as lowly as they,
> With a turf on my breast and a stone at my head,
> Ere another such grove shall arise in its stead.

In defense of his metrical choice one could argue that the ternary rhythm, reinforcing the claim that time moves swiftly and that our pleasures are fleeting, might enliven us to seize the day. The poem concludes:

> 'Tis a sight to engage me, if anything can,
> To muse on the perishing pleasures of man;
> Short-lived as we are, our enjoyments, I see,
> Have a still shorter date, and die sooner than we.

But it is very hard for an English speaker today to take seriously rhyming couplets in this meter when there is no vigorous phrasal counterbalancing and disruption.

Some theorists of meter insist that the goal of metrical analysis is not to help describe poetic rhythms but simply to specify the meter, the abstract normative structure that is the meter of the poem.[39] Most, though, see the task as one of describing the relevant prosodic structure of lines of verse in ways that will illustrate how they should be read and help to account for the experience of their rhythm, which is the case with Attridge's system, where meter is a strictly patterned regularity, within which stresses induced by the prosody of the language and syntactic organization contribute to a rhythm.

2. Rhythm

If one takes meter as the primary name for nonmeaningful pulsation, it is possible to associate rhythm with higher-level functions that put language in motion and make it meaningful, and some theorists of rhythm have tried to make it the basis of meaning in general. Henri Meschonnic, for instance, whose voluminous writings on the subject criticize all existing approaches to rhythm as excessively narrow, treats "rhythm in language [as] the organization of marks by which linguistic and extralinguistic signifieds produce a specific semantics, distinct from lexical meaning," a semantics which he calls *la signifiance*. Rhythm governs meaning as "the continuous movement of *signifiance* constructed by the historical activity of a subject." It involves all of discourse, not just sound and meter: he claims "la métrique est la théorie du rhythme des imbeciles" ("metrical analysis is the theory of rhythm of imbeciles").[40] A central problem in his work, in fact, is the expansion of the concept of rhythm to be very nearly all-encompassing. A rhythm is "une forme-sujet," a fusion of speaker and subject, and thus the organization of the speaking subject in and by discourse. Not content with this conjunction, he seeks a single theory for language and history, with rhythm as not only the principle that produces subjects but the mechanism for possible historical change.[41] He does develop his own mode of scansion, which supplements the French tradition of scansion by promoting accent and various forms of hierarchization, a valuable contribution, but he stresses that rhythm cannot be captured by any form of scansion.

The failure of Meschonnic's many works to exercise much influence, even in France, seems due to the fact that rhythm can no longer be contrasted with anything else, or even identified in a text, since it is the movement of meaning and of history. More precise in its analyses, though equally ambitious, is the work of Richard Cureton, whose account of rhythm and meter in *Rhythmic Phrasing in English Verse* will be expanded into a full-scale "Temporal Poetics."[42] Cureton brings together different levels of organization in verse, from the basic beating of meter to temporal structures that function at the level of the work as a whole, as versions of rhythm in a broad sense: forms of temporal organization. For Cureton rhythm is multilevel, variable, and complex. It is strictly hierarchical, with a fractal structure: local events are perceived as more or less prominent elements within longer events, which are themselves perceived as more or less prominent within yet longer events, and so on throughout the entire text. His goal in this temporal poetics is to synthesize metrical, syntactic, rhetorical, and thematic choices, rather than treating them separately, and to relate these different kinds of choices to four different kinds of "rhythmical time" which, as a paradigm of four contrasting categories, can be found everywhere: the four seasons, four ages of man, four basic elements, four directions, and so on. This last venture into the fourfold prompts considerable skepticism about the larger enterprise, but one should doubtless reserve judgment, since the crucial volume has yet to be published. The basic work on rhythm distinguishes meter, which organizes stronger and weaker beats into hierarchical structures with duple or triple patterning, from grouping, or phrasing, a countervailing force bringing to bear norms of the language and syntactic structures.

Whether the completed theory can successfully synthesize textual organization through an expanded concept of rhythm remains to be seen, but the distinction between meter and phrasing is useful for discussion of free verse, which deploys forms of organization different from traditional meters. At various moments in the history of lyric, free verse forms connote freedom of various sorts (to put it crudely, freedom of escape from classical meters into a direct relationship with the divine, in Klopstock and to some degree in Hölderlin; a limited freedom for fixing the infinite differently, in Mallarmé; a freedom for individual expression, in the ideology of much twentieth-century American verse).[43] Sometimes we read lines of free verse against meter, recognizing there, as one title has it, *The Ghost of Meter*.[44] In other cases the principles of organization seem quite different, as here:

so much depends

upon

a red wheel

barrow

glazed with rain

water

beside the white

chickens.

As I mentioned in Chapter 1, Williams's poem has a well-defined structure—three stanzas with a first line of three words and a second line of one word—but since the word is not a relevant unit for meter, this is a different sort of construction. The enjambment prompts readers to treat each line as if it were a breath group and to pause, however awkwardly, isolating the single word of each second line from the prior element with which it belongs.[45]

This is what Attridge calls "extrinsically-segmented verse," where lineation is not prompted by syntax or phrasal structure but is externally imposed; here the visual arrangement is crucial to the effect. The other main possibility, "intrinsically-segmented" verse, organizes lines according to syntactic units or breath groups.[46] Paul Celan's "Todesfuge" ("Death Fugue") lineates by syntactic units and creates its distinctive, powerful rhythm by the relentless repetition of entire words and phrases, not just particular sounds. Here is Stanza 1:

Schwarze Milch der Frühe wir trinken sie abends
wir trinken sie mittags und morgens wir trinken sie nachts
wir trinken und trinken
wir schaufeln ein Grab in den Lüften da liegt man nicht eng
Ein Mann wohnt im Haus der spielt mit den Schlangen der schreibt
der schreibt wenn es dunkelt nach Deutschland dein goldenes Haar
 Margarete
er schreibt es und tritt vor das Haus und es blitzen die Sterne er
 pfeift seine Rüden herbei

er pfeift seine Juden hervor läßt schaufeln ein Grab in der Erde
er befiehlt uns spielt auf nun zum Tanz

                ☞

Black milk of daybreak we drink it at evening
we drink it at midday and morning we drink it at night
we drink and we drink
we shovel a grave in the air there you won't lie too cramped
A man lives in the house he plays with his vipers he writes
he writes when it grows dark to Deutschland your golden hair
   Margareta
he writes it and steps out of doors and the stars are all sparkling,
he whistles his hounds to come close
he whistles his Jews into rows has them shovel a grave in the ground
he orders us strike up and play for the dance.

                              [Trans. John Felstiner]

The poem alludes both to the repetition of musical fugues and to German drinking songs but the repetition of words and phrases, continued in subsequent stanzas, with all the verbs in the present tense, takes on a numbing quality, beating us into submission: this is what happens, over and over. The combination of hyperbolic repetition with the variable line length is one striking possibility in lyric (Whitman offers a very different example, as does Hopkins, in a superb poem I consider in the next section). But Celan and Williams illustrate the extraordinary range of rhythmical possibilities of free verse, for which we still lack a plausible set of organizing categories that would capture its rhythmical resources—so important to lyric of the nineteenth and twentieth centuries.

The boldest account of rhythm that I have encountered, but which does not really take on free verse, is Amittai Aviram's *Telling Rhythms*. There are three possible relations between rhythm and meaning, he claims: (1) rhythm is a rhetorical device subordinated to meaning, to which it can contribute (the most common view); (2) there is no significant relation between rhythm and meaning; and (3) meaning is subordinate to and refers to rhythm. Intrepidly opting for the last, he maintains that seeing meaning or content as a representation of the form is the only way of relating the two without reducing form to content. The meaning of a poem, he claims, allegorically represents "aspects of the power of the poem's own rhythm to bring about a physical response, to engage the readers or listener's body and thus to disrupt the orderly process of meaning." Thus, for example, in Blake's "Tyger," "Much of the power and thrill of the poem comes from the insistent repetitiveness and parallelism that gives the poem a strong, relentless beat. It makes sense, then, to see the Tyger himself as a local habitation and a name for the powerful rhythm that comes into existence at the same moment as the language and images but with which the language of the poem is also trying to come to terms—and failing in the effort. The result is a feeling of the awesome ineffability of reality itself—of God's creation."[47]

If poems tell allegorically about their rhythm, this does not eclipse other meanings; it is a claim that they are in some way about what he calls the sublime power of their rhythm—sublime in that it resists or lies beyond efforts of representation and can only be experienced, not comprehended. Either the thematic material can be construed as an allegory of the power of rhythm or its failure to represent the rhythm is itself, we might say, testimony to the way in which the sublime power of rhythm escapes representation.

It is easy to find particular poems, such as Blake's "Tyger," where the thematic surface does seem to provide an allegory of the power of rhythm. Aviram offers a range of examples, such as Goethe's "Der Zauberlehrling" ("The Sorcerer's Apprentice"):

Hat der alte Hexenmeister
sich doch einmal weggebegeben!
Und nun sollen seine Geister
auch nach meinem Willen leben!
Seine Wort' und Werke
merkt' ich, und den Brauch,
und mit Geistesstärke
tu ich Wunder auch.

Walle, walle,
manche Strecke,
dass zum Zwecke

Wasser fliesse,
und mit reichem,
vollem Schwalle
zu dem Bade
sich ergiesse!

        ☞

Good! The sorcerer, my old master
left me here alone today!
Now his spirits, for a change,
my own wishes shall obey!
Having memorized
what to say and do,
with my powers of will I can
do some witching, too!

Go, I say,
Go on your way,
do not tarry,
water carry,
let it flow
abundantly,
and prepare
a bath for me!

[Trans. Brigitte Dubiel]

This poem addresses the power of its own rhythm, "registering anxiety over the fact that the power, once discovered, cannot be controlled" (as the apprentice shortly loses control of the forces he has brought into action with the spell).[48] It is certainly possible to interpret the poem as allegorizing its changing rhythms: the masterful four-beat meter of the opening quatrain, suggesting control, is succeeded in the second quatrain by the more halting, indeterminate rhythm, of five or six syllable lines in which the final beat of each line is not realized, followed then by the spell itself, where the charm-like rhythmical solidity of the two-beat lines contrasts with the absurdity of the command: "Water, fill the bath!"

In claiming that the meaning of a poem is an allegory of its rhythm, Aviram may seem to yield to the hermeneutical orientation of most criticism and its assumption that the test of a theory is whether it can assist in the production of interpretations that are new yet still plausible, but he recognizes that interpreters will not be satisfied with this broad, common, allegorical meaning and admits that often his theory will not enrich an understanding of the poem. If his theory has not been taken up, it is doubtless because critics want theories to help them discover hidden meanings or at least produce new and different interpretations. His theory is not a hermeneutical one, though, and he suggests that the test of a theory of poetry should be at once the vision it gives us of poetry and its pedagogical efficacy. For the first, he stresses that by physically engaging us and distracting us from the semantic dimension of language, rhythm "confers upon us a momentary feeling of freedom from any particular, finite construction of the world." In focusing on the rhythm we increase the possibility that the poetic use of language will renew perception, through its new orderings, "undermining the distinctions and definitions of reality as we ordinarily live them."[49] For the second, he suggests, with good reason, that an account of poetry predicated on the priority of rhythm over meaning will pedagogically encourage the forging of relations between poetry and other valued rhythmic activities and help resist students' turn away from poetry.

His theory does have the signal virtue of directing attention to the problem of grasping the action of the rhythm. We have been rather too inclined to neglect this, though it is a mystery of the first order. What makes a rhythm work on us? What makes a rhythm "catchy"? What do these lyric rhythms accomplish? Invoking the Kantian account of the sublime, the exhilaration of the mind's response to what seems to escape representation, may seem excessive for discussing the rhythm of lyrics, but it is defensible. For Kant, the inability to comprehend a sublime event demonstrates the inadequacy of one's intellectual capacities, but one's ability to identify such an event as escaping one's grasp can be exhilarating confirmation of one's supersensible powers. We doubtless do better to speak of rhythms such as Goethe's as "catchy" rather than "sublime," but it certainly is not exorbitant to think of rhythm as a force that works on us but lies beyond our comprehension. In the case of Blake's "Tyger," it seems appropriate to say that the image of the tiger and the questions about what forces brought it into being, all of which are part of the meaning of the poem, reinforce the effect of the powerful rhythm, which engages readers but for which we don't know how to account.

Experientially it is often the case that that meaning is subordinate to rhythm, at least in the sense that what attracts us to a poem is its rhythm, not its meaning, which may be rather banal. This power is rather awesome, really, deserving of attention. After all, we often have trouble remembering facts that are quite important to us, but poems have the power to make us remember bits of language that concern us not at all. Why do I remember "Little Boy Blue, / Come blow your horn"? It is certainly not because it makes sense or even because it was drummed into me as a child. Or why has Verlaine's "Les sanglots long / Des violons / De l'automne / Blessent mon coeur / D'une langeur / Monotone" inscribed itself in mechanical memory, when this meaning is of no possible consequence to me? This power of rhythm, whether we choose to call it "sublime" or not, is certainly something we should acknowledge and try to factor into our dealings with poetry. I have suggested that critics conceal the seductive power of rhythm by undertaking for poems that attract us a complex interpretive process, to find something worthy of the hold it has on us—in which case what we conclude to be the meaning of the poem is designed to repress that other meaning, which Aviram calls allegorical but is better thought of as force, a force operating independently of what we usually call meaning.

The claim that the meaning of a poem is an allegory of the power of its rhythm stresses the separation of these levels, even as it seeks then to relate them. Their separation is asserted by Mutlu Blasing, who maintains that a lyric, "far from being a text where sound and sense, form and meaning, are indissolubly one, is a text where we witness the *distinct* operation of the two systems. We can always yield to the seductive call to 'stop making sense' and attend to the patterning of the non-sense. Or we can choose to switch to the symbolic and make sense. We cannot do both at once." The stipulation that we cannot do both at once functions, as much of her theory does, as a critique of other accounts of the lyric that seek fusion and that thereby end by granting priority to the fictional mode, which the ritual mode is said to support.

For Blasing, rhythm is especially important as the crux of language acquisition. Children learn by imitating speech rhythms: "training in vocal rhythmization, in the prosody of human speech, . . . precedes speech, which could not happen without it." Rhythm therefore has a fundamental, somatic aspect, bodily but social rather than individual: "the rhythmic body is the socially-constructed body; rhythmization *is* socialization. And it is difficult to tell apart bodily responses to poetic rhythm from our total memory of verbal rhythm. Our sensory experience of the materials of words is already emotionally and historically charged, and we cannot experience verbal rhythm in a way that is distinguishable from a mental experience."[50]

Boldly asserting that "Lyric poetry is not mimesis," Blasing calls it "a formal practice that keeps in view the linguistic code and the otherness of the material medium of language to all that humans do with it—refer, represent, express, narrate, imitate, communicate, think, reason, philosophize. It offers an experience of another kind of order, a system that operates independently of the production of meaningful discourse that it enables." Lyric is not a deviation from rational language; rather, lyric deploys formal, nonrational orders, as "the ground on which complex thought processes and figurative logics can play and on which disciplinary discourses, of criticism, for instance, draw boundaries, construct their histories, their oppositions." "Poetry," she writes, "is a cultural institution dedicated to remembering and displaying the emotionally and historically charged materiality of language, on which logical discourse would establish its hold."[51]

In her account, lyrics do generate lyric subjects, an "I" necessary to "intentionalize the linguistic code," to present repetition, pattern, and so on, as if it were willed, chosen—the "authoredness" of lyric is important—but this "I" is a product, not a source. That subject is a collective one: phonic patterning is a summons to membership in this collective subject of the mother tongue that emerges from the inhuman order of language. "In poetry we hear, as [Wallace] Stevens puts it, 'the inhuman making choice of a human self.'"[52]

Such accounts of rhythm raise the question broached at the beginning of this chapter, in Isobel Armstrong's account of haunting by the pulse of a

rhythm and Valéry's sense that someone else was using his *machine à vivre:*
How to conceive of lyric's relation to the bodily experiencing of beats?
Northrop Frye notes that if lyric has its roots in song and chant, for moderns this means in the rhythmical language of nursery rhymes. When you
recite to a child

> Ride a cock horse
> To Banbury Cross,
> To see a fine lady
> Upon a white horse . . .

the child does not need a footnote explaining Banbury or even cock horse;
"all he needs is to get bounced. If he is, he is beginning to develop a response to poetry in the place where he ought to start. For verse is closely
related to dance and song; it is also closely related to the child's own speech,
which is full of chanting and singing, as well as of primitive verse forms
like the war cry and the taunt song."[53] Young children generally like poetry: they are engaged by its rhythms, entranced by its repetitions, and
perhaps at some level deeply pleased by a regime of adult language so full
of nonsensical rhyming and chiming. By the time they leave school, they
have generally come to avoid it, perhaps because it has been linked to a
poorly orchestrated practice of interpretation, even though their attraction to rhythmic language has not diminished. Their attention has shifted
to music but, strikingly, songs with lyrics are vastly more popular among
the young than music without lyrics—a fact that ought to be suggestive
for thinking about lyric in general.

Since the somatic character of rhythm is undeniable, there have been
many attempts over the years to relate lyrical form directly to such bodily
rhythms: claims that iambic rhythm corresponds to the heart beat or to
the rhythm of our pulse; that a particular rhythm corresponds to the
rhythm of marching or of walking.[54] But the correlation between the tactus
of rhythmical beating (the rate at which one taps one's foot or beats time)
and the pulse rate, for example, is rather loose and covers a broad possible range: in music "the tactus is invariably between about 40 and 160
beats per minute," write Fred Lerdahl and Ray Jackendorff, and the range
in verse would seem to be narrower but in the middle, say between 60

and 120 beats per minute. "The relationship of this rate to the human pulse has often been noted," they add, "though an explanation of why there should be such a relation between physiological and psychological rates us far less obvious than one might at first think."[55] Stephen Cushman calls "the physiological fallacy" the idea that "the physiological organization of the body regulates the prosodic organization of verse. A line is a certain length because breathing takes a certain amount of time; accents recur regularly in a line because heartbeats recur regularly in the chest; lines are indented from the left margin because the eye has trouble moving to the left. Of course prosody can represent physiology, suggesting the rhythms of respiration, pulse, eating, speaking, or walking, . . . but we cannot assign bodily functions a causal role in relation to prosody. If we did, how would we account for the range of prosodies throughout the world?"[56]

What is crucial is not whether poetic rhythm derives from bodily rhythms, but rather the bodily, experiential dimension of rhythm itself—our somatic participation in rhythm—which seems to achieve two distinguishable though closely related effects. "It is almost only via rhythm and the sensory properties of language," Valéry writes, "that literature can reach the organic being of a reader with any confidence in the conformity between intention and the results."[57] At a basic level rhythm seems not so much a matter of interpretation as a direct experience, the result of a rhythmic competence, though mediated by culture; it thus offers a somatic experience that seems to have a different status than the comprehension of a poem. Bringing someone to hear or feel a rhythm is procedurally different from trying to explain the meaning of a poem. Even though we know that rhythms are constructed, this experience seems to give rhythms an exteriority to the mind, as if they were an external force. The words of the poem may be signs for which we have to supply the signifieds, but the rhythm seems independent of us. Roland Barthes writes, "Le plaisir du texte, c'est ce moment où mon corps va suivre ses propres idées, car mon corps n'a pas les mêmes idées que moi" (The pleasure of the text is that moment when my body follows its own ideas, for my body does not have the same ideas as I).[58] Rhythm prompts and appeals to the body's own ideas.

This brings us to the second effect: in its somatic dimensions, rhythm is a source of pleasure—a topic not much discussed in the critical literature, but not easily denied. Barthes was not a lover of poetry, except haiku, and does not write of pleasure in verse rhythms, but in *Le Plaisir du texte* he notes that when he tries to analyze a text that has given him pleasure, what he finds is not his subjectivity but his "corps de jouissance" (his ecstatic body), the body caught up in scenarios of pleasurable entrapment.[59]

One of the most vital manifestations of the English verse tradition today is rap, which illustrates the continuing appeal of rhythmical language with vigorous patterns of prominences. Given the ease of recording today and the ubiquity of musical instruments that can play melodies, it is surprising that one of the most popular forms of music—for it still seems to be seen as music—mostly breaks with the tradition of sung lyrics, taking rhythm rather than melody as its basis, and in the process reviving the kind of purely accentual meter that we find in Old English verse and in such metrical experiments as Hopkins's sprung rhythm. Rap frequently uses a four-stress line, with an indeterminate number of syllables between each stress point, along which heavy internal rhyming as well as end rhyme.[60]

Melle Mel's classic rap song, "The Message" from 1982, is a fine example of rap's use of familiar rhythmic technique. After the opening chorus (which is also accentual: "It's like a **júng**le some**tímes** it makes me **wón**der/How I **kéep** from going **ún**der" [*bis*]), each verse receives four strong stresses, with a timed (isochronous) beat, though the first line has six syllables and the second thirteen:

> **Bró**ken **gláss** **éver**y**whére**
> People **pís**sing on the **stáirs,** you know they **júst** don't **cáre.**

The subsequent lines in the opening stanza (again, all four-beat lines) alternate between verses with a medial caesura and verses that run on to the end—a classic verse technique.

> I **can't** take the **smell,** I **can't** take the **noise,**
> Got no **money** to move **out,** I guess I **got** no **choice.**
> **Rats** in the **front** room, **roa**ches in the **back,**
> **Jun**kies in the alley with the **base**ball **bat.**
> I **tried** to get a**way,** but I **could**n't get **far,**
> Cause a **man** with a **tow**-truck repos**sessed** my **car.**

The unexpected rise of rap, a form of heavily rhythmical language that relies on rhythm and imagery, and its enormous persisting popularity among the young of all social strata, suggests a hunger for rhythmic language that might find some satisfaction in lyric, if poems were differently conceived and presented. The fact that rhythmic language could to some extent replace melodic language in the affections of the young seems a sign of the profound appeal of patterned language—and perhaps a monitory lesson for modern poetry that has abandoned the more explicit forms of linguistic patterning, including meter and vigorous rhythm. In the case of pop music our sense of the success, of the catchiness, the memorability of a song, is at least as much dependent on rhythm as on meaning, since words of songs we repeat and those we love (not necessarily the same— such is the seduction of rhythm) can be wholly banal or even unintelligible. A greater foregrounding of rhythm as central to lyric might enable the teaching of poetry to regain some of the ground lost in recent years and also might lead to a different sort of poetics. One could thus imagine an approach more connected with evaluation, which has not been central to literary studies recently: What works and what doesn't? What engages our attention, our *corps de jouissance*—to use Barthes's term—and what does not? For such a poetics an important part of the teaching of poetry would be accustoming students to hearing and experiencing the rhythms of traditional verse—they have a surprisingly hard time hearing iambic pentameter without the practice of recitation, for instance, though they fare much better with four-beat rhythms.

3. Sound and Repetition

Wallace Stevens reminds us, in strangely jerky prose, "that, above everything else, poetry is words; and that words, above everything else, are, in poetry, sounds." "However central the sound dimension is to any and all poetry," writes Marjorie Perloff, "no other poetic feature is currently as neglected." No doubt the reason is, as Reuven Tsur explains, that while the sound stratum "clearly is of the greatest literary significance, it is difficult to say anything meaningful about its contribution to the whole that can be defended in any systematic way." The difficulty comes from the fact that we are dealing less with necessary effects than with the seduction—what Baudelaire called the "sorcellerie evocatoire" ("evocative sorcery")—or enchantment always at work in lyric, even when poems thematically resist or debunk such enchantment.[61]

For instance, the whole question of the mimetic suggestiveness of sounds is a vexed one. Sounds deemed onomatopoeic, notoriously, vary from one language to the next, and one may certainly be skeptical about alleged mimetic connections between qualities of sound or rhythm and qualities of the objects or topics evoked. Dr. Johnson was inclined to kick this stone: "The fancied resemblances, I fear, arise sometimes merely from the ambiguity of words; there is supposed to be some relation between a *soft* line and a *soft* couch, or between *hard* syllables and *hard* fortune."[62] It is well attested that when one retains the key phonemes of a passage thought to be mimetically suggestive but changes the meaning, the new line will no longer seem to suggest what the old one did, which only shows that it is awareness of a meaning that activates readers' or critics' conviction that the sound is in some way echoing the sense. On the other hand, experiments on the associations of sounds convincingly show agreement, even across languages, about the contrastive values of sounds: asked to pair the two vowels *i* and *u* in *pit* and *put* with pairs of qualities such as *bright/dark, high/low, light/heavy, big/small, thick/thin,* subjects largely agree.[63] Some relate these effects to the fact that speakers of all languages use the same vocal apparatus to produce sound, so that the place and manner of articulation should be the key to sound symbolism, but the literature on this subject does not lead to reliable conclusions, and such connections would in any event doubtless be relative rather than absolute. How far such relative perceptions are relevant to the experience of reading verse is difficult to determine. It seems likely that the sounds have an effect not individually, for any particular value, but, like rhythm, through patterning which foregrounds them and either calls attention to particular words or phrases, creating the associational rhythm of which Frye speaks, or creates a memorable musical surface. In a shrewd discussion of the music of poetry, Robert von Hallberg notes that "The separable syntactic and prosodic structures of a poem vie with one another for the focused attention of readers. Critics reassuringly show how sound echoes sense, but it does so only occasionally; sonics are often bewildering, even in poems as shapely as Shakespeare's sonnets." In the end, "the sound effects that matter most are not merely local to one statement" but those that contribute to the seductive, charm-like autonomy of the larger poetic sequence.[64]

I return to this dimension of lyric below when discussing rhyme, but first there is the question of the relation of sound to voicing, the idea of "voice," and the lyric subject. Blasing stresses that poetic rhythm evokes the historical subject of the language, a general rather than individual subject. Citing a virtuoso passage from Seamus Heaney, she describes the production of the poetic subject through a reawakening of primal linguistic functions. And indeed, the operations of the vocal apparatus in the production of sounds may release all sorts of psychosexual impulses.[65] The concluding lines of Heaney's short "Death of a Naturalist" present an adolescent encounter with frogs:

> Then one hot day when fields were rank
> With cowdung in the grass the angry frogs
> Invaded the flax-dam; I ducked through hedges
> To a coarse croaking that I had not heard
> Before. The air was thick with a bass chorus.
> Right down the dam gross-bellied frogs were cocked
> On sods; their loose necks pulsed like sails. Some hopped:
> The slap and plop were obscene threats. Some sat
> Poised like mud grenades, their blunt heads farting.
> I sickened, turned, and ran. The great slime kings
> Were gathered there for vengeance and I knew
> That if I dipped my hand the spawn would clutch it.

Without attempting to explicate an infantile psychosexual orality, Blasing writes,

> This passage is a staged poetic performance of what predates—and remains the "underbelly"—of referential language itself. The "poetic" conventions of rhymes, alliteration, and consonance, together with the exploitation of the tonal, expressive qualities of different phonemes, render audible the imbrication of the alimentary, sexual, and speech functions in the oral zone. The birth of a poet is at once a relearning of language, a reliving of what infantile amnesia forgets, and a "turning"

away from it again, now into poetic language. This sequential history is remembered in the simultaneous annulment and reinscription of the subject in poetry, of the dissolution of the subject and its return as illusion.[66]

To call the reinscription of the subject an illusion is to stress that we are dealing with an effect, not the biographical individual. The passage from Heaney gives us sounds with a remarkable potency, along with a first-person figure undergoing this experience, but it presents voicing rather than voice. A particularly intriguing feature of lyric is the paradox, to which I have already alluded, that the more a poem foregrounds vocal effects, as here, the more powerful the image of voicing, oral articulation, but the less we find ourselves dealing with the voice of a person. "Poetic language rescripts the body into verbal language once again," Blasing writes, "and the language that keeps the pleasures of verbal sound in play courts—explicitly in incantatory or hypnotic verse—a hysterical regression, jeopardizing the 'I', the linguistic construct of a psychosocial subject."[67]

"Hysterical regression" is itself a psychologizing of the linguistic movement that blocks ascribing poetic sounding to a speaking voice, for the "I" is jeopardized by the movement of incantatory verse, which may foreground the labile pleasure of poetry for the reader, in rhythmical articulation driven by metrical, phrasal or assonantal patterns. Gerard Manley Hopkins's "The Leaden Echo and the Golden Echo" is an especially striking example of sound patterning that is not metrical, that relies on the proliferation of chiming verbal forms to produce amazing energy, independent of its meaning. The verbal rhythm of this poem is immensely seductive, despite its hyperbolic doctrinal claims. It is a poem that perversely can seduce even those who find its assertions both absurd and sentimental.

THE LEADEN ECHO AND THE GOLDEN ECHO

THE LEADEN ECHO

HOW to kéep—is there ány any, is there none such, nowhere known
　　some, bow or brooch or braid or brace, láce, latch or catch or key
　　to keep

Back beauty, keep it, beauty, beauty, beauty, . . . from vanishing
    away?
Ó is there no frowning of these wrinkles, rankèd wrinkles deep,
Dówn? no waving off of these most mournful messengers, still
    messengers, sad and stealing messengers of grey?
No there's none, there's none, O no there's none,
Nor can you long be, what you now are, called fair,
Do what you may do, what, do what you may,
And wisdom is early to despair:
Be beginning; since, no, nothing can be done
To keep at bay
Age and age's evils, hoar hair,
Ruck and wrinkle, drooping, dying, death's worst, winding sheets,
    tombs and worms and tumbling to decay;
So be beginning, be beginning to despair.
O there's none; no no no there's none:
Be beginning to despair, to despair,
Despair, despair, despair, despair.

THE GOLDEN ECHO

        Spare!
There ís one, yes I have one (Hush there!);
Only not within seeing of the sun,
Not within the singeing of the strong sun,
Tall sun's tingeing, or treacherous the tainting of the earth's air,
Somewhere elsewhere there is ah well where! one,
Oñe. Yes I cán tell such a key, I dó know such a place,
Where whatever's prized and passes of us, everything that's fresh
    and fast flying of us, seems to us sweet of us and swiftly away with,
    done away with, undone,
Úndone, done with, soon done with, and yet dearly and dangerously
    sweet
Of us, the wimpled-water-dimpled, not-by-morning-matchèd face,
The flower of beauty, fleece of beauty, too too apt to, ah! to fleet,
Never fleets móre, fastened with the tenderest truth

To its own best being and its loveliness of youth: it is an everlasting-
    ness of, O it is an all youth!
Come then, your ways and airs and looks, locks, maiden gear,
    gallantry and gaiety and grace,
Winning ways, airs innocent, maiden manners, sweet looks, loose
    locks, long locks, lovelocks, gaygear, going gallant, girlgrace—
Resign them, sign them, seal them, send them, motion them with
    breath,
And with sighs soaring, soaring síghs deliver
Them; beauty-in-the-ghost, deliver it, early now, long before death
Give beauty back, beauty, beauty, beauty, back to God, beauty's self
    and beauty's giver.
See; not a hair is, not an eyelash, not the least lash lost; every hair
Is, hair of the head, numbered.
Nay, what we had lighthanded left in surly the mere mould
Will have waked and have waxed and have walked with the wind
    what while we slept,
This side, that side hurling a heavyheaded hundredfold
What while we, while we slumbered.
O then, weary then why should we tread? O why are we so haggard
    at the heart, so care-coiled, care-killed, so fagged, so fashed, so
    cogged, so cumbered,
When the thing we freely fórfeit is kept with fonder a care,
Fonder a care kept than we could have kept it, kept
Far with fonder a care (and we, we should have lost it) finer, fonder
A care kept.—Where kept? Do but tell us where kept, where.—
Yonder.—What high as that! We follow, now we follow.—Yonder, yes
    yonder, yonder,
Yonder.

Here the rhythm is not determined by metrical considerations but by
alliteration (which partly stands in for meter) and by phrasing, and of course
readers have considerable leeway as to how to pace and structure the
poem.[68] These four concluding "yonders," which can be hard to bring
off without half-smirking grandiloquence, encapsulate the problem. For
secular readers the poem is embarrassing because it depends so utterly

on a hyperbolic version of the Resurrection of the Body, which cannot seem anything but wishful. It is the dream to which the cosmetics industry ministers, for example: you will be preserved forever as the truly beautiful you, with a better body, no lines or wrinkles, not a hair lost, no bad hair days. It is wishful and thus sentimental in the sense of a wished-for self-delusion. But the hyperbolic literalization of claims in the poem—"not a hair is, not an eyelash, not the least lash lost"—makes it different from, say, the merely sentimental belief that our true selves will live on forever. To deny utterly what we know of bodies and their transience is to enter what we might call hypersentimentality, of a sort hard to comprehend except with reference to language and its surprising incarnational effects, so dramatically staged by the linguistic patterning here. The materiality yet iterability of the signifier may indeed suggest that things are preserved in all the particularity with which they can be named, even though naming negates the object.

The work of poetry here is linked with the power of formalization: the way in which a formal principle allows a system to repeat itself. This poem seduces by lists, in a structure that makes it seem as if any list could go on forever: there will always be more names for similar things, and it is impossible to exhaust all possible terms. Witness the sequence

> O why are we so
> haggard at the heart, so care-coiled, care-killed, so fagged
> so fashed, so cogged, so cumbered . . .

where the proliferation of participles is cheering, positively enlivening, despite the fact that they speak of exhaustion and oppression. As these lists grow, often by varying elements while keeping something stable—"bow or brooch or braid or brace, lace or latch or catch or key,"—they illustrate less any mimetic properties of language than the ability of language to proliferate. The words work to engage us in a proliferation of particularities. Such lists bring the reader into the process of naming and to the pleasure of repeating the series. The poem tells us to give up beauty, but in the telling, in the energetic naming, the poem values it, celebrates beauty in language that proliferates. It is not that language is made beautiful by the crafting of subtle euphony, for instance; rather, by giving into language, letting it proliferate, running through the verbal possibilities of closely related terms, a beauty of linguistic iteration and alliteration is released.

There is some minimal patterning in the wordplay that is can be seen as mimetic—"sighs soaring, soaring sighs . . ."—patterning which readers can of course make mimetic by allowing their voices to soar at this point.[69] But this is unimportant compared with the compelling force of "not an eyelash, not the least lash lost . . ." This is language engaged not in description but in energetic play—a labile pleasure. "Nay, what we have light-handed left in surly the mere mold / Will have waked and have waxed and have walked with the wind what while we slept." That *"what while we"* is splendidly gratuitous, an extra *wh* for the echo—pure energetic excess. Or "Fonder a care kept, . . . kept/ Far with a fonder care, . . . finer fonder a care kept," with the reversals not suggestive of fondness but producing a kind of phonic enveloping.

The force of poetry here is linked with its ability to get itself remembered, in words that may structure or inform or produce experience. This survival becomes especially striking when, as in Hopkins's poem, what gets remembered and repeated is arguably not wisdom but verbal froth, such as "not the least lash lost," or "will have waked and have waxed and have walked with the wind, what while we slept." It is hard to work out what is happening in cases like this—a modulation of sounds not mimetic. The sonics of lyrics are often bewildering, as von Hallberg says. Indeed, in "lace or latch or catch or key" the effect is very nearly the opposition of suggesting that there is something, a key or lock, that would tie down, fix beauty once and for all. There are so many things that no fixing is needed or possible. The superfluity installs us in a proliferation of echoing signs.

As does rhyme. Rhyme in English poetry, writes T. V. F. Brogan, "is historically its single most consistent characteristic." This is especially true for lyric, whose short lines and complex stanzas often make rhyme especially prominent. "What belongs particularly to lyric," Hegel notes, "is the ramified figuration of rhyme which, with the return of the same letters, syllables and words, or the alternation of different ones, is developed and completed in variously articulated and interlaced rhyme-strophes." But rhyme has often been thought dubious, unnecessary: the Greeks and Romans did not use it; Milton called it "the Invention of a barbarous

Age to set off wretched matter and lame Meter." Rhyme can be rejected
as too potent—sensuously bewitching—and as a trivial jingling. The
suspicion of rhyme persists in what, since Alexander Pope, has been the
reigning critical conception: to avoid being mere bauble, rhyme should
be thematically productive, suggesting an unexpected connection between
the meanings of the two words that rhyme. Ideally, to avoid facile connections, the rhyme words should be different parts of speech. It is as
though "good rhyme has to be serious rhyme, which does work; it must
not be evasive; it must not jingle and tinkle."[70]

Poets in the twentieth century often fought shy of rhyme, not as a con-
straint on expression but as a mark of commitment to sound at the expense
of meaning. When granted prominence, it may be given radically unorthodox forms, as in Marianne Moore's "The Fish," whose stanza consists
of a sequence of lines of 1, 3, 9, 6, and 8 syllables:

> The Fish
>
> wade
> through black jade.
> 　　　Of the crow-blue mussel-shells, one keeps
> 　　　adjusting the ash-heaps;
> 　　　　　opening and shutting itself like
>
> an
> injured fan.
> 　　　The barnacles which encrust the side
> 　　　of the wave, cannot hide
> 　　　　　there for the submerged shafts of the
>
> sun,
> split like spun
> 　　　glass, move themselves with spotlight swiftness
> 　　　Into the crevices—
> 　　　　　in and out, illuminating
>
> the
> turquoise sea
> 　　　of bodies. . . .

Rhyme involves an echoing of stressed syllables, so to rhyme what should be the unstressed syllables of articles is to use rhyme to impose a different order on language; rhyming "an" with "fan" and "the" with "sea" and stacking the two rhyme words so close to each other works against any aligning of sound and sense.[71]

In fact, as a number of critics have argued, there is an alternative view of rhyme that has much to be said for it. Historically, the conception of rhyme as nonsemantic chiming fits much rhyming practice better than the modern view that rhyme should serve meaning. English Renaissance poets, writes von Hallberg, knew that vowel magic—the repetition of vowel sounds, as in rhyme—constitutes the better part of poetic eloquence. This is especially true in lyrics with short lines that highlight the rhyme, such as Clément Marot's "A une Damoiselle malade" ("To a Sick Damsel").

Ma mignonne,	My sweet dear
Je vous donne	I send cheer—
Le bon jour;	All the best!
Le sejour	Your forced rest
C'est prison.	Is like jail.
Guerison	So don't ail
Recouvrez,	Very long.

[Trans. Douglas Hofstadter]

And so on for twenty-eight three-syllable lines of rhyming couplets.[72]

Contrasting the rhyming practice of Chaucer and other poets, who are not attempting witty, semantically productive rhymes, with that called for by Pope, James Wimsatt distinguishes two systems of sound in poetry: in the symbolic system, phonemes and intonation patterns carry meaning through differential organization of the sound plane, but in the prosodic system, which includes line division, syllable count, stress, rhyme, and refrain, sounds produce what "may be called music, not for employing a harmonic or melodic organization of tones but for its mathematical organization of phonetic units, sometimes marked by stress and rhyme." There

may be local semantic effects but its main effect is iconic rather than semantic: it is self-reflexive and nonsymbolic, signifying the instantiation
of poetry but not directly related to verbal meaning. Describing the increasing and subsiding density of rhymes in John Skelton's two- and three-
beat lines, Susan Stewart notes that the insistent rhymes of "Mistress Margaret Hussey" "effect the turns and metamorphoses of praise by something
akin to uttering spells":

> Merry Margaret,
> As midsummer flower,
> Gentle as falcon
> Or hawk of the tower
> With solace and gladness,
> Much mirth and no madness . . .

Rhyme is "always a showcase for the arbitrary nature of the sign and limits
our efforts to dominate meaning; rhyming draws us beyond ourselves with
its potential for aural pleasure."[73]

Rhymes mark out lines and stanzas, contributing in a major way to
rhythm (rhyme and rhythm both come from *rhythmus*), and they work
to signify, iconically, the poetic event. Hegel identifies an erotic, teasing
dimension to rhyme: in the different stanza forms of lyric, "it is as if the
rhymes now find one another immediately, now fly from one another and
yet look for one another, with the result that in this way the ear's attentive
expectation is now satisfied without more ado, now teased, deceived, or
kept in suspense owing to the longer delay between rhymes, but always
contented again by the regular ordering and return of the same sounds."
Mallarmé treats this structure as magical: "one cannot deny the similarity
between the circle perpetually opening and closing with rhymes and the
circles in the grass left by a fairy or magician."[74]

Whether we call it magic or not, one effect is to lend authority to lyric
pronouncements. It is no accident that so many proverbs rhyme: "A stitch
in time saves nine," not eight or ten. The rap artist Jay-Z notes that rhyming
allows hip-hop to contain contradictions and "make sense of the world
in a way regular speech can't." He contrasts his spoken introduction to a

song, which offers the beginning of an argument ("You can agree or dis-agree") with a line from the song itself:

I'd rather die enormous than live dormant/that's how we on it.

"That's it. No argument. It is what it is. Why? The rhyme convinces you. The words connect. That simple couplet takes the idea of the spoken intro and makes it feel powerful, almost unassailable. Think about it: O. J. Simpson might be a free man today because 'glove don't fit' rhymed with 'acquit.' It was a great sound bite for the media, but it was also as persuasive as the hook on a hit song. That's the power of rhymes."[75] But the authority of rhyme is presumed, not earned, not guaranteed, which is why people speak, sometimes boldly, sometimes tentatively, with embarrassment, of the enchantment of rhyme, the magic of sound patterning: it is alluring but can be resisted; the return of rhyme satisfies, as Hegel says, but rhyme can always be dismissed as empty echoing. The return of rhymes is strangely satisfying, an event whose value is hard to explain or justify but that all readers of poetry have experienced.

"The poem must resist the intelligence/Almost successfully," writes Wallace Stevens.[76] Usually this is taken as a warrant for obscure poetry, but poetry can resist the intelligence without being obscure: by offering linguistic echoing without obvious thematic purport, and by so doing get under the guard of intelligence, as it were, into memory, where it can pro-vide form for the mind to espouse. Perhaps language must run the risk of dismissal as empty sound if it is to get under the guard of intelligence. Charms disguise themselves as harmless.

In a wonderful book, *Precious Nonsense,* now largely neglected, Ste-phen Booth uses the examples of nursery rhymes to illustrate poems' ability to let us understand something that does not make sense as if it *did* make sense. We seem to take pleasure in accepting nonsense, he writes, "as sense is usual among us."[77] What is the attraction of this strange jingle that we don't understand?

One for the money,
Two for the show,

Three to get ready,
And four to go!

Why "One for the money"—what is that about? Is it just for the *one/mon* echo? Perhaps the lines allude to betting on races—to have a chance of real money, bet to win (one)—but "to show" in a race is to place third, not second, so this association does not help generate sense. The most salient feature of this jingle, which we never notice but which is blatant once called to our attention, is the strange collision of irrelevant numbers produced by the prepositions in each line: *one four, two four, three two, four two*. This subliminal collocation, the jumbling of numbers, however unintelligible, must be part of its attraction. Or in "Little Boy Blue, / Come blow your horn. / The sheep's in the meadow, / The cow's in the corn," the rhyme horn/corn makes *corn* seem right; the parallelism between sheep and cow, and the fact that *Blue* of "Little Boy Blue" is the past tense of *blow,* all bolster the poem's ability to deafen us to the illogic of its claim about the sheep, since the meadow seems a fine place for a sheep.

"What does the human mind ordinarily want most?" Booth asks. "It wants to understand what it does not understand. And what does the human mind customarily do to achieve that goal? It works away—sometimes only for a second or two, sometimes for years—until it understands. What does the mind have then? What it wanted? No. What it has is understanding of something that it now understands. What it wanted was to understand what it did not understand." The poem, in giving us an impression of the rightness of what we don't understand, the sense that we control what we don't understand, has "the ability," he writes, "to free us from the limits of the human mind," in, I would add, a miniature version of the sublime, to which rhythm, along with other forms of repetition, energetically ministers.[78]

FIVE

Lyric Address

Along with rhythmical sound patterning, what I have called triangulated address—address to the reader by means of address to something or someone else—is a crucial aspect of the ritualistic dimension of
lyric. "Lyric is pre-eminently the utterance that is overheard," writes
Northrop Frye, taking up John Stuart Mill's famous formulation distinguishing poetry, which is overheard, from eloquence, which is heard. "The
lyric poet," Frye continues, "normally pretends to be talking to himself
or to someone else: a spirit of nature, a muse, a personal friend, a lover, a
god, a personified abstraction, or a natural object. . . . The radical of presentation in the lyric is the hypothetical form of what in religion is called
the 'I-Thou' relationship. The poet, so to speak, turns his back on his listeners, though he may speak for them and though they may repeat some
of his words after him."[1]

Triangulated address is the root-form of presentation for lyric, underlying even those poems that do not engage in the strange forms of address
and invocation endemic to the genre. But it is scarcely clear that "overheard" is best way to speak of this pretense to address someone or something else, while actually proffering discourse for an audience. After all,

we encounter lyrics in the form of written texts to which readers give voice. What we "hear" is our own ventriloquizing of ambiguously directed address, though we may, and in some cases certainly do, construe this as overhearing a distinctive poetic voice. Poems addressed to no one, such as Leopardi's "l'Infinito" and Williams's "Red Wheelbarrow" discussed in Chapter 1, may be conceived by readers as meditations overheard, but song-like poems such as Goethe's "Heidenröslein" or even Lorca's "La Luna asoma" are scripts for performance more than a voice overheard.[2] Whatever its inadequacies, though, Frye's formulation has the virtue of stressing the importance of voicing and of indirection, both central to the experience of lyric. This radical of presentation foregrounds the event of address, by making it an operation not determined by its apparent communicative purpose. To invoke or address something that is not the true audience, whether a muse, an urn, Duty, or a beloved, highlights the event of address itself as an act, whose purpose and effects demand critical attention. To avoid confusion, I will use the term *addressee* for whomever or whatever is designated by the pronouns of address and the term *audience* for the presumed beneficiaries of lyric communication—most often listeners or readers.

The most blatant manifestation of triangulated address is the invocation of impossible addressees, such as unseen powers: "O wild West Wind, thou breath of autumn's being" (Shelley, "Ode to the West Wind"), or creatures and things unlikely to answer—a lion, a ship, death, a swan, the earth:

> Lion! J'étais pensif, ô bête prisonnière, / Devant la majesté de ta grave crinière
> ("Lion! I was pensive, o prisoner-beast, / before the majesty of your weighty mane"; Victor Hugo, "Baraques de la foire")

> O navis, referent in mare te novi / fluctus. O quid agis?
> ("O ship, the fresh tide carries you back to sea again. What are you doing?"; Horace, *Odes* 1.14)

> Or ài fatto l'extremo di tua possa, / o crudel Morte.
> ("Now you have done the worst that you can, O cruel Death"; Petrarch, *Canzoniere* 326)

¿Qué signo haces, oh Cisne, con tu encorvado cuello/al paso de los
    tristes y errantes soñadores?
("What sign do you give, O Swan, with your curving neck,/when the
    sad and wandering dreamers pass?"; Reuben Darío, "Los Cignes")

Erde, du liebe, ich will!
("Earth, you darling, I will!"; Rilke, *Duino Elegies,* 9)

Address to someone or something gives the poem a character of event,
and the less ordinary the addressee, the more the poem seems to become
a ritualistic invocation. Nor is this address to absent or impossible
interlocutors an outworn poetical fashion, as we are likely to believe, a
feature of romantic poetry now left behind by a more ironic age. There
are many apostrophes in modernist poetry; among the best known are
D'Annunzio's address to a torpedo boat ("Naviglio d'acciaio, diritto ve-
loce guizzante/bello come un'arme nuda" ["Ship of steel, straight, swift,
flashing, lovely as a naked weapon"]) and Apollinaire's to the Eiffel Tower
("Bergère ô tour Eiffel le troupeau des ponts bêle ce matin" ["Shepherdess,
o Eiffel Tower, the herd of bridges is bleating this morning"]). And a surprising range of recent poems engage in address, not just to friends and
lovers or enemies (as in Sylvia Plath's "Daddy, Daddy, you bastard, I'm
through!") or to indeterminate "you"'s, which can be the reader or the
poet him- or herself, but also to such things as the sun, a flower, a leaf.[3]

Wordsworth, turning away from the roses of tradition, had warmly
hailed the humble daisy and the invasive celandine. What, then, is left
for a modern poet if not the weed.

WEEDS

    The pigrush, the poverty grass,
The bindweed's stranglehold morning glories,
    The dog blow and ninety-joints—
They ask so little of us to start with,
    Just a crack in the asphalt,
Or a subway grate with an hour of weak light.
    One I know has put down roots

As far as a corpse is buried, its storage stem
  As big as my leg. That one's called
Man-under-ground. That one was my grudge.

  And suddenly now this small
Unlooked for joy. Where did *it* come from,
  With these pale shoots
And drooping lavender bell? Persistent
  Intruder, whether or not
I want you, you've hidden in the heart's
  Overworked subsoil. Hacked at
Or trampled on, may you divide and spread,
  Just as, all last night,
The wind scattered a milkweed across the sky.

[J. D. McClatchy]

That sudden "you" is a very effective touch—one we don't expect. It moves the poem from poetic reflection to invocation, event, and makes it more than a musing on the resilience of some plants: a celebration of their energy and overcoming of adversity, as the address to a "you" brings speaker and plant together in the hope of dissemination. McClatchy's last line recalls the conclusion of Shelley's "Ode to the West Wind":

Drive my dead thoughts over the universe
Like withered leaves to quicken a new birth,
And by the incantations of this verse,
Scatter, as from an unextinguished hearth
Ashes and sparks, my words among mankind!

More modest than Shelley's "Scatter my words," McClatchy's "may you divide and spread" evinces the same desire for the scattering or dissemination of the lyric words.

Or here in "Les Étiquettes Jaunes" is the supposedly prosaic, down-to-earth Frank O'Hara, who felt ill-at-ease when not near a subway station:

Leaf! you are so big!
How can you change your
color, then just fall!

(The poem concludes, "Leaf! don't be neurotic/like the small chameleon.")

Such blatant apostrophes have been central to the lyric tradition and mark the vatic aspect of that tradition: invoking all manner of things, and thus presuming the potential responsiveness of the universe, in what is the acme of poetic presumption. The vatic stance is a potential embarrassment to poets, as we shall see: they frequently revolt against it, mock it, or retreat from it, while still relying on it at some fundamental level. It is also an embarrassment to critics, who are inclined to ignore it or transform apostrophic address into description. Though apostrophic address is rife in poems of the Western tradition, the lyric device of address to absent or improbable addressees has been largely ignored in the critical literature.[4] Earl Wasserman wrote fifty pages on Shelley's highly apostrophic "Adonais" without mentioning it. Even M. H. Abrams's classic essay, "Style and Structure in the Greater Romantic Lyric," declines to discuss this figure, which to any untrained observer seems an obvious and pervasive feature of the great poems Abrams discusses, which are mainly odes. Ignoring urns, nightingales, clouds, rivers, castles, mountains, and personified abstractions such as Duty, Melancholy, and Autumn, Abrams seeks out human addressees, speaking of the poet's "sustained colloquy, sometimes with himself or with the outer scene, more frequently with a silent human auditor, present or absent." Apostrophe is a palpable embarrassment, because it is a figure of all that is most radical, pretentious, and mystificatory in the lyric: the flights of fancy or proclamations of vatic action that critics prefer to evade, as they discuss instead, for instance, the *theme* of the power of poetic imagination—a serious matter that they are reluctant to link to an empty "O" of address: "O wild West Wind . . ."[5]

I will return later in the chapter to this sort of apostrophic address, but there are other cases of lyric address to consider first.

1. Address to Listeners or Readers

This might seem to be the model of direct communication for lyric, its default mode, in which the actual audience is addressed directly, but it is actually surprisingly rare: lyric address is usually indirect. Ben Jonson gives us the basic instance of direct address, a straightforward dedicatory poem, "To the Reader."

> Pray thee, take care, that tak'st my booke in hand,
> To reade it well: that is, to understand.

Often such address comes at the beginning of a volume, to welcome the reader in and to frame the collection, as in Petrarch's "You who hear within these scattered verses . . ." (discussed in Chapter 1) which, using the figure of hearing for what is obviously to be reading, expresses the hope for forgiveness and understanding from readers for the spectacle he has made of himself in these poems. Baudelaire's opening poem, "Au Lecteur," on the contrary, adopting the first-person plural, as it describes our calamitous propensities, charges the reader with hypocrisy if he claims not to be familiar with the whole menagerie of our vices depicted in the collection: "Hypocrite lecteur, mon semblable, mon frère." Such poems are experienced as exceptional, explicitly metapoetic, dependent on the collection they introduce.[6]

Readers are also occasionally addressed in poems that are not prefatory. Ben Jonson's compelling performance of simplicity, "To Elizabeth L.H.," is an outstanding example:

> Wouldst thou hear what Man can say
> In a little? Reader, stay.
> Underneath this stone doth lie
> As much Beauty as could die:
> Which in life did harbour give
> To more Virtue than doth live.
> If at all she had a fault,
> Leave it buried in this vault.
> One name was Elizabeth,
> The other, let it sleep with death:

Fitter, where it died, to tell
Than that it lived at all. Farewell.

The conventional "Stay, traveler," of the poetic epitaph is here a refigured as address to the reader, who is enjoined to attend to the epitaphic text. Epideictic poems that offer advice and tell the reader what to value may use direct address. Frost's "Provide, Provide," for instance, citing the fate of the fallen Hollywood star reduced to washing the steps with pail and rag, urges, tongue-in-cheek:

Make the whole stock exchange your own!
If need be occupy a throne,
Where nobody can call you crone.

Some have relied on what they knew;
Others on simply being true.
What worked for them might work for you.

. . . . .
Better to go down dignified
With boughten friendship at your side
Than none at all. Provide, provide!

But address to a "you" construable as the reader is rare even in Frost, and the authoritative *Handbook of Literary Rhetoric* claims that such address has the effect of an apostrophe since it is an unusual turning away from the anonymity of readership.[7]

Walt Whitman is the great exception here: address to readers returns frequently, hyperbolically, in *Leaves of Grass,* not only interpellating readers but insisting on their affinity with the author, as in "Song of Myself":

I celebrate myself, and sing myself,
And what I shall assume you shall assume,
For every atom belonging to me as good as belongs to you.[8]

Addressing its readers, the poem claims to offer "you" special benefits from reading Whitman:

Have you practis'd so long to learn to read?
Have you felt so proud to get at the meaning of poems?

Stop this day and night with me and you shall possess the origin of
    all poems,
You shall possess the good of the earth and sun, (there are millions
    of suns left,)
You shall no longer take things at second or third hand, nor look
    through the eyes of the dead, nor feed on the spectres in books . . .

But often the activities Whitman predicates of "you" go well beyond reading, complicating the situation of address, as in John Ashbery's "This Room," where the concluding line, "Why do I tell you these things? You are not even here," functions beautifully, tellingly, as an address to the reader, but could also be read as address to a lover or even, in the poem's context of dream and self-division, self-address. Whitman's poem "To You" addresses readers necessarily unknown, boldly claiming intimacy:

Whoever you are, now I place my hand upon you, that you be my
    poem,
I whisper with my lips close to your ear,
I have loved many women and men, but I love none better than you.

O I have been dilatory and dumb,
I should have made my way straight to you long ago,
I should have blabbed nothing but you, I should have chanted
    nothing but you.

I will leave all, and come and make the hymns of you;
None have understood you, but I understand you,
None have done justice to you, you have not done justice to yourself,
None but have found you imperfect, I only find no imperfection in
    you.[9]

The more the poem predicates feelings or experiences of "you," the more complicated the situation of address becomes, as "you" is figured in ways not so easily identified with a reader. In fact, the poem was previously entitled not "To You" but "Poem of You, Whoever you Are," as though it were not just addressed to you the reader but also a poem *of* or about an as-yet unknown lover. The final poem of *Leaves of Grass*, "So Long," announces the triumph of a new world and its people, but returns to embrace the reader:

> My songs cease, I abandon them,
> From behind the screen where I hid I advance personally solely to
>   you.
> Camerado, this is no book,
> Who touches this touches a man,
> (Is it night? are we here together alone?)
> It is I you hold, and who holds you,
> I spring from the pages into your arms—decease calls me forth.

With the reference to the death that makes the author live in and spring forth from the book, Whitman seems to be seeking the sort of uncanny effect achieved by Keats in "This Living Hand," discussed below. But once we are given details of this "you" that don't apply to most readers, we may have a case of what has been called the "blurred you," which gestures toward the reader but is also plausibly taken as either the poet himself or someone else.[10] Antonio Machado writes in his *Proverbios y cantares*, 50:

> Con el tú de mi canción,   But that you in my song
>   non te aludo compañero;   doesn't mean you, pal;
>   ese tú soy yo.   that you is me.

Goethe's second "Wanderers Nachtlied" ("Wanderer's Nightsong") is a classic example of this indeterminacy:

> Über allen Gipfeln
> Ist Ruh,
> In allen Wipfeln

Spürest du
Kaum einen Hauch;
Die Vögelein schweigen im Walde.
Warte nur, balde
Ruhest du auch.

☞

Above all summits
it is calm.
In all the tree-tops
you feel
scarcely a breath;
The birds in the forest are silent,
just wait, soon
you will rest as well!

Here the two "du"s are at least ambiguous. The first can be an impersonal "one" but the second, because of the command, "just wait," is read either as self-address—the speaker too will rest soon—or, as the poem is generally interpreted because of the universality of death, as a broader address in which readers are implicated as well. Rilke's great "Archaïscher Torso Apollos" ("Archaic Torso of Apollo") is a similar case:

Wir kannten nicht sein unerhörtes Haupt,
darin die Augenäpfel reiften. Aber
sein Torso glüht noch wie ein Kandelaber,
in dem sein Schauen, nur zurückgeschraubt,
sich hält und glänzt. Sonst könnte nicht der Bug
der Brust dich blenden, und im leisen Drehen
der Lenden könnte nicht ein Lächeln gehen
zu jener Mitte, die die Zeugung trug.
Sonst stünde dieser Stein entstellt und kurz
unter der Schultern durchsichtigem Sturz
und flimmerte nicht so wie Raubtierfelle;
und bräche nicht aus allen seinen Rändern

aus wie ein Stern: denn da ist keine Stelle,
die dich nicht sieht. Du musst dein Leben ändern.

                  ⁓

We did not know his legendary head
with eyes like ripening fruit. And yet his torso
is still suffused with brilliance from inside,
like a lamp, in which his gaze, now turned to low,
gleams in all its power. Otherwise
the curved breast could not dazzle you so,
nor could a smile run through the placid hips
and thighs to that dark center where procreation flared.
Otherwise this stone would seem defaced
beneath the translucent cascade of the shoulders
and would not glisten like a wild beast's fur:
would not, from all the borders of itself,
burst like a star: for here there is no place
that does not see you. You must change your life.

                          [Trans. Stephen Mitchell]

The poem begins in the first-person plural, "We," but then, crucially, shifts to address "you." The first "you" in line 6—"Otherwise / the curved breast could not dazzle you so [dich blenden]"—with its presupposition that someone is dazzled, would seem to mean any observer of the torso, but the increasing uncanniness of the torso, in which, finally, there is "no place that does not see you" establishes a situation where the final "you"—"You must change your life"—seems inexorably to address the reader. This is, of course, an effect deliberately sought. Even though it is quite possible to take the command to change your life as a meditative inference of the speaker/poet, generalized to others by readers, it is hard for a reader not to feel addressed. Ashbery writes, "We are somehow all aspects of a consciousness, . . . and the fact of addressing someone, myself or someone else, is what's the important thing . . . rather than the particular person involved."[11]

Finally, the most stunning instance of an address to the reader, which flaunts the poem's ability to make such address an event, is Keats's "This

Living Hand." More successful than Whitman's claim to touch the reader, this poem challenges time and seems to win.

> This living hand, now warm and capable
> Of earnest grasping, would, if it were cold
> And in the icy silence of the tomb,
> So haunt thy days and chill thy dreaming nights
> That thou wouldst wish thine own heart dry of blood
> So in my veins red life might stream again,
> And thou be conscience-calmed—see here it is—
> I hold it towards you.

This is a daring attempt to produce a poetic event by exploiting the resources of direct address to the reader, boldly collapsing into one the time of articulation—the *now* when "this living hand" is "warm and capable of earnest grasping"—and the time of reading: "See, here it is, I hold it towards you." The poem dares assert that this hand is being held toward us at the moment of reading, and we might expect to smile ironically at this misplaced poetic pretension: the claim to survive the icy silence of the tomb and reach out to us here and now. But seldom do readers react in this way.[12] Rather, we accede to the poem's claim, granting it the power to make us imaginatively overcome the death with which it simultaneously threatens us. Contrasting the poet's life with his death, it proleptically claims that if this hand were dead, it would haunt us, and make us wish to transfer our blood to it, if only that would make it live, and that we would feel better for it. While we don't actually wish to sacrifice ourselves, readers do temporarily sacrifice their sense of reality in allowing the poem to create for them a temporality in which the hand lives and is held toward them. The poem predicts this mystification, dares us to resist it, and shows it to be irresistible. It is a tour de force that shows what lyric is can do and why it is memorable.

I have maintained that direct address to the audience is rare, but in *The Idea of Lyric* Ralph Johnson claims that lyric as inherited from the Greeks was in fact sung to an audience, so that there is a "you" as well as an "I," a speaker, or a singer, talking to, singing to, another person or persons:

"The rhetorical triangle of speaker, discourse, and hearer is the essential feature of the Greek lyric, of the Latin lyric that continued and refined the Greek tradition, and of the medieval and early modern European lyric that inherited and further refined the Graeco-Roman lyric tradition." This model of an "I" speaking to a "you", he argues, remains central to the best lyric tradition, though the modern conceptions of the lyric have obscured this and led us to imagine that the lyric in general is to be understood as the solipsistic meditation of an individual, expressing or working out personal feelings. In the classical model, "I" and "you", speaker and listener, are (according to Johnson) directly related to one another in a community; with the modern lyric, he writes, "the disintegration of pronominal form entails the disintegration of emotional content, for in lyric, too, form and content are interdependent."[13]

Johnson takes as his principal cases Horace and Catullus, the two most appreciated lyric poets of the classical canon for whom we possess a substantial lyric corpus, and contrasts their poems addressed to another person or persons with what he calls the "meditative poem, in which the poet talks to himself, or to no one in particular or, sometimes, calls on, apostrophizes, inanimate or non-human entities, abstractions, or the dead." Only 9 percent of Horace's poems and 14 percent of Catullus's are meditative in this sense (soliloquizing or apostrophizing), while 87 percent of Horace's and 70 percent of Catullus's are addressed to another person.[14]

There is something of a puzzle here. Johnson's argument distinguishing the good classical model of direct address to the audience from the bad modern model of solipsism or indirection depends on the assumption that if a poem addresses a person, that person counts as the audience. "The most usual mode in the Greek lyric (probably) and in the Latin lyric (certainly)," he writes, "was to address the poem (in Greek, the song) to another person or persons. What this typical lyric form points to is the conditions and the purposes of the song: the presence of the singer before his audience." And he maintains that in Rome, "even after the singer sang no more," this remained the typical form.[15] But while 87 percent of Horace's odes do address another person (sometimes fictional, sometimes historical), only once does Horace address the Roman people or any group that might be the actual audience for his poems: the exception is Ode 3.14, celebrating Augustus's return from the wars and the possibility of enjoying peace (and wine and women). This begins with an address to the public, "O plebs."

> Herculis ritu modo dictus, o plebs,
> morte uenalem petiisse laurum,
> Caesar Hispana repetit penatis
> > victor ab ora.

☞

> O citizens, conquering Caesar is home
> from the Spanish shores, who, like Hercules, now
> was said to be seeking that laurel, that's bought
> > at the price of death.

> > > > > [Trans. A. S. Kline]

This address to the public rather than to a real or fictional individual is the exception rather than the rule.[16] Horace cannot be said to address his audience except by the indirection of apostrophic address to another. The lyric address to a "you" is fundamental to lyric, as Johnson rightly concludes, but it does not signal direct address to the audience.

"Directness" seems a primary value for many scholars of Greek literature, who frequently emphasize that the archaic lyric was addressed to its audience as part of a public ceremony. Whether pronominal structures reflect this is another matter. With Greek poetry the extraordinarily fragmentary nature of what survives makes it difficult to know what are the norms are for lyric address. Seldom do we have a complete text, and so we cannot confidently determine what the frame of address would have been. Johnson himself notes that "the Greek lyric . . . is essentially inaccessible to us," while admitting that we cannot resist trying to imagine it in its full splendor.[17] The existing corpus, though, certainly challenges the idea that the Greek lyric is characteristically framed as direct address to the audience that would have heard it. There are few specimens to justify such an idea. Critics cite Archilochus 109, Callinus 1, and Solon 4, as evidence of the tradition Horace is allegedly following in Epode 7, where he addresses an audience—"Where, where are you wicked people rushing?"—or Epode 13, where he addresses friends—"amici." But these examples are scarcely enough to justify the claim that direct address to the audience is the norm of the Greek lyric.

Is this not a myth of Greece, the "full splendor" critics are wont to imagine? While there are numerous second-person pronouns in the fragments of Greek lyrics, they very rarely designate a community the poet could be said to address directly. Even Pindar, maker of ceremonious odes, whose public victory odes have the undeniable social function of assembling a community around its champions, almost never addresses the citizens of the city of the victor. His epinikian odes address the victors, numerous gods, Truth, Peace, my lyre, my song, and my soul. They are ceremonious, ritualistic, and highly voiced, but of forty-five odes only Nemean 2 addresses a collective group of people: "Celebrate him, O citizens,/in honor of Timodemos upon his glorious return,/and lead off with a sweetly melodious voice."[18] This surprising failure of Pindar's odes to address the audiences makes one wonder whether there may have been, unbeknownst to us, some generic rule against addressing the citizens, since otherwise it would seem such an obvious thing to do in odes of this sort. Is it to facilitate reperformance in a wide variety of contexts that the odist declines to address a specific audience?[19]

Pindar, then, scarcely supports the claim of directness. And Sappho's only complete poem, discussed in Chapter 1, which Johnson, seeking directness, imagines addressed to the new beloved who "sits listening in the audience," is of course, addressed to Aphrodite and only indirectly, if at all, to a beloved.[20] A better case is "Phainetai moi," the poem of Sappho quoted by Longinus and discussed in Chapter 2, which addresses the beloved:

> He seems to me equal to the gods that man
> whosoever who opposite you
> sits and listens close
>   to your sweet speaking . . .

But Longinus takes these lines as a rhetorical performance directed at readers, rather than a poem for which the "you" is the true and present audience. I take up this question below, when considering love poems.

It would not be surprising if there never had been a moment when poetic address was simple and straightforward: an originary simplicity then transformed into conventions of indirectness. Address is not simple in the Greek lyric: direct address to the audience sitting in front of the performer is the exception rather than the rule, and of course even where it does take place, the possible separation of the performer from the figure that says "I," which arises immediately not only for choral lyric but wherever there is reperformance, gives us those structures of iterability and textuality that complicate poetry in the modern and early modern world as well. One of the most characteristic structures of lyric, amply represented in the archaic Greek lyric as in all periods of the modern lyric, is the triangulation whereby a speaker ostensibly addresses a beloved, as a way of speaking indirectly to the audience. Johnson suggests that "the person addressed (whether actual or fictional) is a metaphor for readers of the poem and becomes a symbolic mediator, a conductor between the poet and each of his readers and listeners," but of course then what we have is indirection, as in address to a goddess or an urn, rather than address to the audience. I now turn poems addressing people other than readers.

2. Addressing Other People

This is doubtless the most common structure in the Greek and Latin lyric. In Horace's first three books, for instance, 52 odes are addressed to named individuals, 17 to gods and goddesses, including the muses, and only 6 to other nonhuman addressees (and only 15 to no one). Of the human addressees, 26 are judged to be historical individuals and 26 to be fictional or conventional—in general, all of the women and the men with Greek names: Pyrrha, Chloe, Lydia, Lyce, Glycera, Thaliarchus, Lycidas, etc.[21] Scholars have worked to identify the historical addressees but attempts to interpret the odes in relation to particular named hearers have, Gregson Davis notes, "generally failed to win assent." Ode 2.3 tells Dellius, "Remember to keep your mind level when the path is steep . . . for Dellius, you must die . . ." Why Dellius? No one knows. Licinius, in 2.10, is urged to follow the golden mean. Subsequently, Licinius was executed for treason, but if Horace had intimations of his political inclinations, different advice might have been more apposite. In 2.11 Hirpimus is advised to relax and reflect how little life requires, and in 2.14 it is Postumus who is told to remember our mortality: you can't take it with you. Since Postumus was a name given to boys born after their fathers had died, the advice might seem unnecessary, though not inappropriate. Address, writes Davis, "is most usefully regarded as providing a context for lyric utterance. It is part of the necessary fiction of this dyadic lyric model that the poet 'sings' to a 'hearer,' single or multiple," and the address functions much like a dedication, treating the addressee as "a worthy member of a lyric audience." Richard Heinze argued convincingly long ago that the claim to be singing to the lyre to a particular auditor is clearly a fiction—there is no evidence that Horace ever played the lyre or that these poems were sung—and thus the whole discursive situation should be taken not as a reality of performance but as a poetic device, one whose function we need to interrogate.[22]

Consider, for convenience, the shortest of these odes addressed to an individual, 1.11.

Tu ne quaesieris—scire nefas—quem mihi, quem tibi
finem di dederint, Leuconoë, nec Babylonios
temptaris numeros. Ut melius quicquid erit pati,
seu pluris hiemes, seu tribuit Iuppiter ultimam,
quae nunc oppositis debilitat pumicibus mare
Tyrrhenum. Sapias, vina liques, et spatio brevi
spem longam reseces. Dum loquimur, fugerit invida
aetas: carpe diem, quam minimum credula postero.

Don't ask, we're not allowed to know, what end
The gods have assigned to me, to you, Leuconoe,
And don't try Babylonian horoscopes. How much
Better to accept whatever comes, whether Jupiter
Has allowed us many winters or one last one, which now
Wears out the Etruscan sea on opposing cliffs.
Be wise, strain the wine, cut back large hopes to small compass.
While we speak, envious time flies past. Seize the day,
Trusting as little as possible in tomorrow.

[Trans. Niall Rudd, modified]

The famous tag "carpe diem" is offered as general advice, not a response to a specific situation. This is quite characteristic of the Horatian lyric, which freely offers moral admonition. But the pretense of uttering it now to an undefined someone gives it a distinctive character. Although the homiletic wisdom the odes dispense is not the sort of thing one would say to someone out of the blue, the moral disquisition becomes less platitudinous when ostensibly directed to a second-person addressee than if addressed directly to the reader or declared as a conclusion without address of any kind; and the marks of articulation, such as the minimal address and the link to an undefined *now,* make it more of an event. Poems of this sort tread a fine line: on the one hand, they do not become dramatic monologues, where we need to ask who is speaking to whom on what occasion—nothing is gained by trying to imagine a particular characterizable speaker here or an occasion of address—yet it is important that they are addressed. Perhaps because the addressee is no more than a proper name, readers are free to feel addressed without being directly interpellated by a moralizing poet.

Catullus is a poet who appears by his practice to conceive of the poem as a discourse addressed to another individual. Not only are most of his poems addressed to people presumed to be friends or acquaintances, or at least living people (very few are addressed to no one or to inanimate objects); he also provides a model for subsequent love lyrics in devoting a series of poems to a possibly fictional mistress, Lesbia. The most explicit address to a known individual is to the poet Licinius Calvus—a poem about writing poetry which is also a love poem.

Hesterno, Licini, die otiosi
multum lusimus in meis tabellis,
ut convenerat esse delicatos:
scribens versiculos uterque nostrum
ludebat numero modo hoc modo illoc,
reddens mutua per iocum atque vinum.
atque illinc abii tuo lepore
incensus, Licini, facetiisque,
ut nec me miserum cibus iuvaret

nec somnus tegeret quiete ocellos,
sed toto indomitus furore lecto
versarer, cupiens videre lucem,
ut tecum loquerer simulque ut essem.
at defessa labore membra postquam
semimortua lectulo iacebant,
hoc, iucunde, tibi poema feci,
ex quo perspiceres meum dolorem.
nunc audax cave sis, precesque nostras,
oramus, cave despuas, ocelle,
ne poenas Nemesis reposcat a te
est vemens dea: laedere hanc caveto.

⤚

Yesterday, Licinius, while we were at leisure,
we played at length upon my tablets,
(We had made an agreement to be *delicati*.)[23]
Scribbling out verses, each of us
would play now in this mode, now in that,
rendering like for like in wit and wine.
And I went away, Licinius, so
enflamed by your charm and your jokes
that food could give no pleasure in my pain
and sleep refused to put my poor eyes to rest.
Instead, wild with utter madness, I tossed
in bed, kept waiting for the daylight
to talk to you and be with you again.
But when my limbs, exhausted from their struggle,
were lying, nearly dead, on the mattress,
I made this poem, my dear,
so you could see from it the extent of my pain.
Now don't you dare be brazen, my darling,
and don't you dare reject my prayers,
or Nemesis might just come around and get you.
She's one wild goddess: do not dare offend her.

[Trans. David Wray, modified]

This poem addresses Calvus three times, progressing from more formal "Licini" to terms of increasing endearment: "iucunde," "ocelle." One commentator calls this poem "a letter in verse" to Calvus, but the opening lines' description of yesterday's activities would be superfluous for the partner in those activities: they recount what readers need to know.[24] The first three lines, with their account of young men idling away the day in erotic verse play are doubtless designed to scandalize censorious elders while disclosing a pleasurable experience.

We have here a hyperbolic performance: not just "I had a really great time; let's do this again tomorrow," but I am enflamed—"incensus"—and carried away, overcome by the madness of passion, "indomitus furore" (*furor* is a strong word). And the poet threateningly invokes Nemesis if his reader doesn't respond to his offering—not the best epistolary strategy. What we have here is possibly "a petulant plea cast in the traditional language of the abandoned lover," or a jokingly hyperbolic version of such a plea, as the language of Wray's own translation above tends rather to suggest. Paul Veyne notes that in the Latin love elegy mythology was resource for playful pedantry ("une science plaisante, un jeu de cuisterie"), source of a good deal of amusement. The poem earlier alludes to the opening scene of the last book of the *Iliad,* where Achilles can't sleep or eat while thinking of Patroclus—a mock heroic touch. All in all, this is not a letter of invitation but "a self-consciously outrageous poetic performance," as the poem emphasizes, presenting itself as a poem.[25]

How does the address to Calvus affect readers' relation to the poem? First, it makes it an event, rather than simply a reflection on what happened last night. Second, the address to Calvus renders the poem more tantalizing to readers by highlighting the erotic excess, its hyperbolic performativity: this is not just idle recollection of an erotic encounter but a claim to the male beloved to have been overcome with erotic desire, stimulated by the exchange of verses, which the poem is continuing. The invocation of Nemesis at the end marks the sense that this description of erotic engagement might not titillate every reader, raising the question of how Calvus will react but also implicitly how other readers—positioned as potentially active participants—will take it. Indeed, generations of readers *have* been seduced by the charm and wit of Catullus, as he claims to have been seduced by that of Calvus, and their response has been to treat this account of erotic verse play as a profound poetic statement, a manifesto of this group of poets.[26] The poet is playing for an audience, and historically he has won them over.

Critics who discuss the address of classical verse incline less to Mill's figure of the reader "overhearing" a poem addressed to another than to that of the poet "winking at the reader" while addressing someone else. This is perhaps a better way of describing the situation than "overhearing," but what does it mean? Presumably that there are aspects of the poem which do not make sense as spoken to the ostensible addressee but are crucial to the address to a wider audience of readers. This is a phenomenon with which we are all familiar, when we speak ostensibly to one person but with an eye to how our discourse will be received by others who will hear it and so insert some elements specifically chosen for them. Poems in the Western tradition addressed to friends invariably say things that would be superfluous for friends, and this gives poems a ritualistic air, much as prayer tells God things that God already knows, and much as love poems ritualistically rehearse what would presumably be well known to an actual lover.

Love poems, addressed to a beloved, named or unnamed, real or imagined, accessible or inaccessible, are the primary example of poems ostensibly addressed to another individual that indirectly address an audience. Some poems that address actual or potential lovers may actually be communicated to them in the first instance, and many people through history have adopted this model for attempting to communicate their feelings to a lover, but in choosing to compose a poem rather than a little speech or a letter they have opted not just for a supplement of form and the effortful merit this made thing implies, but also for a degree of indirection that reorganizes communication. The love poems that are central to the Western lyric canon are not, though, communications of lovers which are later recognized and assembled as poems, but compositions by poets for an audience other than a particular lover, where address is a rhetorical strategy of triangulated address. Andrew Marvell's "To his Coy Mistress" urges the lady, "Now let us sport us while we may," addressing her throughout the poem, but the title, which is addressed to readers, not to the lady, makes clear who is the poem's audience, as does its mockery of the sort of leisurely wooing that the coy lady is alleged to want and deserve. A French critic argues that the address of love poems is double, to the beloved and to readers, which is quite possible in principle, but in many cases the beloved may be invented, or explicitly out of reach, like Dante's Beatrice or Petrarch's Laura, and the address even to real objects of veneration is far from direct. Reading Shakespeare's sonnets, we are not overhearing his communications to a fair youth and the dark lady, if such existed, but are being offered highly original performances of sonnets. Baudelaire's poems of love allegedly concern three different women, and in one case he did send five of these poems, one by one, over a course of fifteen months, to a woman, the salon beauty Apollonie Sabatier; but he did so anonymously, treating them not as communications of variable amorous affect but as tributes in the form of poems, destined, of course, for his collection. Paul Veyne writes of the Latin love elegy (Catullus, Propertius, Tibullus, and Ovid), "these sweet words are proposed to amuse the reader and not to please the addressee; in Rome the lover-poet poses for his public and displays his mistress for them." Just as a song, though addressing "my love," is offered as singable, repeatable language, for audition and performance by others, the love poems of the tradition are for others to read and repeat, an erotic liturgy, as C. S. Lewis puts it.[27]

The range of love poetry in the Western tradition is immense, though the stances and figures it adopts are familiar: longing, exaltation and despair, vituperation and veneration, adoration from afar, regret for what has been lost or for what never was, anticipation of what might be and— much less frequent, this—quiet satisfaction. Despite its predictable forms, the range of affects is great and love poetry can easily stand as paradigmatic for the lyric tradition. Allen Grossman writes of lyric in general, "in the most primitive terms, the presence of a poem involves a complete triadic state of affairs, in which there is a self, and the beloved of that self which always has a transcendental character ascribed to it, and a third—the third being the audience, the ratifier, the witness, and the inheritor of the drama of loving relationship to which the poem gives access."[28] Love poems are the clearest instance of Grossman's model, where the beloved addressed acquires a transcendental, nonempirical character, less a person than a poetic function, addressed for poetic purposes and for the benefit of what Grossman cannily calls the "inheritors" of the poetic relationship to which the verse gives access.

What does address to the beloved accomplish? First, it gives us an event in the lyric present, the moment of address, when one longs for or praises the beloved or complains about his or her unresponsiveness. This permits a more vivid expression of feeling, not as something to be described from a past which is narrated but rather as an act of praise or blame in the present or, often, an active questioning of the process in which one is engaged. Baudelaire's *Les Fleurs du Mal* includes love poetry that is extraordinary for the variety of tones and possible relations it articulates. By turn reverent, vicious, tender, sententious, suppliant, declamatory, mocking, and insinuating, these poems enact the hyperbolic instabilities of fantasy so central to passion. Within a stretch of a dozen poems we have the modes of surrender:

> I cry in every fiber of my flesh:
> "O my Beelzebub, I worship you!"
>
> > ["Le Possédé"]

Of tender reminiscence:

> Evenings . . .
> We often told ourselves imperishable things
>
> > ["Le Balcon"]

Of vituperation:

> You'd entertain the universe in bed,
> Foul woman!
>
> > ["Tu mettrais l'univers . . ."]

Of fond mocking:

> Your childlike head lolls with the weight
>   Of all your idleness,
> And sways with all the slackness of
>   A baby elephant's.
>
> > ["Le Serpent qui danse"]

Of supplication:

> I beg your pity, you, my only love.

> > ["De profondis clamavi"]

Of amorous fantasy:

> I want to sleep! To sleep and not to live!
> And in a sleep as sweet as death, to dream
> Of spreading out my kisses without shame
> On your smooth body, bright with copper sheen.

> > ["Le Léthé"]

and of an attitude too complex to be named, when a declaration of veneration—"I love you as I love the night's high vault"—turns into a sordid evocation of lovemaking:

> I rise to the attack, mount an assault
> A choir of wormlets mounting on a corpse,
> And cherish your unbending cruelty,
> This iciness so beautiful to me.

> > ["Je t'adore à l'égal de la voute
> > nocturne" ; all translations by
> > James McGowan]

The structure of address to a real or imagined lover enhances the possibility of enacting the most complex, surprising, or perverse movements of desire.

For a quieter, more reflective but equally inventive example of amorous address, consider Sonnet 17 from Neruda's *Cien sonetos de amor*:

> No te amo como si fueras rosa de sal, topacio
> o flecha de claveles que propagan el fuego:

te amo como se aman ciertas cosas oscuras,
secretamente, entre la sombra y el alma.

Te amo como la planta que no florece y lleva
dentro de sí, escondida, la luz de aquellas flores,
y gracias a tu amor vive oscuro en mi cuerpo
el apretado aroma que ascendió de la tierra.

Te amo sin saber cómo, ni cuándo, ni de dónde,
te amo directamente sin problemas ni orgullo:
así te amo porque no sé amar de otra manera,

sino así de este modo en que no soy ni eres,
tan cerca que tu mano sobre mi pecho es mía,
tan cerca que se cierran tus ojos con mi sueño.mi s

☙

I do not love you as if you were salt-rose, or topaz,
or the arrow of carnations the fire shoots off.
I love you as certain dark things are to be loved,
in secret, between the shadow and the soul.

I love you as the plant that never blooms
but carries in itself the light of hidden flowers;
thanks to your love a certain solid fragrance,
risen from the earth, lives darkly in my body.

I love you without knowing how, or when, or from where.
I love you straightforwardly, without complexities or pride;
so I love you because I know no other way

than this: where *I* does not exist, nor *you,*
so close that your hand on my chest is my hand,
so close that your eyes close as I fall asleep.

[Trans. Steve Tapscott]

If the beloved were really the audience, she would doubtless be perplexed
by this communication—"a plant that never blooms"?—especially given
the claim to straightforwardness, though she might ease that perplexity
by admiring this discourse as a poem, which does not aim to commu-

nicate but to celebrate, evoking, through its proliferation of figures, a wonderfully original, nearly unimaginable relationship and positing a closeness that perhaps can only occur in language, which can make your hand my hand and make your eyes close as I fall asleep. If we replace "you" by "her" throughout, the poem becomes rather more fanciful, narcissistic even, whereas address in love poems evokes for readers the interpersonal relation and possibilities of enactment, here quite magical, that are fundamental to the genre. There is a reason why love poems are addressed.

3. Apostrophe

There seems no limit to the range of things that can be addressed by a lyric. Horace addressed a ship, a tree on his estate, a wine flask, his lyre, the ship of state, and a spring. Catullus addresses poems to a sparrow, to Colonia (thought to be Verona), to the peninsula of Sirmio, to his papyrus, to Volusius's *Annals,* to his farm, to his hendecasyllabic verse form, which he asks to engage in invective, and to a door, which is privy to many secrets. These poems make patently obvious what emerges from consideration of the poems addressed to individuals: that the strategy of positing an addressee is a way of securing particular effects, producing distinctive impressions of voice through unusual utterance, while in fact writing for the reader. Pablo Neruda wrote 225 odes, addressing everything from the abstractions Happiness, Poverty, Time, Laziness, Gratitude, Life, and Criticism, on the one hand, to ironing, a pair of socks, barbed wire, the dictionary, scissors, and soap, on the other. Here is the "Oda al jabón":

Eso	That's what
eres,	you are
jabón, delicia pura	soap, pure delight
aroma transitorio	fleeting smell
que resbala	that slips
y naufraga como un	and sinks like a
pescado ciego	blind fish
en la profundidad de la bañera.	in the depths of the bathtub.

[Trans. Ilan Stavans]

Kenneth Koch, exploiting the comic possibilities of apostrophe in a daring book of *New Addresses*, wagers that there is nothing that cannot occupy this position, addressing World War II ("You were large"), Piano Lessons ("You didn't do me any good"), My Fifties, Jewishness, The Roman Forum, Psychoanalysis, My Father's Business, Orgasms, and even My Old Addresses. If this is amusing, it is because it takes to an extreme a fundamental gesture of lyric, mocking its pretensions to transform objects of attention into potential auditors, yet slyly expanding our imaginative possibilities: we sometimes curse computers, busses, and other inanimate objects that resist our will; why not also apostrophically admonish psychoanalysis or piano lessons?

In an essay on his contemporary Théodore de Banville, Charles Baudelaire writes of lyric, "Let us note, first of all, that hyperbole and apostrophe are the forms of language not only most agreeable but also most necessary to it."[29] Lyric is characteristically extravagant, performing unusual speech acts of strange address, and the empty "O" that often accompanies apostrophe—"O wild West Wind"—beautifully illustrates the semantically empty play of language, as in sound patterning, that organizes and distinguishes lyric.

Quintilian, speaking of oratory, defines apostrophe as "a diversion of our words to address someone other than the judge"; and though he cautions against it, "since it would certainly seem more natural that we should specifically address ourselves to those whose favor we desire to win," he allows that occasionally "some striking expression of thought is necessary, . . . which can be given greater point and vehemence when addressed to some person other than the judge." In forensic rhetoric, apostrophe is a turning from the actual audience to address someone or something else (the opponent, the fatherland, justice), and the etymology of the term emphasizes the turning rather than the anomalous address; but outside the courtroom, apostrophe has long denoted address to someone or something other than the actual audience; it includes address to individuals, but it especially denotes address to what is not an actual listener: abstractions, inanimate objects, or persons absent or dead.[30]

Apostrophe! we thus address
More things than I should care to guess.

Apostrophe! I did invoke
Your figure even as I spoke.[31]

As Barbara Johnson writes, summing up the modern usage of the term, "Apostrophe in the sense in which I will be using it involves the direct address to an absent, dead, or inanimate being by a first-person speaker. . . . Apostrophe is thus both direct and indirect: based etymologically on the notion of turning aside, of digressing from straight speech, it manipulates the I/thou structure of direct address in an indirect way."[32]

Quintilian treats apostrophe as a seeking "greater point or vehemence"—which does not, of course, distinguish it from other tropes; but apostrophe is different because it makes its point by troping not on the meaning of a word but on the circuit of communication itself, foregrounding the fact that this is utterance of a special kind, marked as voicing (the gratuitous "O" that accompanies many apostrophes gives us pure voicing) but not as mundane communication. In foregrounding the lyric as act of address, lifting it out of ordinary communicational contexts, apostrophes give us a ritualistic, hortatory act, a special sort of linguistic event in a lyric present.

Rhetoricians, in the tradition of Quintilian, posit that apostrophes serve as intensifiers, images of invested passion. In so doing they draw upon a dubious psychology, treating apostrophic address as the natural result of an unexceptionable cause. In 1715 Bernard Lamy observes that "apostrophe occurs when, being extraordinarily moved, a man turns every which way, addressing himself to the heavens, to the earth, to the rocks, to the woods, and to insensible things." A century later Pierre Fontanier, in his *Figures du discours,* asks "But what can give rise to apostrophe? It can only be feeling [*le sentiment*], and only feeling stirred up within the heart until it breaks out and spreads itself about outside, as if acting on its own, . . . the spontaneous impulse of a powerfully moved soul."[33] Apostrophe allegedly signifies, metonymically, the passion that caused it. "O rose, thou art sick" would differ from "The rose is sick" or "This rose is sick" as the reflection of a more intense feeling.

There may be some truth in this, but apostrophe is a distinct poetic operation, a linguistic artifice, and if it does signify intensity, this is not because passion naturally provokes it. There are many apostrophes that do not lend themselves to this story of the natural outpouring of passions. Baudelaire's "Sois sage, ô ma Douleur, et tiens-toi plus tranquille," uses what one says to a child—"Behave yourself, be good, stop fidgeting, settle down"—to address pain: we have not a bursting forth of emotion but an intimate restructuring of affective space. Or consider Petrarch's famous address in *Canzoniere* 126 to the water, tree, grass, flowers, and air of the site where he was first smitten with love:

> Chiare, fresche et dolci acque,
> ove le belle membra
> pose colei che sola a me par donna;
> gentil ramo ove piacque
> (con sospir' mi rimembra)
> a lei di fare al bel fiancho colonna;
> erba e fior' che la gonna
> leggiadra ricoverse
> co l'angelico seno;
> aere sacro, sereno,
> ove Amor co' begli occhi il cor m'aperse:
> date udïenza insieme
> a le dolenti mie parole estreme.

☙

> Clear, sweet fresh water
> where she, the only one who seemed
> woman to me, rested her beautiful limbs;
> gentle branch where it pleased her
> (with sighs, I remember it)
> to make a pillar for her lovely flank:
> grass and flowers which her dress
> lightly covered,
> as it did the angelic breast:
> serene, and sacred air,
> where Love pierced my heart with eyes of beauty:
> listen together
> to my last sad words.

[Trans. A. S. Kline]

This address to all the natural elements of the site, and the request that they listen, is not the product of an uncontainable emotion—though the affect itself may be intense—but a characteristic lyric indirection or displacement of great delicacy.

Even for exuberant poems, it is may be difficult to argue that apostrophes work above all to intensify a situation described. Blake addresses the spring in his "Poetical Sketches":

> O thou with dewy locks, who lookest down
> Through the clear windows of the morning, turn
> Thine angel eyes upon our western isle,
> Which in full choir hails thy approach, O Spring !
> The hills tell one another, and the listening
> Valleys hear; all our longing eyes are turn'd
> Up to thy bright pavilions: issue forth
> And let thy holy feet visit our clime!
> Come o'er the eastern hills, and let our winds
> Kiss thy perfumèd garments; let us taste
> Thy morn and evening breath; scatter thy pearls
> Upon our lovesick land that mourns for thee.
> O deck her forth with thy fair fingers; pour
> Thy soft kisses on her bosom; and put
> Thy golden crown upon her languish'd head,
> Whose modest tresses are bound up for thee!

Though this act of address suggests intense feeling, it seems to attach less to the season itself than to the act of addressing or convoking it. Geoffrey Hartman remarks that with Blake's four poems on the seasons, "We feel at once their intensely vocative nature—that the prophetic or speaking out and the invocational or calling upon are more important than their conventional subject. Their mood is never purely descriptive but always optative or imperative: what description enters is ritual in character. It evokes an epiphany so strongly as to carry the poet toward it."[34]

We can see why this might be the case if we ask why rhetoricians should claim that passion spontaneously seeks apostrophe. The answer would seem to be that to apostrophize is to will a state of affairs, to attempt to bring it into being by asking inanimate objects to bend themselves to your desire—as if apostrophe, with all its rhetorical fragility, embodied an atavistic casting of spells on the world. In these terms, the function of apostrophe would be to posit a potentially responsive or at least attentive universe, to which one has a relation. Apostrophes invoke elements of the universe as potentially responsive forces, which can be asked to act, or refrain from acting, or even to continue behaving as they usually behave. The key is not passionate intensity, but rather the ritual invocation of elements of the universe, the attempt, even, to evoke the possibility of a magical transformation. This is manifestly central to the tradition of song, ancient and modern, from the anonymous sixteenth-century poem,

> Westron wynde, when wilt thou blow,
> The small raine down can raine.
> Cryst, if my love were in my armes
> And I in my bedde again!

to a famous twentieth-century lyric,

> Hello Darkness, my old friend,
> I've come to talk with you again,

> [Paul Simon's "The Sound of Silence."]

As a figure endemic to poetry that finds little place in other discourses, apostrophe works as a mark of poetic vocation. Asking winds to blow or seasons to stay their coming or mountains to hear one's cries is a ritual action, whereby voice calls in order to be calling, and seeks to manifest its calling, to establish its identity as poetical voice. A maker of poems constitutes him or herself as poet, by presuming to address various "you"s, whether in love poems or odes, or elegies, or just poetic observations, with address to leaves, or weeds. In an operation that sounds tautological, the vocative of apostrophe is a device which the poetic subject uses to establish with the object a relationship that helps to constitute the subject itself as poetic, even vatic. Apostrophic address works to establish a relation to the poetic tradition (critics who dismissed apostrophe as merely an inherited classical convention admit this much), as if each address to winds, flowers, mountains, gods, beloveds, were a repetition of earlier poetic calls. So Milton's "Lycidas" begins

> Yet once more, O ye laurels, and once more,
> Ye myrtles brown, with ivy never sere,
> I come to pluck your berries harsh and crude . . .

"Yet once more" inscribes this opening in the tradition of the pastoral elegy, where such plants have been addressed before, as in Virgil's second eclogue, "et vos, o lauri, carpam et te, proxima myrte, / sic positae quoniam suavis miscetis odores" ("And you, O laurels, I will pluck, and then you, myrtle, since you are placed so as to mingle your sweet scents"). The empty "O" of apostrophe, which has no semantic force, could be said implicitly to allude to all other apostrophes of the tradition.

But with apostrophic address a range of effects are possible. Let us look at three examples, one from each of the classical, renaissance, and romantic periods.

Horace's most famous ode to an inanimate addressee invokes a fountain (3.13).

> O fons Bandusiae, splendidior vitro,
> dulci digne mero non sine floribus,
>   cras donaberis haedo,
>   cui frons turgida cornibus
>
> primis et venerem et proelia destinat;
> frustra: nam gelidos inficiet tibi
>   rubro sanguine rivos,
>   lascivi suboles gregis.
>
> te flagrantis atrox hora Caniculae
> nescit tangere, tu frigus amabile
>   fessis vomere tauris
>   praebes et pecori vago.
>
> fies nobilium tu quoque fontium,
> me dicente cavis impositam ilicem

saxis unde loquaces
    lymphae desiliunt tuae.

                          ⌒

O fountain of Bandusia, brighter than glass,
well do you deserve an offering of sweet wine
    and flowers, and tomorrow you will receive a kid
            with new horns bulging on his brow,
marking him out for love and war—
to no avail, since he will stain your cold stream
    with his red blood, this offspring
            of the amorous flock.
The cruel hour of the blazing Dog-star
cannot touch you. You give delicious
    coldness to oxen weary of the plough
            and the straggling flock.
You too will become a famous fountain
as I sing of the holm-oak
    above your cave in the rock
            where your waters leap down chattering.

                                    [Trans. David West]

The classical models of lyric genres have the virtue of providing a pan-
oply of poetic speech acts of praise, invocation, celebration and complaint,
so there is no need to imagine a fictional speaker or occasion. The poem
is the occasion. This poem emphasizes its link with other rituals of ceremonious praise by announcing that tomorrow the spring will receive a
special sacrifice of a young goat; but the poem's separation from "tomorrow's" event emphasizes that this encomium is not the fictional representation of some other sort of speech act. It performatively sets out to
accomplish what it declares, that this spring will become a famous spring,
like the springs of the Muses—Arethusa, Hippocrene, Dirce, or the Pierian
spring—and it has succeeded.[35] Although no one knows where this spring
is or even whether there is any such spring, it is famous; and the sacrifice
of the kid is repeatedly enacted, as the apparently gratuitous celebration
of his budding horns—"marking him out for love and war"—confers value

that is swiftly sacrificed, as—no doubt with a twinge—we are compelled to imagine him killed off.[36]

It is evident here that the praise addressed to the spring is in in fact addressed to us, despite the vocative and second-person verbs, yet it makes a difference that the poem does not just praise the spring to us but addresses it. Consider what happens if we remove the second-person address:

> *The spring* of Bandusia is brighter than glass;
> *and well* deserves an offering of sweet wine
>   and flowers, and tomorrow *it* will receive a kid. . . .
>
> The cruel hour of the blazing Dog-star
> cannot touch *this spring. It* gives delicious
>   coldness to oxen weary of the plough
>   and the straggling flock.
> *It* too will become a famous fountain
> as I sing of the holm-oak
>   *above its* cave in the rock
>   where *its* waters leap down chattering.

The changes are minimal. They do not destroy the poem, but they do substantially change its character, as when we changed the pronouns in Neruda's love poem earlier. The spring is no longer imagined as potentially responsive. The poem becomes resolutely descriptive from the outset rather than invocatory, and the "dicente" ("as I sing") at the end comes more as an afterthought than a continuation and climax of a performativity.

One notable loss in my transmutation of the poem is *"your* chattering waters," which makes the poem conclude with attribution of speech—*loquaces*—to an invoked "you". What is lost is not just the possibility that the spring become something other, raised to a different plane with a life of its own, in a move analogous to the singularizing operation of the fame that the poem in both versions promises; lost also is "the reciprocity between the speaking of the poet and the prattling of the spring," as if the spring's natural response were made verbal by the poetic address; and thus is lost above all a sense of lyric as a ceremonialized performance: conjuring, endowing, acting.[37] For Horace, addressing a spring seems eminently possible, a regular lyric strategy, enabling him to evoke a form of otherness in which pleasure is implicated. This is not private meditation but an act of public celebration.

Next we move from Roman celebration of a spring to Edmund Waller's seventeenth-century commands to a rose, entitled "Song."

> Go, lovely rose!
> Tell her that wastes her time and me
> That now she knows
> When I resemble her to thee,
> How sweet and fair she seems to be.
>
> Tell her that's young,
> And shuns to have her graces spied,
> That hadst thou sprung
> In deserts where no men abide,
> Thou must have uncommended died.
>
> Small is the worth
> Of beauty from the light retired;
> Bid her come forth,
> Suffer herself to be desired,
> And not blush so to be admired.
>
> Then die, that she
> The common fate of all things rare
> May read in thee;
> How small a part of time they share,
> That are so wondrous sweet and fair!

Addressing the rose and urging it to speak and then to die is a distinctively poetic act, which imagines and invokes a responsive flower, but the poem's own gesture is fundamentally a social one: offering a rose to the lady is an age-old gesture. The rose, lovely like the lady, is asked to serve as a concrete instantiation of the poetic act of comparison, but it is also the messenger, the go-between, a metonymical extension of the speaker. It "replicates the verbal artifact," Paul Alpers writes, "in that it is both the gift sent and a means of sending a message to the lady" (though, unlike the rose, the poem is endowed with longevity). By invoking the rose, this poet does not so much animate it in bardic fashion as engage in social indirection. By apostrophizing the rose rather than addressing the beloved directly, and by telling the rose what to say to the beloved, the poem makes the argument about virginity more elegant, less aggressive and self-serving, than it would be if a speaker directly told the imagined beloved, "suffer yourself to be desired." "By deflecting his address from the lady to the flower who resembles her," Alpers writes, "the speaker makes the various arguments against virginity less insistent and thus gives an air of graciousness to his pointed wit."[38] This apostrophic poem does indeed involve a turning away from a possible empirical listener, the lady, to another addressee, which is animated by this poetic address, but the animation seems less an intensification or an instantiation of bardic power than gracious and witty indirection, a social gesture, staged for the audience, which doubtless includes ladies. The trope of apostrophe here seems to install us in a social situation rather than extract us from it, as so often happens in the apostrophic lyrics of the romantic period, but it still involves an operation of enlisting elements of the universe in one's love, as well as a poetic extravagance and exercise of poetic authority in willing the rose to speak, giving it lines to speak, and directing it to die.

But "Go, Lovely Rose" is quite different from a later address to the rose, Blake's celebrated "The Sick Rose."

O rose, thou art sick;
The invisible worm
That flies in the night
In the howling storm

Has found out thy bed
Of crimson joy,
And his dark secret love
Does thy life destroy.

Blake's lyric has provoked a good deal of critical discussion, especially because other texts of Blake's do *not* treat sexuality as a dark, destructive secret—except insofar as a perverted religious and social order constrains and represses it. Critics argue about this poem's take on beauty and human sexuality: Is this is a poem of beauty destroyed by evil, or a critique of the myth of female flight and male pursuit, or a representation of a puritanical, misogynistic male speaker who imputes sickness to any rose or woman whose bed is a site of sexual pleasure? We seem to have a scenario in which a phallic force has invaded the rose's bed. But Blake in one draft changed "his dark secret love" to "her dark secret love," making the invisible worm feminine, before changing it back again, suggesting that, for him at least, this is not a straightforward male-female scenario, with the rose as the woman and the worm as male sexuality. One line of argument links the invisible, flying worm to invisible spirits, *lares* or *larvae,* part of the demonic lore of the Middle Ages and the Renaissance. Paracelsus's *De Origine morborum invisilibium* discusses the imagination as cause of invisible diseases, among them illnesses deriving from overactive sexual fantasy. Blake himself seems to have been convinced that social and religious structures which keep fantasies from leading to action were a source of illness: "He who desires and acts not breeds pestilence," he wrote.[39] And there is a highly relevant sequence in Shakespeare's *Twelfth Night:* "She never told her love, / But let concealment, like a worm i' the bud, / feed on her damask cheek" (and of course "damask" is a rose).

In arguments about the meaning of the poem, none of the critics ask why the speaker *addresses* the rose, rather than observing that the rose is sick: "Oh this rose is sick" or "The rose here is sick." It makes a considerable difference. Alpers notes that if the poem is rewritten without the second-person pronouns, it is difficult to tell what state of affairs is represented: is it a gardener's lament?[40] In Blake's version, that question does not even arise: instead of describing with some detachment the nature of the sickness of the rose, the poem tells the rose that it is sick—apostrophic poems, like prayers, often tell the addressee something the addressee presumably already knows. It thus acquires a ritual character. Or else the address declares the rose to be sick, as if the rose did not know that its condition were a sickness and its life were being destroyed. Since addressing the rose constitutes it as sentient creature, a potential listener, or rather, *presupposes* an animate listener, the question of the rose's relation to its crimson joy and its sickness is explicitly raised.

The energy of poetic address creates a surprisingly strong sense of prophetic revelation and marks this speech act as poetic discourse. If one has trouble saying what a speaker would be doing in saying "O Rose, thou art sick," it is because this does not correspond to any everyday speech act, and the simplest answer to what the speaker is doing is something like "waxing poetical." Address to the rose, which personifies it as a sentient creature with a life of its own, creating an I–thou relation between poetic subject and natural object, works to create the poetic "I" as a bardic, visionary voice, inscribing the poem in the tradition of poetry that seeks to make things happen by acts of naming. Paradoxically, the more such poetry addresses natural or inanimate objects, the more it offers tropes of voice only, voice-events or instances of what I have called voicing, and the more it reveals itself at another level as not spoken, but as writing that through its personification enacts voicing, for the readers to whom it repeatedly presents itself.

In all three cases apostrophic address foregrounds the poetic act: an act of celebration in Horace, the act of transmitting a poetic message in Waller, and the act of visionary self-constitution in Blake. The poetic act has a different character in the three cases: ceremonial-ritualistic, in Horace, socially adept in Waller, and prophetic in Blake. In each case, though, the ritualistic dominates the fictional, as the poem seeks to establish itself as an event of memorable language and not the fictional representation of a past event. "Poetry makes nothing happen," writes Auden, speaking for an ironic age in his elegy "In Memory of W. B. Yeats." But, Auden continues, "it survives . . . / A way of happening, a mouth." The "O" of apostrophic address connects mouth and event.

A primary force of apostrophe is to constitute the addressee as another subject, with which the visionary poet can hope to develop a relationship, harmonious or antagonistic; apostrophe treats that bringing together of subject and object as an act of will, something accomplished poetically in the act of address. A subtle and self-conscious metacommentary on this aspect of apostrophe comes at the end of Rilke's ninth Duino Elegy. When you speak to the angel, tell him things: "Sag ihm die Dinge."

         Und diese, von Hingang

lebenden Dinge verstehn, daß du sie rühmst; vergänglich,

traun sie ein Rettendes uns, den Vergänglichsten, zu.

Wollen, wir sollen sie ganz im unsichtbarn Herzen verwandeln

in—o unendlich—in uns! Wer wir am Ende auch seien.

Erde, ist es nicht dies, was du willst: *unsichtbar*

in uns erstehn?—Ist es dein Traum nicht,

einmal unsichtbar zu sein?—Erde! unsichtbar!

Was, wenn Verwandlung nicht, ist dein drängender Auftrag?

Erde, du liebe, ich will.

             ☞

        These things that live on departure

understand when you praise them: fleeting, they look for

rescue through something in us, the most fleeting of all.

Want us to change them entirely, within our invisible hearts

into—oh, endlessly—into ourselves! Whosoever we are.

Earth, is it not just this that you want: to arise

invisibly in us? Is not your dream

to be one day invisible? Earth! invisible!

What is your urgent command, if not transformation?

Earth, you darling, I will!

      [Trans. J. B. Leishman and Stephen Spender]

Addressing earth, the poem embraces the apostrophic wish: that the things of the earth function as *thous* when addressed. If they are subjects, they seek, like all subjects, to transcend a purely material condition. If earth can be addressed and has desires, it wants to be spirit also and to become at least in part invisible, conceptual rather than material, through a rearising in us, whether as a function of our will or by taking over our will. That we, the agents of this transformation, are "the most fleeting of all" adds to the irony of the situation, but the poem goes further in boldly promising to respond to the earth's command for transformation. Has it done so, giving earth a spiritual rearising, in the moment of the poem?

The figure of apostrophe, which seems above all to seek to establish relations between self and other, can also on occasion be read as an act of radical interiorization and solipsism, which either parcels out the self to fill the world, or internalizes what might have been thought external. Examples of the first would be apostrophes of Baudelaire's that people the world with fragments of the self: "Sois sage, o ma Douleur" ("Behave yourself, pain") "Mon esprit, tu te meus avec agilité" ("My spirit, you move around with agility"), "Recueille-toi, mon âme, en ce grave moment" ("Collect yourself, my soul, in this solemn moment"). For the second, we have Rilke's claim that things "want us to change them entirely into ourselves." The logic of this second move would be that since every I implies a you (in that "I" means "the person addressing you refers to himself/herself"), to name as you that which we usually believe cannot be a you (such as the earth), is to fill that place with what can only occupy it through "an invisible rearising in us."

The internalizing force of apostrophe comes out with special clarity in poems that multiply apostrophes to different figures. Wordsworth's "Ode," later subtitled "Intimations of Immortality from Recollections of Early Childhood," brings together in a single unreal space "Thou child of joy," "ye blessed creatures," "Thou whose exterior semblance doth belie thy soul's immensity," "ye birds," and "ye fountains, meadows, hills, and groves." Brought together by apostrophes, they function as nodes or concretizations of moments of poetic reflection.

This internalization is important because it works against narrative and its accompaniments: sequentiality, causality, linear time, teleological meaning. As Shelley put the matter with high poetic disdain, "There is this difference between a story and a poem, that a story is a catalogue of detached facts, which have no other connection than time, place, circumstance, cause and effect; the other is the creation of actions according to the unchangeable forms of human nature."[41] This puts the case for apostrophic poetry against narrative. If one brings together in a poem a boy, some birds, a few blessed creatures, and some mountains, hills, and groves, one tends to place them in a narrative where one thing leads to another, events demand to be temporally located, and soon one has a poem that would provoke Shelley's strictures. But if one puts into a poem

"thou shepherd boy," "ye birds," "ye blessed creatures," etc. they are immediately associated with what might be called the timeless present but is
better seen as a temporality of lyric articulation or enunciation. Even if the
birds were only glimpsed once in the past, to apostrophize them as "ye
birds" is to locate them in the time of the apostrophe, a special temporality which is the set of all moments at which writing can say "now."
This is a time of discourse rather than of story. In the case of Wordsworth's "Ode," much of its energy derives from the tension between a
narrative of development and loss, progressing from the child to the man,
and the apostrophic temporality, in which the birds, creatures, boys, and
so on, resist being organized into events, as they become moments of the
event that the poem is attempting to be.[42]

The fundamental characteristic of lyric, I am arguing, is not the description and interpretation of a past event but the iterative and iterable
performance of an event in the lyric present, in the special "now," of lyric
articulation. The bold wager of poetic apostrophe is that the lyric can
displace a time of narrative, of past events reported, and place us in the
continuing present of apostrophic address, the "now" in which, for readers,
a poetic event can repeatedly occur. Fiction is about what happened next;
lyric is about what happens now.[43]

I discussed earlier the tension between ritual and fictional elements
in lyric. Here, with the apostrophic and the narrative, we encounter specific versions of this interplay. A poem can recount a series of events,
which acquire the significance lyric requires when read synecdochi-
cally or allegorically (I return to this topic in the Chapter 6) Avoiding
apostrophe, Wordsworth wrote lyrical ballads: anecdotes which signify.
Alternatively, poems can invoke objects, can people a space of the lyric
"now" with forms and forces that may have pasts and futures, certainly,
but that are convoked as presences. Nothing need happen in an apostrophic poem, as the great romantic odes amply demonstrate. In lyric
there is characteristically dominance of the apostrophic and ritualistic.
Nothing need happen in the poem because the poem is to be itself the
happening.

The tension between the narrative and the apostrophic can be seen as
the generative force behind a whole array of lyrics. One might identify,
for example, as instances of the dominance of the apostrophic, poems

which, in a very common move, substitute a nontemporal opposition for a temporal one, or substitute a temporality of discourse for a referential temporality. In lyrics of this kind a temporal problem is posed: something once present has been lost or attenuated; this loss can be narrated but the temporal sequence is irreversible, like time itself. Apostrophes displace this irreversible structure by removing it from linear time and locating it in a discursive time. The temporal movement from A to B, restructured by apostrophe, becomes a reversible alternation between A' and B': a play of presence and absence governed not by time but by poetic ingenuity or power.

The clearest example of this structure is the elegy, which replaces an irreversible temporal disjunction, the movement from life to death, with a reversible alternation between mourning and consolation, evocations of absence and presence. In Shelley's "Adonais," for example, as in Milton's "Lycidas," the apostrophes give us an alternation rather than a narrative sequence.

> Oh weep for Adonais—he is dead!
> Wake, melancholy Mother, wake and weep!
> Yet wherefore? Quench within their burning bed
> Thy fiery tears, . . .
> Most musical of mourners, weep again!
> Lament anew, Urania! . . .
>   but his clear Sprite
> Yet reigns o'er earth; the third among the sons of light.
> Most musical of mourners, weep anew! . . .
>
> Awake him not! surely he takes his fill
> Of deep and liquid rest, forgetful of all ill. . . .
>
> Mourn not for Adonais.—Thou young Dawn,
> Turn all thy dew to splendour, for from thee
> The spirit thou lamentest is not gone;
> Ye caverns and ye forests, cease to moan!

Moving back and forth between these two postures, the poem displaces the temporal pattern of actual loss; to focus on these alternating apostrophic commands, mourn or cease to mourn, makes the power of its own evocativeness the central issue.

A poem of a very different sort, Yeats's "Among School Children," embraces a similar pattern: reiterated contrasts between age and youth form a structure from which the poem suddenly turns in the penultimate stanza with an apostrophe:

> —O presences
> That passion, piety or affection knows,
> And that all heavenly glory symbolise—
> O self-born mockers of man's enterprise;

The transcendental presences invoked here, the images which are objects of strong feelings that generate them, make the transient projects of human life seem paltry, but a second apostrophe calls forth against these images another set of presences that seem both empirical and transcendental and that are presented as possible examples of organic unity:

> O chestnut-tree, great-rooted blossomer,
> Are you the leaf, the blossom or the bole?
> O body swayed to music, O brightening glance,
> How can we know the dancer from the dance?

The opposition is no longer an irreversible temporal move from youth to age but an atemporal juxtaposition of two sorts of images evoked as presences by apostrophes. The question of whether we can choose between these alternatives and precisely what such a choice would entail is a difficult one, but the poem has, through its apostrophic turn, made this a central issue.

Poems claiming to narrate a loss they recognize as irreversible—not holding out hope of transcendence—may have that knowledge undermined by the apostrophes they use. Wordsworth's "Elegiac Stanzas" recount a loss:

> A power is gone, which nothing can restore . . .
> A deep distress hath humanized my Soul.

But by *addressing* Peele Castle—

> I was thy neighbor once, thou rugged Pile!
> Four summer weeks I dwelt in sight of thee:
> I saw thee every day . . .

—the narrator places it outside a narrative temporality, denying the claims of narrative time by the very phrases—recollections—that acknowledge it. Because the apostrophes make the castle a present addressee, the narrator can identify with the "huge castle standing here sublime," and he can find in his poetic ability to invoke it a sense of his own continuity.

Apostrophe resists narrative because its "now" is not a moment in a temporal sequence but a special "now" of discourse: of writing and of poetic enunciation. This temporality of discourse, to which I return in Chapter 6, is scarcely understood, difficult to think, but it seems to be one of the things toward which lyric strives: that iterable time when language can say "now."

If one major effect of lyric address is the replacement of a narrative temporality with temporality of the poetic event, this contributes to what is perhaps its most important effect, the evocation of poetic power. I have already raised this issue in different forms, speaking, for example, of apostrophe as the embodiment of poetic pretension—daring to address the sun, the winds, the stars—and as a source of embarrassment. Apostrophe treats the subject's relation to the world as a specular relationship, a relation between subjects, and it has a highly optative character, expressing wishes, requests, demands that whatever is addressed do something for you or refrain from doing what it usually does. Heinz Schlaffer maintains that lyric is at bottom a resistance to the disenchantment of the world, a resistance to the secular rationality that has overtaken older forms of thinking in which the ritual played an important part; and that lyric persists in modes of invocation and magical operations that seem anachronistic.[44] But as it persists, it displays its skepticism in various ways. In fact, one of the central features of the lyric is the tension between enchantment and disenchantment, or between the presumption to involve the universe in one's desires and doubts about the efficacy of such poetic acts. This is splendidly played out in A. R. Ammons's "Dominion":

> Glittery river, I said,
> rise, but
> it didn't:
>
> stop, then, damn
> it, but it
> didn't:
>
> O river, I said,
> ruffle
> blurring
>
> windknots up
> (and
> that was nice
>
> like perch striking roils
> at surface
> flies):
>
> river, I said, don't
> turn back,
> and it eased on
>
> by,
> majestic in the sweetest
> command.[45]

Finally the poet finds a command that works, easing the poem on as it complies with what is called the river's sweet command. But doubts about poetic power are featured not only in modern poems, which may address socks, or the sun or Jewishness or my old addresses in ways that border on joking; they also play a central role in poems squarely in the romantic tradition that explicitly court prophetic effects. Consider Alphonse de Lamartine's "Le Lac," famous for its apostrophic call for time to stop: "O temps, suspends ton vol!"

If any poem is emblematic of apostrophic discourse, it is "Le Lac," which incorporates in its address to nature a powerful line of complaint about the passage of time and human loss—the sort of thing that helps justify the notion of apostrophe as the bursting forth of a powerful emotion: "Temps jaloux, se peut-il que ces moments d'ivresse . . . s'envolent loin de nous . . . ?" ("Jealous time, can it be that these moments of ecstasy . . . fly far away from us?"). And two stanzas later:

Éternité, néant, passé, sombres abîmes,
Que faites-vous des jours que vous engloutissez ?
Parlez : nous rendrez-vous ces extases sublimes
Que vous nous ravissez?

Eternity, nothingness, dark abyss,
What do you do with the days you engulf?
Speak, will you give us back these sublime ecstasies
That you ravish from us?

[Trans. Gervaise Hittle, modified]

Commanding Eternity to speak is the acme of bardic pretension and boldly sets up its own subsequent deflation, since eternity will not reply.

"Le Lac" begins with a rhetorical question about the possibility of momentarily arresting the passage of time:

Ainsi, toujours poussés vers de nouveaux rivages,
Dans la nuit éternelle emportés sans retour,
Ne pourrons-nous jamais sur l'océan des âges
Jeter l'ancre un seul jour?

Thus driven forth forever toward new shores,
Into eternal night borne without respite,
Can we never on the Sea of Ages,
Drop anchor for one day?

The second stanza addresses the lake and asks it both to witness the poet's present isolation, now that his beloved is gone—"Look, I come

alone to sit upon this stone"—and to recall his past visit with his beloved. He asks the lake, in particular, to recall *her* apostrophe at that time:
"O temps, suspends ton vol, / Et vous, heures propices, suspendez vos
cours" ("O time, suspend your flight, and you, propitious hours, suspend your course"). This famous apostrophe, an apostrophe within an
apostrophe, as she asked time to let them savor their all-too-fleeting happiness, is one to which, we are told, the lake paid attention ("le flot fut at-
tentif"), though not, apparently, time itself. Here, as elsewhere, the fundamental gesture of apostrophe is to make something which cannot
normally be addressed into an addressee, treating it as a subject capable
of hearing, and thus in principle capable of acting and of responding.

This posture of complaint is ironized in Baudelaire's "La Béatrice," a
satire on romantic poetic stances: the poet spends his walk complaining
to nature:

> Dans des terrains cendreux, calcinés, sans verdure,
> Comme je me plaignais un jour à la nature,
> Et que de ma pensée, en vaguant au hasard,
> J'aiguisais lentement sur mon cœur le poignard

☞

> In an ashy, cindery terrain without greenery,
> One day as I was complaining to nature,
> And, wandering haphazardly, was slowly
> Sharpening thought's dagger on my heart . . .

> [Trans. James McGowan, modified]

But this poem exploits the structure and stance it mocks and demystifies.
Hearing him, demons in a cloud start chuckling and whispering about
this foolish creature:

> "Contemplons à loisir cette caricature
> Et cette ombre d'Hamlet imitant sa posture,
> Le regard indécis et les cheveux au vent.
> N'est-ce pas grand' pitié de voir ce bon vivant,
> Ce gueux, cet histrion en vacances, ce drôle,

Parce qu'il sait jouer artistement son rôle,
Vouloir intéresser au chant de ses douleurs
Les aigles, les grillons, les ruisseaux et les fleurs,
Et même à nous, auteurs de ces vieilles rubriques,
Réciter en hurlant ses tirades publiques?"

"Take your time to look at this caricature,
This shadow-Hamlet, who takes the pose—
The indecisive stare and blowing hair.
A pity, isn't it, to see this fraud,
This posturer, this actor on relief,
Because he artfully can play his role,
He thinks his shabby whining can engage
The eagles and the insects, brooks and flowers,
Even to us, who wrote these trite charades,
He shouts aloud all his public tirades."

When this poet complains to nature he gets a response—from the demons, who make fun of his pretension to interest the universe in his complaints, even as they take an interest. While the poem mocks this poetic posturing, it nevertheless confirms the structure of this relation in which the poet can address the universe and expect a response, albeit an ironic one. Demons in the clouds not only pay attention and respond, mockingly, but emerge as successful rivals for his mistress. Poems like this one, where mockery seems primary, nonetheless make clear that mockery depends upon the vatic presuppositions of the figure of apostrophe. The figure helps construct a hostile universe as well as a benign or responsive one, and the mockery of poetic pretension provides what William Empson calls a "pseudo-parody that disarms criticism."[46]

"Le Lac" does not mock the apostrophic stance but adopts another strategy. It demands that eternity speak, that the lake look, and that time stop, but like many apostrophic lyrics, it also recognizes that such requests are vain. Stanza 8 admits that time will not stop: "But in vain I ask for a few moments more. / Time escapes me and flees." And the poem—this is quite characteristic—progresses from the impossible requests to these nonhuman addressees to requests that are more plausible, that could even be imagined as fulfilled, like Ammons's command to the river not to turn back. Having demanded that eternity speak, the poem moves on to conclude by asking the lake, the silent rocks, grottoes, and woods to preserve the memory of their love. How will they do that? By allowing it to live on in the regular action of wave and breeze, in everything we hear or breathe.

> Ô lac! rochers muets! grottes! forêt obscure!
> Vous, que le temps épargne ou qu'il peut rajeunir,
> Gardez de cette nuit, gardez, belle nature,
> Au moins le souvenir!
> . . . . .
> Qu'il soit dans le zéphyr qui frémit et qui passe,
> Dans les bruits de tes bords par tes bords répétés,
> Dans l'astre au front d'argent qui blanchit ta surface
> De ses molles clartés.
>
> Que le vent qui gémit, le roseau qui soupire,
> Que les parfums légers de ton air embaumé,
> Que tout ce qu'on entend, l'on voit ou l'on respire,
> Tout dise : Ils ont aimé!

☞

> O lake! silent rocks! caves! dark forest!
> You whom Time spares or can make young again,
> Keep of that night, keep, lovely nature
> at least the memory!
> . . . . .
> May it be in the soft wind that shivers and passes,
> in the sounds of your banks, by your banks repeated,
> in the star with silver brow that whitens your surface
> with limpid clearness.
>
> May the wind that groans, the reed that sighs,
> May the soft scent of your fragrant air,
> May everything that can be heard, seen or breathed
> All say: they have loved!

If the poem is successful, it will not have made eternity speak or time stop, but it will have produced a more plausible effect, making us think of the activities of nature as repeating "ils ont aimé!" "Le Lac" gives us, then, first a vatic posture of address to entities treated as subjects, second, impossible requests, already recognized as impossible, and, finally, requests that could be accomplished through the poem. Despite the proliferation of impossible requests, by treating natural forces as addressable subjects and then formulating more modest demands, the poem may succeed in its quasi-magical quest of enlisting the universe in the scenario of commemoration.

Apostrophic poems display in various ways awareness of the difficulties of what they purport to seek. Poems that boldly apostrophize often end in questions and withdrawals. Keats's "Ode to a Nightingale" presents an ecstatic engagement with the nightingale and all that it might represent but concludes, "the fancy cannot cheat so well / as she is famed to do, deceiving elf." She deceives by not deceiving effectively and leaving us with questions:

Was it a vision or a waking dream?
Fled is that music:—Do I wake or sleep?

The questions about the status of the encounter render uncertain any claims that might be made for what it could impart—James Longenbach speaks of "the tissue of equivocations that constitutes our experience of the poem"—but they leave us with the poetic event itself.[47]

Other poems, instead of posing questions about the efficacy of the apostrophic act, foreground and parody their own apostrophic procedures. Baudelaire's "Le Cygne" begins with an apostrophe "Andromaque, je pense à vous" ("Andromaque, I think of you"). Then the swan of the title, nostalgically seeking his "beau lac natal" in "un ruisseau sans eau" ("the beautiful lake of his birth in a stream without water") apostrophizes "Eau" itself: "Eau, quand donc pleuvra tu? quand tonneras-tu, foudre?" ("Water, when will you rain? When will you thunder, lightning?") The fact that the sound of "eau" is identical to the apostrophic "O" could prompt various interpretations: the absence of *eau* is what generates the apostrophe, as if the apostrophic "O" implies a lack; the nostalgic quest for a moment or place of origin, the "eau" of a "beau lac natal," yields only an "O" of a trope; or the pun identifies the potential addressee of every apostrophe as the apostrophic "O" itself and makes every apostrophe an invocation of invocation. In any event, the poem foregrounds the apostrophic gesture, and links the apostrophizing swan with the exiled poet Victor Hugo, to whom the poem is dedicated:

> Je pense à mon grand cygne, avec ses gestes fous,
> Comme les exilés, ridicule et sublime
> Et rongé d'un désir sans trêve! . . .
>
> ⤳
>
> I think of my great swan, with his crazed gestures,
> Like all exiles, ridiculous and sublime,
> And gnawed by an unremitting desire. . . .

The poem offers a critique of the apostrophic gesture, which is ridiculous as well as sublime. When it seeks something other than itself *(eau)*, it finds only itself, "O." In these terms, the opening apostrophe to Andromaque, which seeks nothing but merely accomplishes what it declares, "I think of you!" is a demystified apostrophe. But if the swan is presented as ridiculous in its apostrophizing, this futile gesture helps make the swan a powerful symbol of loss and nostalgia for readers, of which the poet, who already sees the swan as a "mythe étrange et fatal," is only the first. The feeble apostrophizing *cygne* becomes, as critics invariably note, a powerful apostrophic *signe,* as readers embrace the feeling that the futility of the swan's apostrophe seems to be exposing. The swan's apostrophe makes nothing happen, but the poem survives, a way of happening, a beak.

Sometimes the apostrophic address works to create the voice of the sublime poet who seeks to arrest time, to harness the winds or the seasons, to call on the gods, though poems usually by the end retreat from such claims. The poet who hails time and urges it to do its work—"Devouring time, blunt thou the lion's paw"—but forbids it "one more heinous crime: / O, carve not with the hours my love's fair brow," in the end concedes his lack of power to forbid and embraces an alternative solution, but one still asserting the privilege of poetry: "Yet do thy worst, old Time! Despite thy wrong,/My love shall in my verse ever live young."[48]

Apostrophes posit a subject asked to respond in some way, if only by listening, but few are the poets who actually have the temerity to imagine an explicit response: Sappho, of course, as we saw in Chapter 1, Victor Hugo, who unabashedly presumes to make nature speak and reports "ce que dit la Bouche d'ombre" ("what the mouth of darkness says"). Some modern poets do so, but with canny strategies. Frank O'Hara, in "A True Account of Talking to the Sun at Fire Island," gives us a comic version of the aubade:

> The Sun woke me this morning loud
> and clear, saying "Hey! I've been
> trying to wake you up for fifteen
> minutes. Don't be so rude, you are
> only the second poet I've ever chosen
> to speak to personally
>
>   so why
> aren't you more attentive? If I could
> burn you through the window I would
> to wake you up. I can't hang around
> here all day."
>   "Sorry, Sun, I stayed
> up late last night talking to Hal."

In a reversal of Donne's "The Sun Rising," instead of the poet complaining to the sun for bringing to an end a night of love, the sun complains to the poet (though the sun goes on to say he likes his poetry and not to worry about the people who say he is crazy).

But joking is not the only strategy. Ammons, in a posthumously published poem, "Aubade," takes up the question of address in the lyric tradition. The "you" of poetic address once associated with natural objects vatically invoked, and which can be read as God or the beloved, continues to have a function, he suggests, but the "you" is now elusive, "nowhere to/be found or congratulated." The second half of "Aubade" expatiates on lyric address:

Sometimes when I say
"you" in my poems and appear to be addressing
the lord above, I'm personifying the contours

of the on high, the ways by which the world
works, however hard to see: for the on high

is every time the on low, too, and in the
middle: one lifts up one's voice to the

lineations of singing and sings, in effect,
you, you are the one, the center, it is around

you that the comings and goings gather, you
are the before and after, the around and

through: in all your motions you are ever still,
constant as motion itself: there with

you we abide, abide the changes, abide the
dissolutions and recommencements of our very

selves, abide in your abiding: but of course
I don't mean "you" as anyone in particular

but I mean the center of motions millions of
years have taught us to seek: now with

space travel and gene therapy that "you" has
moved out of the woods and rocks and streams

and traveled on out so far into space that it
rounds the whole and is, in a way, nowhere to

be found or congratulated, and so what is out
there dwells in our heads now as a bit of

yearning, maybe vestigial, and it is a yearning
like a painful sweetness, a nearly reachable

presence that nearly feels like love, something
we can put aside as we get up to rustle up a

little breakfast or contemplate a little
weight loss, or gladden the morning by getting
off to work. . . . [his ellipsis].

Harold Bloom suggests that in Shelley's highly apostrophic poems, such as "Ode to the West Wind," "to invoke the Spirit that is in the West Wind is not to invoke the wind or the autumn only" but to address an ultimate Thou behind it.[49] Ammons notes that his poetic "you" may appear to invoke an ultimate Thou but is really a personifying of the ways in which the world works, an indeterminate you as a principle of order or source of value. In his account of the flight of the gods the "you" of lyric address has left the woods and rocks and streams, creating for the modern poet the problem of what to praise or "congratulate." What before was outside, in an animated universe, now dwells in our heads as a framework of yearning, a "nearly reachable presence, that nearly feels like love," but Ammons cannot allow himself to halt at that yearning, which easily becomes embarrassing, and must, in his conversational tone, undercut his vision by noting that the yearnings, the presences of these overt and spectral "you"s, are only language, which we can put aside as we rustle up breakfast, contemplate weight loss, and get off to work. The apostrophic gesture can be pushed aside for worldly reasons. I note that the collection in which "Aubade" appears is entitled *Bosh and Flapdoodle*.

Apostrophes work to constitute as addressees things that are not normally addressed and thus to foreground the peculiar and nonmimetic character of the speech events they generate. Frequently, though not always, they work to establish a vatic stance, where voice engages an addressable world, of entities asked to respond in some way, as in Shelley's address to the wild West Wind,

Be thou spirit fierce, my spirit,
Be thou me, impetuous one . . .
Be through my lips to unawakened earth
The trumpet of a prophecy . . .

The poem itself should count as the response of the wind as, scattering thoughts like leaves, it ventriloquizes the prophetic agency of the wind.

Apostrophic poems often seek the risk of conjuring up actions, with the radical gesture of Keats's charioteer in "Sleep and Poetry":

> The charioteer with wondrous gesture talks
> To the trees and mountains; and there soon appear
> Shapes of delight, of mystery and fear.

The Keatsian claim makes apparent the connection between apostrophe and embarrassment. Such vatic pretensions always carry the risk that readers, and indeed poets themselves, with find them excessive. We critics can temper our embarrassment by treating apostrophe as a poetic convention and the summoning of spirits as a relic of archaic beliefs. What is really in question, though, is the power of poetry to make something happen. If, as Auden says, the poem is "A way of happening, a mouth," we can look to apostrophe as more than just the happening of sound. The vocative of apostrophe is an approach to the event because its animate presuppositions are deeply embedded, asserted the more forcefully because they are not what the utterance asserts. Just as the question "Have you stopped beating your wife?" thrusts its presuppositions on the listener with the force of an event, constitutes an event against which one must struggle, so the presuppositions of apostrophe are a force to be reckoned with. A nicely self-reflexive example is Lamartine's apostrophic question, "Objets inanimés, avez-vous donc une âme?" ("Inanimate objects, do you have a soul?"), which presupposes what it purports to ask about.[50] In the difference between asking whether inanimate objects have a soul and asking **them** whether they have a soul lies a key to the effect of apostrophe. The vocative posits a relationship between two subjects even if the sentence containing it denies the animicity of what is addressed, as in Baudelaire's apostrophe to a portion of the self in "Spleen II":

> Désormais tu n'es plus, o matière vivante,
> Qu'un granit entouré d'une vague épouvante.

> Henceforth, o living matter, you are
> But a granite form shrouded in vague horror.

The assertion of the sentence contradicts its presupposition, as in Rousseau's complaint to inanimate objects: "Êtres insensibles et morts, ce charme n'est point en vous; il ne saurait y être; c'est dans mon cœur qui veut tout rapporter à lui" ("Insensible and dead beings, this charm is not in you; it could not be; it is my own heart which brings everything back to itself").[51] The animicity enforced by the apostrophe is independent of any claims about the actual properties of the object addressed.

A particularly daring contemporary project of animation is Louise Gluck's *The Wild Iris,* which posits a responsive nature that actually responds, as various flowers address the poet or gardener (though the perspective of a flower is sufficiently unfamiliar that it is often hard to tell exactly what is happening, and who is saying "you" to whom). In "The Gold Lily" a flower addresses a human gardener.

> As I perceive
> I am dying now and know
> I will not speak again, will not
> survive the earth, be summoned
> out of it again, not
> a flower yet, a spine only, raw dirt
> catching my ribs, I call you,
> father and master: all around,
> my companions are failing, thinking
> you do not see. How
> can they know you see
> unless you save us?
> In the summer twilight, are you
> close enough to hear
> your child's terror? Or
> are you not my father,
> you who raised me?

This is a daring prosopopoeia, in which the poet moves beyond apostrophes that make the flower a potentially animate subject to give the flower a voice and a radically different perspective on the world, as it addresses us. Poems like this, when they effectively imagine and animate an otherness to which we can lend credence, however briefly, fulfill a long-standing lyric task of making a planet into a world.[52]

A specific effect of apostrophic address is to posit a world in which a wider range of entities can be imagined to exercise agency, resisting our usual assumptions about what can act and what cannot, experimenting with the overcoming of ideological barriers that separate human actors from everything else. "This function of invocation appears to me so important," writes Friedrich Kittler, "because thereby the limits of the human are transgressed."[53] It posits a third realm, neither human nor natural, that can act and determine our world. Ideologies always allow some hypostasized entities to figure as the subject of active verbs: today we can say "Time will tell," "the Heart knows," and "the Market will determine the winners," or at least "History will judge"—poetic figures all. For us, "Speed kills," but for the lyric tradition "Beauty kills." Why cannot flowers ask that we save them? Would we not be better off had we more vividly imagined nature as an actor rather than matter to be exploited for our purposes? Theodor Adorno remarks that we have lost nature and can only hope to restore or regain it through personification: "Only after transformation into human form can nature regain anew that which human rule has taken away." Various recent philosophical developments, from actor-network theory to object-oriented ontology and ecological theory, have questioned the exceptionality of the human subject, the notion that only humans can act, or as Jane Bennett puts it in *Vibrant Matter*, our "habit of parsing the world into dull matter (it, things) and vibrant life (us, beings)." How would things change, she asks, if we were to take seriously the vitality of non-human bodies, their ability not only to frustrate our plans (we've always known that) but to act as quasi-agents, as well?[54] Bruno Latour's actor-network theory describes the "distributed cognition" that makes it plausible to consider many sorts of things as agents if the universe is to become intelligible to us.[55] The poets, though, were here first. They have risked embarrassment in addressing things that could not hear in an attempt to give us a world that is perhaps not more intelligible but more in tune with the passionate feelings, benign, hostile, and ecstatic, that life has inspired. The testing of ideological limits through the multiplication of the figures who are urged to act, to listen, or to respond is part of the work of lyric.

I take the structure of indirect address to be central to the lyric. In fact, it is surprising that this has not been more widely accepted, since to address someone directly—an individual or an audience—one would not write a poem. Composing a poem, even a poem to a lover that one hopes no one else will ever see, introduces a certain indirection. I would suggest that there is always an indirect "you" in the lyric—"one lifts one's voice to the lineations of singing," writes Ammons, "and sings, in effect, you"—as lyrics strive to be an event in the special temporality of the lyric present. Often that "you" is expressed—the "you" of the beloved, or God, the wind, a flower. But sometimes it is not, and lingers as a spectral presence, a yearning, something like love.

SIX

Lyric Structures

What different sorts of lyrics should we distinguish? What structures or modes of organization, in addition to rhythm and sound patterning, are particularly important or distinctive? In the tradition of composing and reflecting on lyric, we have, of course, well-attested sub-genres, such as ode, elegy, song, epitaph, hymn, and others, more adventitious. The historian of genre Alastair Fowler makes the surprising claim that "Most short poems of our time belong to well-defined subgenres. But these modern subgenres are so numerous that, being mostly unlabeled, they are unrecognized in the main and hard to describe." It seems rather strange—perhaps reflecting the deep desire of an expert on genre?—to say that most poems belong to well-defined subgenres, if one then notes that these are not only mainly unrecognized but also hard to describe. If they are well defined, should one not be able to define them? Is the idea that they are recognized by the poets but not by readers or critics, or that they are recognized and defined only by a few knowledge-able professionals who have not deigned to reveal these secrets to the world? Fowler himself writes of these unrecognized subgenres, "A few can be designated briefly, however: the confessional poem, the satirical last will and testament; the epigram on a historical personage; the message from a symbolic country; and the sinister catechism."[1] Aside from the confessional poem, the others are so oddly specific and unusual—is he, perhaps, pulling our leg with this Borgesian list?—that one would have to imagine many dozen such types to have a chance of providing genres for the range of modern poems. Unfortunately, Fowler does not see this as his task, even in a book entitled *Kinds of Literature*. Modern poetry awaits the description of its many "well-defined" genres.

For want of information about the unrecognized subgenres of lyric, we could revert to the recognized ones, whose extraordinarily heterogeneity is testimony both to the unsystematic character of much theorizing about literature and to the way in which literary forms develop unpredictably from other prior forms. Some, such as sonnet, villanelle, rondeau, sestina, haiku, are defined by verse and stanza structure, though they are likely to have acquired thematic associations because of the topics they have most memorably articulated. Others are defined by their ostensible occasions: the aubade, the epithalamion, the epitaph, the elegy in the modern sense, the hymn, the invitation poem or carpe diem. Still others by a combination of formal qualities and thematic orientation: an ode is a poem in stanzas of celebration or commemoration; the ballad (not the French ballade) is a poem in four-beat quatrains, usually rhyming abcb, sometimes alternating four-beat and three-beat lines, deploying a narrative of popular character. Helen Vendler's influential textbook lists possible types of poem by form and occasion, of course, but also by speech act (confession, meditation, prayer, prophecy, praise), and by subject (flower poem, bird poem, travel poem, sea poem).[2]

Such lists may seem haphazard and do not pretend to divide the domain of lyric, but are pedagogically useful, alerting readers to the sorts of things poems may be doing, and they do capture a salient fact about the lyric tradition: if I write a poem about a bird I doubtless have in mind other poems about birds from the tradition. Insofar as poems about birds are a recognized type, it will matter whether I write about a nightingale, a thrush, a swan, an oven bird, or a crow because of the role accorded to these birds in prior poems. Contributions to the study of the lyric often take the form of identifying a particular sort of poem—a tradition not previously recognized but which seems significant once it is identified: the country house poem, the walk poem, the lyric of inconsequence.[3] Grouping poems as instances of a type both singles out something notable that poets have done and makes salient the variations within this type.

Such categories are valuable as a way of indicating the sorts of things that lyrics do and identifying different possibilities of lyric structure. As should be abundantly clear by now, defense of the lyric as a general category is not a claim for sameness but the promotion of a framework within which a history and/or pedagogy of lyric possibilities can be explored. What sorts of distinctive lyric structures can we discover? I speak of "lyric structures" both because the term *lyric form* is best reserved for types defined by formal structure, such as the sonnet, villanelle, or sestina, and because my interest in the possibilities of lyric focuses as much on aspects of lyric and particular strategies and configurations within lyrics as on recognized types of lyric.

1. Mapping the Lyric

There is one ambitious attempt to map the domain of the lyric that we ought to consider, both because it identifies a wide range of lyric types and because as a concrete proposal that seeks to be comprehensive it provides grounds for discussion: Is this a good way to get at the possibilities of lyric or are there better? In the *Anatomy of Criticism*, after defining lyric in terms of a "radical of presentation" (lyric as overheard), Northrop Frye proceeds, in a discussion of what he calls "specific thematic forms," to list various sorts of lyric. He notes that his list "will not give, and is not intended to give, a classification of specific forms of lyric: what it attempts to give is an account of the chief conventional themes" and "to show empirically how conventional archetypes get embodied in conventional genres."[4] But of course many lyric subspecies are named after themes, whether carpe diem poem, dream vision, or epitaph. Though the entries sound like types of lyric, one should no doubt accept Frye's disclaimer and think of the terms used in the diagram below, created by Robert Denham, as lyric conventions or thematic possibilities rather than lyric species, conceived as a continuum.[5]

These possibilities are arranged on the perimeter of a circle which is defined in relation to several oppositions. First there is the opposition between spectacle and mimesis, with forms nearer to the top tending to epiphany and ritual and those at the bottom to plot or representation. Running clockwise, then, the circle represents a movement from spectacle to mimesis and back to spectacle again. There is also, for Frye, a movement from innocence to experience and from something like inner-directedness to outward-directedness and back again. It is also obvious to a reader of Frye that there is a movement from an orientation toward God at the top to an orientation toward a godless world at the bottom, where the nadir is an ironic emptiness. Equally important, what distinguishes the right-hand side of the circle from the left is the opposition between the fundamental elements of lyric, *melos* and *opsis,* or charm and riddle, sound patterning and puzzle.

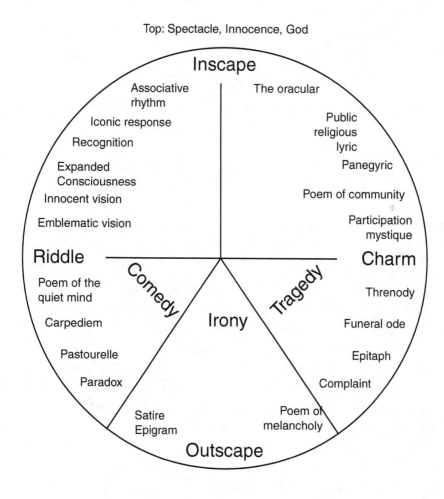

Top: Spectacle, Innocence, God

Inscape

Associative rhythm

The oracular

Iconic response

Public religious lyric

Recognition

Panegyric

Expanded Consciousness

Poem of community

Innocent vision

Emblematic vision

Participation mystique

Riddle — Charm

Comedy

Tragedy

Poem of the quiet mind

Threnody

Carpediem

Irony

Funeral ode

Pastourelle

Epitaph

Paradox

Complaint

Satire Epigram

Poem of melancholy

Outscape

Bottom: Mimesis, Experience, the Fallen World

At the top, then, are forms most invested in what Frye calls the oracular associative rhythm of lyric (see Chapter 4), here seen as the combination of incantatory sound patterns (charm) and ambiguous meaning
(riddle).[6] One of the "most direct products" of oracular associative rhythm,
he writes, "is a type of religious poetry marked by a concentration of sound
and ambiguity of sense." Between this inner-focused epiphanous poetry
and the cardinal point of *melos,* charm, lie poems in an oracular tradition, including religious poetry, psalms and hymns. The religious poem,
as it becomes more dignified and less ambiguous, moving away from riddle
toward charm, becomes more public: "the 'I' of the poem is one of a visible community of worshippers, and the syntax and diction become less
ambiguous"—whence such forms as the "Apollonian paean, the Hebrew
psalm, the Christian hymn, or the Hindu Vedas," which he calls "poems
of community." This category proves rather vast: it includes not only
panegyric—odes to gods and heroes, poems of triumph, festivity, and pro-
cession, epithalamia—but also praise of the courtly love mistress. The
poem of community approaches the rightmost cardinal point of the
lyric, *charm,* which involves "some kind of physical or quasi-physical
compulsion—perhaps propulsion is the word." "One's education in this
type of charm," Frye writes, "begins with nursery rhymes, where the infant is swung or bounced to the rhythm . . . It continues through college
yells, sing-songs, and similar forms of *participation mystique*" (293–295).

As we pass from the upper half of the circle, lyric innocence, to the lower
half, lyric experience, we find, first, forms with prominent sound patterning but of more tragic content, threnodies and funeral odes, and then,
as we descend toward representation, elegies and epitaphs, increasingly
ironic in mode (the three divisions of this lower half represent the lyric
counterparts of the tragic, ironic, and comic forms of drama). Moving toward irony, we encounter "the complaint, the poem of exile, neglect or
protest at cruelty," including complaint at the cruelty of the disdainful mistress, and then poems of melancholy or ennui, moving toward the low point
of experience or *outscape,* "a convention of pure projected detachment,
in which an image, a situation, or a mood is observed with all the imaginative energy thrown outward to it and away from the poet" (297).[7]

At the point in his notebooks when he expresses most confidence in
his chart ("the lyric wheel has cleared wonderfully and now seems to be

as it should, the simplest of all"), Frye has not yet added the *opsis/melos* dimension, and the progression down this side is a simple one: hymn to God, ode to hero or exalted mistress, poem to friend or lover, and epistle or satire focused on ordinary men.[8] Adding the dimension of charm and the move from innocence to experience and death, through the tragic, has complicated the chart. And the left-hand side is more complicated still. Moving around the *opsis*/riddle side of the diagram, we find epigram and satire. Then within the comic comes paradox: Frye mentions Shakespeare's sonnet "Th' Expense of Spirit in a Waste of Shame," the paradoxical conventions of metaphysical poetry, and the riddling poems of Emily Dickinson. He also places here the *pastourelle,* a medieval French lyric form in which a knight engages in a battle of wits with a shepherdess, and, finally, what he calls the "less ambiguous" forms of lyric comedy that we find in the carpe diem poem, which posit the possibility of pleasure in experience and can certainly be an instance of cleverness, like a riddle. Then, more mysteriously, comes what he calls the "poem of the quiet mind": he mentions descriptive poetry and Wordsworth. It seems especially odd for descriptive poetry and the quiet mind to come at what should be the maximum point of riddle, which usually disquiets the mind, but riddling haiku and koans may be used for meditation.

The last quadrant of the diagram, moving from *opsis* to innocence and associative rhythm, is somewhat hard to fathom from the terms in the diagram, though Frye's comments make clear that it contains a good deal of important poetry. Riddle and wit, prominent in the lower left-hand quadrant, seem to be replaced by the visual dimension of *opsis: opsis* as image (as opposed to sound on the right-hand side), so emblem poems, such as Herbert's "The Pulley," then poems of innocent vision (he mentions Herrick and pastoral poetry), poems of vision in which the emblem is confronted, or "imaginative confrontation" (an important term not mentioned in Denham's diagram—an example is Keats's "Ode on a Grecian Urn,"), and then visionary "poems of expanded consciousness," such as Eliot's *Four Quartets* or Rilke's *Duino Elegies.* As we come back toward the beginning of the cycle we find more rhapsodic poems of "recognition" or "self-recognition," such as Coleridge's "Kubla Khan," Yeats's "Sailing to Byzantium," or Rilke's *Sonnets to Orpheus,* and finally more oracular poems of associative rhythm, such as mad songs.

The fundamental contrasts in Frye's scheme are between *melos* and *opsis,* sound patterning and riddle/image, and between an inner-focused, associative lyric ("inscape") and an outer-focused mimetic one ("outscape"), though, as befits an eminent Blake scholar, he also labels this second opposition "innocence" versus "experience." In addition, Frye elsewhere gives weight to the distinction between the hieratic and the demotic. "The hieratic poet finds, with Valéry, that the kind of poetry he wants to write depends, like chess, on complex and arbitrary rules, and he experiments with patterns of rhythm, rhyme and assonance, as well as with mythological and other forms of specifically poetic imagery. The demotic tendency is to minimize the difference between literature and speech, to seek out the associative or prose rhythms that are used in speech and reproduce them in literature."[9] This pair of terms, together with the three traditional rhetorical levels, can produce yet another matrix of classes: high, middle, and low hieratic; high, middle, and low demotic. The hieratic/demotic distinction would be hard to fit into the wheel, since demotic forms may belong both with the simplicity of innocence and with satire or comedy's tough-minded avoidance of or deflation of intricacies of sound and sense. And "high hieratic" might be either the oracular lyric of Hopkins's "Windhover,"

> Flesh fade, and mortal trash
> Fall to the residuary worm; ' world's wildfire, leave but ash:
> In a flash, at a trumpet crash,
> I am all at once what Christ is, ' since he was what I am . . .

or a poem of elegant melancholy, such as Keats's ode of that name:

> No, no, go not to Lethe, neither twist
> Wolf's-bane, tight-rooted, for its poisonous wine.

How should one evaluate a mapping of this sort? The fact that, despite the general importance of Frye's book, critics do not often discuss this scheme, even to attack it, suggests that they have not generally taken it to be an important or successful summary of lyric possibilities; but others have not come up with better ways of classifying literary themes, so quite possibly Frye's scheme seems too overwhelming to take on. Alastair Fowler, in a brief indictment of the general project of mapping genres (not the lyric diagram), maintains that "the comprehensive map is a chimera," and mapping genres is theoretically unsound since maps order things in relation to only two axes: the presence, to a greater or lesser degree, of two qualities and their opposites.[10] Frye provides a diagram rather than just a list of themes in order to show that the domain of lyric (like that of literature in general, in Frye's account) is a not just a random collection of works: there is a structure of knowledge, which readers gradually build up, predicated on the range of possible imaginative engagements with human experience. His chart does suggest this: though ever-finer discriminations of themes and types of poems are possible, they take place within an order, an overall structure. The fact that one can quarrel with his chart, arguing that a particular sort of poem should be closer to charm, or that descriptive poetry should not go with riddle, suggests that the domain of lyric is not felt to be completely unordered and that Frye's goal is not a preposterous one, even if success seems unlikely.

At one point in his notebooks Frye writes, "I wish I had some rudimentary notion of how to go about classifying lyrics: even a fertilizing suggestion about it would be something."[11] He has, at least, succeeded in this: the chart and catalogue set forth the great range of things lyrics do in what is considerably more than a list: a claim about the principal oppositions that structure this conceptual space.

Difficulties arise, as I have suggested, especially through the attempt to include more than two parameters at once: the god/hero/mistress/friend/man sequence, the opposition between the individual and the social, innocence versus experience, and self-reference versus mimesis are all on one axis, set against the opposition between riddle and charm or visual patterning versus sound; and this latter (horizontal) axis also deploys the tragic/ironic/comic continuum, for instance. Since there are very many oppositions that could be used to chart lyric themes, the restriction to two dimensions necessarily jumbles together possibilities which may coincide but may also be quite unlike. If one were seriously to treat lyric as a domain to be mapped, one would need a multidimensional space.

But of course lyric is not a domain in which spatial relations among poems or types of poems are there to be discovered and mapped. It is an open-ended tradition of poems that can be related to one another in myriad ways, through features they share or modify. Mapping suggests that lyric is a domain set off from other sorts of poetry, but of course the oppositions used to chart this alleged domain involve features that appear in other poems as well—a fact one needs to accept rather than conceal. Since I am less interested in attempting to describe lyric themes than in particular aspects of lyrics and the different ways in which lyrics are structured, mapping a domain as a continuum is not the best approach; but for some aspects of lyric, a spatial organization can certainly aid reflection—it is a way of representing some relations among possibilities. In order to consider further what I have called the ritualistic dimension of lyric, I will therefore pursue Frye's distinction between *melos* and *opsis,* sound patterning and visual patterning, as a space to be mapped, after which I will abandon mapping in order to discuss other aspects of lyric and its structures, particularly the hyperbolic character of lyric and the ritual framing or deploying of lyric's fictional elements.

Melos and *opsis,* or *babble* and *doodle, charm* and *riddle,* are aspects of lyric that help it establish itself in its specificity as iterable form. One mode of *opsis* crucial to the ritualistic dimension of lyric is the visual delineation of lines and stanzas. Poems organized in stanzas, for instance, have a structural potential visually given in advance: a set of units that are equivalent but disjoined, so that the question of how the stanzas relate to each other necessarily arises. In Lorca's "La Luna asoma," discussed in Chapter 1, the separation of stanzas visually emphasizes the disjunction between "No one eats oranges / Under the full moon" and the coins of silver that "Start sobbing in the pocket" when the moon rises. How can they be related? How does the order of stanzas matter? The separation of stanzas offers the possibility of a progression or else a nonprogressive set of alternative statements or images. For lyrics without rhymes especially, or those where rhymes are infrequent and do not demarcate the ends of lines, the visual form of the poem both confers an identity as poem and marks the units which are to be treated as equivalent. In free verse especially, those silent breaks are the most salient markers of verse structure.[12]

Conceived as a spatial domain, lyric lies between the pictorial and the musical, and *opsis* and *melos* are its poles. The melic limit of lyric would be pure babble: meaningless magic spells or tongue-twisters such as "How much wood could a woodchuck chuck if a woodchuck could chuck wood"—not lyric but deploying techniques fundamental to lyric. Wallace Stevens's "Bantams in Pine Woods" gives us a remarkable display of orality, rivaling tongue-twisters:

Chieftain Iffucan of Azcan in caftan
Of tan with henna hackles, halt!

The other limit would be visual pattern, as in concrete poetry. Frye mentions the poems of e. e. cummings and George Herbert's "Easter-wings," a poem in the shape of angel's wings, as lyrics on the border of the pictorial.[13]

But Frye's examples make it clear that charm and riddle, or babble and doodle, each have two dimensions, two rather different ways of manifesting themselves. *Melos* can take the form of intense sound patterning, with nonsense as its limit, what Hegel called the *tra-la-la* function, as in the "hey nonny, nonny" of songs, or Max Jacob's famous line, "Dahlia! dahlia! que Delila lia," where the patterning it is fun to repeat takes precedence over any question of Delilah tying up dahlias.[14] The more such sound patterning is foregrounded, the more it evokes orality or voicing, but the less it represents any imaginable voice. We should, thus, distinguish *melos* as voicing from *melos* as an attempt to instantiate sound as voice, as the sound of speech, a goal in some of Frost's poems, for instance, or in poems that use dialect to provide an image of distinct voices (though often here we get not imitation of actual speech so much as a making strange of language through its material dimensions).

At the opposite pole, *opsis* (visual pattern, riddle, or doodle), we find two analogous possibilities: the poem as babble has as its counterpart the poem as doodle, an image that does not invite oral articulation, as in collages or various sorts of concrete poetry. In "Le sceptre miroitant," a poem by Michel Leiris (p. 254), reading in different directions one can make out the words *amour, miroir, mourir, moi,* and even *roi* ("love," "mirror," "die," "me," "king") and can try to put them together conceptually, but one cannot, for instance, recite the poem: the image takes precedence over vocalization.

M O U R
   O
  M   U R I
A   I   R
   R
   O
   I
   R

In Guillaume Apollinaire's "Il pleut" ("It is raining"; p. 255), words can scarcely be made out—some easily, others less so; they are used as design elements.

If one labors to make out the words, one finds:

It's raining women's voices as if they had died even in memory
And it's raining you as well marvelous encounters of my life O little drops
Those rearing clouds begin to neigh a whole universe of auricular cities
Listen if it rains while regret and disdain weep to an ancient music
Listen to the bonds fall off which hold you above and below

[Trans. Roger Shattuck]

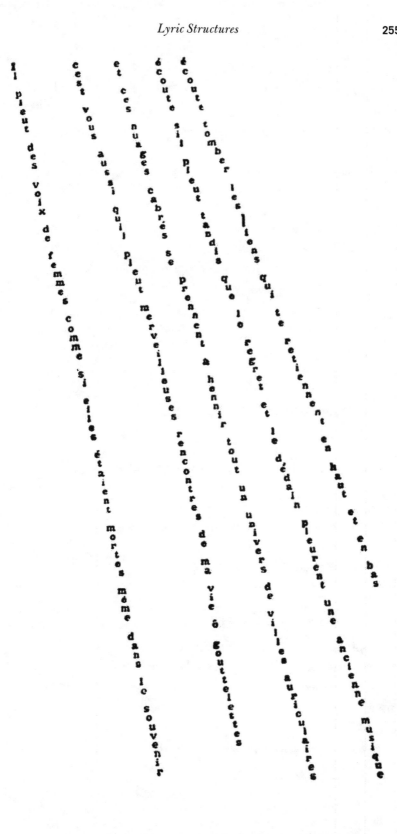

il pleut des voix de femmes comme si elles étaient mortes même dans le souvenir

c'est vous aussi qu'il pleut merveilleuses rencontres de ma vie ô gouttelettes

et ces nuages cabrés se prennent à hennir tout un univers de villes auriculaires

écoute s'il pleut tandis que le regret et le dédain pleurent une ancienne musique

écoute tomber les liens qui te retiennent en haut et en bas

The "opsic" counterpart of poem as representation of voice would be the poem as articulation or representation of an image, as in William Carlos Williams's scene of a red wheelbarrow beside the white chickens, or Pound's "In a Station of the Metro":

> The apparition of these faces in the crowd;
> Petals on a wet, black bough.

This manifestation of the visual pole, where the lyric is seen as above all a display of vivid images—striking ways of depicting the world—differs substantially from the poem which is itself a visual image. We thus have, diagramatically, for the opposition *opsis/melos:*

opsis	*melos*
the poem **is** a visual construction	the poem **is** sound patterning (voicing)
or	or
the poem **produces/represents** images	the poem **produces/represents** voices

The opposition between *melos* and *opsis* thus needs to be articulated with another opposition between the language as material form, letter, or sound, and language as mode of representation. In some respects this opposition corresponds to Frye's vertical axis, but that axis (innocence/experience, inner-directed/outer-directed) has other dimensions as well, all of which cannot be grouped together without conflating lyric possibilities that seem to ask to be distinguished.

There is a further complication entailed by Frye's specification of *opsis* as both riddle and doodle, two forms of puzzle. Frye's *opsis* as puzzle is both visual image (Herbert's "Easter-wings") and semantic riddle (Dickinson's "I like to see it lap the miles")—possibilities that rarely coincide but do come together in a poem such as e. e. cummings's "r-p-o-p-h-e-s-s-a-g-r," a visual poem, one that can scarcely be read in linear fashion but must be observed—a visual rather than auditory construction, where letters need to be rearranged in space.

r-p-o-p-h-e-s-s-a-g-r
  who
a)s w(e loo)k
upnowgath
  PPEGORHRASS
    eringint(o-
aThe):l
    eA
     !p:
S   a
      (r
rIvInG   .gRrEaPsPhOs)
             to
rea(be)rran(com)gi(e)ngly
,grasshopper;

But Frye also places under *opsis* verbal riddles without a visual dimension, such as Emily Dickinson's

> It sifts from Leaden Sieves—
> It powders all the Wood.
> It fills with Alabaster Wool
> The Wrinkles of the road—

Here reading involves working out what the poem is talking about through its sequence of images (the answer is *snow*). Frye notes that there has long been a close link between the conceptual and the visual, which might justify his treating a semantic puzzle and a visual representation as the same pole in his diagram, though there is also, of course, a tradition of melic riddles based on puns.

Opsis and *melos* form a fundamental axis of opposition for the lyric, and each concept also points toward one boundary of the genre (visual art on the one hand; musicality on the other), but they do not form a simple opposition since each has at least two distinct manifestations, as represented by the diagram below.

LYRIC

Ritualistic

opsis   **melos**

poem as   poem as sound

visual image

(PURE PATTERN)   (NONSENSE)

VISUAL ART   MUSICALITY

poem articulates   poem articulates

images   voice

Dramatic monologue   *ballad*

Fictional

DRAMA   NARRATIVE

Opsis and *melos* are not equally essential: *melos* is fundamental to the lyric, but its visual form can be insignificant, except to mark lineation. Both, however, are versions of the dominant ritualistic dimension or pole of lyric. But to complete this mapping operation, we should note that there is another pole of lyric that points toward a boundary: fictionality. Narrative fiction, whether in verse or prose, drama or novel, can be added to our diagram, as lying beyond the domain of lyric. Dramatic monologues and ballads fall within lyric but on the borders of drama and fiction.

Using just two oppositions, as here, between *opsis* and *melos* and the ritualistic and fictional, it seems possible to give diagrammatic representation to something like a domain for the lyric, though the attempt to work this out reveals ambiguities in Frye's concepts, in *opsis* in particular. But if a diagram can help one think about a range of lyric strategies and poets' ways of pushing at what might seem to be the limits of the genre, an investigation of the genre needs also to focus on aspects that cannot easily be mapped.

2. Lyric Hyperbole

Before turning to lyric's ways of dealing with fictionality, which is both a feature of lyric and a border, I should take up one aspect of lyric I have frequently emphasized but not addressed directly: what I have called, after

Baudelaire, its hyperbolic character. This might seem a feature that could be treated as scalar, with at one pole the ecstatic, exaggerated claims so common to lyrics, from Baudelaire's description of a woman's eye as the livid sky where hurricanes breed, to the warning by Goethe's rose that the youth will always think of her, and at the other pole, the laconic notation of Frank O'Hara's "I-do-this, I-do-that" poems, for instance, where the effect in part derives from the contrast between the apparent triviality, the foregrounded aimlessness of miscellaneous acts or observations, and the presumption of lyric significance.

> Now when I walk around at lunchtime
> I have only two charms in my pocket
> an old Roman coin Mike Kanemitsu gave me
> and a bolt-head that broke off a packing case
> when I was in Madrid the others never
> brought me too much luck though they did
> help keep me in New York against coercion
> but now I'm happy for a time and interested

His "Personal Poem" continues on in much the same vein: nothing hyperbolic here, certainly. The presence or absence of hyperbole might therefore seem another opposition in an ideal mapping of lyric as a multidimensional space. But the hyperbolic character of lyric, I would argue, is like indirect address, which I take to be a fundamental underlying structure of lyric, sometimes explicitly realized in address to impossible auditors, at others times virtually at work in inflecting the circuit of communication in poems ostensibly addressed to others (Sappho's invocation of Aphrodite, Petrarch's sonnets to Laura), or in poems explicitly addressed to no one (Williams's "Red Wheelbarrow," Leopardi's "L'Infinito"). Like indirect address, hyperbole is a fundamental characteristic of the lyric which, when not manifest, takes the form of an underlying convention: that apparently trivial observations are of considerable significance. This is the convention that determines our response to Pound's "In the Station of the Metro" quoted earlier: that the apparition of faces in the crowd which look like petals on a wet black bough is somehow significant, a moment of epiphany, even, however hard this may be to explain.

What the philosopher H. R. Grice calls the "cooperative principle" is a fundamental axiom of communication: assume that your interlocutor is cooperating and saying something relevant, even if its relevance is not immediately evident. When we confront a work of literature, the cooperative principle is "hyper-protected," in that we go a long way in accepting obscurity, disjunction, or apparent irrelevance, on the assumption that these are deliberate and will turn out to be in some way efficacious.[15] With the lyric, the convention that whatever is written will prove to be important is particularly powerful, and crucial to the functioning of many modern lyrics especially, which end by noting a minor occurrence: a leaf falls; an old man sits on a doorstep; a dog barks in the distance. The notations of haiku figure as epiphanies, as in Richard Wright's

> Whitecaps on the bay:
> A broken signboard banging
> In the April wind.

This presumption of significance is what permits one to speak, however counterintuitively, of the hyperbolic character of laconic poems: there is an implicit claim that whatever is lyrically noted is of overweening importance, even in one of Williams's observational poems, such as

THE POOR OLD WOMAN

> munching a plum on
> the street a paper bag
> of them in her hand
> They taste good to her
> They taste good
> to her. They taste
> good to her.

No exaggeration here, though the experimentation with three ways of lineating the proposition "They taste good to her" makes it clear that we are expected to take this as relevatory, a suggestion that such simple pleasures as eating a plum that tastes good should be central to our experience of the world.

The tradition of overt hyperbole in lyric is evident in poems I have already discussed, such as Sappho's sublime response to the mere act of looking at the beloved:

> for when I look at you, even a moment, no speaking
> is left in me
>
> no: tongue breaks and thin
> fire is racing under the skin
> and in eyes no sight and drumming
> fills ears
>
> and cold sweat holds me and shaking
> grips me all, greener than grass
> I am and dead—or almost
> I seem to me.
>
> [Trans. Anne Carson]

Or there is Rilke's "Archaischer Torso Apollos," discussed in Chapter 5, which reverses the gaze: as you contemplate this statue, the torso observes you, and you must change your life. Lyrics in the Petrarchan tradition celebrate the extreme beauty, virtue, or cruelty, of the beloved, whose glance can slay—no need to multiply examples—and even ostensibly anti-Petrarchan lyrics, such as Shakespeare's Sonnet 130, verge on hyperbole:

> And yet, by heaven, I think my love as rare
> As any she belied with false compare.

Praise is one of the basic functions of lyric, but is often better accomplished with understatement, since the convention of significance gives understatement hyperbolic force.

Particularly striking in lyric is the way in which the hyperbolic presumption enables a poet to make a poem out of nothing at all. Yves Bonnefoy takes a stab at this:

LE PEU D'EAU

A ce flocon
Qui sur ma main se pose, j'ai désir
D'assurer l'éternel
En faisant de ma vie, de ma chaleur,
De mon passé, de ces jours d'à présent,
Un instant simplement: cet instant-ci, sans bornes.
Mais déjà il n'est plus
Qu'un peu d'eau, qui se perd
Dans la brume des corps qui vont dans la neige.

⌒

THE BIT OF WATER

This flake
Which alights on my hand, I desire
To make eternal,
By making my life, my warmth,
My past, my present days
Into a moment: the boundless moment of now.
But already it is no more
than a bit of water, which vanishes
In the fog of bodies moving through the snow.

[Trans. Hoyt Rogers]

The hyperbolic urge is manifest in the desire to condense one's life to an unbounded instant to assure eternity for this snowflake—something the poem itself can overweeningly attempt to do, so that the utterly predictable melting of the snowflake in the hand becomes a loss to be mourned, a symbol of transience.

Emily Dickinson rises to the occasion even more splendidly, avoiding the topoi of the snowflake and of the desire for eternity, in this remarkable poem:

A Thought went up my mind today—
That I have had before—

But did not finish—some way back—
I could not fix the Year—

Nor where it went—nor why it came
The second time to me—
Nor definitely, what it was—
Have I the Art to say—

But somewhere—in my Soul—I know—
I've met the Thing before—
It just reminded me—'twas all—
And came my way no more—

This little poem could be read as metacommentary on poets' vatic pretensions—as though any poetic thought would necessarily be significant and worth striving to preserve. But if the poem is making fun of that assumption, it also, of course, shows that even the most evanescent thought— one that cannot be specified at all—allows the self-realization of a poem. The thought itself is not invested with significance except as the occasion of a poetic event, created above all by the stanza form, which is the more impressive for the nullity of its referent. This little poem is paradigmatic for lyric in its exploitation of language's ability to make much of nothing, even as it slyly mocks that procedure. It also helps to justify the otherwise admittedly strange notion that there is an underlying hyperbolic character, part of the conventions of the genre, to even the most modest lyric poem.

3. Dramatic Monologue

I turn now to another set of lyric possibilities, involving the lyric control of fictional elements. In Chapter 2 I called the tension between the ritualistic and the fictional constitutive for lyric. Discussing this tension within lyric sequences, Roland Greene occasionally speaks of the *artifactual* and *nominative* dimensions of lyric—terms which make it clear that the two are not mutually exclusive. (The nominative elements work to construct a character/speaker and the artifactual to create an artifact available for iteration.)[16] At issue, then, for the lyric are relations between two forces rather than a continuum on which poems are situated, for while one or the other mode may explicitly predominate in a particular poem or group of poems, readers often may grant precedence to one or the other of these forces: reading the poem above all as instructions for performance, as language destined for recitation and repetition, or seeking to bypass ritualistic elements to find in the poem a plot and the representation of a character. The tension is especially palpable in the lyric sequence—Petrarch's *Canzionere,* Shakespeare's *Sonnets,* Baudelaire's *Les Fleurs du Mal,* Rilke's *Sonnets to Orpheus*—where the reader who chooses to read more than isolated poems works to construct character and plot from the discontinuous lyrics but always encounters ritualistic elements that do not contribute to any construction of fictions: metrical schemes, rhymes, and sound patterns, elaborate figuration, and lyric address. Käte Hamburger is fundamentally correct, I have argued, in asserting that lyric is not fictional discourse but disquisition about the world, but lyrics frequently contain fictional elements—representations of characters and events—so the various ways in which these elements are organized or controlled is of major interest for any account of lyric. I take up first the lyric production of fictional speakers, of which the dramatic monologue is the extreme example, and then turn to the representation of events and especially the temporal strategies deployed to bring these events into the predominately ritualistic structure of lyrics.

Chapter 3 described the strange process by which the dramatic monologue has come to serve as the implicit model for the lyric in general in Anglo-American criticism and lyric pedagogy. As Randall Jarrell already observed in 1953, it went from being an exception to being the norm.[17] If the lyric is bordered by sonorous nonsense on one side and the purely visual arrangements of concrete poetry on the other, the dramatic monologue lies at the limit of lyric on a third side, in the direction of narrative fiction and drama, at the borderline between lyric and fiction. While large numbers of lyrics, from Goethe's "Heidenröslein" to cummings's "r-p-o-p-h-e-s-s-a-g-r," do not project a speaker and we gain nothing by trying to imagine one, there are, of course, many poems that do project a speaker. Driven by a desire to resist the notion of the lyric as the poet's cri de coeur, critics since the mid-twentieth century have made it an article of faith that, as John Crowe Ransom put it, "The poet does not speak in his own but in an assumed character, not in the actual but in an assumed situation, and the first thing we do as readers of poetry is to determine precisely what character and what situation are assumed. In this examination lies the possibility of critical understanding and, at the same time, of the illusion and the enjoyment." From there it takes only a small leap for Ransom to conclude that the poem "may be said to be a dramatic monologue . . . Browning only literalized and made readier for the platform or the concert hall the thing that had always been the poem's lawful form."[18] It takes a powerful ideology to imagine other forms of lyric as unlawful.

As I argued in Chapter 3, the dramatic monologue is only a particular form of lyric and not the general model for lyric, but it is crucial to a theory of the lyric both to give this form its due and to delimit it, to prevent it from functioning as a lazy general model for all poetry, as it easily may for those accustomed to narrative fiction. The dramatic monologue can be said to have developed in nineteenth-century England as an attempt at a more "objective" form of lyric, and in the hands of Robert Browning especially, who called these poems of his "dramatic lyrics." They vividly dramatize distinct historical characters (generally fictional) in specific circumstances, as they respond to a situation, debate with themselves, or interact with implied audiences. There are, of course, precedents for poems presenting particular speakers in defined situations, from Alcaeus through Wordsworth, but with Browning it becomes a recognized type.

One should note at the outset, though, that there are really two traditions of dramatic monologue.[19] Browning's dramatic monologues attempt to portray a fictional speaker through his or her own words and thus often involve a mimesis of speech (this is what underlies Barbara Herrnstein Smith's theory of the lyric as a fictional imitation of personal utterance). But there is another strain, largely French, which owes much to the formal speeches of classical French drama: monologues in balanced alexandrines and self-consciously poetic language that do not at all attempt to imitate actual speech. Important poems by Mallarmé and Valéry are presented as the inner or overt speech of fictional speakers, mythological rather than historicized personages: a faun in Mallarmé's "L'Après-midi d'un faune" ("The Afternoon of a Faun") who muses about an amorous encounter with nymphs that morning; the youngest of the three Fates in Valéry's "La jeune parque" ("The Young Fate"), who soliloquizes on the seashore about time and eternity, in lines that make no concession to speech; or the Satanic serpent in Valéry's "Ebauche d'un serpent" ("Sketch of a Serpent"), which Yvor Winters called the greatest poem ever written for its engagement with large moral and philosophical issues. Here is the beginning of "L'Après-midi d'un faune":

Ces nymphes, je les veux perpétuer.
                    Si clair,
Leur incarnat léger, qu'il voltige dans l'air
Assoupi de sommeils touffus.

                    Aimai-je un rêve?
Mon doute, amas de nuit ancienne, s'achève
En maint rameau subtil, qui, demeuré les vrais
Bois mêmes, prouve, hélas! que bien seul je m'offrais
Pour triomphe la faute idéale de roses.
Réfléchissons . . .

                    ou si les femmes dont tu gloses
Figurent un souhait de tes sens fabuleux!

These nymphs, I would perpetuate them.
                    So bright
Their crimson flesh that hovers there, light
In the air drowsy with dense slumbers.
                    Did I love a dream?
My doubt, mass of ancient night, ends extreme
In many a subtle branch, that remaining the true
Woods themselves, proves, alas, that I too
Offered myself, alone, as triumph, the false ideal of roses.

Let's see . . .
                    or if those women you note
Reflect your fabulous senses' desire!

                              [Trans. A. S. Kline]

The faun muses about an encounter with two nymphs, which he fears he may only have dreamt, as reflections of his own desire ("Did I love a dream?"). Mallarmé puts several sections of the poem in quotation marks and italics, as if they were speech. These are sequences in the past tense, somewhat clearer than the rest of the poem, one block introduced as "SOU-VENIRS" ("memories") and another by the command, ostensibly to Sicilian shores, to "CONTEZ" ("tell"), but these lines too are first-person discourse of the faun, like the rest. It is a poem of sensuous imagery and indeterminate musing about the reality of the encounter with the nymphs, cast in rhymed alexandrine couplets, though these are mildly disguised by breaking up lines and skipping lines between fragments (so "Ces nymphes, je les veux perpétuer. . . . Si clair" forms a single twelve-syllable alexandrine). The poem is not a depiction of character or of speech but the euphonious imagination of a lush, indeterminate sensuality of a sort easy to attribute to a world of fauns and nymphs.

Many other poems in the French tradition give us a first-person speaker, often easy to identify with the poet, in an identifiable situation—I discussed Valéry's "La Dormeuse" in Chapter 4—but as in that case, such poems generally do not take the form of a particular sort of fictional speech act. Those that do so most plausibly tend to be love poems, ostensibly addressed to the beloved, where the focus falls on the particular amorous gesture that seems to be undertaken. Baudelaire's "Une Charogne" ("A Carcass") is one of the most notorious: a speaker reminds his mistress, going into considerable detail, of a rotting carcass they encountered this morning, and end ends by telling her,

> —Et pourtant vous serez semblable à cette ordure,
> À cette horrible infection,
> Etoile de mes yeux, soleil de ma nature,
> Vous, mon ange et ma passion!

> —And yet you will be like this excrement,
> This horrible infection,
> O star of my eyes, sun of my being,
> You, my angel, my passion.

> [Trans. Geoffrey Wagner]

This poem in quatrains, with prominent rhyming of alternating alexandrines and octosyllabic lines, turns out, strangely, not to be a carpe diem poem. Instead of urging the woman to make love while she is not yet rotting, the poem suggests that when that day comes she tell the worms, "who will devour you with kisses, / That I have preserved the form and divine essence of my decomposed loves." This turns out to be, implausibly, a poem about the achievements of poetic form, even though what is here preserved is scarcely a divine essence but a description of a rotting carcass set upon by flies and larvae. Though quite different from the poems by Valéry and Mallarmé mentioned above, this poem, like them, does not attempt to capture a character through his or her speech. Unlike the English dramatic monologue, it is more ritualistic than fictional, despite its presentation of grotesque incident.

The attractions of the English dramatic monologue are rather different. Browning's "My Last Dutchess," the most famous of the tradition, is written in rhymed pentameter couplets but with so much enjambment that the rhymes are quite unobtrusive and students frequently recall it as a poem in blank verse rather than in rhymed couplets. The concealment of artifactuality, the creation of the impression of someone speaking, is at the center of its achievement and, along with the sense that the Duke is revealing his evil character without fully meaning to, is responsible for its fame.

> . . . Sir, 'twas not
> Her husband's presence only called that spot
> Of joy into the Duchess' cheek: perhaps
> Frà Pandolf chanced to say, "Her mantle laps
> Over my lady's wrist too much," or "Paint
> Must never hope to reproduce the faint
> Half-flush that dies along her throat": such stuff
> Was courtesy, she thought, and cause enough
> For calling up that spot of joy. . . .

In other monologues by Browning, though, the verse form is very prominent: "Soliloquy in a Spanish Cloister" uses much colloquial language— "Gr-r-r-there go, . . ." it begins—but in tetrameter quatrains rhymed *abab*, so that the ritualistic element is foregrounded and, though it is very lively language, it is not, for modern readers at least, a mimesis of speech:

> Gr-r-r-there go, my heart's abhorrence!
> Water your damned flower-pots, do!
> If hate killed men, Brother Lawrence,
> God's blood, would not mine kill you!
> What? your myrtle-bush wants trimming?
> Oh, that rose has prior claims—
> Needs its leaden vase filled brimming?
> Hell dry you up with its flames!

"Porphyria's Lover," the soliloquy of a young man who murdered his lover, is another four-beat poem with a stanzaic rhyme scheme, *ababb*, where the rhymes make themselves felt. It is quite a tour de force to make highly rhymed four-beat verse seem remotely like the mimesis of speech, and the tension between the ritualistic and the fictional thus remains centrally at work in the dramatic monologue. Readers cope with it by bracketing the artifice of the poem and concentrating on the fictional speaker, whom by convention we treat as if *not* speaking in verse. That is to say, by convention, in reading we separate the fiction from the artifact and attribute the latter—the verse itself, sound patterning, and intertextual references—to the author, while treating the content of the speech as generated by the fictional character. Certainly the effect of "Porphyria's Lover" would be very different if we thought this murderer was a poet composing his elaborate stanzas about the murder he has committed, but our conventions permit us to bracket the ritualistic form as we read for fictional character.

In his pioneering book on the dramatic monologue, *The Poetry of Experience*, Robert Langbaum notes that Browning gives us speakers in particular situations, but they seldom accomplish anything except self-expression, and that the lyric element, as he calls it, triumphs over the dramatic: "It is the lyric instead that arises as an expression of pure will, an expression for which the dramatic situation, if any, provides merely the occasion."[20] Despite this unambiguous judgment from an authoritative source, in subsequent criticism and pedagogy the dramatic, fictional element has been emphasized over the ritualistic. Poems with a fictional speaker revealing his or her character in a speech act quickly became a normative type for English poetry, with Pound and Eliot and others undertaking them, and it then became possible to read other poems of the tradition as dramatic monologues, breaking the link between poet and dramatized speaker, in poems such as "Tintern Abbey" and even Coleridge's "Frost at Midnight." Eventually some classicists began to read earlier poems by this model as well, and since Horace's odes are presented as addressing someone or something, they can help show what is involved in treating lyrics as dramatic monologues.

There are odes of his that clearly do require such an approach; for example, to make sense of "Natis in Usum," Ode 1.27, we need to imagine it as speech in a situation we must reconstruct. The poem begins:

> Natis in usum laetitiae scyphis
> pugnare Thracum est: tollite barbarum
>   morem, verecundumque Bacchum
>   sanguineis prohibete rixis.
>
> vino et lucernis Medus acinaces
> immane quantum discrepat: impium
>   lenite clamorem, sodales,
>   et cubito remanete presso.

> Cups are made for joy. Only Thracians use them
> for fighting. Put a stop to this barbarous practice.
>   Bacchus is a respectable god. Keep him well away
>   from brawling and bloodshed.
> Wine and lamplight don't belong in the same world
> as that Persian dagger. Moderate
>   your unholy noise, friends,
>   and keep the weight on the elbow.

> [Trans. David West]

The statement that only Thracians fight with large wine cups ("scyphis") is clarified by the commands to "Stop this barbarous practice" and to keep wine and brawling well apart. We are incited to imagine a speaker at a gathering where people are throwing wine cups, someone has a Persian dagger, and he tells the guests to quiet down and lie back down on the couches to continue eating and drinking. By contrast, for the ode to Pyrrha discussed in Chapter 1, any attempt to reconstruct a situation of utterance raises irrelevant questions: the poem makes better sense if we don't try to imagine a scene of discourse but take it as poetic discourse about love, made vivid by apostrophic address to Pyrrha. An intermediate case, which helps us to see what is at issue in treating a poem as a dramatic monologue, is Ode 1.9, a version of the carpe diem poem, which some critics treat as a dramatic monologue because the opening phrase appears to position speaker and listener looking at a particular mountain:

Vides ut alta stet nive candidum
Soracte, nec iam sustineant onus
   silvae laborantes, geluque
      flumina constiterint acuto.

dissolve frigus ligna super foco
large reponens atque benignius
   deprome quadrimum Sabina,
      O Thaliarche, merum diota.

permitte divis cetera; qui simul
stravere ventos aequore fervido
   deproeliantis, nec cupressi
      nec veteres agitantur orni.

quid sit futurum cras, fuge quaerere et
quem Fors dierum cumque dabit lucro
   appone, nec dulcis amores
      sperne puer neque tu choreas,

donec virenti canities abest
morosa. Nunc et Campus et areae
   lenesque sub noctem susurri
      composita repetantur hora;

nunc et latentis proditor intimo
gratus puellae risus ab angulo

pignusque dereptum lacertis
  aut digito male pertinaci.

☞

You see Soracte standing white and deep
with snow, the woods in trouble, hardly able
   to carry their burden and the rivers
         halted by sharp ice.
Thaw out the cold. Pile up the logs
on the hearth and be more generous, Thaliarchus,
   as you draw the four-year-old Sabine
         from its two-eared jug.
Leave everything else to the gods. As soon as
they still the winds battling it out
   on the boiling sea, the cypresses stop waving
         and the old ash trees.
Don't ask what will happen tomorrow.
Whatever day Fortune gives you, enter it
   as profit, and don't look down on love
         and dancing while you're still a lad,
while the gloomy grey keeps away from the green.
Now is the time for the Campus and the squares
   and soft sighs at the time arranged
         as darkness falls.
Now is the time for the lovely laugh from the secret corner
giving away the girl in her hiding place,
   and for the token snatched from her arm
         or finger feebly resisting.

[Trans. David West]

Critics are divided about how to interpret this poem. "You see Soracte"
and "Pile up the logs" suggest a winter setting in a cabin or house in the
mountains somewhere north and east of Rome, from which Mount Soracte
is visible. But as commentators have often noted, the more we mentally
envision the winter scene, the harder it is to explain the later statements—
first that storm winds are roiling the sea, which does not fit well with the

cold clear day of the first stanza, and second that now is the time for amorous games in the evening in the Campus Martius, which requires warmer
weather. If we treat the poem as dramatic monologue, we need to establish the situation of speech and then find for the apparently unrelated elements some other function—perhaps as general remarks about changing
fortunes or about appropriate activities for young men. We also must work
out what the speaker is doing in saying these things to the listener. Here
is where things get complicated. David West argues that piling logs on
the fire would be the task of a slave, so that Thaliarchus must be a slave,
and the master's injunction to be "more generous" in pouring out the wine
would be an "affectionate tease." But why would the speaker be interested
in urging his slave to indulge in love-play with girls while he is still young?
West suggests that that the young slave, whose charms the master has hitherto enjoyed, is growing older and perhaps less attractive as a lover, so
the time has come for him now to be active in his pursuit of girls.[21]

If we read this as a dramatic monologue we need to worry about the
obscure motivations of the speaker and work out the true relation between
speaker and listener, which leads down this path of fictional speculation.
But if we read the poem not as the representation of a speaker's engagement with a particular person but as a poetic utterance for a convivial
occasion then its diverse elements make more sense: winter prompts the
injunction to seize the day; don't worry about the future; build up the
fire, pour the wine. Young men, you should make love while you can. If
we take the opening evocation of winter not as the setting of a dramatic
scene of speech to be fleshed out but as images reminding us to enjoy life
while we can (drinking by the fire in the winter, chasing girls in the arcades in the summer), then we do not need to deem Thaliarchus a slave,
in our pursuit of scenic consistency, and we can also give equal weight to
the two other evocations of scenes, especially the most vivid one of twi-
light in the arcades around the Campus Martius.

What matters is not which of Horace's odes should be read as dramatic
monologues but that we should be able to discriminate and not presume
that all must involve a fictional speaker performing a speech act in a particular situation. There are two possible models here: by the dramatic
monologue model a fictional speaker in a house with a view of the mountain in the winter speaks to another character for reasons to be worked

out; in the lyric model, we have a poetic disquisition where elements such as "You see Soracte" are figural devices, vividly evoking a moment of the year for epideictic purposes.[22] Since dramatic monologues have fictional speakers, some of the features that identify them include the naming of speakers (many put the speaker's name in the title: "Child Roland to the Dark Tower Came," "Ulysses," "The Love Song of J. Alfred Prufrock"). We may be offered details about the social condition of the speakers, and of course information about the situation in which they find themselves (such details may not be fleshed out but they are at least implied). And, most important, the speech event that a dramatic monologue fictionally depicts is itself not literary discourse but a real-world speech event. In the lyric model, on the other hand, there may not be an identifiable "speaker" at all and the speech event is a literary one.

"The Love Song of J. Alfred Prufrock," for instance, gives us a named speaker warily contemplating a teatime visit, about whose hesitations and indecisions we learn a good deal, and while the situation is indeterminate (to whom is he saying "Let us go and make our visit"?), a particular social context is certainly implied. Above all, while we take the words of the poem to be those spoken by this fictional character, we do not, I think, imagine him to be speaking verse. It is not Prufrock but T. S. Eliot who ironically rhymes "come and go" with "Michelangelo":

> In the rooms the women come and go,
> Talking of Michelangelo.

Similarly, in "My Last Duchess," we take the words of the poem to be words spoken by the Duke to the Count's envoy, but the rhymed pentameter couplets are supplied by the author, not the Duke. (The Duke is not showing the envoy that he can speak in heavily enjambed rhyming couplets.) Thus, we do not think he speaks ironically when he says, "even had one skill in speech—as I have not," though manifestly this is most skillful rhyming verse.

Ralph Rader calls our judgment that the Duke does not provide the rhymes "a small but potent fact," as indeed it is—distinguishing the dramatic monologue from other first-person lyrics.[23] Consider, in contrast, Baudelaire's "Invitation au voyage":

Mon enfant, ma soeur,	My child, my sister
Songe à la douceur,	Imagine how sweet to
D'aller là-bas vivre ensemble!	Go far off to live together!
Aimer à loisir,	To live at leisure
Aimer et mourir,	To live and to die
Au pays qui te ressemble!	In that land resembling you!

Here the poet's verse, the short lines that emphasize the harmonious rhyming and the sound patterning, are part of the invitation to an idyllic sojourn, not form added by the poet to represent an act of invitation by a fictional character in some concrete situation.

In the dramatic monologue, in sum, the tension between the ritualistic and fictional elements of the poem yields, by convention, a dissociation of levels: readers unconsciously separate the act of communication by the fictional speaker in his or her situation from the verse produced by the poet. The ritualistic frames the fictional, but as a separable embedded level. In other lyrics, however, there is no reason to posit a fictional speaker performing some real-world speech act separate from the poetic discourse that the verse provides, and fictional elements are assimilated in other ways, to which I now turn.

4. Framing Past Events

Lyrics very often offer representations of events: a boy picks a rose; a woman crosses a street; a quail is induced to be served to us. At one extreme we have the ballad, a form that, like dramatic monologue, is an extreme case of lyric, but in some ways the opposite of dramatic monologue: little delineation of character but a bare-bones narration of incident. Ballads are narratives but framed for lyric by a highly rhythmical ballad stanza and often by refrains or other forms of repetition that interrupt narrative and place us in a present of poetic articulation. The frequent recourse to the present tense, which I discuss below, also contributes to the ritual effect. The ballad stanza in Northern European traditions consists of quatrains of alternating four-beat and three-beat lines, usually with rhyme at the second and fourth lines. And the stripped-down, formulaic nature of ballad narratives, often with repetitive, balancing dialogue, emphasizes their character as verse to be repeated, if not sung. "Sir Patrick Spens," one of the most popular Scottish ballads, gives us a minimal narrative, in the past tense, of a tragic voyage reluctantly undertaken, in which such events as the shipwreck itself are elided (we are told at the end in the present tense that Sir Patrick lies "fifty fathom deep"); but echoing stanzas tell us that the ladies wait in vain.

> O lang, lang may the ladies sit,
>   Wi' their fans into their hand,
> Before they see Sir Patrick Spens
>   Come sailing to the strand!
>
> And lang, lang may the maidens sit
>   Wi' their gowd kames in their hair,
> A-waiting for their ain dear loves!
>   For them they'll see nae mair.

Like many popular ballads, this exists in numerous versions, which may expand details, but a constant is the foreboding of an ill-omen:

> "Late, late yestre'en I saw the new moon
>   Wi' the old moon in his arm,
> And I fear, I fear, my dear master,
>   That we will come to harm."

Most ballads are impersonal, without identifiable narrators, though many use dialogue by speakers identified or unidentified. There is little delineation of character or motive; transitions are abrupt; and lyric themes of tragic love and sudden disaster predominate. Possibly the most famous of the Anglo-Scottish ballads, "Lord Randal," which exists in numerous other languages as well, consists entirely of question and answer, with no framing narrative:

> "Oh where ha'e ye been, Lord Randall, my son?
> O where ha'e ye been, my handsome young man?"

"I ha'e been to the greenwood: mother, make my bed soon,
For I'm weary wi' hunting, and fain wad lie down."

The first phrase of Lord Randal's response varies according to the question, but "mother, make my bed soon, / For I'm weary wi' hunting, and fain wad lie down," is repeated in each quatrain. In the final section the questions become more ritualistic—"What d'ye leave to your mother [sister/brother/true-love], Lord Randal, my son . . . ?"—and in the response, "For I'm weary wi' hunting" is replaced by "For I'm sick at the heart." Strangely, this ballad often cited as exemplary is metrically anomalous, in triple meter with four-beat lines and a five-beat third line. Literary ballads, such as Keats's "La Belle Dame sans merci" and Goethe's "Der Erlkönig" (discussed below), though they also may deviate in significant ways from the ballad stanza, retain the dialogic structure and symmetries of syntax and phrasing.[24] The ritual elements frame and ultimately dominate the narrative of events, as the artifact presents itself as a poem to be repeated, or at the very least is received as a text that *is* often repeated—the very nature of a ballad.

Outside of ballads, fictionality in lyrics most often takes the form of minimal narrative of events in the past tense, but in fact lyrics that remain in the past tense, recounting incidents, are not so common, especially prior to the twentieth century. In *The Norton Anthology of Poetry,* for example, only 123 of 1,266 poems are in the past tense, and 21 of these are ballads.[25] The relative rarity of lyrics in the past tense, though a topic seldom discussed, is not hard to understand: the past tense is a narrative tense and provokes the desire to know what happens next. So when a poem begins

> I leant upon a coppice gate
>   When Frost was spectre-gray,
> And Winter's dregs made desolate
>   The weakening eye of day.

The natural question is, "So what happened?" whereas if the poem— Thomas Hardy's "The Darkling Thrush"—had begun "I *lean* upon a coppice gate/When frost *is* spectre-gray . . ." we could anticipate reflections, meditation, more than narrative. What does happen next in this case is that in bleak winter surroundings the thrush produces a song "of joy unlimited," unexpectedly suggesting cause for hope:

> So little cause for carolings
> Of such ecstatic sound
> Was written on terrestrial things
> Afar or nigh around,
> That I could think there trembled through
> His happy good-night air
> Some blessed Hope, whereof he knew
> And I was unaware.

Although the poem reports past happenings, the conclusion implies the present relevance of the incident, even though the present of lyric articulation is not explicitly marked.

Narrative lyrics cast in the past tense have ways of indicating the significance of the incident narrated, so that the report of incident becomes subordinated to a meaning in the lyric present. One common structure for lyrics framed as past is a description of a situation in the past tense, followed by an account of what someone thought or said there, as in Hardy's poem or in the most famous of Spenser's *Amoretti:*

> One day I wrote her name upon the strand,
> But came the waves and washèd it away:
> Agayne I wrote it with a second hand,
> But came the tyde and made my paynes his prey.
> "Vayne man," sayd she, "that dost in vain assay
> A mortal thing so to immortalize;
> For I my selve shall lyke to this decay,
> And eke my name bee wypèd out lykewize."
> "Not so," quod I, "Let baser things devize
> To dye in dust, but you shall live by fame;
> My verse your vertues rare shall eternize,

And in the heavens wryte your glorious name:
>Where, whenas death shall all the world subdew,
>Our love shall live, and later life renew.

Though the entire poem is framed as something that happened in the past, the utterance quoted gives a present claim about significance. Many ballads also have this structure of a past-tense narrative frame and present-tense reported speech or, more often, dialogue. "The Twa Corbies" begins:

>As I was walking all alane,
>I heard twa corbies makin a mane;
>The tane unto the ither say,
>"Whar sall we gang and dine the-day?"

But the rest of the poem consists of the crows planning in the present to feast on the body of a slain knight, whose hawk, hound, and lady fair have abandoned him. It concludes with the corbies' observation:

>"Mony a one for him makes mane,
>But nane sall ken [shall know] whar he is gane;
>Oer his white banes, whan they are bare,
>The wind sall blaw for evermair."

Poems that remain in the past throughout often acquire an allegorical character. Readers wonder why we are being told about these past events, and if the poem declines explicitly to draw a present moral or conclusion, the implications may be easy to infer from cultural conventions. Goethe's "Heidenröslein," discussed in Chapter 1, recounts a series of events, most of which, in ballad fashion, are remarks by the youth and the rose, and concludes that her "weh" and "ach" could not help her—she just had to suffer it—a situation that invites interpretive elaboration. George Herbert offers a number of poems in the past tense—"The Collar," "Artillerie," and "The Pulley,"—which, like poems mentioned above, cite speech. His "Redemption" is a narrative of past events:

Having been tenant long to a rich Lord,
Not thriving, I resolved to be bold,
And make a suit unto him, to afford
A new small-rented lease, and cancell th' old.
In heaven at his manour I him sought:
They told me there, that he was lately gone
About some land, which he had dearly bought
Long since on earth, to take possession.
I straight return'd, and knowing his great birth,
Sought him accordingly in great resorts;
In cities, theatres, gardens, parks, and courts:
At length I heard a ragged noise and mirth
Of theeves and murderers: there I him espied,
Who straight, *Your suit is granted,* said, and died.

The sudden, chilling turn at the end powerfully jolts the reader out of the narrative of leases and landlords and into the Christian allegory. Walt Whitman's "When I heard the Learn'd Astronomer" is a less dramatic example from a more modern era, relying on readers' ability to recognize as self-evident a value-charged opposition between book learning and a more direct contact with nature:

When I heard the learn'd astronomer,
When the proofs, the figures, were ranged in columns before me,
When I was shown the charts and diagrams, to add, divide,
    and measure them,
When I sitting heard the astronomer where he lectured with
    much applause in the lecture-room,
How soon unaccountable I became tired and sick,
Till rising and gliding out I wander'd off by myself,
In the mystical moist night-air, and from time to time,
Look'd up in perfect silence at the stars.

Many of Emily Dickinson's enigmatical past-tense poems take on this allegorical character, as in "I felt a Funeral, in my Brain," where the sequential narrative becomes an allegory of an experience otherwise impossible to recount, as the ending makes clear:

> And then a Plank in Reason, broke,
>> And I dropped down, and down—
> And hit a World, at every plunge,
>> And Finished knowing—then—

These two principal strategies for linking a past anecdote to reasons why it might be offered for repetition at the point of lyric enunciation—the citation of discourse in the present and the activation of a value-charged allegorical meaning—are supplemented by other strategies for evoking significance while remaining in a narrative in the past. Dylan Thomas's "Fern Hill" offers the rich evocation of a dreamy childhood without giving it a present function.

> Now as I was young and easy under the apple boughs
> About the lilting house and happy as the grass was green,
>> The night above the dingle starry,
>>> Time let me hail and climb
>> Golden in the heydays of his eyes,
> And honoured among wagons I was prince of the apple towns
> And once below a time I lordly had the trees and leaves
>> Trail with daisies and barley
>>> Down the rivers of the windfall light.

The past is maintained even in the final stanza, when we might expect an explicit retrospective regret for the lost world:

> Nothing I cared, in the lamb white days, that time would take me
> Up to the swallow thronged loft by the shadow of my hand,
>> In the moon that is always rising,
>>> Nor that riding to sleep
>> I should hear him fly with the high fields
> And wake to the farm forever fled from the childless land.

Oh as I was young and easy in the mercy of his means,
   Time held me green and dying
      Though I sang in my chains like the sea.

But the claim not to have cared in the past of childhood that the farm would be forever fled and that to be green is to be already dying makes clear the nostalgic cast of this evocative narrative.

In the twentieth century especially, however, we find lyrics that remain resolutely in the past, without tying themselves to a function in the present of enunciation. Theodore Roethke's well-known "My Papa's Waltz" is one such:

The whiskey on your breath
Could make a small boy dizzy;
But I hung on like death:
Such waltzing was not easy.

We romped until the pans
Slid from the kitchen shelf;
My mother's countenance
Could not unfrown itself.

. . . . .

You beat time on my head
With a palm caked hard by dirt,
Then waltzed me off to bed
Still clinging to your shirt.

This poem, entirely in the past tense, a report of habitual incidents, is an example of what Barbara Herrnstein Smith calls the "pointless anecdotes" that suffuse modern poetry: "anecdotes of which the only point could be, 'This is a kind of thing that happens.'"[26] She suggests that the paradoxical effect of what she calls the "non-assertive conclusion" of such lyrics, the failure to indicate the significance of the events, is in fact to heighten the importance of what is presented, even if that significance is left for the reader to imagine.

This effect is the result of fundamental lyric convention of significance: the fact that something has been set down as a poem implies that it is important now, at the moment of lyric articulation, however trivial it might seem. But it may be that the apparently trivial event is not so much rendered important in itself as marked as an occasion for poetic power. There often seems a movement from the claims of experience to the claims of writing: the poem can make a poetic event out of an insignificant experience. Dickinson's poems—"A Thought went up my mind today" is a telling example—exploit this presumption to become something more than the narrative of trivial past events. Even her "lyrics that appear to narrate more conventional stories," writes Sharon Cameron, "may be seen on closer scrutiny to throw their weight not on the plot and its end but rather on some issue to which the end is mere preface." They "push their way into the dimensions of the moment, pry apart its walls."[27] Often, as in "A Bird Came Down the Walk," the mysteriousness of the conclusion lifts us away from a sequential logic of narrative to a figurative register where the question is no longer, "And then what happened?" The bird came down the walk, bit a worm in two, stepped aside to let a beetle pass, and then

> . . . rowed him softer home
> Than Oars divide the Ocean,
> Too silver for a seam,
> Or Butterflies, off Banks of Noon,
> Leap, plashless, as they swim.

The flight of the bird drops away as the question becomes what to make of these aquatic metaphors and plashless, leaping butterflies. The end is mere preface.

5. The Lyric Present

As might be suggested by these last examples, where even a narrative in the past manages to suggest value for the present, the present tense is the dominant tense of lyric. I mentioned that in the *Norton Anthology* only 123 of 1,266 lyrics are consistently in the past tense; for example, only two of Shakespeare's 154 sonnets remain in the past throughout. The use of the present tense is "the most notable characteristic of lyric poetry," writes Suzanne Langer. While this might suggest that the lyric is a poem in which the poet expresses his or her momentary feelings and thoughts, in fact "the present tense proves to be a far more subtle mechanism than either grammarians or rhetoricians generally realize, and to have quite other uses than the characterization of present acts and facts."[28]

Even ballads, which function perfectly well in the past tense, often draw on the present for vividness and to enrich their ritualistic dimension, intermittently pulling themselves out of a narrated past and into a present of enunciation, especially at the beginning and the end. "Sir Patrick Spens" actually begins in the present—"The king sits in Dumferline town,/Drinking the blude-red wine"—before reverting to the past for narrative, until the end, when the ladies weep in vain and Sir Patrick lies offshore, fifty fathom deep. Goethe's ballad "Der Erlkönig" ("The Elfking") achieves a remarkable effect with its orchestration of past and present. Beginning with a present question—

> Wer reitet so spät durch Nacht und Wind?
> Es ist der Vater mit seinem Kind.

> Who is riding so late through night and wind?
> It is the father with his child.

> [Trans. Susanne Langer]

—the poem continues through dialogue alone, as the child complains of the torments of the ghostly Elfking and the father replies reassuringly, until the final stanza:

> Dem Vater grauset's, er reitet geschwind,
> Er hält in den Armen das ächzende Kind,
> Erreicht den Hof mit Mühe und Not,
> In seinen Armen das Kind war tot.

> The father is shaken, he rides apace,
> The child is moaning in his embrace;

He reaches the house, in fear and dread;
The child within his arms was dead.[29]

The jarring introduction in the final line of a past tense where the present would have been perfectly possible ("The child within his arms *is* dead") gives a supplementary finality to this discovery, as already past in the present of articulation.

But the move from a pervasive present tense to a past at the end is very unusual—doubtless one reason for its power here. A very common structure is the move from past to present: the past anecdote explicitly pulled into the lyric present at the end, with a present-tense reflection on the significance of the incident recounted or other references to a present of enunciation. This is more widespread as a lyric structure than the lyric narrative completely in the past. A classic example is Wordsworth's "I wandered lonely as a cloud," where the evocative description of the scene of daffodils in the past tense yields at the end to a claim of present significance:

I gazed—and gazed—but little thought
What wealth the show to me had brought:
For oft, when on my couch I lie
In vacant or in pensive mood,
They flash upon that inward eye
Which is the bliss of solitude;
And then my heart with pleasure fills,
And dances with the daffodils.

Even more economically, his "She dwelt among the untrodden ways" concludes "But she is in her grave, and, oh, / The difference to me!" Shelley's "Ozymandias" begins in the past: "I met a traveler from an antique land, / Who said, "Two vast and trunkless legs of stone / Stand in the desert. . . ." The rest of the poem quotes what was said and concludes in a present tense that offers the implicit reflection: "Round the decay / Of that colossal wreck, boundless and bare, / The lone and level sands stretch far away."

In Petrarch's *Canzoniere* a quarter of the poems are structured by the contrast between *then* and *now,* past and present: they recount a past experience which now affects the lover in a certain way. The persistence of this structure works to undermine narrative continuity in the collection as a whole and thus is another counterbalance to the pull of fictionality.[30] The structure is so common that it seems almost pointless to cite examples. Among poems considered in Chapter 1, Leopardi's "L'Infinito" begins with the past love for this scene, which now in the present suggests infinite depths. Baudelaire's "À une passante" begins as an incident in the past, is pulled into the present of enunciation with the apostrophe to the "Fugitive beauté," and concludes with the melancholic reflection that neither knows where the other is going.

There would be many ways of classifying the structures of lyrics deploying the present tense. The German theoretician Wolfgang Kayser defines the *lyrische Grundlagen* or three major possibilities of lyric as *nennen, ansprechen,* and *leidhaft sprechen:* naming, addressing, and speaking songlike.[31] In Chapter 5, I discussed apostrophic poems, which characteristically center on the present of enunciation, as they address persons, things, abstractions, calling them to do something, to respond, or just to hear. Another major group is what might be called poems of naming or definition, which use the simple present for supposedly atemporal truths: "Th'expense of spirit in a waste of shame / Is lust in action." "La nature est un temple où de vivant pilliers / Laissent parfois sortir de confuses paroles." " 'Hope' is a thing with feathers—/ That perches in the soul."[32] This present tense used to describe what is generally the case subtends a large class of present-tense poems of an epideictic character, which make general claims about the world: so much depends upon a red wheelbarrow; they fuck you up, your mum and dad; nothing gold can stay. Sometimes these are cast in a minimal narrative form, as in Dickinson's stunning account of the heart's propensities in a sadistic world, quoted previously:

> The Heart asks Pleasure—first—
> And then—Excuse from Pain—
> And then—those little Anodynes
> That deaden suffering—
> And then—to go to sleep—
> And then—if it should be
> The will of its Inquisitor
> The privilege to die—

But while structured as a narrative, for suspense and surprise, this is evocation of a present, continuing condition. Sometimes there is a framework of reasoning, as if the claim needed to be worked out and justified, as in Hopkins's "As kingfishers catch fire":

> As kingfishers catch fire, dragonflies draw flame;
> As tumbled over rim in roundy wells
> Stones ring; like each tucked string tells, each hung bell's
> Bow swung finds tongue to fling out broad its name;
> Each mortal thing does one thing and the same:
> Deals out that being indoors each one dwells;
> Selves—goes itself; myself it speaks and spells,
> Crying What I do is me: for that I came.
>
> I say more: the just man justices;
> Keeps grace: that keeps all his goings graces;
> Acts in God's eye what in God's eye he is—
> Christ. For Christ plays in ten thousand places,
> Lovely in limbs, and lovely in eyes not his
> To the Father through the features of men's faces.

Another possibility is a meditative structure, foregrounding reflections on one's own thoughts, which may, of course include references to past experiences. Baudelaire's "Le Cygne," as I mentioned earlier, opens by apostrophizing Andromaque and pursues recollections prompted by a recent sighting of the exiled swan. The second half of the poem then begins, "Paris change, mais rien dans ma mélancholie n'a bougé / Et mes chers souvenirs sont plus lourds que les rocs" ("Paris changes, but my melancholy has not budged / And my dear memories are more heavy than boulders"). It then reviews and exacerbates these memories in a process somewhere between ritual and obsession.

The present tense is important is lyric in all the languages of the Western tradition, but in English there is an especially distinctive lyric use of the simple present: lyrics use a special nonprogressive present with verbs of action to incorporate events while reducing their fictional, narrative character and increasing their ritualistic feel. In English, to

note *occurrences* in the present, we use the present progressive tense:
I am walking. When we encounter the unmarked nonprogressive present
tense with occurrences, we can guess that we are dealing with a foreigner
or a poem.

I sit in one of the dives
On Fifty-second street,
Uncertain and afraid . . .

[Auden]

I taste a liquor never brewed,
From tankards scooped in pearl;

[Dickinson]

I wander through each chartered street
Near where the chartered Thames does flow
And mark in every face I meet
Marks of weakness, marks of woe.

[Blake]

I walk through the long schoolroom questioning;
A kind old nun in a white hood replies
                    . . . the children's eyes
In momentary wonder stare upon
A sixty-year-old smiling public man.

[Yeats]

In both colloquial and formal English, such action verbs require the progressive form—*I am walking through the long schoolroom*—without which
they would mark a habitual action and lead one to expect a temporal indication: "I *often* sit in one of the dives on Fifty-second Street"; "I taste a
liquor never brewed *whenever I get a chance.*" It is the combination of
simple present and lack of temporal specification with action verbs that
makes this a distinctive tense in English poetry.

Rodney Huddleston and Geoffrey Pullum's authoritative *Cambridge Grammar of the English Language* treats the English present tense as simply nonpast. It notes that with the unmarked, nonprogressive present tense "there is no explicit reference to any feature of the temporal flow (such as whether the situation is conceived as instantaneous or having a duration through time)." This unmarked nonprogressive present tense, or the simple present, "combines freely with states but not with occurrences." It is used both for states that are temporary, "She has a headache," and those that last or are outside of time, "She is Austrian." "But the use of the simple present with verbs of action is quite restricted."[33] Five of the possible uses one can identify are worth mentioning briefly, since some of their effects are relevant to this lyric present, which works to assimilate events to a ritualistic poetic discourse.

The most common use of the simple present is with temporal qualifiers that make the verb in effect designate a serial state more than an occurrence: "I do the *Times* crossword every morning." Without such qualifiers, in ordinary speech, we presuppose them: "I do the *Times* crossword" means I do it regularly. Now, "I walk through the long schoolroom questioning" does not mean "I do this regularly," but there is an implication, if not of repetition, at least of iterability. Certainly one effect of the lyric present is to make what is reported something more than what I am doing at a particular moment. "I sit in one of the dives / On Fifty-second street, / Uncertain and afraid . . ." comes across as something more than a report on what I am doing right now. It happens now, in time, but in an iterable *now* of lyric enunciation, rather than in a now of linear time.

These lyric presents are not the gnomic present, of truths, which sometimes does use verbs of action: *A rolling stone gathers no moss; water boils at 100 degrees centigrade.* As I have emphasized, lyrics regularly seek to tell truths about this world, so some lyric presents can take on something of a gnomic character. Consider Byron's

She walks in beauty, like the night
Of cloudless climes and starry skies;
And all that's best of dark and bright
Meet in her aspect and her eyes.

Is this like doing the *Times* crossword?—she walks in beauty every day, or is this is a truth of her being, such that questions about how often she walks are irrelevant—something she *is* rather than something she does?

Relevant also to this special lyric present is the performative present: "I promise to pay you tomorrow." As I have noted, there are regular performatives in lyrics, such as Herrick's "I sing of brooks, of blossoms, birds and bowers"; and there may even be hints of performativity in a range of lyric presents, which are accomplished in the act of utterance. In ordinary English one cannot say "I hereby wander through each chartered street," but does Blake's "I wander through each chartered street," carry a suggestion of "I *hereby* wander . . ." through the agency of this poem? Does Hopkins's "I wake and feel the fell of dark, not day" not imply something like "I hereby feel the fell of dark"—by virtue of this incantation or articulation?

Another use of this simple present tense, particularly interesting for comparison with the lyric use, comes in jokes or oral narrative. "Have you heard this one?" we say: "A nun, a priest, an Irishman, a Scotsman, a rabbi, and a blonde walk into a bar. The bartender looks at them and asks, 'Is this some kind of joke?'" The simple present (as opposed to the past) marks this as a story independent of any particular context, as iterable utterance, a quasi-mythic narrative with only slight claim to reality, as we indicate in asking, "Have you heard this one?" If you tell a story about what you did yesterday in this tense—"So I walk into the office and the boss says to me . . ." instead of "I walked into the office and the boss said to me . . ."— the effect may be greater vividness but the implication is that this is a detachable story that will be amusing, tellable, a story that could be repeated, not just a representation of what happened. But the simple present also marks it as informal, whereas in lyric the simple present is more formal than either the present progressive or the past: "I walk through the long schoolroom questioning" as opposed to "I am walking . . ." or "I walked . . ."

We don't usually pay attention to this tense—it just comes to seem natural in lyric—but it has strange effects. Robert Frost's "Stopping by Woods" presents itself as a dramatic monologue; we need to imagine a fictional speaker (people often think "country doctor") who stops in "these woods," who delays the fulfillment of obligations to "watch these woods fill up with snow." A curious feature of this poem, which opposes Nature, woods, snow, and death to the human world of promises and obligations, is that the norms and values of the human world are delegated to the horse ("My little horse must think it queer / To stop without a farmhouse near"). But then we are told:

> He gives his harness bells a shake
> To ask if there is some mistake.
> The only other sound's the sweep
> Of easy wind and downy flake.

Here we have something other than the observation of an event by a speaker. We hear a different note. A speaker describing what is happening at a given moment would say something like "he is shaking his harness bells." Frost's formulation, "He gives his harness bells a shake," introduces a distance from any particular fictional moment and marks this as a different kind of discourse, a ritualistic act not tied to a specific observable moment. We still need a speaker, of course, but the special temporality of this utterance moves us into a different discursive region. What makes this poem more than an anecdote is this simple present, on the one hand, and on the other the repetition of the final line,

> And miles to go before I sleep,
> And miles to go before I sleep.

As critics have often noted, this repetition moves us, anecdote and all, into a figurative, poetic register.

Consider a different example without a speaker, Emily Dickinson's

> Further in Summer than the Birds,
> Pathetic from the Grass,
> A minor Nation celebrates
> > Its unobtrusive Mass.

Lyric pedagogy encourages us to imagine a speaker/persona observing this celebration, but of course the more one tries to imagine a concrete fictional situation the odder becomes the nonprogressive present, which a real speaker would not utter. What difference does it make that the minor nation "celebrates" rather than "is celebrating"? It pulls it out of a world of empirical observation and indicates that we need not imagine a speaker at all but can take this as a lyrical discourse about the world, a ritualistic celebration of the world's sounds as a mass, where, as the poem concludes, "a Druidic Difference / Enhances Nature now."

In Yeats's "Leda and the Swan" the nonprogressive present does not come until the end of the first quatrain:

> A sudden blow: the great wings beating still
> Above the staggering girl, her thighs caressed
> By the dark webs, her nape caught in his bill,
> He *holds* her helpless breast upon his breast.

The violent action is carried by participles, not the main verb. The definite articles—"*the* great wings" etc.—refer deictically to a presupposed scene that has not been presented, making this seem like the description of a painting, perhaps. But the nonprogressive present-tense verb of the first tercet undercuts a pictorial perspective:

> A shudder in the loins *engenders* there
> The broken wall, the burning roof and tower
> And Agamemnon dead.

Describing an event that can't be depicted, "engenders" suggests a different sort of model. By convention—this is the fifth use of the simple present and perhaps the most relevant—we use this tense to describe what happens in works of literature. The *Cambridge Grammar* notes that we talk about authors, works, and characters "from the perspective of their present and potentially permanent existence rather than that of their past creation."[34] "Othello kills Desdemona," for example. Is that what is going on in "Leda": an account of what happens in the myth? "Hamlet delays" and "Othello kills Desdemona" seem rather more timeless than "A shudder

in the loins engenders . . ." but they are at the same time instances of it-
erated action. The simple present is appropriate, for the delaying and the
killing happen again and again as well as always.

A poem like Auden's "The Fall of Rome," even though its narrated
events are thoroughly idiosyncratic, seems to give us something like a
mythic situation:

> The piers are pummeled by the waves;
> In a lonely field the rain
> Lashes an abandoned train;
> Outlaws fill the mountain caves.

"Lashes," as if the rain were always lashing the train. If we move to a poem
that is harder to assimilate to myth—that can't be taken to refer to an imagined myth—what do we find? Consider Elizabeth Bishop's "At the
Fishhouses":

> Although it is a cold evening,
> down by one of the fishhouses
> an old man sits netting,
> his net, in the gloaming almost invisible,
> a dark purple-brown,
> and his shuttle worn and polished.
> The air smells so strong of codfish
> it makes one's nose run and one's eyes water.

Here the sense of a *now* is palpable—the very lack of first-person pronouns
intensifies the sense of a scene being presented to the reader. The singularity of the scene may be stressed, but it takes on a peculiar aspect, as
something that happens, not just something that is happening: "he sits
netting" rather than "he is sitting netting."

The end of Keats's "Ode to Autumn" is a fascinating, rather eerie case:

> Hedge-crickets sing; and now with treble soft
> The redbreast whistles from a garden-croft;
> And gathering swallows twitter in the skies.

Here the vivid yet indeterminate *now* of an undetermined time of articulation that is implicit in other examples is made explicit. Perhaps we should call it a "floating now," repeated each time the poem is read. There is a subtle distinction between "The redbreast *is whistling* from a garden-croft" (or we could say, to preserve the meter, "The wren is whistling from a garden-croft") and "The redbreast *whistles* from a garden-croft." The former indicates something happening at a particular, locatable time; the latter puts us into this strange time of the lyric now.

In *Feeling and Form* Suzanne Langer notes that while the simple present is treated as fundamental and taught as the base form of the verb in English, we seldom use it; and she singles out this special lyric use as creating "an impression or an idea as something experienced in a sort of eternal present."[35] Following her lead, in the best discussion of the subject, George T. Wright takes up Yeats's line: "I walk through the long schoolroom questioning." We admire such a line, he writes, "as simple, ordinary natural English. It reports an event that has happened—is happening—happens. Such a confusion in our own verbs may show us that the Yeats is not so speechlike as it at first seems." Wright concludes that "In effect what we find in such verbs is a new aspect or tense, neither past, nor present but timelesss—in its feeling a lyric tense." Wright does admit, "If we do not know when the action is taking place, however, we still feel that it takes time." But he repeats, "It is outside of time but it has duration—a special state but common to all art."[36]

Wright's analysis is excellent, but the allure of the timeless—doubtless the assumption that great art should be timeless—leads him, I think, to neglect the oddity of the lyric time of enunciation, which is both that of a speaker/poet and that of the reader, who may speak these words also. Wright is thinking in terms of representation, artistic representation, which leads him to timelessness. If we think of the time of enunciation, of the lyric attempt to be itself an event rather than the representation of an event, this changes the perspective on the lyric present, as well as much else. Lyrics have a variety of strategies for framing fictional elements—fictional speakers and represented events—and bringing them into the lyric present, which is a present of enunciation. Ever since Pindar and doubtless before, lyrics have been constructed for reperformance, with an iterable *now:* not timeless but a moment of time that is repeated every time the poem is read, and the English simple present only intensifies that underlying possibility of lyric. Its structure, like that of triangulated address or of hyperbole is only dissimulated, never eliminated, and provides a framework for a great range of lyric invention.

SEVEN

Lyric and Society

Lyric is often characterized as language cut off from worldly purposes—so framed by its form and its conventions. "Over every poem which looks like a poem," declares John Crowe Ransom, "is a sign which reads: This road does not go through to action." Theodor Adorno begins his famous essay "On Lyric Poetry and Society" by evoking his audience's supposed discomfort at an approach to lyric that is thought inimical to its fundamental nature: "You experience lyric poetry as something opposed to society, something wholly individual. You feel strongly that it should remain so, that lyric expression, having escaped from the weight of material existence, should evoke images of a life free from the coercion of reigning practices, of utility, of the relentless pressures of self-preservation." But Adorno, notoriously, finds utopian potential in the lyric: set against society, it may offer resistance to its assumptions through a language not yet entrammeled in society's preoccupations. Jacques Rancière declares, "The poet belongs to politics as one who does not belong there, who ignores its customs and scatters its words."[1] Not belonging in a realm one inhabits, ignoring or resisting its customs, and scattering or dispersing the words that organize life and

296

social value certainly make possible social engagement but scarcely insure social and political effects.

1. Engagement and Disengagement

Horace is an interesting case. He writes some poetry on public, political
themes, such as the odes in book 4 that celebrate Augustus for bringing
peace and plenty to Rome, but he frequently asserts the nonpolitical character of his odes: his is "the peaceful lyre," in contrast to the public, political epic. Ode 1.6 declines to praise the exploits of the martial hero
Agrippa: let Varius, an epic poet, write of your victories, he declares:

> Nos, Agrippa, neque haec dicere nec gravem
> Pelidae stomachum cedere nescii
> nec cursus duplicis per mare Ulixei
>   nec saevam Pelopis domum

☞

> Agrippa, I don't try to speak of such things,
> not Achilles' ever unyielding bad temper,
> nor duplicitous Ulysses' sea-wanderings,
>   nor the cruel house of Pelops.

[Trans. A. S. Kline]

He rewrites the incipits of the *Iliad* and the *Odyssey,* as if to show how
the lyric would reduce or mangle heroic qualities: the wrath of Achilles
becomes prosaic "bad temper," *stomachus,* and Ulysses's *polytropos* becomes simply duplicitous. Lyric subjects are different: "I sing of banquets,
of battles fought by fierce virgins / with nails cut sharp to wound young
men: / as always, I sing idly, whether / fancy free or burning with love."[2]
But he inhabits the political world by declining to inhabit it: in the classic
gesture of the *praeteritio,* which disingenuously recites what it claims to
pass over or refuse, he writes a stanza about the praise of heroic exploits
that he will not attempt. Such *recusatio* both defines the space for lyric
in opposition to political and heroic poetry and, by its praise of Agrippa
and Caesar as too glorious for his lyric talent, ambiguously projects a hierarchy of social values.

Other Horatian odes explicitly mark the vicissitudes of love and the pleasures of private life as the domain of lyric, yet the very act of demarcation involves reflection on the attitudes with which to approach life, and his lyrics became known for the articulation of values and the production of apothegms that for many generations of educated Europeans served as ethical points of reference, if not actual guides to conduct: *Dulce et decorum est pro patria mori;* or *Integer vitae scelerisque purus,* or perhaps, *Carpe diem.* The majority of his odes do not in fact describe amorous dalliance but question how to live, with details of personal experience marshaled for general homiletic wisdom: Take things as they come. Do not be too eager to ask what the future will bring. Take the middle way: the tallest pine shakes most in a windstorm. Live modestly. Do not forget that death may come at any moment. While many of poems preach the virtues of withdrawal from the public sphere, this is not made to seem incompatible with praise of those political figures who insure a society that makes this possible. The best society, these poems suggest, is one that encourages the exercise of private virtues and moderate pleasures, including lyric reflection.

Interestingly, Baudelaire, who could not be more different from Horace—no judicious advisor, he!—adopts a similar ironic strategy of distinguishing lyric from a poetry treating social themes, which he nevertheless pursues. What poem does he choose to open the *Tableaux parisiens?* This section of *Les Fleurs du Mal* features the ordinary inhabitants of the great city—prostitutes, thieves, beggars, the blind, little old women and decrepit old men, and a haggard negress, exiled from Africa—but it opens with "Paysage," a term for landscape painting. The poet proposes to compose his "eclogues," while contemplating an urban tableau of noisy workshops with smoke rising:

> Je veux, pour composer chastement mes églogues,
> Coucher auprès du ciel, comme les astrologues,
> Et, voisin des clochers écouter en rêvant
> Leurs hymnes solennels emportés par le vent.
> Les deux mains au menton, du haut de ma mansarde,
> Je verrai l'atelier qui chante et qui bavarde;
> Les tuyaux, les clochers, ces mâts de la cité,
> Et les grands ciels qui font rêver d'éternité.

Il est doux, à travers les brumes, de voir naître
L'étoile dans l'azur, la lampe à la fenêtre
Les fleuves de charbon monter au firmament
Et la lune verser son pâle enchantement.

☞

I would, to compose my eclogues chastely,
Lie down close to the sky like an astrologer,
And, near the church towers, listen while I dream
To their solemn anthems borne to me by the wind.
My chin cupped in both hands, high up in my garret
I shall see the workshops where they chatter and sing,
The chimneys, the belfries, those masts of the city,
And the skies that make one dream of eternity.

It is sweet, through the mist, to see the stars
Appear in the heavens, the lamps in the windows,
The streams of smoke rise in the firmament
And the moon spread out her pale enchantment.

[Trans. William Aggeler]

It sounds as though this is going to be urban pastoral, poetically processing an urbanized landscape—with smoke instead of clouds, steeples instead of masts—to find a strange beauty there. But in fact the poet will shut himself off from this scene:

Je fermerai partout portières et volets
Pour bâtir dans la nuit mes féeriques palais.
Alors je rêverai des horizons bleuâtres,
Des jardins, des jets d'eau pleurant dans les albâtres,
Des baisers, des oiseaux chantant soir et matin,
Et tout ce que l'Idylle a de plus enfantin.
L'Émeute, tempêtant vainement à ma vitre,
Ne fera pas lever mon front de mon pupitre;
Car je serai plongé dans cette volupté
D'évoquer le Printemps avec ma volonté,

De tirer un soleil de mon coeur, et de faire
De mes pensers brûlants une tiède atmosphère.

☞

I shall close all the shutters and draw all the drapes
So I can build at night my fairy palaces.
Then I shall dream of pale blue horizons, gardens,
Fountains weeping into alabaster basins,
Of kisses, of birds singing morning and evening,
And of all that is most childlike in the Idyll.
Riot, storming vainly at my window,
Will not make me raise my head from my desk,
For I shall be plunged in the voluptuousness
Of evoking the Springtime with my will alone,
Of drawing forth a sun from my heart, and making
Of my burning thoughts a warm atmosphere.

Flaunting a disengagement from the urban scene to build his imaginative creations, he claims he will not even notice *l'émeute,* workers' riots, as he produces a childlike idyll in a scene generated from within, from his own thoughts. This image of the lyric poet at work, closing himself off from the outside world, proves not to be an accurate description of what follows: the poems of this section do not ignore the poor, the miserable, though the central focus is still on what the poetic imagination does with these urban figures, in empathy or hostility. In his poetry of the city Baudelaire develops the lyric poet's way of belonging by not belonging, pursuing the theme of the relation between the poetic imagination and society.

The two major difficulties of describing that relation are first, that the subject is so vast—the lyric in general and society in general, with a great deal of historical variation. But second, the choice of what one might call the level of analysis can produce an exasperating range of possibilities. We have just seen that poets themselves may project a relation between lyric and society which their own poetic practice may undercut and require one to frame differently, and that is without even taking a broader historical perspective. Baudelaire's poems were so shocking that he was prosecuted (and found guilty) for outrage to public morals, but today every French schoolchild studies his work as one of the great cultural monuments of the nation. How, then, to conceive of the social bearing of his lyrics?

The multiple levels at which lyric practice can be situated—the poet wants to impress a patron, the poet is engaging an inherited poetic practice, the poet is contributing to a new structure of feeling, the poet is unconsciously protesting the social norms of the day, the poet offers an imaginary solution to a social antagonism—mean that the situation one describes is generated retrospectively: in effect, the relations between lyric and society are constructed retrospectively, by those who experience the history that these lyrical practices help create and who thus register the effects of these poems or explicitly reconstruct one of the histories to which they contribute. When we think about Baudelaire, we do so from a perspective formed in part by his creation of the figure of the *poète maudit,* social outcast, but which has since become a cultural icon. The situation is scarcely a simple one.

One of the things that lyrics may do is project a distinction between the immediate historical, communicative situation and the level at which the work operates in its generality of address and its openness to being articulated by readers who will be differently situated (situated in part by the history of these works themselves). This means that the claims later ages can make about them will be multiple also and open to reversals, through recontextualizations and changes of scale. What becomes evident in any discussion of sociopolitical implications of concrete literary works is the unpredictability of their historical efficacy. What at one level might seem contestation is complicity at another. A socially oriented criticism can treat the work as its recurrent coming into being in a social space, which is itself in part the effect of that work and always to be constructed by a reading of one's own relation to it. The possible social meanings available are likely to be enormously varied, depending upon the level and scope of analysis.

Still, one can sketch some possibilities. I have repeatedly evoked the epideictic character of lyric, its assertion of claims about the world, and will revisit this function shortly with the example of the ancient Greek lyric. There is a long tradition of lyrics explicitly engaging sociopolitical issues, such as Celan's "Todesfuge," discussed in Chapter 4, or protest poems of the twentieth century. Victor Hugo's collection *Les Châtiments* attacks Napoleon III through a variety of lyric forms—ballads, elegies, odes, satires. Horace, in Ode 3.6, pillories the decadence of Roman society, where every generation is less virtuous, more self-indulgent than the last:

> Damnosa quid non imminuit dies?
> aetas parentum, peior avis, tulit
>   nos nequiores, mox daturos
>   progeniem vitiosiorem.

☞

> What has not cankering time made worse?
> Worse than our grandparent's generation,
> Our parents then produced us, even worse
> And soon to bear still more sinful children.

William Blake's "London" is a complex indictment of oppression in a now thriving city with its charters of privilege:

> I wander thro' each charter'd street,
> Near where the charter'd Thames does flow,
> A mark in every face I meet,
> Marks of weakness, marks of woe.
>
> In every cry of every man,
> In every Infant's cry of fear,
> In every voice, in every ban,
> The mind-forg'd manacles I hear:
>
> How the Chimney-sweeper's cry
> Every blackning Church appalls,
> And the hapless Soldier's sigh
> Runs in blood down Palace walls.
>
> But most thro' midnight streets I hear
> How the youthful Harlot's curse

Blasts the new-born Infant's tear,
And blights with plagues the Marriage hearse.

This poem works to render rhythmically and syntactically equivalent, without the need of argument, the various cries that illustrate forms of social bondage, the "mind-forg'd manacles" that blight a whole range of institutions: the church, the government, and marriage itself, in that striking concluding compression, "the Marriage hearse."

Lyrics may also offer outright diatribe, as in Shelley's "England in 1819":

An old, mad, blind, despised, and dying king,—
Princes, the dregs of their dull race, who flow
Through public scorn, mud from a muddy spring,—
Rulers who neither see, nor feel, nor know,
But leech-like to their fainting country cling,
Till they drop, blind in blood, without a blow,—
A people starved and stabbed in the untilled field,—
An army which liberticide and prey
Makes as a two-edged sword to all who wield,—
Golden and sanguine laws which tempt and slay;
Religion Christless, Godless, a book sealed,—
A Senate—Time's worst statute unrepealed,—
Are graves from which a glorious Phantom may
Burst to illumine our tempestuous day.

While implicitly acknowledging that poets are not yet the unacknowledged legislators of mankind and so must do battle, this powerful condemnation of a corrupt and shortsighted governing elite nevertheless ends on an optimistic note, with the meter emphasizing that a glorious phantom *may* burst forth. Such optimism is less present in later political poems, such as Yeats's "The Second Coming" ("The best lack all conviction, while the worst / Are full of passionate intensity"), which condemns the state of Europe after World War I, and "Easter 1916," which performatively memorializes the Irishmen slain by the English. Like Auden's "September 1, 1939," which I take up at the end of this chapter, this

poem gains solemnity from the three-beat meter with a virtual beat or
pause at the end of each line:

> We know their dream; enough
> To know they dreamed and are dead;
> And what if excess of love
> Bewildered them till they died?
> I write it out in a verse—
> MacDonagh and MacBride
> And Connolly and Pearse
> Now and in time to be,
> Wherever green is worn,
> Are changed, changed utterly:
> A terrible beauty is born.

No one doubts that lyrics often have explicit social or political themes and
are the vehicle of protest as well as praise, though the question of their
social effects is hard to determine.[3]

Second, at least as difficult to estimate are the effects of lyric language,
for which various claims can plausibly be made. The indeterminacy of
meaning in poetry provides an experience of freedom and a release from
the compulsion to signify. With its apparently gratuitous chiming and
rhyming, its supplemental metrical organization and uses of lineation—
in short its determination by a host of sensuous factors—lyric language
works against instrumental reason, prosaic efficiency, and communicative
transparency, quite independently of the thematic content of particular
lyrics. The ways of creating memorable language and ways of resisting
what Merleau-Ponty calls "the prose of the world" go together in lyric.
Hegel argues that once prose has taken dominion of the world, and
"the mere accuracy of the prosaic way of putting things has become the
ordinary rule," to lyric falls the task of transforming "the prosaic consciousness's ordinary mode of expression into a poetic one," working
"out of the mind's habitual abstractness into a concrete liveliness" and
creating estrangement from the prosaic perception of the world.[4] Lyric's
sonorous structures, as they acquire a formal solidity, convey a feeling,
Robert Kaufman argues, that we can glimpse alternatives to the concepts

that have structured our world.[5] Readers' encounters with anomalous verbal combinations, along with the kinetic effects of rhythm, offer a challenge to homogenized experience. Song has always ministered to pleasure more than industry, and often has been a form of resistance to the political organization of life; and as the written version of song, lyric operates in the same fashion, but with greater verbal artistry and precision. Like song, lyric can work subliminally to these ends, enlisting its readers and performers in language processes that are not determined by communicational efficiency and propositional meaning but memorability, ceremoniousness, harmony, charm.

Lyric language doubtless works subliminally, and much of its social efficacy may depend on its ability to embed itself in the mind of readers, to invade and occupy it, to be taken in, introjected, or housed as instances of alterity that can be repeated, considered, treasured, or ironically cited. Rhythm, repetition, and rhyme work to create formulations that are in some way striking, often with an opacity that gives them an existence independent of a message, makes them stick in the memory, where they come to play a role in thought and action, enlarging imaginative resources, channeling thought in particular ways.

Finally, there is the lyric contribution to the construction of a community, to which I turn in a moment: a pan-Hellenic community through the reperformance of ancient Greek lyric; a European intellectual and affective community through European Petrarchism; and a national middle-class readership through the construction of an English literary tradition rooted in popular ballads. Although in some cases themes may be important here, the effects of lyric may come also from lyric as a formal structure that can be repeated: if the most popular ancient Greek poems are widely performed, that helps to create this audience as a community, just as the proliferation of Petrarchan sonnets spread structures of feeling and modes of virtuosity that contributed to a Renaissance culture. Benedict Anderson's account of the role of newspapers in the nineteenth century in creating the imaginative communities that are nations might find an analogy in the earlier functioning of lyric.[6]

Walter Benjamin writes that there has been no success on a mass scale in lyric poetry since Baudelaire, but there have certainly been circumstances where later poets' work plays a role in the production of community identity: in addition to such well-known Caribbean poets as Aimé Césaire and Kamau Braithwaite, one might cite Louise Bennett. Much of her poetry in Jamaican Creole or patois in the 1940s and 1950s was published weekly in a Jamaican newspaper and achieved great popularity, as satirical comments on Jamaican affairs and world news. Her most famous poem, "Colonization in Reverse," satirizes the invasion of Britain by Jamaicans who are looking for "a big-time job."

> Wat a joyful news, Miss Mattie,
> I feel like me heart gwine burs'
> Jamaica people colonizin
> Englan in reverse.
>
> By de hundred, by de t'ousan
> From country and from town,
> By de ship load, by de plane-load
> Jamaica is Englan boun.

Other poems repurpose the language of journalism, infusing it with Creole expressions in a popular talking-back to the formal English of Jamaican officialdom. Daniel Tiffany argues that the use of popular dialects—whether underworld canting songs, local argot, cockney slang—is one of the ways in which lyric most effectively generates social impact, engaging issues of class. Bennett herself, writing in ballad stanzas with prominent rhymes and colloquial language, produces a popular poetry dealing with public issues of the day, and by instantiating this dialect in iterable poems helps constitute the actual and potential readers of that language as a community.[7]

I now turn to three different cases that illustrate a range of social engagement: the epideictic lyric of ancient Greece, the Renaissance sonnet, and Wordsworth's *Lyrical Ballads*. I then take up Adorno's celebrated argument about the lyric in "On Lyric Poetry and Society" and conclude with two twentieth-century examples of the complex relations between lyric and ideology.

2. Three Examples

A. *The Epidectic Lyric in Ancient Greece*

In archaic Greece, even after the development of writing, melic or lyric verse was performed on various social occasions, which inclines critics to posit for lyric a fundamental social role: it works to constitute such groups of listeners as social groups, offering discourse about the relations of men to the gods and about what is to be valued. The Pindaric ode, writes Leslie Kurke, "does the work of mediating and finessing the divergent interests and claims of individual and community, elitist and middling values." Jeffrey Walker maintains that lyric is the original form of epideictic rhetoric—what later became the rhetoric of praise and eloquence—which works to shape communal judgments about what is right and thus to create values. The archaic lyric predates the emergence of both poetry and rhetoric as discursive modes; it is a medium for persuasion rather than self-expression. "In that archaic realm, epideictic or 'poetic' discourse is the 'primary' form of 'rhetoric,' on which pragmatic discourse, and especially formalized pragmatic, depended for the major source of its power—the culturally authoritative paradigms of eloquence and wisdom on which it draws."[8]

According to Hesiod, both the *basileus,* the wise prince, and the singer produce "honeyed words of eloquence": the princes "persuade with gentle words"; the singers chant the glorious deeds of men and gods and turn people from their sorrows. Both speakers receive their eloquence from the muses—the muses' sacred gift to humankind—and have the power of persuasion. Plutarch reports that "Thales passed as a lyric poet, and screened himself behind this art, but in reality he did the work of one of the mightiest of lawgivers. For his odes were so many exhortations to obedience and harmony, and their measured rhythms were permeated with ordered tranquility, so that those who listened to them were insensibly softened in their dispositions, insomuch that they renounced the mutual hatreds which were so rife at the time and dwelt together in a common pursuit of what was high and noble."[9] Efficacious words indeed.

It was the poets, especially Homer, who gave the Greeks their gods. They had no other prophet to provide a sacred or foundational text. Early Greek poetry, explains Marcel Detienne, belongs to a ritualized performative speech, possibly of divine origin: the seer, the poet, and the king are the three masters of truth, *aletheia*—a conception of truth which is contrasted not with falsity but with *lethe,* oblivion. Poetic discourse confers fame; it is not a representation of fame but fame itself, *kleos,* glory, passed by word of mouth. As Pindar, the inheritor of this discursive function puts it, "mortal men forget / what has not intermingled in the glorious stream of verses / and come to flower through a poet's skill."[10] Of course, this notion does not live on uncontested, and with the rise of philosophy poetry comes to be seen as an art of deception rather than a ritual of truth, a charm or drug, *apate,* illusion, rather than *aletheia.* If Plato claims that there is an ancient quarrel between philosophy and poetry (which he did much to exacerbate) it is partly because both arose from epideictic discourse about what was to be valued.

In public eloquence, public performance, Greek lyrics often strive for wisdom, offering views on topics of general concern, as in Sappho's priamel, which begins as follows (the brackets mark gaps in the papyrus):

O]ἰ μὲν ἰππήων στρότον οἰ δὲ πέσδων
οἰ δὲ νάων φαῖσ᾽ ἐπὶ γᾶν μέλαιναν
ἔ]μμεναι κάλλιστον ἔγω δὲ κῆν᾽ ὄτ-
    τω τις ἔραται.

Some men say an army of horse and some men say an army on foot
and some men say an army of ships is the most beautiful thing
on the black earth. But I say it is
    what you love.

[Trans. Anne Carson]

Sappho cites the example of Helen, who left everything for the one she loved, but the poem suddenly turns at the end to Anactoria, who is now gone:

τᾶ]ς κε βολλοίμαν ἔρατόν τε βᾶμα
κ]ἀμάρυχμα λάμπρον ἴδην προσώπω

ἢ τὰ Λύδων ἄρματα κἀν ὅπλοισι
  πεσδομ]άχεντας

         ☞

I would rather see her lovely step
and the motion of light on her face
than chariots of Lydians or ranks of
    footsoldiers in arms.

This poem champions, against the epic values that formed the normative
view of a warrior society, what has become a modern view of love and of
what in general is to be preferred. The turn to Anactoria at the end is unexpected but links the individual thought and situation to the general
theme in a way that comes to be characteristic of lyric. It does not so much
express an individual's view as counter a sociopolitical orthodoxy.

Another famous example of the lyric of dissent is a fragment of
Archilochus's:

Ἀσπίδι μὲν Σαΐων τις ἀγάλλεται, ἥν παρὰ θάμνῳ
  ἔντος ἀμώμητον κάλλιπον οὐκ ἐθέλων·
αὐτὸν δ' ἐξεσάωσα· τί μοι μέλει ἀσπὶς ἐκείνη;
  ἐρρέτω· ἐξαῦτις κτήσομαι οὐ κακίω.

         ☞

Some Saian exults in my shield which I left
   —a faultless weapon—beside a bush against my will.
But I saved myself! What do I care about that shield?
   To hell with it! I'll get one soon just as good another time.

                            [Trans. Richmond Lattimore]

The declaration that abandoning his shield and saving himself was preferable to fighting on is scandalous for a culture of martial honor. This poem
is said to have led to Archilochus being driven out of Sparta.

Lyrics mount challenges to orthodoxies but can also, in modernity as
in antiquity, offer memorable apothegms that put on display alleged truths,
provide material for reflection, and are repeatable in appropriate circumstances. Lyrics are good to think with—as Lévi-Strauss said of myths.

Pindar's odes, for instance, contain many gnomic statements, purporting to be truths about the world: "The race of gods and men is one, we both draw our breath from a single mother," controversially declares the sixth Nemean Ode. In Plato's *Protagoras,* where the protagonists discuss the arguments of a poem by Simonides about whether it is truly hard to be good, everyone takes it for granted that, as Protagoras says, the most important part of a man's paideia is to be capable of making judgments about the sayings of poets: "I consider, Socrates, that the greatest part of a man's education is to be skilled in the matter of verses; that is, to be able to apprehend in the utterances of the poets, what has been rightly and what wrongly composed, and to know how to distinguish them and account for them when questioned." Socrates dismisses this as a vulgar practice— "For it seems to me that arguing about poetry is comparable to the wine-parties of common market-folk"—the sort of thing that happens at dinner parties; and he argues, against the received view which took poetic sayings seriously, that people ought to discuss dialectic rather than poetry, or at least to articulate their own opinions rather than make use of the verses of poets in their discussions of what is right or best. But at the very beginning of the dialogue, in response to joshing that Alcibiades, whom Socrates has been pursuing, is losing his youthful beauty and has a beard coming, Socrates replies, "And what of that? Do you mean to say that you do not approve of Homer, who said that the youth has the highest grace in him where the beard is appearing, as now in the case of Alcibiades?" Plato has Socrates appeal to the poets as source of wisdom, and it seems evident that in the fourth and fifth centuries BCE poetry is a form of epideictic discourse, an instrument of ethical education. "The assumption that poetry could be taken as the prime educative medium," writes Simon Goldhill, "conforms both to what is known about the practice of schooling of Athenian young boys and to what is regularly assumed about the function of poetry by ancient commentators and poets—namely that poetry has an ethical and normative thrust designed to inform, improve, and exhort the citizen, as well as to give pleasure."[11]

Plato's *Laws,* a late dialogue describing ways in which the state should attempt to mold good citizens, complains about the proliferation of poems and poets, "on whose writings we are told by our tens of thousands of people, we ought to rear and soak the young, if we are to give them a correct education, making them, by means of recitations, lengthy listeners who learn off whole poets by heart." In earlier times, faced with a threat of Persian attack, Athenians were united and reverent and each type of lyric had its own music: "one class of song was that of prayer to the gods, which bore the name of 'hymns,' contrasted with this was another class, best called 'dirges'; 'paeans' formed another; and yet another was the 'dithyramb.' named as I fancy, after Dionysius. 'Nomes' also were so called as being a distinct class of song; and these were further described as 'citharoedic nomes' [solemn poems accompanied by the lyre]. So these and other kinds being classified and fixed, it was forbidden to set one kind of words to a different class of tune."[12]

Then, "the populace willingly submitted to orderly control." But after the Athenians' defeat of the Persians, there was a fall into decadence and irreverence that required concerted state action: "there arose as leaders of unmusical illegality poets who, though by nature poetical, were ignorant of what was just and lawful in music; and they, being frenzied and possessed by a spirit of pleasure mixed dirges with hymns and paeans with dithyrambs, and imitated flute-tunes with harp-tunes, and blended every kind of music with every other; and thus through their folly bore false witness against music, as a thing without any standard of correctness . . . By compositions of such character, set to similar words, they bred in the populace a spirit of lawlessness." Lawless or licentious taste in music and poetry led to contempt for the law, "For, thinking themselves knowing, men became fearless; and audacity bred effrontery. For to be fearless of the opinion of a better man, owing to self-confidence, is nothing else than base effrontery." Next came a refusal to be subject to rulers, then "the shirking of submission to one parents and elders," and finally, "the effort to disregard the laws, while the last stage of all is to lose all respect for oaths or pledges to divinities."[13] Mixing poetic genres is the first step on the road to anarchy or revolution.

No wonder poetry must be strictly controlled by the state. *The Republic* notoriously concludes that "we can admit no poetry into our city, save only hymns to the gods and the praises of good men. For if you grant admission to the honeyed muse in lyric or epic, pleasure and pain will be lords of your city, instead of law."[14] Exception is being made for the sort of lyric associated above all with Pindar.

Among the fragments that have come down to us, one of the few poetic corpora that survived in manuscript are the epigrams in elegiac verse of Theognis, from around 544 BCE. They not only offer advice to the boy Cyrnus, to whom many of them are addressed, but make judgments and seek to persuade listeners, or at least induce them to reconsider their attitudes and dispositions, as in Theognis 183–186:

> Κριοὺς μὲν καὶ ὄνους διζήμεθα, Κύρνε, καὶ ἵππους
>   εὐγενέας, καί τις βούλεται ἐξ ἀγαθῶν
> βήσεσθαι· γῆμαι δὲ κακὴν κακοῦ οὐ μελεδαίνει
>   ἐσθλὸς ἀνήρ, ἤν οἱ χρήματα πολλὰ διδῷ.

☙

> We seek out rams and asses and horses that are purebred, Cyrnus,
>   and everyone wishes that they mount (females) of good stock;
> but a noble man does not mind marrying the base daughter of a base
>   father
>   if the latter gives him a lot of money. . . .

[Trans. Douglas Gerber]

Though these poetic performances are often presented as addressed to the youth Cyrnus, Theognis is acutely interested in the survival of his verse and represents it as repeatable text, insisting that his work will be read and live on:

> Κύρνε, σοφιζομένῳ μὲν ἐμοὶ σφρηγὶς ἐπικείσθω
>   τοῖσδ' ἔπεσιν, λήσει δ' οὔποτε κλεπτόμενα,
> οὐδέ τις ἀλλάξει κάκιον τοὐσθλοῦ παρεόντος·
>   ὧδε δὲ πᾶς τις ἐρεῖ· Θεύγνιδός ἐστιν ἔπη
> τοῦ Μεγαρέως· πάντας δὲ κατ' ἀνθρώπους ὀνομαστός.' [19–23]

☙

> Kyrnos, this is my work; let a seal be stamped on the writing
>   of these words, so that none who steals them shall ever deceive,
> so that none in the presence of good work can substitute forgery.
>   Thus shall each reader say: "These are the words of Theognis
> of Megara, a great name, the world knows it."

[Trans. Richmond Lattimore]

These lines are distinctive not only for the early celebration of the ability of lyric to transcend any particular occasion of performance to establish a name but also for the vision of a Panhellenic community created in part by poetry and poetic performance. Describing "the Panhellinization of the lyric," Gregory Nagy notes that while Pindar's victory odes celebrate a specific event, each of them "aimed at translating its occasion into a Panhellenic event, a thing of beauty that could be replayed by and for all Hellenes for all time to come."[15]

The poetry of praise and immortality contributes to this creation as it imagines its own the dissemination. Theognis gives a nice twist to this theme in lines addressed to Cyrnus:

Σοὶ μὲν ἐγὼ πτέρ' ἔδωκα, σὺν οἷσ' ἐπ' ἀπείρονα πόντον
    πωτήσῃ, κατὰ γῆν πᾶσαν ἀειρόμενος
ῥηϊδίως· θοίνῃς δὲ καὶ εἰλαπίνῃσι παρέσσῃ
    ἐν πάσαις πολλῶν κείμενος ἐν στόμασιν,
καί σε σὺν αὐλίσκοισι λιγυφθόγγοις νέοι ἄνδρες
    εὐκόσμως ἐρατοὶ καλά τε καὶ λιγέα
ἄισονται. καὶ ὅταν δνοφερῆς ὑπὸ κεύθεσι γαίης
    βῆς πολυκωκύτους εἰς Ἀίδαο δόμους,
οὐδέποτ' οὐδὲ θανὼν ἀπολεῖς κλέος, ἀλλὰ μελήσεις
    ἄφθιτον ἀνθρώποις αἰὲν ἔχων ὄνομα,
Κύρνε, καθ' Ἑλλάδα γῆν στρωφώμενος, ἠδ' ἀνὰ νήσους
    ἰχθυόεντα περῶν πόντον ἐπ' ἀτρύγετον,
οὐχ ἵππων νώτοισιν ἐφήμενος· ἀλλά σε πέμψει
    ἀγλαὰ Μουσάων δῶρα ἰοστεφάνων.
πᾶσι δ', ὅσοισι μέμηλε, καὶ ἐσσομένοισιν ἀοιδή
    ἔσσῃ ὁμῶς, ὄφρ' ἂν γῆ τε καὶ ἥλιος.
αὐτὰρ ἐγὼν ὀλίγης παρὰ σεῦ οὐ τυγχάνω αἰδοῦς,
    ἀλλ' ὥσπερ μικρὸν παῖδα λόγοις μ' ἀπατᾷς. [237–254]

☞

I have given you wings with which you will fly, soaring easily
over the boundless seas and all the land. You will be present
at every dinner and feast, lying on the lips of many,
and lovely youths accompanied by the sounds of pipes will sing of
    you

in orderly fashion with beautiful, clear voices.
And whenever you go to Hades' house of wailing, down the dark
   earth's depths,
never even in death will you lose your fame, but you will be in men's
   thoughts,
your name ever immortal, Cyrnus, as you roam throughout the land
of Greece, among the islands, crossing over the fish-filled, und-
   raining sea,
not riding on the backs of horses, but it is the splendid gifts
of the violet-wreathed Muses that will escort you.
For all who care about their gifts, even for future generations,
you will be alike the subject of song, as long as earth and sun exist.
And yet I do not meet with a slight respect from you,
but you deceive me with words, as if I were a small child.

[Trans. Andrew Miller]

Theognis uses the language of memorialization to highlight disappoint-ment and deception in an erotic affair. The promise of immortalization in words assumes, of course, the performance of this poetry of praise for multiple audiences at feasts, where the boast is performatively fulfilled again and again. Deceived by words, the poet takes revenge, through tri-angulated address, and in a manner that fits the crime, since we may re-alize at the end that despite the lengthy celebration of the addressee, we have been told nothing of his virtues or memorable qualities. The verse that instructs, chides, and cajoles the audience works to create what Nagy calls the "ostensibly integral community of *philoi* that is the *polis* of Megara"—a posited community of listeners ready to be influenced and to judge.[16]

B. The Renaissance Sonnet

If the sphere of private life is demarcated as the domain of the lyric by Horace and by the practitioners of the Latin love elegy, it is not typically treated as a domain of private reflection and expression or exploration of a tumultuous inner life, but rather as a set of social attitudes. Some ten centuries later, the troubadours introduced what must be seen as a new structure of feeling, a social disposition culminating in European Petrarchism: love as a spiritualized activity constructed around the inaccessibility of the beloved and the impossibility of realization. Love is taken to structure one's existence, which becomes an oscillation between affective extremes rather than a teleological development (as in the Christian scenario). As Petrarchism became a courtly mode practiced by a politically influential class across Europe, playing the lover through lyric becomes a form of refinement and self-distinction. And this set of conventions and topoi provided an incentive and resource for exercising and refining national vernaculars: a language proved its mettle by developing its own Petrarchan poetry.[17] This complex of discursive possibilities, building on the *finz amour* of the troubadours, was a powerful force in the social world, and of course quite surprisingly persists in our own day despite considerable skepticism about love and numerous changes in sexual mores over the centuries.

The opening sonnet of Petrarch's *Canzoniere,* discussed in Chapter 1, presents the poet less as lover than as a social subject ostensibly embarrassed to have made a spectacle of his amorous complaining. Petrarchism suggests a division of the world into the private space of unhappy passion and the public world in which the lover still moves and in which his tragic entrammelment may even seem comical. Such a division is, of course, an ideological operation of some significance, initiating a process that culminates in nineteenth-century novels, which suggest that one's true life is an interior and affective one, rather than one's worldly existence.[18] In *The History of Sexuality,* Michel Foucault sketches the operations whereby what the ancients had seen as a something of an illness, if not form of madness—sexual desire—becomes in the nineteenth century central to the identity of individuals; but this is a process that begins with the troubadours and Petrarchism. This poetry produced what Rancière calls a new *partage du sensible,* a new organization of experience presuming the centrality of unrealized amorous passion, which has animated the lyric and popular song ever since.[19] Petrarch also developed a new form of praise: refusing to submit a poetic discourse of love to a rational calculus, the sonnets do not evaluate; they do not try to show that you, Laura, surpass other women in this or that respect. "You are the one," they claim, "the only one for me"; I would sacrifice anything for "one glance from those eyes."[20] This lyric mode thus promotes a notion of the individual subject as distinct from others. It is not that everyone loves the most beautiful or most accomplished woman around; subjects are individuated by their distinctive obsession with one woman, real or imagined. And of course, that subject is characterized by inner divisions, as it experiences hope and despair, thrills at the sight or thought of the beloved, or is crushed by her cruelty or indifference.

The formal structure of the sonnet, whether Petrarchan or Shakespearean, is a device for the public exploration of a host of subjects as they relate to an often idealized passion. The sonnet worked to promote a common ideology—of alleged individuality. "Each sonnet," writes Roland Greene, "seems a uniquely personal event or artifact—and its speaker often declares the singularity of his or her experience—and yet the multiplication of the form . . . enables European cultures to share a technology of ideation and feeling, to think through a common medium, all the while professing the particular identity of each society, poet, and speaker."[21]

Shakespeare's *Sonnets* are frequently read as the exploration of a peculiar individual amorous tension but are replete with public themes. The first seventeen sonnets are often difficult for modern readers to engage, especially readers hoping to explore the place where "Shakespeare unlocked his heart."[22] Why would the first concern be that a young man breed, reproducing himself by producing offspring? Why would a speaker in love be eager for the man he loves to father a child, which presumably would require significant concourse with a wife or female lover? This group of sonnets can be seen as a mode of courtly compliment—you are so splendid that we need you to go forth and multiply—and Shakespeare shows therein his own poetic fecundity, breeding so many sonnets on a single unusual theme; but it seems strangely obsessional to give flattery this particular cast for a whole series of sonnets. Sonnets 1–17 are most comprehensible as urging civic responsibility (breeding is what such a beautiful young man owes the world)—not what we have come to expect in love sequences, which usually ignore worldly responsibilities.

The first sonnet approaches the issue of breeding as the syllogistic consequence of a social truth: "from fairest creatures we desire increase"; you are extraordinarily fair, therefore you should breed.

From fairest creatures we desire increase,
That thereby beauty's rose might never die,
But as the riper should by time decease,
His tender heir might bear his memory:
But thou, contracted to thine own bright eyes,
Feed'st thy light's flame with self-substantial fuel,
Making a famine where abundance lies,
Thyself thy foe, to thy sweet self too cruel.
Thou that art now the world's fresh ornament
And only herald to the gaudy spring,
Within thine own bud buriest thy content
And, tender churl, makest waste in niggarding.
Pity the world, or else this glutton be,
To eat the world's due, by the grave and thee.

This sonnet, Helen Vendler observes, enumerates "values considered by the speaker as axiomatic and self-evidently good" in the sequence as a whole: "beauty, increase, inheritance, memory, light, abundance, sweetness, freshness, ornament, springtime, tenderness, and the world's rights." Like so many of the sonnets, this poem develops through clashing metaphors—the candle and the bud—slipping from one frame of reference to another and trying to bind them together in the couplet. But it ends with the alternatives of pitying the world (by breeding) or gluttonously eating the world's due, two forms of social behavior. The second sonnet poses the question of beauty by asking what the fair youth could say when asked "where thy beauty lies," and it casts the answers in terms of social morality: one should act so as to receive praise and avoid shame. In the seventh sonnet the childless man is "found by onlookers to be of no social consequence." Throughout the first seventeen sonnets there is continual reversion to how you will be viewed by the world and what you owe the world. Such questions are not only put to the youth but also arise for the speaker ("The age to come would say, This poet lies"). "Love poetry's political character," writes Christopher Martin, "is determined by the writer's awareness of the way that the audience responds to the poet's self-presentation."[23]

The sonnets that come later in the collection achieve remarkable complexity of thought—a major innovation in the Petrarchan tradition—by their deployment of often conflicting images or discourses, in quatrains that are set in uncertain relation to one another, and by virtue of the unusual situation of the speaker and the peculiar moral and amatory tensions he explores. It is striking, though, how many of the most justly celebrated sonnets, while helping create the impression of a speaker-subject, reflect on central social and ethical questions and seem to belong more to the mode of epideictic discourse than to anything like personal amorous confession. One need only think of famous incipits: "Th'expense of spirit in a waste of shame / Is lust in action"; "Tis better to be vile than vile esteemed"; "Let me not to the marriage of true minds / Admit impediments"; "They that have power to hurt and will do none . . ."[24] Sandra Bermann observes that though Shakespeare probably did not intend the *Sonnets* for publication, they are among the most public ever written in demanding the reader's insight into a complex world, as—she is speaking about Sonnet 87, but the point is a general one—they tap into "a societal, altogether worldly dimension in which contracts are made and broken and courts of common law pass judgment in property cases."[25]

Like most lyrics, Shakespeare's *Sonnets* function at several different levels. First, there is what Roland Greene calls the fictional aspect of this sequence: its projection of a speaker-character who addresses the objects of his affections, not only in different affective states but with a wide range of arguments and complex forms of praise. At this level the *Sonnets* propose a conception of the subject that seems modern and discontinuous, often at odds with itself in ways different from the Petrarchan subject, which oscillates between emotional poles. "The subject of Shakespeare's sonnets," writes Joel Fineman, "experiences himself as his difference from himself . . . an identity of ruptured identification." Reading the *Sonnets* in relation to the lyric tradition of epideictic praise, Fineman argues that the Dark Lady sonnets in particular mark a radical departure and "manage to give off the subjectivity effect required by a post-idealist literariness."[26]

Second, in the content of its amorous engagement, the collection takes the radical step of positing a bisexual subject, enamored of the Fair Youth while deeply involved with the Dark Lady. One may certainly question the potency of this conceptual event, since this aspect of the *Sonnets* seems not to have been salient for readers prior to what Foucault calls the invention of homosexuality in the nineteenth century, but it is very striking for modern readers.

Third, individual sonnets with their apothegms, sometimes relativized to the particular situation of a speaker but often not, continue a tradition of epideictic poetry that Shakespeare certainly complicates but does not abandon. Modern complaints about the unsatisfactory concluding couplets of many sonnets may derive from the fact that modern readers have been trained to expect an organic drama and find that the laconic declarations of many couplets make the metaphoric quatrains into rhetorical performances rather than deeply felt positions that would require more labor to resolve. But rhetorical performance was central to the practice of sonnets.

Finally, the very writing of sonnets at the end of the sixteenth century, at the climax of the sonnet vogue in England, contributes to the sense of a cultural coming-of-age in England both through the mastery of a prestigious Renaissance form and through the adaptation of that form to a less idealizing epideictic performance.

Another form of this social efficacy can be observed in an earlier sonnet from the other side of the Channel, Joachim Du Bellay's "Heureux qui comme Ulysse" ("Happy he who like Ulysses"). This poem about nostalgia for one's native land has had a remarkable fortune in French culture, as it became one of the most frequently memorized poems in the French canon—an example of the way in which particular poems may quite unexpectedly become powerful nationalist affirmations.

> Heureux qui, comme Ulysse, a fait un beau voyage,
> Ou comme cestuy-là qui conquit la toison,
> Et puis est retourné, plein d'usage et raison,
> Vivre entre ses parents le reste de son âge!
> Quand reverrai-je, hélas, de mon petit village
> Fumer la cheminée, et en quelle saison
> Reverrai-je le clos de ma pauvre maison,
> Qui m'est une province, et beaucoup davantage?

Plus me plaît le séjour qu'ont bâti mes aïeux,
Que des palais Romains le front audacieux,
Plus que le marbre dur me plaît l'ardoise fine
Plus mon Loire gaulois, que le Tibre latin;
Plus mon petit Liré, que le mont Palatin
Et plus que l'air marin la douceur angevine.

Happy the man who, journeying far and wide
As Jason or Ulysses did, can then
Turn homeward, seasoned in the ways of men,
To live life out, among his own again!
When shall I see the chimney-smoke divide
The sky above my little town: ah, when
Stroll the small gardens of that house again,
Which is my realm and crown, and more beside?
Better I love the plain, secluded home
My fathers built, than bold façades of Rome;
Slate pleases me as marble cannot do,
Better than Tiber's flood my quiet Loire,
Those little hills than these, and dearer far,
Than great sea winds the zephyrs of Anjou.

[Trans. Richard Wilbur]

A poem of choice of life as well as of nostalgia, Du Bellay's sonnet performs the neat ideological operation of presenting attachment to the nation and implicitly to the primacy of French culture as attachment to landscape, to the countryside (*terroir*, in modern parlance) which is figured as home for even the most cosmopolitan—for Du Bellay, living in Rome, and for later generations of Parisians. As such, one critic writes, "it may well function as France's most powerful political poem of all."[27]

Renaissance sonnets, though produced in diverse circumstances in different countries over several centuries, were a potent form of social action: positing a conception of an intense, often divided inner affective life, promoting literate culture through their success as a socially valued virtuoso display in courtly or aristocratic settings, and advancing the prestige of national languages.

C. Wordsworth

The Romantic era serves as something of a crux in any account of the sociopolitical status of lyric or of the relation between lyric poetry and society. It is here that arises the widespread modern conception, partly due to John Stuart Mill, of lyric as anti-social, a discourse of withdrawal, private vision, addressed to no one and overheard. Mill distinguished poetry not from prose but from eloquence, which of course seeks an audience, tries to persuade and teach. "Eloquence supposes an audience; the peculiarity of poetry appears to us to lie in the poet's utter unconsciousness of a listener. Poetry is feeling confessing itself to itself in moments of solitude."[28] This opposition between poetry and eloquence would have been unintelligible to the Greeks, for whom poetry was a very model of eloquence, nor does it describe much of the poetry of the romantic period, which is neither "feeling confessing itself to itself" nor opposed to eloquence.

Wordsworth presents a particularly interesting case. Though his poetry was important for Mill, Mill's theoretical formulations deviate substantially from Wordsworth's, whose Preface to the *Lyrical Ballads* is very much concerned with audience and with the social effect of his poems, as I discuss below. But first, Wordsworth's choice of low or rustic characters and situations gives him a central role in the transformation of the conceptual framework governing literary productions, especially in England.

The literary tradition of the eighteenth century passed down what Rancière calls the "representational regime of art," an Aristotelian framework where particular genres were hierarchically organized according to the type of action imitated and the characters and diction appropriate to each. Wordsworth appears initially to situate his writing in such a framework by taking up the ballad, a popular form of poetry, and peopling his newly defined "lyrical ballads" with cottagers, children, vagrants, thieves, an idiot boy and a mad mother; but his experiment, as he called it, proved to be a transformative and democratizing one. Wordsworth chose characters from rustic life, not because he was writing comedy or pastoral, but to capture elemental feelings, which he claimed to be those of everyone, and to be more easily observable in those whose social condition leaves them less exposed to "the action of social vanity." "Humble and rustic life was generally chosen because in that situation the essential passions of the heart find a better soil in which they can attain their maturity, are less under restraint, and speak a plainer, more emphatic language; because in that situation our elementary feelings exist in a state of greater simplicity and consequently may be more accurately contemplated and more forcefully communicated."[29]

The emancipation of the lyric is not just a matter of "shaking off the dust of obsolete rules and the pomp of conventional expressions," observes Rancière. "Isn't a new form of political experience necessary to emancipate the lyrical subject from the old poetico-political framework?" Taking up what he calls "the most famous poem in the English language, Wordsworth's 'Daffodils' [or "I Wandered Lonely as a Cloud"]," he asks, "How does the 'I' that is present in it, the 'I' of 'I wandered lonely as a cloud,' relate to the history of revolutionary subjectivity, whatever the well-attested versatility of the poet's political opinions and the equally attested political indifference of the daffodils?"[30]

For Rancière, "Politics is the construction of a specific sphere of experience in which certain objects are posited as shared and certain subjects are regarded as capable of designating these objects and arguing about them," and literature intervenes "in the carving up of objects that form a common world, the subjects that people that world, and the powers they have to see it, name it, and act upon it." The tradition inherited from Aristotle defined a hierarchy of literary genres and subject matters and principles of appropriateness that adapts forms of expression to the subjects represented and deploys notions of verisimilitude and appropriate action as criteria of judgment. This involved a particular *partage du sensible* or organization of what is to be apprehended by the senses, what is perceived as self-evident in a common world, and the organization of roles within this perceptual universe. The poetic revolution of the late eighteenth century disrupted the representative regime. "The most visible aspect of this dismantling," he writes, was the suppression of any hierarchy of subjects and characters, of any principle of correspondence between a style and a subject or a character."[31] Wordsworth's rejection of poetic diction in favor of the language of a "man speaking to men" and his choice in *Lyrical Ballads* and in the *Poems in Two Volumes,* which contain his most famous lyrics, of "low" subjects to illustrate the common mental operations of all mankind are central to this process.

Rancière does not, though, focus on character and diction alone: "The liberty that shaped the modern poetic revolution is a way the poet has of accompanying his utterance. This accompaniment has as its condition of possibility a new political experience of the sensory [*du sensible*]." An autonomy of sensory experience, open to anyone, "appears as the germ of a new humanity, a new form of individual and collective life." Poetry, in this new order, entails a particular form of sensory apprehension rather than speech in accordance with the conventions of generic hierarchies. The speaker wanders lonely as a cloud, which may evoke the crowd, but the subject is constituted *as* the subject of this sensory experience, which is available to any wanderer. The preface to *Lyrical Ballads* announces as the principle of the new poetics the communication of feelings and of natural associations of ideas in a state of excitement. This poetics, Rancière claims, "is first of all the utopian production of the *we* of the community which gave face to this sensory community that authorizes the stroll of the 'I' toward the daffodils, and identifies this movement with the writing of the poem conceived as communication of the movement of sensation."[32]

Rancière even goes so far as to posit, surprisingly, a relationship between Wordsworth's "I Wandered Lonely as a Cloud" and the opening of "La Marseillaise": "Allons, enfants de la patrie" ("Let us go," or "Come on, children of the nation"), a deep relationship not just "between the two stories about going," the speaker's wandering and the patriots' marching, and between the joyful army of patriots and the "host" of daffodils, but between the nonmimetic, nonallegorical signifying in the two cases. The wandering speaker sees the joy of the daffodils as the poet/speaker of *The Prelude* had seen on the roads of France, as he wandered there in 1790, joy shining in the people's faces as they danced "the dances of liberty":

On the roads of France, in that summer of 1790, no image imitates any model . . . what the poet sees, along the roads, along the Saone, or in the solitude of the mountains, is what makes the presentation of community possible, to know the self-presence of nature . . . The community is made up of the people who, while walking, see the same images rise up. Nature has dethroned the king by suppressing his place, his point-of-view—Nature in the double sense that will establish for the new age the core of politics in sensory experience: in one single notion, the power that causes being and holds beings together and the place where one goes, without privilege, to talk and look about.[33]

This is the Wordsworth who announced at the beginning of *The Prelude* that even "should the chosen guide" for his poetic enterprise "Be nothing better than a wandering cloud, / I cannot miss my way."

Wordsworth's poetic practice in "I Wandered Lonely as a Cloud" corresponds with the Kantian precept of the aesthetic revolution, that the beautiful is able to make itself appreciated without any concept. And the focus of the poem is the process of a generalized subject's self-understanding, as the speaker not only appreciates the joyful beauty of the host of daffodils but is surprised by the pleasure that the recollection of the joyful scene will afford, as

They flash upon that inward eye
Which is the bliss of solitude.

While emphasizing the relation of the poetic revolution and its contribution to the organization of the perceptual field to the political revolution in France that abolished the monarchy, Rancière also notes that the particular form Wordsworth's poetic utterance takes involved a distancing from the Revolution, as his hopes were disappointed by the transformation of the Revolution into the Terror. "Lyric subjectivity and its horizon of community are established only at the price of a critical effort that separates the wandering of the poetic 'I' from the poetic utopia of politics. . . . Poetry asserts itself as the ability of a sensory community to grasp anyone and anything in poetic *wandering* by going back over the route of the inaugural walk, by dissociating the rhythm of its walk from that of citizen armies, the clouds of summer sky from political storms."[34] But that separate lyric "I," wandering lonely as a cloud or experiencing the bliss of solitude, is still constituted in its similarity to others, as it accompanies itself on its lyric trajectories.

The assumption that lyric poetry is a form of social action is everywhere manifest in the Preface to *Lyrical Ballads*. In addition to explicitly choosing his subjects from low and rustic society rather than from urban society, Wordsworth conceives of writing as an engagement of his language with the mind of the public, thus with public taste and thus with the state of society. To present these experimental poems properly would require, he writes, "a full account of the present state of public taste in this country, and to determine how far this taste is healthy or depraved: which again could not be determined without pointing out in what manner language and the human mind act and react on each other, and without retracing the revolutions not of literature alone but likewise of society itself." Later he specifies that "a multitude of causes unknown to former times are now acting with a combined force to blunt the discriminating powers of the mind, and unfitting it for all voluntary exertion to reduce it to a state of almost savage torpor. The most effective of these causes are the great national events which are daily taking place [above all, the war with France] and the increasing accumulation of men in cities, where the uniformity of occupations produces a craving for extraordinary incident which the rapid communication of intelligence hourly gratifies." Under these circumstances, encouraging and enlarging the capabilities of the human mind to be "excited without the application of gross and violent stimulants"—that is, the capacity to be affected by the vicissitudes of ordinary circumstances—is, he writes, "one of the best services in which, at any period, a writer can be engaged, but this service, excellent at all times, is especially so at the present day."[35]

Since a poet is more subtly attuned to the imaginative recollection of experience than others, he can work to train the mind of reader and generate an appropriate readership, an imagined community of sympathetic readers. Wordsworth's prefaces and his lyrics, Thomas Pfau maintains, "were meant to counter the dissolution of the 'public' into regionally, demographically, and spiritually incompatible smaller communities" by reconfiguring a heterogeneous middle-class public into a more cohesive aesthetic community that would be moved in common ways.[36]

There are several different aspects to this process. First, Wordsworth took the ballad, a traditional, anonymous, popular form, often the formal condensation of tragic social incident, and transformed it into a literary form, helping to invent a tradition and produce the idea of national literature with roots in the past and the countryside. Pfau describes a self-reinforcing process by which the modern ballad continuously tells the story of its emergence from a traditional rustic culture by referring to a "hypostatized prehistory of authentic feeling and communal simplicity," and in the process establishing a literature thereby endowed with the capacity to maintain roots in the past and bolster its legitimacy in the present. The modern ballad shows literature at work, "transferring allegedly unselfconscious life forms from a simple past" to the poetry of a canon that will survive with its audience, a middle-class audience that is itself largely the product of the socioeconomic forces that are leading to the demise of the rural culture that ballads allegedly enshrine. "Solicitous of local and regional poverty as a matter of intense dramatic potential and spiritual 'interest' to an emergent national reading culture, Wordsworth's balladic encounters between the 'virtual' estate of the British middling classes and the fictive historicity of an English pre-capitalistic 'rustic' sphere generate an interpretive paradox" not easy to resolve, a social contradiction.[37]

In *Lyrical Ballads* a poet figure recovers, for a posited audience that can profit from their examples, rural characters deemed examples of a primitive, simple relation to objects and landscape. But the ballads sometimes expose the "ideological colonization" of that past by an arrogant or obtuse narrator—think of the narrator of "Resolution and Independence," appropriately satirized by Lewis Carroll in "A Sitting on a Gate," who ignores the responses of the leech-gatherer and shows no interest in his actual predicament. At other times they elegiacally emphasize the demise of rural simplicity, creating a kind of fictive history, and potentially drawing readers' attention to the contemporary antagonisms that make this world something of a nostalgic dream. "Precisely insofar as it succeeds in mobilizing flexible interpretive responses," Pfau claims, "the middle-class audience of *Lyrical Ballads* becomes a historically distinct formation in its own right."[38]

The second aspect of this production of a readership involves the transformation of landscape through the emphasis on its capacity to stimulate the imagination, thereby working to constitute a readership that learns how to respond in this way. "Tintern Abbey" takes as a theme the transformation of landscape into spiritual stimulation and of the possibilities that such an aesthetic consciousness holds for affective investment and spiritual depth:

> Once again
> Do I behold these steep and lofty cliffs,
> That on a wild secluded scene impress
> Thoughts of more deep seclusion . . .

Readers are encouraged to empathize with the speaker's meditative mood as he contrasts the youthful, unthinking pleasure in the natural scene of "sounding cataract" and "the deep and gloomy wood" with the later joy "Of elevated thoughts, a sense sublime / Of something far more deeply interfused," that now attends the natural scenes. With the figure of the poet's sister Dorothy as surrogate for the reader, the poem imagines that she will experience the same process that the speaker has reported:

> Thy memory [will] be as a dwelling-place
> For all sweet sounds and harmonies; oh! then,
> If solitude, or fear, or pain, or grief,
> Should be thy portion, with what healing thoughts
> Of tender joy wilt thou remember me,
> And these my exhortations!

The success of the poem depends on "the transferential construction of a sympathetic community of readers."[39]

The manuscript of Wordsworth's *The Ruined Cottage* is explicit about this project of producing a new aesthetic consciousness or affective organization of the perceptual realm, a collective disposition as moral basis of a community:

            by contemplating these forms
    In the relations which they bear to man
    We shall discover what a power is theirs
    To stimulate our minds, and multiply
    The spiritual presences of absent things.
    The weariness will cease—We shall acquire
    The [ ] habit by which sense is made
    Subservient still to moral purposes . . .
    All things shall speak of man and we shall read
    Our duties in all forms . . .[40]

On the basis of poems like these, Pfau suggests, "Wordsworth and his still-indistinct audience engage in a process of mutual projection and transference that furnishes them, almost imperceptibly, with more distinctive cultural and political identities."[41] The potentially oppressive project of making us read our duties in all forms gives poetry a particularly central role in trying to help readers overlay the world of cities and nascent capitalism with another, more vital and humanized world.

But "Tintern Abbey" has also served as example of a rather different version of the social action of poetry. The very explicitness with which the poem designates a time and place in its full title, "Lines Written a few Miles above Tintern Abbey, on Revisiting the Banks of the Wye during a Tour, July 13, 1798," has led historicist critics to focus on what they see as its obfuscation of social and political realities in the interest of imaginative transcendence. Marjorie Levinson, in what has become a notorious critique, argues that the primary social action of this poem, like Wordworth's other major lyrics, is the imaginative suppression of the social. The specific date of the poem's prolix title, July 13, 1798, underlines many anniversaries, national and personal: it is the eve of Bastille Day, anniversary of the fall of the Bastille nine years previously, eight years since Wordsworth's July visit to Revolutionary France, and five years since the murder of Marat on July 13, 1793, so in its own day it should signal the political context of the Revolution and the collapse of revolutionary hopes. In the opening lines of the poem itself, Wordsworth transforms aspects of the scene he would have confronted along the Wye when visiting the abbey and its surrounds: the beggars living in the ruins of the abbey itself, the industrial landscape of iron forges nearby whose furnaces burned night and day, and commercial traffic on the busy river itself.[42]

In fact, the title specifies that the poem is composed a few miles *above* Tintern Abbey, where there is a spot from which neither vagrants nor the iron mills could be seen, but his decision to include this salient date (however coincidental it may have been) and to choose this particular spot is certainly germane to the strategy that Levinson analyzes. Here is a descriptive passage near the beginning of the ode:

> Once again I see
> These hedge-rows, hardly hedge-rows, little lines
> Of sportive wood run wild: these pastoral farms,
> Green to the very door; and wreaths of smoke
> Sent up, in silence, from among the trees!
> With some uncertain notice, as might seem
> Of vagrant dwellers in the houseless woods,
> Or of some Hermit's cave, where by his fire
> The Hermit sits alone.

The small farms are green to the cottage door because the peasants lack other land to cultivate, as a result of the enclosure of common land, and the hedgerows, products of enclosure, become picturesque "lines of sportive wood run wild." The smoke from the fires of charcoal burners—one of the few ways that inhabitants could make a living—becomes wreaths in the landscape, and instead of vagrants living in the ruins of the Abbey we are offered the uncertain possibility of vagrants in the woods or, better, some poetic Hermit, with a capital H, a figure for retreat from society.

Levinson's detailed interpretation of the transformative strategies of the poem, which replaces the picture of a place with an imaginative image, has been read as an indictment of poet and poem, which at one level it certainly is. It treats the poem as if it were a falsified representation rather than "lines composed" in a particular spot, which the poet does not need to represent. But Levinson emphasizes that, for her, recovering the social and political resonance of that date and site "did not dilute, discredit, or remain extrinsic to the poem's psychological and metaphysical argument. Quite the contrary, these new meanings, that related Wordsworth's existential *Angst* to his own less mediated experience, as to the truths of his moment and his nation, materialized what has come to seem an impossibly displaced and textualized meditation. It became clear, for example, that many of 'Tintern Abbey's' most innocent affirmations—doctrinal and iconic—signified within the universe of contemporary social discourse as negations."[43]

Converting history to poetry, through the workings of memory and imagination, Wordsworth "establishes a literary immortality for the endangered farms and woods," which become in summary "beauteous forms." For Levinson, " 'Tintern Abbey' originates in a will to preserve something Wordsworth knows is already lost. At the same time, it arises from the will to deny this knowledge." Aspirations to liberty attached to the French and the Industrial revolutions must now be transferred to the mind; memory functions as barricade to resist the violence of historical change and contradiction. These scenes must be transformed, "because to entertain their concrete social reality would have meant confronting his own enabling insertion in a system he could not consciously abide." In sum, "Far from seeking to deprecate Wordsworth's transcendence or to trivialize profoundly moving works," Levinson writes, "I hoped to renew our sense of their power by exposing the conditions of their success: that recalcitrant facticity with which they had to contend, explicitly *and* unconsciously." "Tintern Abbey's" insights "level a fierce protest against the psychic effects of a newly industrializing and urban economy, and the protest is deepened by the fact that it takes the form of a meditative lyric, a form that gives no space to the representation of the social."[44]

Here, then, would be one possibility for lyric. It has some affinity with Adorno's conception—to which we next turn—of the lyric as potent negation, whose "distance from mere existence becomes the measure of what is false and bad in the latter."[45] Levinson's account of the social engagement of Wordsworth's lyrics is very different from Rancière's or Pfau's, both of whom maintain—as my previous two examples have shown as well—that there are other ways to participate in the social than to represent it. Lyric is not mimesis and can work, in very different historical circumstances, to generate a community that it addresses, to assert social values, to participate in a restructuring of the sensuous and affective domain of life. There is, of course, great historical variation, but also a good deal of commonality in the social engagement of lyrics. Above all, their effects are unpredictable and, as I have mentioned, our sense of them may largely depend on the particular social or political theories with which we approach the work of lyrics, so that what seems radical or resistant at one level can be seen as complicitous or reactionary at another. But for the most striking modern example of this dialectical reflection, I turn to Adorno's account of the lyric as "a philosophical sundial telling the time of history" (46).

3. Adorno's Dialectic

A classic essay on the lyric's relation to society that merits extended discussion is Theodor Adorno's "On Lyric Poetry and Society." It exemplifies a dialectical thinking that is easy to mock, and he himself imagines his audience accusing him of saying "it is precisely what is not social in the lyric poem that is now to become its social aspect," as if one were to give Louis XVI credit for the French Revolution; but he notes that there might be more truth here than common sense allows (42). He embraces the claim of his collaborator Max Horkheimer that "art, since it became autonomous, has preserved the utopia that evaporated from religion," insofar as art constitutes a resistance to the economic system, and that "an element of resistance is inherent in the most aloof art."[46] In its aloofness, the lyric is nonetheless "always the subjective expression of a social antagonism"; the greatness of works of art lies in their power "to give voice to what ideology conceals" (45, 39). Historical relations and social antagonisms are the more effectively constellated when the poem does not make the relation between self and society an explicit theme and this relation is allowed to crystalize "involuntarily" within the poem.

Such crystallization occurs through a "collective undercurrent" or substratum which emerges at various points in the work of art: "In every lyric poem the historical relationship of the subject to objectivity, of the individual to society, must have found its precipitate in the medium of a subjective spirit thrown back on itself," whereby the lyric subject "always stands for a far more general collective subject," even though the lyric "I" presents itself as in opposition to the collective (45, 42, 46). For Adorno the oppositional or utopian force of lyric emerges above all in its language, as the evacuation of or resistance to a language of commerce and alienation. Thus Adorno's dialectical critique finds utopian promise in unexpected places, such as a lyric by the explicitly reactionary poet Stefan George, whose verse rescues a language sullied by commerce.[47] Hearing German "as though it were a foreign tongue," George "overcomes its alienation, which is an alienation of use, by intensifying it until it becomes the alienation of a language no longer actually spoken nor even imagined and in that imaginary language he perceives what would be possible but never took place" (52). Here is the poem:

Im Windesweben	In the winds-weaving
War meine Frage	My question was
Nur Träumerei	Only daydreaming.
Nur Lächeln war	Only a smile was
Was du gegeben.	What you gave.
Aus nasser Nacht	From a moist night
Ein Glanz entfacht—	A gleam ignites—
Nun drängt der Mai,	Now May urges,
Nun muß ich gar	Now I must
Um dein Aug' und Haar	For your eye and hair
Alle Tage	Every day
In Sehnen leben.	Live in yearning.

[Trans. Paul Fleming]

At one level Adorno's argument is not difficult to grasp: through a process of self-divestment, albeit in reactionary opposition to the bourgeois society of his day, to which he could see no alternative, George is able to empty himself into language and make himself the spokesman of a pure language, constructing what Adorno calls "lines that sound as though they were not written by him but had been there since the beginning of time and would remain as they were forever" (53). Since this is a quixotic enterprise, "language's chimerical yearning for the impossible becomes an expression of the subject's insatiable erotic longing, which finds relief from the self in the other," and evokes "a vanished condition of the soul" (53, 51). But it is hard for someone who is not a native speaker of German to understand the source of the effects claimed here. How can the *gar* of

line 9, which Adorno calls short for "ganz und gar" ("completely"—
though this does not make it into the translation) and says was "shoved
into the line," doubtless for the rhyme with *Haar*, be "what establishes
the poem's status, with the force of a déjà-vu." As used in the line, *gar*
"has no proper meaning," he says, and is a "Goethean 'residue of the
absurd,' in which language escapes the subjective intention that occa-
sioned the use of the word" (53). The last four lines of the poem, Adorno
says, are among "the most irresistible in German poetry," like a quotation from a lost language, or something "language has irrevocably failed
to achieve [*aus dem von der Sprache unwiederbringlich Versäumten*—
perhaps "an irrecoverable omission from language"], a linguistic melody
beyond mere signifying (53). It is as though a word determined by the
rhyme and escaping a signifying intention of the author evokes, in its rightness, an ideal language, one never consummated in the world and which
thus implicitly condemns the world. Perhaps it is the simplicity of this
expression of unfulfillable longing that makes this a case of the lyric word
that "can no longer bear anything but the universal" and "represents language's deepest being as opposed to its service in the realm of ends" (53).

The one poem that Adorno cites in full in his *Aesthetic Theory* offers
an even more striking dialectical claim about the social significance of a
brief lyric. "Mausfallen-Sprüchlein"("Mousetrap Rhyme") is a poem of
Eduard Mörike's in the form of a child's chant for catching a mouse:

MAUSFALLEN-SPRÜCHLEIN

Das Kind geht dreimal um die Falle und spricht:

Kleine Gäste, kleines Haus.
Liebe Mäusin, oder Maus,
Stell dich nur kecklich ein
Heut nacht bei Mondenschein!
Mach aber die Tür fein hinter dir zu,
Hörst du?
Dabei hüte dein Schwänzchen!
Nach Tische singen wir
Nach Tische springen wir
Und machen ein Tänzchen:

Witt witt!

Meine alte Katze tanzt wahrscheinlich mit.

☞

The child circles the mousetrap three times and chants:

Little guests, little house.

Dearest tiny or grown-up Mouse,

Boldly pay us a visit tonight

When the moon shines bright!

But close the door behind you tight,

You hear?

And careful for your little tail!

After supper we sing,

After supper we spring,

And do a little dance;

Swish! Swish!

My old cat probably dances along.

[Trans. Hullot-Kentor, modified]

Despite the ostensible "sadistic identification" with what civilized custom does to an animal disdained as a parasite, Adorno claims that the concluding taunt—"if it really is a taunt and not the involuntarily friendly image of child, cat, and mouse dancing, the two animals on their hind legs—once appropriated by the poem no longer has the last word." The poem, he continues, "is the non-judgmental reflex of language on a miserable, socially conditioned ritual, and as such it transcends it by subordinating itself to it" ("ein Urteilsloser Reflex der Sprache auf einen abscheulichen, sozial eingeübten Ritus, übersteigtes diesen, indem es ihm sich einordnet"). On first reading, this is quite astonishing: the poem transcends the ritual by subordinating itself to it, judges it by failing to judge it. He continues, "The poem's gesture, which points to this ritual as if nothing else were possible, holds court over the gapless immanence of the ritual by turning the force of self-evidence into an indictment of that ritual. Art judges exclusively by abstaining from judgment . . . Form, which shapes verse into the echo of a mythical epigram, sublates its way of thinking.

Echo reconciles."[48] These are bold statements about the functioning of art—judgment is effected by abstaining from judgment—by presenting the ritual in an innocent fashion. But there is also something of a puzzle here. Whether or not we think that the final image is really a "friendly" dance of mouse with cat and child rather than victory dance of cat and child around the trapped mouse, it is doubtless true that the apparently cheerful celebration in verse of this spell to lure mice into the trap has a critical edge, by virtue of nothing more than artistic performance, its form as a poem rather than a child's ritual chant. But it is not clear how "echo reconciles." Why should we not say "echo ironizes"?

Adorno goes on to refer to the purposiveness without purpose of aesthetic objects: in a society that worships power, purposelessness becomes an implicit or de facto critique of power. If the social functioning of poetry in archaic Greece is sometimes linked to a sense of the power of words, in modern societies it may have come to be linked to a sense of the strange power of powerlessness.[49] In "Che cos'è la poesia?" Derrida links the poem, which asks to be learned by heart, which seeks its effectiveness by augmenting our linguistic resources and thus our vision of the world, to the figure of a hedgehog, *l'hérisson,* a vulnerable little creature which has as defense only its prickly outside. Threatened, it can only roll into a ball, making itself vulnerable, easily crushed on the roads. "No poem without accident," Derrida writes. "No poem that does not open itself like a wound."[50] It must risk itself in the world. The poem asks to be read, but can only offer itself and is easily ignored, dismissed, as the world sweeps on, as a mousetrap rhyme will usually find only oblivion.

Discussions of the relation between lyric and society generally treat lyric as a form of social practice and are thus inclined to focus on the micro- or macrohistorical circumstances in which lyrics are produced, circulated, and consumed, and the purposes, conscious or unconscious, which they might aim to serve. But, as I have mentioned, the multiple levels at which a poet's lyric practice can be described means that later ages can make many different claims about them, and these will always be subject to dialectical inversions: what at one level seems reactionary at another can be hailed as resistant, and vice versa. Adorno's claim that the poem is most socially engaged when it refuses to make the social a theme, and his remarkable assertion that the poem transcends a social ritual by subordinating itself to it, emphasize the dialectical character of literary works' historicity, but if these claims are cast as general laws, they obscure what is evident in any discussion of particular literary works: the unpredictability of their historical effects (a point on which Adorno would certainly agree). In the George poem it is supposedly the anomalous *gar*, which we don't even translate, that for Adorno makes the poem a powerfully utopian work for readers; and in the case of the other poem he discusses in "On Lyric and Society," Mörike's "Auf einer Wanderung," it is the surprising address to the muse at the end that enables it to succeed in offering "the signs of an immediate life that promised fulfillment precisely at the time when they were already condemned by the direction history was taking" (50). "The single word 'Muse' at the end of the poem is decisive," Adorno writes. "It is as if this word, one of the most overused of German classicism, gleamed once again, truly as if in the light of the setting sun, by being bestowed upon the *genius loci* of the friendly little town, and as though even in the process of disappearing it were possessed of all the power to enrapture which an evocation of the muse in the modern idiom, comically inept, usually fails to capture" (48).

The comically inept can prove the most adept. Adorno's dialectical thinking shows the difficulty of producing a convincing analysis of the social implications of a work, let along its historical efficacy. If a socially oriented criticism treats the work as a repeated event in a social history which is itself in part the effect of that and other works, there is an almost irredeemable indeterminacy, depending upon assumptions about politics and language. Literary works are fatefully entangled with the ideologies that they both help to produce and seek to resist, and the results of a critical analysis can be quite different, depending upon the level at which it is offered. A pair of concrete examples from recent American poetry will illustrate the problem.

3. Tangling with Ideology

The great paradox of lyric, as a ritualistic form with occasional fictional elements, is that while frequently it constitutes a complaint about or resistance to the status quo, its social effectiveness may ultimately depend upon some sort of catchiness or memorability. One way to succeed is by being read and assimilated in some form, conscious or unconscious, so that its language infiltrates the ideology that it may have sought to engage. Vast numbers of poets have sought to challenge common sense, stretch the language, present unimagined or unexpected juxtapositions, in poems that can be presented as "purifying the language of the tribe" or as undertaking guerrilla action against it, but often readers of these poems have not yet given effect to their performance. It is when poems establish themselves as memorable, live as poems, that they are most likely to tincture or fracture ideology, to structure our approach to the world, and thus to have a chance of bringing into play their critical edge, but they also run the risk that what readers will find most memorable is what neatly formulates an insight readers might already be inclined to espouse. Memorability may promote an ideological apothegm but also makes it potentially open to a critique performed by the rest of the poem. Here are two poems whose memorability has given them a broad audience and thus a potent social role and at least a potential for critique.

Robert Frost's "The Road Not Taken" is a much-loved American poem, held to offer important wisdom in a homespun guise.

> Two roads diverged in a yellow wood
> And sorry I could not travel both
> And be one traveler, long I stood
> And looked down one as far as I could
> To where it bent in the undergrowth;
>
> Then took the other, as just as fair
> And having perhaps the better claim,
> Because it was grassy and wanted wear;
> Though as for that, the passing there
> Had worn them really about the same,
>
> And both that morning equally lay
> In leaves no step had trodden black.
> Oh, I kept the first for another day!
> Yet knowing how way leads on to way,
> I doubted if I should ever come back.

> I shall be telling this with a sigh
> Somewhere ages and ages hence:
> Two roads diverged in a wood and I—
> I took the one less traveled by,
> And that has made all the difference.

These tightly rhymed stanzas of four-beat verse are taken to offer a memorable lesson: take the less-traveled road, my boy, and that will make all the difference. The belief that the less-traveled road is not just the more adventurous choice but also the better one is deeply embedded in a conformist culture in which everyone believes in the uniqueness of the individual and the value of that uniqueness. The poem is read and cited as an encouragement to take the least obvious or least common way when confronted with life choices. This point might even be emphasized by the poem's stress on the fact that the two roads were nearly same: both lay "In leaves no step had trodden black." When you have two options, the poem seems to be saying, even if there don't seem to be grounds for choosing between them, take the slightly less-traveled, less usual one.

The poem concludes that this choice has made all the difference (which we assume to be a favorable difference, though the "sigh" could raise doubts on that score), but in fact, as critics have often noted, it presents this conclusion not as the fruit of experience—not "looking back on my life I see that this was a good choice that has paid off"—but as a claim I will no doubt make in the future, when I shall be telling the story of my life. Inevitably—because of the powerful desire to give narrative shape to our lives—I will claim that this arbitrary choice between two nearly identical paths made all the difference, and that my choice was the riskier one. The poem wryly reflects on the propensity to regret roads not taken or options one could not pursue, and to dramatize past choices as decisive, even when one does not know what the other options would have yielded. In offering its prediction of what I will doubtless say many years hence when I recount my choice, the poem foregrounds the ideological character of the operation of conferring meaning on our lives, the predictability of the subject's response to experience, even as it appears to offer a memorable rendition of the superiority of independence and originality. It exposes the ideology even as it helps to compose it. How to assess this relationship?

Frost, a great poet, knew well that poetry can function in this way. In 1917 he wrote to Louis Untermeyer, "You get more credit for thinking if you restate formulae or cite cases that fall in easily under formulae, but all the fun is outside saying things that suggest formulae that won't formulate—that almost but don't quite formulate. I should like to be so subtle at this game as to seem to the casual person altogether obvious. The casual person would assume I meant nothing or else I came near enough meaning something he was familiar with to mean it for all practical purposes. Well, well, well."[51] Writing memorable lines that articulate a view with which the "casual person" is already familiar, Frost found his fun in subtly devising a formula that wouldn't quite formulate, or that would disformulate the formula, for those readers less casual than most persons. I emphasize that we are not dealing with a matter of subtle interpretation here but with an implication often recognized and in fact quite obvious once it is pointed out, even to a casual person.

Frost seems to follow a similar logic of formulas that don't quite formulate in "Mending Wall," where the adage twice repeated by the neighbor, "Good fences make good neighbors"—which is perhaps the line readers are most likely to remember and on which the poem ends—is challenged by the rest of the poem, both circumstantially ("There where it is we do not need the wall") and more broadly ("Before I built a wall I'd ask to know / What I was walling in or walling out"). If the poem suggests that the speaker fails in his mischievous quest to "put a notion in [his neighbor's] head" and get him to question his adage, it may have better success with readers, who are lured to contemplate the question of what that something is "that doesn't love a wall, / that wants it down."[52]

In "The Road Not Taken," what is most often remembered from the poem is the assertion that taking "the road less travelled by" makes all the difference, but the poem's actual formulation exposes this conception as the wishful construction it is, in a slyly effective critique of the ideology that the poem is casually taken to reinforce. The critique is potentially the more effective since the poem is entangled in the ideology in question. A poem that stood aloof or denounced the formula would have much less potential purchase, and the memorability of the poem gives it at least a chance of effecting its critique.

A more complicated case is W. H. Auden's poem "September 1, 1939." His elegy for "a low dishonest decade" is one of his most famous poems. Ironically, it is also a poem that he rejected. Readers and critics often accept Sir Philip Sidney's dictum, "Now for the *poet*, he *nothing affirmeth*, and therefore never *lieth*," but Auden famously rejected this poem because he thought it lied. The poem was first published in the *New Republic* in October 1939, and then in the 1940 collection *Another Time*, but when Auden came to produce his *Collected Poems* of 1945 he dropped the entire stanza containing the famous line, "We must love one another or die":

> All I have is a voice
> To undo the folded lie,
> The romantic lie in the brain
> Of the sensual man-in-the-street
> And the lie of Authority
> Whose buildings grope the sky:
> There is no such thing as the State
> And no one exists alone;
> Hunger allows no choice
> To the citizen or the police;
> We must love one another or die.

Twenty years later, in 1964, he wrote, "Rereading the poem of mine, 'September 1, 1939,' after it had been published, I came to the line 'We must love one another or die,' and said to myself, 'That's a damned lie! We must die anyway.' So in the next edition I altered it to 'We must love one another and die.' This didn't seem to do either, so I cut the stanza. Still no good. The whole poem, I realized, was infected with an incurable dishonesty—and must be scrapped."[53]

Readers have not agreed and continue to treasure the poem, even with the disputed stanza, or perhaps especially with this stanza. It is a poem many people know, at least in part, and many more came to know it after

9/11, when it was read aloud on National Public Radio and cited repeatedly in the media, on the Web, and in private emails. The poem begins:

> I sit in one of the dives
> On Fifty-second Street
> Uncertain and afraid
> As the clever hopes expire
> Of a low dishonest decade:
> Waves of anger and fear
> Circulate over the bright
> And darkened lands of the earth,
> Obsessing our private lives;
> The unmentionable odour of death
> Offends the September night.

The coincidence between the aftermath of the terrorist attack on the World Trade Center and some of the poem's references is striking: the September date, the Manhattan location, the "blind skyscrapers," in their full height and vulnerability, and the feeling of stupor ("Defenseless under the night / Our world in stupor lies"), but above all the "Waves of anger and fear" and pervasive "odour of death" that "Offends the September night."

Such convergences led readers to take this poem as particularly apt, particularly true. The television station MSNBC reported, "In the wake of September 11, 2001, many have turned to one poem in particular in search of understanding and insight." Daniel Swift wrote in the *Times Literary Supplement:* "As New York explains the bombing to itself, Auden's words are everywhere." "Written at the outset of World War II," claimed another source, "this poem captures so much of what we are struggling to come to terms with after the September 11 attacks."[54] It was thought to embody some sort of truth. For both author and readers, the poem has functioned not as a dramatic monologue by a fictional speaker but as epideictic discourse, a modern version of choral lyric in which the words are offered for repetition by readers or singers. This seems to be how both Auden and his modern audience took the poem, as declaring supposed truths, which we can repeat, including "We must love one another or die."

But while readers read and recirculated this poem because they thought it told them something true, it is obvious that they found it compelling because it is poetry, because it is not just some political or ethical statement that condemns dictators and recommends loving one another (there are many such statements around). As a poem, rather than a political statement, it has an autonomy, an independence from any particular situation, so that when it then seems to apply to a given situation, that is striking, unexpected, reason enough to email it to friends. It is the more pointedly effective for not being written about the event: a poem composed on September 12 about the attack would have lacked the potency of autonomous poetry but would have been just another piece of commentary.

It is hard to overestimate the importance of this sense of the independence or autonomy of the poem. Despite the singular date, September 1, 1939, which marks it as testimony, it has a solidity as a piece of crafted language, with a rhythm that seems stately and deliberative, no doubt because the deep default structure of English verse is four-beat verse, so that three-beat lines seems to call for a virtual beat or pause at the end of each line. (Here I put a **B** under beats, **o** under offbeats, **-o-** under double offbeats, and **[B]** for a virtual beat.)

Into the neutral air,
B   -o-   B   o   B   [B]

Where blind skyscrapers use
o   B   B   -o-   B   [B]

Their full height to proclaim
  o   B   B   -o-   B   [B]

The strength of collective man.
  o   B   -o-   B   o   B   [B]

Each language pours its vain
  o   B   o   B   o   B   [B]

Competitive excuse.
  o   B   o   B   o   B   [B]

The occasional rhymes and half rhymes in each eleven-line stanza may reinforce the tendency to pause on the virtual beats, which helps give this poem its solemnity, its solidity.

Especially important is the poem's diagnosis:

The windiest militant trash
Important Persons shout
Is not so crude as our wish:
What mad Nijinsky wrote
About Diaghilev
Is true of the normal heart;
For the error bred in the bone
Of each woman and each man
Craves what it cannot have,
Not universal love,
But to be loved alone.

Even the dogmas spouted by political figures on the right or left are less potent and significant than what Auden calls the deep human wish, not just for "universal love, / But to be loved *alone*" (as the dancer Vaslav Nijinsky wrote of the imperious ballet impresario Sergei Diaghilev). This crazed egotistical wish, to be the only one loved, is "true of the normal heart," "bred in the bone / Of each woman and each man," and the deep cause of human catastrophe.

But while readers valued the poem for the truths or understanding it offered, including that of its most famous line, "We must love one another or die," it is striking that what this poem proclaims as a more elemental truth, known at some deep level to everyone, is a truth not allowed to enter public discourse. This truth is unequivocally stated at the end of the second stanza, as something learned by schoolchildren and known to everyone:

I and the public know
What all schoolchildren learn,
Those to whom evil is done
Do evil in return.

Yet after 9/11, few in the United States dared utter such a thought, much less suggest, as the poem does, that we should look at ourselves in the mirror and consider our complicity:

> Out of the mirror they stare,
> Imperialism's face
> And the international wrong.

This was an unpalatable truth. Anyone who articulated such views, and they were very few, was treated as a pariah. One might say that the poem was competing with ideological discourse and on this particular point it lost—was unable to penetrate. It was not taken as asserting that Americans have committed an international wrong that has come back to haunt them. Though the poem was taken to articulate truths and valued for that, it was not received as a comprehensive argument.

Part of the problem of poems' social efficacy is that they may function at various levels, through their parts rather than as coherent wholes, so that while they may be read as offering truths, readers can treat poems is if they were smorgasbords of truth, where various offerings are laid out for you to pick what you want to consume, what to offer to friends, what to skip over—whereas in a prose argument you would need at least to confront the array of claims that are made. A function of epideictic poetry of this sort is to tell truths, some of which will be remembered and repeated, but others of which will work only subliminally and can be ignored, as if they were not articulated but only part of the fabric of this poetic act. Poems offer memorable formulations, which can inform your thought or your life, but they are not thought to offer an argument, which may sometimes enable them to get under the guard of a wary intelligence, but may also lead to selective recall and repetition and evasion of what might be important. This makes it especially difficult to assess the sociopolitical implications of a poem, since what the poem quite obviously declares may not be what is taken in, assimilated. And ideology may determine what is remembered, though the memorability of a poem at least gives it a chance of working in other ways and at other levels, especially for attentive and curious readers.

Though we are operating in a mode of truth, the seductions of poetic form, which make the poem attractive in the first place and create the possibility of affecting people's lives, are also what enable us to avoid explicitly engaging some assertions or having to cope with potential incoherence. For example, much of the power of Auden's poem comes from its rhythmical articulation of common human propensities: desiring to be loved alone, we are "Lost in a haunted wood, / Children afraid of the night / Who have never been happy or good." We are all complicitous with evil or wrong and driven by unconscious desires. But the poem also draws power from its satirical treatment of others:

> From the conservative dark
> Into the ethical life
> The dense commuters come,
> Repeating their morning vow;
> "I will be true to the wife,
> I'll concentrate more on my work,"
> And helpless governors wake
> To resume their compulsory game:
> Who can release them now,
> Who can reach the deaf,
> Who can speak for the dumb?

The dense commuters and the helpless governors, who are lumped together into a general *they*, along with "the sensual man-in-the-street," are treated as blind and deaf: someone else must see and speak for them. If at some level we all know that "Those to whom evil is done / Do evil in return," this understanding is covered up or covered over by various lies, which must be undone:

> All I have is a voice
> To undo the folded lie,
> The romantic lie in the brain
> Of the sensual man-in-the-street
> And the lie of Authority
> Whose buildings grope the sky:

The "folded lie"—in the first instance, for example, the newspaper—and the lie of authority, the assertion of the primacy of the state, are resisted by explicit assertions:

> There is no such thing as the State
> And no one exists alone;
> Hunger allows no choice
> To the citizen or the police;
> We must love one another or die.

The poem ends on what is seen as a note of defiance, wishing to "Show an affirming flame" while "Our world in stupor lies." The source of hope is "the just" scattered across the world, who exchange messages, like this poem. What differentiates them from the rest of humanity? The final lines of the poem encapsulate this unresolved problem:

> Defenceless under the night
> Our world in stupor lies;
> Yet, dotted everywhere,
> Ironic points of light
> Flash out wherever the Just
> Exchange their messages:
> May I, composed like them
> Of Eros and of dust,
> Beleaguered by the same
> Negation and despair,
> Show an affirming flame.

The concluding lines suggest a common humanity: we are all composed of Eros and of dust and all experience despair. But grammatically "them" in "composed like them," is the *just:* at the point where the poet seems to be confirming the commonality of all humanity, he is aspiring to commonality with the company of the just. The poem leaves us with an unresolved problem, but one that we do not experience as a problem. It is not experienced as a problem, because poems can be of two minds, and readers are happy to be of two minds also, repeating the experience of a common humanity while satirizing the dense commuters and aspiring if not to join "the just"—a mysterious group—at least to favor their cause.

In Chapter 4, I quoted Stephen Booth's claim that the human mind is disappointed by ordinary understanding, since what it wants is to understand something that it does not understand. Auden's poem is compelling because it offers through a poetic event something other than a regular understanding—after 9/11 there was far too much analysis around; that was not what was wanted. The poem appealed to readers and listeners after 9/11 because it was a formal structure, independent of current discourse and commentary, which both spoke uncannily to a horrific event that one needed language to cope with and provided a mood and wisdom of a sort. It was language to be repeated, whose independence from the event itself yet pertinence to it was a source of power and pleasure. One can scarcely imagine a more interesting example of "lyric in society." But to try to analyze its precise relation to the social is to find oneself grappling with a complex entanglement with ideology: What in the poem is perceived? what is remembered? what is repressed? "September 1, 1939" provides words to repeat in response to the horror of an event of devastation while also offering both ambiguities about how to situate oneself and claims that passed unnoticed or were resolutely ignored, such as "Those to whom evil is done / Do evil in return."

Reflection on lyric and society cannot but identify multiple levels at which lyric can function and make it clear that there is no one form of social efficacy for the lyric. There has been, of course, a great historical variation in the social functioning of lyrics. Pindar's odes of public celebration have a quite different social presence and role from a modern lyric published by a small press. It is obvious that today, with the multiplication of other media, poetry plays a much less central cultural role than it once did. But if there is less praise of gods and heroes in our public poetry, this may say more about us and our habits than about the lyric itself. Nonetheless, poems that do similar things appear in many different historical periods: poems that affirm a particular value against a dominant ideology; poems that articulate despair or alienation; elegies that detail the loss to the world a particular death has brought; odes that celebrate a significant achievement or imaginative possibility; poems of complaint that imagine a better condition; poems of nostalgia for lost happiness or innocence. It is certainly possible to attribute to them various social roles: contribution to structures of feeling, community formation, instantiation of ideology or its disruption and exposure, subversion or containment. But above all it is the unpredictability of lyric's efficacy and the different kinds of framings to which it is subject that make any reflection on lyric and society a process in which the analyst cannot but be humbled and dismayed by the contingency of his or her own discourse. A historical account of lyric, taking its own vision into account, also needs to explore the ways in which conceptions of lyrics' relations to society are a function of the theoretical discourses of criticism itself, as well as of the seductions of striking phrasing and sonorous form.

Conclusion

What can one say in conclusion? I have not attempted to determine what is or is not a lyric but have been asking what is the best model of the lyric for encouraging a capacious appreciation of these poems. The range of lyrics examined here makes it clear that there is no simple model that fits them all. Nor can we realistically imagine that the lyric was once one thing and then became something else—as if there were one model for the lyrics of one era, to be replaced by a different model in a later age. The range of examples considered in these pages illustrates the existence of a variety of lyrics and lyric forms at any given time, and whatever one sees them doing in one era—praising the world, bemoaning unhappy love, staging an epiphany, urging the universe to comply with one's desires—can also be discovered elsewhere. Historical change, in the realm of lyric poetry, does not yield linear progression or a succession of discrete models.

I have been concerned, in these chapters, to show that each of the two most widespread current models has serious disadvantages: the model of lyric as intense expression of the subjective experience of the poet does not fit a great many poems, whether ancient or modern. More important, it leads away from the language of the poem to an experience of the poet, which a reader is supposed to try to reconstruct. But our attention should be directed to experiencing the poem itself as an event, not to discovering what the author might have experienced. The dramatic monologue also demands of the reader a reconstruction—this time of the situation and motives of a fictional speaker/character rather than the author. But for many poems of the tradition, attempting to work out who is speaking brings no benefits and obscures rather than clarifies what the poem itself is doing. Even when it is possible to imagine a speaker, this orientation emphasizes the fictional dimension of the poem, neglecting those ritualistic and musical elements that make the poem compel our attention in the first place.

Käte Hamburger's modification of the Hegelian model so as to differentiate lyric from fiction offers a promising framework. The lyric is, at bottom, a statement about this world rather than the projection of a fictional speaker and a fictional world. Her principle that the relationship between the lyric "I" and the living poet is indeterminate emphasizes what was already at least implicit in Hegel's version of what I have been calling, somewhat abusively, the romantic model: the subjectivity at work in the lyric is a formal principle of unity more than the consciousness of a given individual. This model can accommodate the strain of lyric, both classical and modern, that I have frequently emphasized: lyric as epideixis—public discourse about meaning and value—made distinctive by its ritualistic elements. With this conception as a starting point, one can then specify that many lyrics incorporate fictional elements, whether identifiable speakers, as in dramatic monologues, rudimentary plots, as in ballads, or simply incidents made notable by their insertion in the fundamentally hyperbolic space of a lyric poem.

Since most approaches to lyric poetry have assumed that interpretation is readers' proper goal and focused on techniques of interpretation, which generally depend upon fictional and thematic elements, I have highlighted the ritualistic dimensions of lyric: rhythm, lyric address and invocation, and sound patterning of all kinds. These incantatory elements are very often what initially attracts us to a poem—prior to exploration of its meaning—and of course they are what make lyrics different from prose reflections on the world. "Musicality authenticates poetry," Robert von Hallberg declares, allowing the pursuit of "significance at the edges of conventions, where no significance is assured. Readers stay with poems, moving into uncertainty and even obscurity, because the history of this art demonstrates utter seriousness, and because shapely sounds draw them on."[1]

But the history of the art is not all seriousness, and the lure of shapely sound draws us into another realm. The ritualistic elements, precisely because they are eminently seductive, are not quite respectable and can even prove embarrassing. Baudelaire speaks of sorcery and Mallarmé evokes magic, but most critics are reluctant to venture far in that direction. Northrop Frye, though, boldly links *melos* to charm and magic: "The radical of *melos* is *charm:* the hypnotic incantation that, through its pulsing dance rhythm, appeals to involuntary physical response, and is hence not far from the sense of magic, or physically compelling power. The etymological descent of charm from *carmen,* song, may be noted. Actual charms have a quality that is imitated in popular literature by work songs of various kinds, especially lullabies, where the drowsy, sleep inducing repetition shows the underlying oracular or dream pattern very clearly."[2] He notes that the language of invocation in lyrics differs rhetorically very little from the language of spells designed to compel.[3]

To emphasize as I have apostrophic address, which presupposes an animated world that might be asked to act or refrain from acting, is implicitly to link lyric to magic, the enchantment of the world—a world inhabited by sentient forces, a world before the flight of the gods. But it was poets who made that world, poets who gave the Greeks their gods. Society is always confronted with the problem of how matter is endowed with spirit or meaning, and poetry is one of several forces that at once makes this happen and explicates it—our sciences, for instance, explore how matter can be sentient, how spirit can arise from an organism of flesh, blood and bone. Call it religion, science, poetry, or ideology, we find ways to imbue a world of forces and magnitudes with meaning, direction, action. Lyric is bolder, more abrupt and disjunctive, in its treatment of the world; it displays more openly its figuration, its rhetorical positing, in lieu of argument or demonstration.

To stress, as I have done, the fundamentally hyperbolic character of lyric is to underline the flagrancy of lyric operations—a flagrancy that makes them both vulnerable to dismissal and acutely attentive to that vulnerability. Poems that boldly demand action, asking time to stop its course or winds to blow, are often the most skeptical about their power to achieve what is desired; as they evoke possible relations to the universe, they also explore what sorts of demands might succeed. They take a risk, they court embarrassment, with figures that can be rejected as overweening or ridiculous, but it is a risk they acknowledge and often make their most intimate theme. One way of thinking about this is to say that the lyric genre is a place where enchantment and disenchantment, opacity and lucidity are negotiated, "a pressure chamber that regulates the balance between enchantment and disenchantment, wonder and sobriety, in a world perpetually deficient in one or the other," as Klas Molde puts it.[4] But one could also say that along with the lyric's varied imagining of the world, our possible relations to it and its to us, which may be a version of enchantment, it pursues, with all the elegance it can muster, a structuring of that linguistic material whose visceral appeal requires a name other than enchantment. If lyric is a form where the leap of the poetic imagination and skepticism about its efficacy are always implicitly at issue, it is also engaged in the very down-to-earth activity of seducing us with its arrangements of letters, sounds, and silences.

I suggested in the Introduction that the historical connection of lyric with song might provide a salutary corrective model for thinking about this literary form. With song we allow ourselves to be seduced without much guilt by sensuous form and to dwell in the realm of sonorous patterning without an insistent quest for the meaning, but this does not imply that our discriminating faculties are somehow switched off, as Frye suggests in his discussion of charms. In our engagement with song, as we pursue our pleasure, we develop considerable expertise—knowledge of what we like and what we dislike, a sense of affinities among particular singers and composers and of different types of music—without necessarily trying to interpret particular musical texts. Something comparable ought to be possible in the realm of poetry—attending to our pleasure while also gaining confidence in our ability to appreciate what secured our attention. Although I do not agree with Robert von Hallberg's claim that "poetry's appeal to the mind's eye and the body's ears is meant to arrest analysis"—for teasing out what is appealing *does* involve analysis— nonetheless he is right to claim that poets do not demand interpretation of readers but "expect instead what Coleridge called 'poetic faith' that their statements require no supplementation, at least for the duration of a reading."[5]

The duration of a reading is the lyric event, which one should keep in view, perhaps especially in an academic study of poetry. Susan Stewart writes, in a way that recalls Hegel's discussion of the workings of rhyme, "I propose that the sound of poetry is heard in the way that a promise is heard. A promise is an action made in speech, . . . something that 'happens,' that 'occurs' as an event and can be continually called on, called to mind, in the unfolding present."[6] It is important that poems are not recalled as a fact is remembered but are, as she says, registered as able to be recalled, to be uttered or experienced again; even if you only remember a few of their words, or sometimes, maddeningly, just a rhythm, there is the promise of an event that can be reproduced in the present of articulation.

The notion of lyric sound as promise points, finally, to the value to which lyric especially ministers—a love of the sonorous phrase, the memorable formulation, whether it is the expression of an attitude one explores in repeating—"I wake and feel the fell of dark, not day"—or an elegant piece of sonority—"the moan of doves in immemorial elms"—these phrases that, as Valéry says, create the need to be heard again. At the end of Chapter 7 I jokingly spoke of people's tendency to use poems as smorgasbords of truth, but they are not buffets of truths only. Found in poems are all sorts of phrases, especially unimaginable ones, which stretch the imagination, offering us reproducible experiences of pleasure and puzzlement, as we speak them to ourselves and occasionally, to others—as we should do more often.

Notes

Introduction

1. Earl Miner, "Why Lyric?" in *Renewal of Song: Renovation in Lyric Conception and Practice* (Calcutta: Seagull Books, 2000), 4–5.
2. Late in his career Barthes displayed considerable interest in the haiku, but this did not lead to reflection on the lyric. Haiku he rather perversely took as the point of departure for thinking about the notational, anti-narrative features of the novel. *La Préparation du roman* (Paris: Seuil, 2003).
3. Erik Martiny, "Preface," in *A Companion to Poetic Genre,* ed. Erik Martiny (Chichester, UK: Wiley, 2012), xxii.
4. See David Caplan, "The Age of the Sestina," in *Questions of Possibility* (New York: Oxford University Press, 2005): 17–41.
5. Lyrics interpret the world, but this does not mean that readers need exercise ingenuity to work out an interpretation of a lyric, as has come to be expected in the classroom—though of course they should feel free to do so, as this is one of the pleasures lyrics offer.
6. There are, of course, very rich lyric traditions in other cultures, which I am not competent to address.
7. The dates of these poets are: Sappho, around 600 BCE, Horace, 65–8 BCE, Petrarch, 1304–1374, Goethe, 1749–1832, Leopardi, 1798–1837, Baudelaire, 1821–1867, Lorca, 1898–1936, Williams, 1883–1963, and Ashbery, 1927–.

1. An Inductive Approach

1. John Winkler, *The Constraints of Desire: The Anthropology of Sex and Gender in Ancient Greece* (London: Routledge, 1990), 167–168, translation modified. (Henceforth, names of translators will be given in brackets, unless I am responsible.) The translation of *deute* as "once again *this* time" is from Gregory Nagy, *Poetry as Performance* (Cambridge: Cambridge University Press, 1996), 100. Winkler and Anne Carson prefer the reading of some of the manuscripts, which make the opening word *poikilophron,* "having a mind that is dappled, variegated, complex," to the reading of most modern editors, *poikilothron,* either "ornately enthroned" (from *thronos,* "throne") or "with variegated embroidered flowers" (from *throna,* "embroidered flowers"). Intricate-mindedness seems more pertinent to the poem.

2. Winkler, *Constraints,* 167.

3. Anne Burnett, *Three Archaic Poets: Archilochus, Alcaeus, Sappho* (Cambridge, MA: Harvard University Press, 1983), 245. Anne Carson, *Eros the Bittersweet* (Princeton: Princeton University Press, 1996), 118–119.

4. Marshall Brown, "Negative Poetics: On Skepticism and the Lyric Voice," *Representations* 86 (2004): 134.

5. Winkler, *Constraints,* 165.

6. Jeffrey Walker, *Rhetoric and Poetics in Antiquity* (Oxford: Oxford University Press, 2000), 232.

7. The contrast between constative utterances, which make true or false statements about the world, and performative utterances, which accomplish the act to which they refer and are not true or false but *felicitous* or *infelicitous,* is introduced by J. L. Austin in *How to Do Things with Words* (Cambridge, MA: Harvard University Press, 1962). For discussion see Chapter 3 below.

8. Brown, "Negative Poetics," 133. Charles Segal finds here "the magnetic, quasi-magical compulsion the ancient poets called *thelxis,* 'enchantment,' or *peitho,* 'persuasion.'" The magical *thelxis* of the words seeks to create—or re-create—the magical *thelxis* of love. The effect of the ritualized structure of the poem is "to lift the daimonic power of eros out of the realm of the formless and terrible" and make this mastery of love's violence comprehensible to others." *Aglaia: The Poetry of Alcman, Sappho, Pindar, Bacchylides, and Corinna* (Lanham, MD: Rowman and Littlefield, 1998), 43, 47–48.

9. See Martin Hägglund, *Radical Atheism: Derrida and the Time of Life* (Stanford: Stanford University Press, 2008).

10. W. R. Johnson, *The Idea of Lyric: Lyric Modes in Ancient and Modern Poetry* (Berkeley: University of California Press, 1982), 139.

11. William Anderson, *Why Horace? A Collection of Interpretations* (Wauconda, IL: Bolchazy-Carducci, 1999), ix.

12. Gregson Davis, *Polyhymnia: The Rhetoric of Horatian Lyric Discourse* (Berkeley: University of California Press, 1991), 225.

13. Paul Allen Miller, *Lyric Texts and Lyric Consciousness* (London: Routledge, 1994). Roland Greene, *Post-Petrarchism* (Princeton: Princeton University Press, 1991), 22, denies that the sequences of Latin poets achieve this effect and convincingly treats Petrarch as the source of the character-generating lyric sequence, though not of lyric per se. It is Petrarch who invents the lyric sequence, because he is the first to develop the conceit of a temporal process (though not a plot) that binds the lyrics and activates "a phenomenology of fiction."

14. The contrast between the generally unlocated present (now) and a past (then) is endemic to the collection and generates an acute sense of time despite the lack of plot or narrative progression. See Greene, *Post-Petrarchism*, ch. 1.

15. Roland Greene, "The Lyric," in *Cambridge History of English Criticism*, vol. 3: *The Renaissance*, ed. Glyn P. Norton (Cambridge: Cambridge University Press, 1999), 222. National languages "illustrat[ing] themselves" comes from Joachim Du Bellay's manifesto, *Défense et illustration de la langue française* (1549).

16. Aristotle's *Rhetoric* distinguishes forensic, deliberative, and epideictic rhetoric. The last is ceremonious rather than legal or political, a rhetoric of celebration, praise or blame, focused especially on virtues and vices. It is directed to an audience that does not make decisions, but forms opinions in response to the discourse, which thus "shapes and cultivates the basic codes of value and belief by which a society or culture lives." Walker, *Rhetoric*, 9, 149.

17. Roman Jakobson, "Linguistics and Poetics," in *Style in Language*, ed. Thomas Sebeok (Cambridge, MA: MIT Press, 1968), 358.

18. Both Margaret Brose, "Leopardi's 'L'infinito' and the Language of the Romantic Sublime," *Poetics Today* 4 (1983): 51, and Timothy Bahti, *The Ends of Lyric* (Baltimore: Johns Hopkins University Press, 1996), 44–46, discuss the tenses and the play of demonstratives here.

19. Albert Thibaudet, *Intérieurs* (Paris: Plon, 1924), 22–24. He writes of the last verse: "every day after these urban encounters people feel this alexandrine arise in their memory, fill a void, calm and complete something in them, associating this spark to millions of sparks . . . and giving this evening its 'substance humaine,' making them go forward into life with a soul for a moment liberated, equilibrated."

20. Walter Benjamin, *Illuminations* (New York: Harcourt Brace, 1968), 169.

21. Hugh Kenner, *A Homemade World* (New York: Knopf, 1975), 59–60.

22. Since the collection as a whole is dedicated to Ashbery's friend Pierre Martory, who died in 1998, it is also possible to imagine him as the "you" who is not even here, but *Your Name Here* claims wider applicability.

23. Eva Muller-Zettelmann, *Lyrik und Metalyrik* (Heidelberg: Winter, 2000).

24. Paul de Man, "The Lyrical Voice in Contemporary Theory," in *Lyric Poetry: Beyond New Criticism*, ed. Chaviva Hošek and Patricia Parker (Ithaca: Cornell University Press, 1985), 55.

25. James Longenbach, *The Virtues of Poetry* (Minneapolis: Graywolf Press, 2013), 157.

26. Charles Baudelaire, *Œuvres complètes,* ed. Claude Pichois (Paris: Gallimard, 1976), vol. 2, 162.

27. Friedrich Hölderlin, "In lieblicher Bläue," in *Gedichte* (Stuttgart: Reclam, 2000), 411.

2. Lyric as Genre

1. Jean-Louis Schaeffer, *Qu'est-ce qu'un genre littéraire?* (Paris: Seuil, 1989), 8. Tzvetan Todorov, "The Origin of Genres," *New Literary History* 8 (1976): 164.

2. Horace, *Ars Poetica,* 1–9. *Satires, Epistles and Ars Poetica,* trans. H. Rushton Fairclough (Cambridge, MA: Harvard University Press, 1978), 451.

3. Fredric Jameson, *The Political Unconscious* (Ithaca: Cornell University Press, 1981), 105.

4. Maurice Blanchot, *Le Livre à venir* (Paris: Gallimard, 1959), 243–244.

5. Benedetto Croce, *Aesthetic as Science of Expression and General Linguistic* (New York: Noonday, 1953), 144.

6. In 2007 *PMLA* devoted a special issue to "Remapping Genre" (*PMLA* 122, no. 5); the so-called new lyric studies (*PMLA* 123, no. 1 [2008]) has sparked debate about genre; and the subject of the 2009 meeting of the English Institute was "Genre," published as *The Work of Genre,* ed. Robyn Warhol. Available at http://quod.lib.umich.edu/cgi/t/text/text-idx?c=acls;idno=heb 90055.0001.001

7. Marie-Laure Ryan, "On the Why, What and How of Generic Taxonomy," *Poetics* 10 (1981): 109–126.

8. Ralph Cohen, "Introduction: Theorizing Genres," *New Literary History* 34, no. 2 (2003): v.

9. David Fishelov discusses the use of various analogies in *Metaphors of Genre: The Role of Analogies in Genre Theory* (University Park: Penn State University Press, 1993).

10. Eleanor Rosch, "Reclaiming Concepts," *Journal of Consciousness Studies* 6 (1999): 65.

11. Northrop Frye, *Anatomy of Criticism* (Princeton: Princeton University Press, 1957), 247.

12. The *Dictarten* are listed alphabetically: "Allegorie, Ballade, Cantate, Drama, Elegie, Epigramm, Epistel, Epopee, Erzählung, Fabel, Heroide, Idylle, Lehrgedicht, Ode, Parodie, Roman, Romanze, Satyre." Johann Wolfgang von Goethe, "Noten und Abhandlungen zu besserem Verständnis des *West-östlichen Diwans*," *Werke* (Munich: Beck, 1981), vol. 2, 187–189.

13. Gérard Genette, *The Architext: An Introduction* (Berkeley: University of California Press, 1992), 65–66. The title obscures the fact that this is an important book about genre.

14. Good discussions of this problem occur in works not known in the English tradition: Michel Charles, *Introduction à l'étude des textes* (Paris: Seuil, 1995); and *La Case blanche: théorie littéraire et textes possibles,* ed. Marc Escola and Sophie Rabau (Paris: Klincksieck, 2006).

15. Allan Grossman, *The Sighted Singer* (Baltimore: Johns Hopkins University Press, 1991), 211.

16. Marcel Detienne, *The Masters of Truth in Archaic Greece* (New York: Zone Books, 1996). Chris Carey, "Genre, Occasion, and Performance," in *The Cambridge Companion to Greek Lyric,* ed. Felix Budelman (Cambridge: Cambridge University Press, 2009), 27.

17. Many classicists use the term in both a narrow and a comprehensive sense. Carey, "Genre," 2. For the broader sense, see W. R. Johnson, *The Idea of Lyric: Lyric Modes in Ancient and Modern Poetry* (Berkeley: University of California Press, 1982); Leslie Kurke, "Archaic Greek Poetry," in *The Cambridge Companion to Archaic Greece,* ed. H. A. Shapiro (Cambridge: Cambridge University Press, 2007), 145–147; Jeffrey Walker, *Rhetoric and Poetics in Antiquity* (Oxford: Oxford University Press, 2000); Gregory Nagy, *Pindar's Homer: The Lyric Possession of an Epic Past* (Baltimore: Johns Hopkins University Press, 1990); J. M. Edmonds, "An Account of Greek Lyric Poetry," in *Lyra Graeca,* ed. J. M. Edmonds (Cambridge: Cambridge University Press, 1980), vol. 3, 583–585. It is worth noting also that throughout the Hellenistic period there were Greek poems that did all the things that lyric poetry in the narrow sense had done (symposia, epinikia, enkomia, hymns, etc.), only they did so in elegiac meter—further warrant for expanding the concept of lyric beyond the meters that had traditionally been accompanied by the lyre.

18. Nagy, *Pindar's Homer*; Walker, *Rhetoric and Poetics in Antiquity.*

19. Harold Bloom, "The Breaking of Form," in Bloom et al., *Deconstruction and Criticism* (New York: Seabury Press, 1979), 17.

20. Kurke, "Archaic Greek Poetry," 142. Andrew Ford, *The Origins of Criticism* (Princeton: Princeton University Press, 2002).

21. See Andrew Ford, *Aristotle as Poet* (New York: Oxford University Press, 2011). Aristotle was allegedly accused of impiety for his "Song for Hermias," in praise of a friend, the ruler of Atarneus.

22. Aristotle, *Poetics,* in *Aristotle: Poetics; Longinus: On the Sublime; Demetrius: On Style,* trans. Stephen Halliwell, W. Hamilton Fyfe, Doreen C. Innes, and W. Rhys Roberts (Cambridge, MA: Harvard University Press, 1995), 29.

23. Plato, *The Republic,* trans. Paul Shorey, book 3 and book 2 (Cambridge, MA: Harvard University Press, 1937), vol. 1, 231, 183.

24. For Plato's discussion of lyric as a form of music in *The Laws,* see Chapter 7.

25. Iambic poetry, named after the meter deemed by Aristotle closest to common speech, was primarily a poetry of invective and scurrility. Elegiac meter consisted of a hexameter line followed by a pentameter line and was used for songs at banquets, epitaphs and inscriptions, and eventually poems of

mourning. The Latin love elegy is so named because of the meter. For the Alexandrian critics, writes Rudolph Pfeiffer, "there never was a general system. Authors were given individual treatment according to the contents or form of their poems." *History of Classical Scholarship from the Beginnings to the End of the Hellenistic Age* (Oxford: Oxford University Press, 1968), 183. Of course, modern accounts of the lyric deploy a similar variety of principles for the delineation of lyric forms: we recognize the sonnet, the ode, and the epithalamion, for instance.

26. Kurke, "Archaic Greek Poetry," 158. Bruno Snell, *The Discovery of The Mind* (Oxford: Blackwell, 1953). For a succinct discussion see Susan Stewart, *Poetry and the Fate of the Senses* (Chicago: University of Chicago Press, 2002), 47–50.

27. Johnson, *The Idea of Lyric,* 123.

28. Horace, *Ars Poetica,* 268–269.

29. Alessandro Barchiesi, "Lyric in Rome," in *The Cambridge Companion to Greek Lyric,* 331. The "Carmen Saeculare" is the only poem of Horace's known to have been performed to music.

30. John Hamilton, *Soliciting Darkness: Pindar, Obscurity, and the Classical Tradition* (Cambridge, MA: Harvard University Press, 2003), 113, 117. In the third century BCE Callimachus had turned against epic and championed writing slender, lightweight songs. His claim that Apollo urges the poet to "Fatten your animal for sacrifice but keep your muse slender" was influential for Latin poetry and for later poets as well.

31. A shrewd and efficient summary is Alessandro Barchiesi, "Carmina," in *The Cambridge Companion to Horace,* ed. Stephen Harrison (Cambridge: Cambridge University Press, 2007).

32. Quintilian, *The Orator's Education,* trans. D. A. Russell, book 10:1.96 (Cambridge, MA: Harvard University Press, 2001), vol. 4, 305.

33. For discussion of the polymetrics as lyric, see Michael Putnam, *Poetic Interplay: Catullus and Horace* (Princeton: Princeton University Press, 2006).

34. To know the number of kisses would give the evil eye power over the lovers. *Conturbare* = to throw one's accounts into confusion, a technical term for fraudulent bankruptcy with concealment of assets. "They will cheat the evil eye as the bankrupt cheats his creditors, by faking their books." C. J. Fordyce, *Catullus: A Commentary* (Oxford: Oxford University Press, 1961), 107–108.

35. In a complex and ingenious reading, William Batstone suggests that "the charge and the joke was that when Catullus asked for many thousand kisses he was taken (and mistaken) to be asking, like a *senex, . . .* for *fellatio,* and that this was a confession of masculine inadequacy." It would take a thousand kisses to produce an erection. See Horace, Epode 8: "If that is what you want from my fastidious groin / your mouth has got some work to do" ("quod ut superbo provoces ab inguine / ore adlaborandum est tibi"). "Logic, Rhetoric, and Poesis," *Helios* 20 (1993): 143–172.

36. Micaela Janan, *When the Lamp Is Shattered: Desire and Narrative in Catullus* (Carbondale: Southern Illinois University Press, 1994), ix.

37. Kathleen McCarthy, "First-Person Poetry," in *The Oxford Handbook of Roman Studies,* ed. Alessandro Barchiesi and Walter Scheidel (Oxford: Oxford University Press, 2010), 443–444. But see Putnam, *Poetic Interplay,* for a rich exploration of Horace's indebtedness to and deviation from Catullus.

38. Richard Tarrant, "Ancient Receptions of Horace," *Cambridge Companion to Horace,* 281–282.

39. Longinus, "On the Sublime," in *Aristotle: Poetics,* 199. I keep the traditional name, Longinus, though the author is unknown.

40. It is no accident that Longinus's examples are in the present tense rather than the past—effects of sublimity want to be felt in the present. His examples also mark the centrality of address to sublimity: not only do most involve address, but Longinus at key moments addresses the reader.

41. Neil Hertz, *The End of the Line* (New York: Columbia University Press, 2005), 4–5.

42. An index of the treatise's influence is Jonathan Swift's comment:

> A forward critic often dupes us
> With sham quotations *Peri Hupsous*
> And if we have not read Longinus,
> Will magisterially outshine us.
> Then, lest with Greek he over run ye,
> Procure the book, for love or money,
> Translated from Boileau's translation,
> And quote Quotation on Quotation.

["On Poetry," 255–262]

43. Ford, *Aristotle,* 78.

44. Walter Cohen, *A History of European Literature* (Oxford: Oxford University Press, 2016), ch. 6, "Medieval Lyric."

45. Peter Dronke, *The Medieval Lyric* (London: Hutchinson, 1968), 14–16, 140–142.

46. Maria Menocal, *Shards of Love: Exile and the Origins of the Lyric* (Durham, NC: Duke University Press, 1994), 24; Ross Brann, " 'The Fire of Love Poetry: Hebrew Lyric in Perspective," in *Medieval Lyric: Genres in Historical Context,* ed. William Paden (Urbana: University of Illinois Press, 2000); but see Cohen, *A History,* ch. 6.

47. Patrick Diehl, *The Medieval European Religious Lyric* (Berkeley: University of California Press, 1985), 99–101.

48. *Anthology of Troubadour Lyric Poetry,* ed. Alan Press (Edinburgh: Edinburgh University Press, 1971), 14–17.

49. William Paden and Frances Paden, *Troubadour Poets from the South of France* (Cambridge: D. S. Brewer, 2007), 10–11, 5. William Paden and Pierre Bec agree that we cannot be sure that *canso, sirventes,* and *cobla* were

distinctive concepts in the minds of the troubadours and their public until very late, when the tradition had become quite self-conscious. Paden, "System of Genres in the Troubadour Lyric," in *Medieval Lyric: Genres in Historical Context,* 32; Bec, "Le problème des genres chez les premiers troubadours," *Cahiers de civilisation médiévale,* 25 (1982): 32–47. Troubadour poetry distinctively includes love lyrics of women troubadours (trobairitz), often quite explicit in their expression of sexual desire. Beatrice, Countess of Die, is the best-known.

50. Curtis Roberts-Holt Jirsa, "Piers Plowman and the Invention of the Lyric in the Middle Ages" (PhD diss., Cornell University, 2008), 27. See Sylvia Huot, *From Song to Book* (Ithaca: Cornell University Press, 1987), 211–241; and Marisa Galvez, *Songbook: How Lyrics Became Poetry* (Chicago: University of Chicago Press, 2012).

51. Judson Boyce Allen, "Grammar, Poetic Form, and the Lyric Ego: a Medieval *a priori,*" in *Vernacular Poetics of the Middle Ages,* ed. Lois Ebin (Kalamazoo, MI: Medieval Institute Publications, 1984), 208.

52. Francisco Petrarca, *Rerum Familiares Libri,* book 24, letter 10, *Poesie minori del Petrarca,* (Milano: Società tipografica de' classici Italiani, 1834) vol. 3, 188. Available at http://babel.hathitrust.org/cgi/pt?id=mdp.39015001611782;view =1up;seq=332

53. Pierre de Ronsard, "Au lecteur" (1557) and "Au lecteur" (1550), in *Œuvres complètes,* ed. Jean Céard, Daniel Ménager, and Michel Simonin (Paris: Gallimard, 1993), vol. 1, 926, 994. Ronsard defined lyric in terms of its themes, which he listed as love, wine, banquets, dances, masques, winning horses, fencing, jousts and tournaments, and rarely some philosophical argument.

54. Joachim Du Bellay, *Défense et illustration de la langue française* (Geneva: Droz, 2001), 131–136.

55. Antonio Minturno, *Arte Poetica* [1563] (Naples: Gennaro Muzio, 1725), book 3, 175. This treatise, in Italian, takes up and extends Minturno's already vast *De Poeta,* in Latin, of 1559, which also divided poetry into the epic, scenic, and melic genres. Gustavo Guerrero, *Poésie et poésie lyrique* (Paris: Seuil, 2000), 92, 130–131.

56. Sir Philip Sidney, *A Defense of Poesy* (Oxford: Oxford University Press, 1966), 46. "Natural problems" means questions of natural philosophy.

57. Roland Greene, "The Lyric," in *Cambridge History of Literary Criticism,* vol. 3: *The Renaissance,* ed. Glyn P. Norton (Cambridge: Cambridge University Press, 1999), 216. John Milton, "Of Education," in *Complete Prose Works,* ed. E. Sirluck (New Haven: Yale University Press, 1959), vol. 2, 405.

58. M. H. Abrams, *The Mirror and the Lamp* (Oxford: Oxford University Press, 1953), 85. John Dennis, *The Grounds of Criticism in Poetry, Critical Works* [1704] (Baltimore: Johns Hopkins University Press, 1943), vol. 1, 338.

59. Charles Batteux, *Principes de la littérature* (reprint of 5th ed., Paris: Saillant et Nyon, 1775: Geneva: Slatkine, 1967), 87–88. Genette, *The Architext,* 31.

60. Robert Lowth, *Lectures on the Sacred Poetry of the Hebrews,* trans. G. Gregory (London: Macmillan, 1847), 188.

61. Sir William Jones, "On the Arts, Commonly Called Imitative," in *Poems, Consisting Chiefly of Translations from the Asiatick Languages* (Oxford: Clarendon Press, 1772), 201–202, 211–212.

62. J. G. Sulzer, *Allgemiene Theorie des schönen Künste* [1771–1774], cited by Abrams, *Mirror,* 88–90. Madame de Staël, *De l'Allemagne* (Paris: Flammarion, 1968), 1, 206–207.

63. John Stuart Mill, "Thoughts on Poetry and Its Varieties," in *Autobiography and Literary Essays,* ed. J. M. Robson and Jack Stillinger (Toronto: University of Toronto Press, 1981), 359.

64. John Addington Symonds, "A Comparison of Elizabethan with Victorian Poetry," *Fortnightly Review* 45, no. 265 (1889): 62, 64. Robert Browning, Letter to John Kenyon, October 1, 1855. Both quoted by Marion Thain, "Victorian Lyric Pathology and Phenomenology," in *The Lyric Poem: Formations and Transformations,* ed. Marion Thain (Cambridge: Cambridge University Press, 2013), 157, 161–162.

65. Mill, "Thoughts on Poetry," 348.

66. Walter Blair and W. K. Chandler, *Approaches to Poetry* (New York: Appleton, 1953), 250. Lawrence Zillman, *The Art and Craft of Poetry* (New York: Macmillan, 1966), 161.

67. Jacques Rancière, *La Parole muette* (Paris: Hachette, 1970). *L'Absolu littéraire* is the title of Philippe Lacoue-Labarthe and Jean-Luc Nancy's account of the theory of German romanticism (Paris: Seuil, 1978).

68. Paul de Man, "Anthropomorphism and Trope in the Lyric," in *The Rhetoric of Romanticism* (New York: Columbia University Press, 1984), 256.

69. His hyperbolic formulation ("it and it alone") seems to borrow something from the lyricizing operations it traces, and thus ultimately links this poem to the possibility of lyric.

70. De Man, "Anthropomorphism," 261–262.

71. I should at least mention de Man's brilliant demonstration that in "Correspondances" the comme of comparison ("like"), which connects the material and the spiritual, turns at the end into a term of sheer enumeration, meaning "such as" ("Like amber and incense, musk, benzoin")—a "stutter" rather than an instrument or guarantor of meaning.

72. *The Lyric Theory Reader,* ed. Virginia Jackson and Yopie Prins (Baltimore: Johns Hopkins University Press, 2014), 270–271. The other main documents of this critique are Virginia Jackson, *Dickinson's Misery: A Theory of Lyric Reading* (Princeton: Princeton University Press, 2005); Jackson's entry for "Lyric" in the latest edition of the *Princeton Encyclopedia of Poetry and Poetics,* ed. R. Greene, S. Cushman, C. Cavanagh, J. Ramazani, and P. Rouzer (Princeton: Princeton University Press, 2012): 826–834; and the papers in "The New Lyric Studies," *PMLA* 123 (2008): 181–234.

73. Jackson, *Dickinson,* 7. Note that what criticism is said to efface are actually different ways of circulating poems rather than particular genres of poetry.

74. Cristanne Miller, *Reading in Time, Emily Dickinson in the Nineteenth Century* (Amherst: University of Massachusetts Press, 2012), 24, 37.

75. Jackson, *Dickinson,* 100.

76. Marjorie Perloff, *Poetic License* (Evanston, IL: Northwestern University Press, 1990), 12.

77. Charles Bernstein, "this poem intentionally left blank," *Jacket* 26 (2004). Available at www.jacketmagazine.com/26/ra-bern.html.

78. René Wellek, "Genre Theory, the Lyric and Erlebnis," in *Discriminations: Further Concepts of Criticism* (New Haven: Yale University Press, 1970), 251–252.

79. Jackson, "Lyric," 827.

80. Greene, "The Lyric."

81. Roland Greene, *Post-Petrarchism: Origins and Innovations of the Western Lyric Sequence* (Princeton: Princeton University Press, 1991), 4–5.

82. Bruce Robbins, "Afterword," *PMLA* 122 (2007): 1648.

3. Theories of the Lyric

1. Julia Kristeva, *La Révolution du langage poétique* (Paris: Seuil, 1974). It is worth mentioning that the English translation consists only of the first 200 pages of this 600-page work and omits the discussions of Mallarmé and Lautréamont. David Nowell-Smith, in his extremely resourceful *Sounding/Silence: Heidegger and the Limits of Poetics* (New York: Fordham University Press, 2013), goes far toward recuperating Heidegger for poetics, arguing that Heidegger "dismisses form in order to rethink form, dismisses beauty in order to rethink beauty, dismisses trope in order to rethink trope, and so on," and that what Heidegger values in *Dichtung* is achieved only through the "ontic" possibilities of its linguistic medium, through verse technique, trope and so on.

2. Parenthetical references are to *Hegel's Aesthetics,* trans. T. M. Knox (Oxford: Oxford University Press, 1975), two volumes but continuously paginated.

3. Isobel Armstrong, "Meter and Meaning," in *Meter Matters,* ed. Jason Hall (Athens, OH: Ohio University Press, 2011), 34. See also her "Hegel: The Time of Rhythm, the Time of Rhyme," *Thinking Verse* 1 (2011): 124–136; and Simon Jarvis, "Musical Thinking: Hegel and the Phenomenology of Prosody," *Paragraph* 28 (2005): 57–71.

4. Benjamin Rutter, *Hegel on the Modern Arts* (Cambridge, MA: Harvard University Press, 2010), 248.

5. Käte Hamburger, *The Logic of Literature,* 2nd ed. (Bloomington: Indiana University Press, 1993), 233–234.

6. Ibid., 235, 241, 266, 269, 271.

7. Ibid., 276–277, 285.

8. See *Figures du sujet lyrique,* ed. Dominique Rabaté (Paris: Presses universitaires de France, 1996); *Le sujet lyrique en question,* ed. J. de Serment, *Modernités* 8 (1996); *Sens et présence du sujet poétique,* ed. M. Brophy (Amsterdam: Rodopoi, 2006); and *Lyrisme et énonciation lyrique,* ed. N. Watteyne (Bordeaux: Presses universitaires de Bordeaux, 2006).

9. W. K. Wimsatt and Cleanth Brooks, *Literary Criticism: A Short History* (New York: Knopf, 1957), 675. For John Crowe Ransom's articulation of this view, see Chapter 6 below. *Perrine's Sound and Sense,* ed. T. Arp and G. Johnson, 14th ed. (New York: Cengage, 2013), 27. Helen Vendler, *Poems, Poets, Poetry* (Boston: Bedford/St. Martins, 2002), xlii, v–vi, 114. Though Vendler's text urges students to identify fictional speakers and fictional speech situations, she distinguishes dramatic monologues, where there are other people in the room, from lyric, where the speaker is alone.

10. Barbara Herrnstein Smith, *On the Margins of Discourse* (Chicago: University of Chicago Press, 1978), 8, 142. Smith, *Poetic Closure: A Study of How Poems End* (Chicago: University of Chicago Press, 1968), 17. *On the Margins of Discourse,* 28.

11. Smith, *Poetic Closure,* 19.

12. Ibid., 127. I take up this special lyric present for actions in Chapter 6. Fortunately, Smith's dubious framework of fictive utterance does not vitiate her compelling insights into the internal structures of poems—which I take to be another indication of its failure as a general theory of the lyric.

13. Ibid., 132.

14. Smith, *On the Margins of Discourse,* 135.

15. Though the dramatic monologue model could be seen as treating poems as drama, what is crucial is its emphasis on a fictional speaker and fictional speech situation, which is why I speak of fiction and novelizing.

16. Herbert Tucker, "Dramatic Monologue and the Overhearing of Lyric," in *Lyric Poetry: Beyond New Criticism,* ed. C. Hošek and P. Parker (Ithaca: Cornell University Press, 1985), 241–242. I consider the dramatic monologue as a particular lyric structure in Chapter 6.

17. Ibid., 243.

18. John Ashbery's "This Room" (discussed in Chapter 1), is another poem that would lend itself to such an investigation. Although it presents a first-person speaker, attempts to interpret it as a dramatic monologue produce unproductive puzzles and distract one from important questions of intertextual reference.

19. Kendall Walton, "Thoughtwriting—in Poetry and Music," *New Literary History* 42 (2011): 462–466. I am grateful to Joshua Landy for discussing Walton with me.

20. C. S. Lewis, *English Literature in the Sixteenth Century* (Oxford: Oxford University Press, 1954), 491.

21. Alessandro Barchiesi, "Carmina: Odes and Carmen Saeculare," in *Cambridge Companion to Horace,* ed. Stephen Harrison (Cambridge: Cambridge University Press, 2007), 150.

22. Pindar, *Olympian* 1, 1–2, and *Olympian* 2, 15–18. Trans. Mark Payne (in the article below).

23. Mark Payne, "Ideas in Lyric Communication: Pindar and Celan," *Modern Philology* 105 (2007): 8.

24. Readers of Larkin, accustomed to a more seriously reflective tone, might be inclined to take this as a dramatic monologue spoken by a vulgar drunk, but the lines "Man hands on misery to man. It deepens like a coastal shelf" ask to be read as poetic assertion.

25. Payne, "Ideas in Lyric Communication," 14.

26. Anthropological accounts of ritual are certainly relevant, although "Anthropology is littered with theories of ritual: a welter of labyrinthine arguments and complex, multi-clause definitions." Caroline Humphrey and James Laidlaw, *The Archetypal Actions of Ritual* (Oxford: Oxford University Press, 1994), 65. The ritualistic is characteristically experienced as (1) external to the actor; (2) involving conspicuous regularity not accounted for by communicative or other ends; (3) its meaning does not depend upon the intention of the actor; and (4) it prompts recognition and offers stimulation more than communication. Engaging works on the subject include Gilbert Lewis, *Day of Shining Red: An Essay on Understanding Ritual* (Cambridge: Cambridge University Press, 1980); Webb Keane, *Signs of Recognition* (Berkeley: University of California Press, 1997); and Roy Rappaport, *Ritual and Religion in the Making of Humanity* (Cambridge: Cambridge University Press, 1999).

27. Roland Greene, *Post-Petrarchism* (Princeton: Princeton University Press, 1991), 5, 7, 10.

28. Ibid., 11.

29. Ibid., 12.

30. J. L. Austin, *How to Do Things with Words* (Cambridge, MA: Harvard University Press, 1975). A simple test in English for the performative is whether one can insert "hereby": "I hereby promise," but not "I hereby read this book," because the action of reading is not accomplished by uttering a particular formula.

31. Jacques Derrida, "Signature, Event, Context," in *Margins of Philosophy* (Chicago: University of Chicago Press, 1984). See Jonathan Culler, "The Performative," in *The Literary in Theory* (Stanford: Stanford University Press, 2007).

32. The bibliography here is vast, but among the highlights over twenty-five years are Mary Louise Pratt, *Toward a Speech Act Theory of Literary Discourse* (Bloomington: Indiana University Press, 1977); Sandy Petrey, *Speech Acts and Literary Theory* (New York: Routledge, 1990); and J. Hillis Miller, *Speech Acts in Literature* (Stanford: Stanford University Press, 2002).

33. For example, W. H. Auden decided that his line "We must love one another or die," in "September 1, 1939" was a lie. See Chapter 7 below.

34. Stanley Cavell, "Performative and Passionate Utterance," *Philosophy the Day after Tomorrow* (Cambridge, MA: Harvard University Press, 2005), 173.

35. Barbara Cassin, "La performance avant le performative, ou la troisième dimension du langage," in *Genèse de l'acte de parole,* ed. Cassin and Carlos Levy (Turnhout: Brepols, 2011), 122–128. Hans Georg Gadamer, working in a different tradition, asks is there not in the poem "a kind of *Vollzugswarheit* [a truth that emerges through performance]? To carry out this performance is the task that the poem imposes." The work is thus "an event [*Ereignis*] that appropriates us into itself." *Gadamer in Conversation,* ed. Richard Palmer (New Haven: Yale University Press, 2001), 76, 71

36. Jacques Derrida, "Che cos'è la poesia?" in *A Derrida Reader,* ed. Peggy Kamuf (New York: Columbia University Press, 1991), 230.

37. Charles Baudelaire, "Fusées," in *Oeuvres complètes,* ed. Claude Pichois (Paris: Gallimard, 1975), vol. 1, 662.

4. Rhythm and Repetition

1. Roman Jakobson, "Linguistics and Poetics," in *Style in Language,* ed. Thomas Sebeok (Cambridge, MA: MIT Press, 1966), 354–355.

2. Northrop Frye, *Anatomy of Criticism* (Princeton: Princeton University Press, 1957), 271.

3. Ibid., 272.

4. Simon Jarvis, "What is Historical Poetics?" in *Theory Aside,* ed. Jason Potts and Daniel Stout (Durham, NC: Duke University Press, 2014), 112. Paul Valéry, "Poésie et pensée abstraite," in *Œuvres,* ed. J. Hytier (Gallimard: Paris, 1957), vol. 1, 1326, 1325. Robert von Hallberg, *Lyric Powers* (Chicago: University of Chicago Press, 2008), 27, 10.

5. Friedrich Nietzsche, *The Gay Science*, trans. Walter Kaufmann (New York: Vintage Books, 1974), 140

6. Susan Stewart's masterful *Poetry and the Fate of the Senses* (Chicago: University of Chicago Press, 2002) sees poetry as rescuing and preserving an experience of the senses increasingly threatened. I would emphasize, though, that the sensuousness of poetry is often impersonal and more inhuman than human.

7. For a fine discussion, see Geoffrey Hartman, *The Unmediated Vision* (New Haven: Yale University Press, 1954), 98–105.

8. Valéry, "Poésie et pensée abstraite," 1322, his italics.

9. Frédéric Lefèvre, *Entretiens avec Paul Valéry* (Paris: Le Livre, 1926), 62. T. S. Eliot, *On Poetry and Poets* (New York: Farrar, Strauss, 1957), 28. W. B. Yeats, "Four Lectures by W. B. Yeats, 1902–4," *Yeats Annual* (1991), 89. Nicolas Abraham, *Rhythms* (Stanford: Stanford University Press, 1995), 123.

10. Jean-Luc Nancy, *A l'écoute* (Paris: Galilée, 2002), 31–32.

11. Isobel Armstrong, "Meter and Meaning," in *Meter Matters,* ed. Jason Hall (Athens: Ohio University Press, 2011), 26–7.

12. Clive Scott, *The Poetics of French Verse* (Oxford: Oxford University Press, 1998), 93.
13. Frye, *Anatomy*, 81, 278–279. Frye, "Charms and Riddles," in *Spiritus Mundi* (Bloomington: Indiana University Press, 1976), 126, 135.
14. Scott, *Poetics of French Verse*, 89.
15. T. V. F. Brogan, "Rhythm," in *New Princeton Encyclopedia of Poetry and Poetics,* ed. Alex Preminger, T. V. F. Brogan, Frank J. Warnke, O. B. Hardison, Jr., and Earl Miner (Princeton: Princeton University Press, 1993), 1068. Valéry writes, "I have read or I have constructed twenty 'definitions' of Rhythm, of which I have adopted none." "Questions de poésie," in *Oeuvres,* vol. 1, 1289.
16. Andrew Welsh, *Roots of Lyric* (Princeton: Princeton University Press, 1978), 8, 196.
17. Brogan, *Princeton Encyclopedia,* 992. The term *prosody* has itself become a possible source of confusion. Long the name for the science of versification, including meter, sound-patterning, stanza forms, rhyme etc., in twentieth-century linguistics it has become the study of the rhythmic ordering of a language in general, including word and phrasal stress and intonation. The two uses are of course closely related, which only increases possibilities of confusion.
18. Paul Kiparsky, "The Role of Linguistics in a Theory of Poetry," *Daedalus* 102 (1973): 231–244, argues that what is relevant for poetry are units that are relevant for linguistics: there are no metrical systems that are based, for example, on number of sounds, but rather number of syllables or stressed syllables; and parallelism always involves units that are the same at some linguistic level of derivation. Even if this is so, this leaves a vast range of linguistic entities that are *not* selected for metrical systems.
19. But see Debra Fried, "The Stanza: Echo Chamber," in *A Companion to Poetic Genre,* ed. Erik Martiny (Oxford: Blackwell, 2012).
20. In *The Rise and Fall of Meter: Poetry and the English National Culture, 1860–1930* (Princeton: Princeton University Press, 2012), a brilliant study of debates about meter in nineteenth and early twentieth century England, Meredith Martin explores their entanglement with conceptions of national culture and demonstrates that there was no stable system of meter disrupted by the modernist embrace of free verse. This is a complex subject that will repay further study.
21. In ordinary spoken French this also varies according to the dialect of the user. Southern French dialects are distinguished by the pronunciation of the *e caduc:* "Cette petite fille" = sɛtə pətitə fijə.
22. The most notable exception is that a terminal *e caduc* can occupy the seventh position in a line if it is elided before a following vowel. Thus in *Oui, je viens dans son temple // adorer l'Eternel,* the *e* of *temple,* would be the seventh syllable, making the caesura fall inappropriately in the middle of a word, were

it not for the initial vowel of *adorer,* which allows the *e caduc* to be elided and the syllable not to count.

23. Benoît de Cornulier, *Théorie du vers* (Paris: Seuil, 1982), 69–76, contests the notion of four-beat alexandrines, as an idea resulting from a confusion of meter and rhythm and the determination to find *feet* in French verse, which he rightly deems unnecessary. His goal is to maintain the precision of metrical analysis and resist confusing it with attention to rhythm, but stress is indispensable to our perception of French verse rhythm and does not require feet.

24. Clive Scott, *Literary Translation and the Rediscovery of Reading* (Cambridge: Cambridge University Press, 2012), 121.

25. Clive Scott, *A Question of Syllables* (Cambridge: Cambridge University Press, 1986), 33–35. Scott, *Translating the Perception of Text* (Leeds: Maney, 2012), 111.

26. Brogan, "Meter," *New Princeton Encyclopedia,* 773.

27. Derek Attridge, *The Rhythms of English Poetry* (London: Longmans, 1982), 13–15. I am much indebted to Attridge's lucid and compelling discussions of English verse, as my frequent references to his books demonstrate.

28. Dana Gioia, "Meter-Making Arguments," in *Meter in English,* ed. David Baker (Fayetteville: University of Arkansas Press, 1986), 93. See Derek Attridge, *Moving Words: Forms of English Poetry* (Oxford: Oxford University Press, 2013), 159–164.

29. Attridge, *Moving Words,* 104.

30. Ibid., 106.

31. Derek Attridge, *Poetic Rhythm: An Introduction* (Cambridge: Cambridge University Press, 1995), 43, 53–54.

32. Attridge, *Moving Words,* 163.

33. Gerard Manley Hopkins, *Letters to Robert Bridges,* ed. Claude Colleer Abbott (Oxford: Oxford University Press, 1955), 246.

34. This powerful poem doubtless deserves some explanation: the Sibyl wrote prophesies on leaves arranged at the mouth of her cave, which had to be put in the right order. What is spelled on Sibyl's leaves is the fate of the *dies irae,* which brings the end of earth in its variety, as night engulfs everything, dismembering and disremembering all selves. The leaves of the Sibyl, like dragons on boughs, stand out against the steel grey of the sky like patterns on a sword (damask), and this oracle tells that life, formerly a multicolored tapestry, now unwinds onto two spools of fate, separating the sheep from the goats, parting, penning, into two groups, white and black, good and evil, which is all that counts now. These two possibilities struggle on the wheel of conscience—am I good, am I bad?—where thoughts grind against each other in torment.

35. Marina Tarlinskaja, "Metrical Typology: English, German, and Russian Dolnik Verse," *Comparative Literature* 44 (1992): 4. The form is common in English and German as well as Russian but in English has been regarded as "loose iambic" rather than having its own name. Here and in *Strict-Stress*

Meter in English Poetry Compared with German and Russian (Calgary: University of Calgary Press, 1993), Tarlinskaja presents compelling evidence that there exists a distinctive form. Derek Attridge's "An Enduring Form: The English Dolnik," in *Moving Words,* 147–187, demonstrates its pervasiveness in English popular and literary verse.

36. Anthony Easthope, *Poetry as Discourse* (London: Methuen, 1983), 64–77.
37. Attridge, *Moving Words,* 124.
38. Tarlinskaja, *Strict Stress-Meter,* 2–3.
39. Cornulier, *Théorie du vers,* and W. K. Wimsatt and Monroe Beardsley, "The Concept of Meter," *PMLA* 74 (1959): 585–598.
40. Henri Meschonnic, *Critique du rythme* (Lagrasse: Verdier, 1982), 216–217, 143.
41. Gabriella Bedetti, "Henri Meschonnic: Rhythm as Pure Historicity," *New Literary History* 23 (1992): 433—a convenient English-language account of Meschonnic's theory.
42. Richard Cureton, *Rhythmic Phrasing in English Verse* (London: Longman, 1992). His *Temporal Poetics,* is a multi-volume work in progress. For a succinct sketch, see his "Rhythm, Temporality, and 'Inner Form,'" *Style,* 2015. For discussion of Cureton's approach, see Attridge, *Moving Words,* ch. 2.
43. For discussion of the first two moments, see Klas Molde, "Lyric Enchantment and Embarrassment" (PhD diss., Cornell University, 2015).
44. Anne Finch, *The Ghost of Meter: Culture and Prosody in American Free Verse* (Ann Arbor: University of Michigan Press, 2000).
45. Needless to say, enjambment does not always lead to pauses at line breaks but sometimes provokes a speeding up to complete the syntactic unit.
46. Attridge, "Poetry Unbound: Observations on Free Verse," in *Moving Words,* 203–221.
47. Amittai Aviram, *Telling Rhythm: Body and Meaning in Poetry* (Ann Arbor: University of Michigan Press, 1994), 232–233, 5, 22.
48. Ibid., 159–160.
49. Ibid., 232–234, 21.
50. Mutlu Blasing, *Lyric Poetry: The Pain and the Pleasures of Words* (Princeton: Princeton University Press, 2007), 14, 53, 58.
51. Ibid., 2–3.
52. Ibid., 14. Wallace Stevens, *The Necessary Angel* (New York: Random House, 1951), 89.
53. Northrop Frye, *The Well-Tempered Critic* (Bloomington: Indiana University Press, 1963), 25–26.
54. For some of the more dubious attempts in the early twentieth century, see Michael Golston, *Rhythm and Race in Modernist Poetry and Science* (New York: Columbia University Press, 2008).
55. Fred Lerdahl and Ray Jackendorff, *A Generative Theory of Tonal Music* (Cambridge, MA: MIT Press, 1983), 73.

56. Stephen Cushman, *William Carlos Williams and the Meanings of Measure* (New Haven, CT: Yale University Press, 1985), 80.

57. Paul Valéry, *Vues* (Paris: la Table ronde, 1993), 291.

58. Roland Barthes, *Le Plaisir du texte, Œuvres complètes,* ed. Éric Marty (Paris: Seuil, 2002), vol. 4, 228.

59. Ibid., 258.

60. Adam Bradley's *Book of Rhymes* (New York: Basic Books, 2009) is a fine account of rap and its affinities with and deviations from the poetic tradition.

61. Stevens, *The Necessary Angel,* 32. Marjorie Perloff and Craig Dworkin, eds., *The Sound of Poetry and Poetry of Sound* (Chicago: University of Chicago Press, 2009), 1. Reuven Tsur, *What Makes Sound Patterns Expressive?* (Durham, NC: Duke University Press, 1992), 101. Baudelaire, "Théophile Gautier," in *Œuvres complètes,* ed. Claude Pichois (Paris: Gallimard, 1976), vol. 2, 118.

62. Quoted in Attridge, *Rhythms of English Poetry,* 289.

63. Tsur, *What Makes Sound Patterns Expressive?,* 20–35.

64. Von Hallberg, *Lyric Powers,* 11, 145.

65. Scott, *Poetics of French Verse,* 133–134.

66. Blasing, *Lyric Poetry,* 101.

67. Ibid., 106.

68. Richard Burton and Geoffrey Hill perform intriguingly different readings of this poem, available on YouTube: both read in a monotone but one very fast, the other slowly, with careful pausing and solemnity. These performances serve as a reminder of how far, as Clive Scott says, rhythm, especially in nonmetrical verse, arises in a reader's negotiation with the text.

69. In fact, much of the mimetic potential of sound patterning lies in readers' ability to slow down and lengthen the vowels as they read the word *slooowlyyy,* or to impart rising or falling rhythms when it seems appropriate. Since we would like our language to be an effective instrument of meaning, especially when reading poems, we can deploy an impressive array of paralinguistic features to that effect.

70. T. V. F. Brogan, *English Versification, 1570–1980* (Baltimore: Johns Hopkins University Press, 1981), 77. G. W. F. Hegel, *Aesthetics* (Oxford: Oxford University Press, 1975), 1137. John Milton, "Preface to *Paradise Lost,*" in *The Complete Poetry of John Milton,* ed. John T. Shawcross, rev. ed. (New York: Doubleday, 1971), 249. Simon Jarvis, "Why Rhyme Pleases," *Thinking Verse* 1 (2011): 30.

71. Anne Ferry, *By Design: Intention in Poetry* (Stanford: Stanford University Press, 2008), 21–25. James Longenbach compares two versions of this poem in which the rhymes are differently arranged. *The Resistance to Poetry* (Chicago: University of Chicago Press, 2004), 16–18.

72. The cognitive scientist Douglas Hofstadter has devoted a splendid 600-page book to this poem and reflections inspired by his multiple translations of it:

Le Ton Beau de Marot: In Praise of the Music of Language (New York: Basic Books, 1997).

73. James Wimsatt, "Rhyme/Reason, Chaucer/Pope, Icon/Symbol," *Modern Language Quarterly* 55 (1994): 24–25. Susan Stewart, "Rhyme and Freedom," in *The Sound of Poetry,* 37–39, 42.

74. Hegel, *Aesthetics,* 1031. Mallarmé, "Magie," in *Œuvres complètes,* ed. Henri Mondor and G. Jean-Aubry (Paris: Gallimard, 1945), 400.

75. Jay-Z, *Decoded* (New York: Spiegel and Grau, 2010), 243. "If the glove don't fit, you must acquit" was a memorable formulation by the defense in O. J. Simpson's trial for murder in 1995.

76. Wallace Stevens, "Man Carrying Thing," in *Collected Poems* (New York: Knopf, 1954), 350.

77. Stephen Booth, *Precious Nonsense* (Berkeley: University of California Press, 1998), 11.

78. Ibid., 5–6.

5. Lyric Address

1. Northrop Frye, *Anatomy of Criticism* (Princeton: Princeton University Press, 1957), 250. John Stuart Mill, "Thoughts on Poetry and Its Varieties," *Autobiography and Literary Essays* (Toronto: University of Toronto Press, 1981), 348.

2. Heinz Schlaffer argues that the lyric tradition has so accustomed readers to hearing poems address someone or something that we understand this to be the case even when there is no explicit addressee. *Geistersprache: Zweck und Mittel der Lyrik* (Munich: Hanser, 2012).

3. For apostrophe in recent American poetry, see Ann Keniston, *Overheard Voices: Address and Subjectivity in Postmodern American Poetry* (London: Routledge, 2006); in recent British poetry, Nancy Pollard, *Speaking to You* (Oxford: Oxford University Press, 2012).

4. When it could not be ignored, it was usually deemed a purely conventional element. A study of the ode, in which the figure is endemic, declares, "The element of address is of no especial significance, being merely a reflection of the classical influence. All the verse of antiquity was addressed to somebody, primarily because it was either sung or read and the traditions of song and recitation required that there be a recipient . . . The Romantic poets were so close to the classical tradition that they accepted the element of address as a matter of course, and we of the present are so remote from it that it seems a thing established in its own right." George N. Shuster, *The English Ode from Milton to Keats* (New York: Columbia University Press, 1940), 11–12. Proximity and distance, it seems, are equally good reasons for denying the significance of apostrophic address.

5. Earl Wasserman, *The Subtler Language* (Baltimore: Johns Hopkins University Press, 1959). M. H. Abrams, "Style and Structure in the Greater Romantic Lyric," in *From Sensibility to Romanticism,* ed. Frederick W. Hilles

and Harold Bloom (New York: Oxford University Press, 1965), 527–528. Since the publication of my essay "Apostrophe," *Diacritics* (1977), collected in *The Pursuit of Signs* (London: Routledge, 1981), the figure has become a topic of serious discussion. In addition to works noted earlier, see Paul Alpers, "Apostrophe and the Rhetoric of Renaissance Literature," *Represen-tations* 122 (2013): 1–22; Barbara Johnson, "Apostrophe, Animation, Abortion," in *A World of Difference* (Baltimore: Johns Hopkins University Press, 1989); William Waters, *Poetry's Touch* (Ithaca: Cornell University Press, 1983); Mark Smith, "Apostrophe or the Lyric Art of Turning Away," *Texas Studies in Literature and Language* 49 (2007): 411–437.

6. In *Les Fleurs du Mal,* for example, although 92 of 127 poems involve address to something or someone, only one poem beyond the inaugural "Au lecteur" addresses the reader (no. 38, "Un fantôme").

7. Heinrich Lausberg, *Handbook of Literary Rhetoric,* trans. D. Orton (Leiden: Brill, 1998), 339.

8. Often such work is done in a prologue: Victor Hugo introduces *Les Contemplations* with "When I speak to you of myself, I speak to you of you. Ah, fool, who believe that I am not you!"

9. Previously, "Poem of You, Whoever You Are," *Leaves of Grass* 1856. Available at www.whitmanarchive.org/published/LG/1856/poems/10. See William Waters's discussion of this poem in *Poetry's Touch,* 122–125. In "Whitman's Lyrics?" *Thinking Verse* 4: 1 (2014): 89–109, John Hicks notes a shift in the "Calamus" section introduced in 1860 from an expansive, encompassing "I" to a more lyrical mode with address to multiple "you"s.

10. See Jonathan Holden, "The Abuse of the Second Person Pronoun," in *The Rhetoric of the Contemporary Lyric* (Bloomington: Indiana University Press, 1980), and John Vincent, *John Ashbery and You* (Athens: University of Georgia Press, 2007).

11. John Ashbery, Interview, in *The Craft of Poetry,* ed. William Packard (New York: Doubleday, 1974), 123–124.

12. Edward Hirsch writes, "Once encountered, though, this fragment of consciousness can't be ignored or forgotten." Available at www.poetrysociety .org/psa/poetry/crossroads/old_school/on_john_keats_this_living_hand/. It has been argued that "This Living Hand" was intended as part of a play, but it is now read as an independent lyric.

13. W. R. Johnson, *The Idea of Lyric* (Berkeley: University of California Press, 1982), 34, 13.

14. Ibid., 3–4.

15. Ibid., 4.

16. "The vocative at the beginning . . . , *o plebs,* is unique." Eduard Frankel, *Horace* (Oxford: Oxford University Press, 1957), 289. There is also an address to Rome in 4.4: "What you owe to the Nerones, O Rome, / the Metaurus River testifies . . ." ("Quid debeas, o Roma, Neronibus, / testis Metaurum flumen . . .)", but this is the invocation of an abstraction, not address to the audience.

17. Johnson, *Idea of Lyric,* 25–26.

18. In addition, Pythian 2 addresses the city of Syracuse, but not as a collection of listeners: "O great city of Syracuse, sanctuary of/Ares mighty in war, divine nourisher of men/and horses delighting in steel,/to you I come from shining Thebes bearing this song." The two other odes that come closest, Isthmian 1 and Isthmian 7, apostrophically address Thebe, the eponymous nymph of Thebes: e.g. "Mother of mine, Thebe of the golden shield, I shall put your concern above even my pressing obligations." But this is only indirectly an address to an audience of Thebans.

19. Hayden Pelliccia, "Two Points about Rhapsodes," in *Homer, the Bible, and Beyond,"* ed Margalit Finkelberg and Guy Stroumsa (Leiden: Brill, 2003), 100.

20. Johnson does admit that "whether or not there was a girl to reject or accept the gift [of the poem] is beside the point." *Idea of Lyric,* 48.

21. The distinction between historical individuals and conventional addressees is not always easy to make: Michele Lowrie gives a census of addressees in *Horace's Narrative Odes* (Oxford: Oxford University Press, 1997), 22 n.3. Mario Citroni also offers a census devoted to finding as many historical addressees as possible: "Occasione e piani di destinazione nella lirica di Orazio," in *Materiali e discussioni per l'analisi dei testi classici* (Pisa: Giardini, 1983), 137.

22. Gregson Davis, *Polyhymnia: The Rhetoric of Horatian Lyric Discourse* (Berkeley: University of California Press, 1991), 6. Richard Heinze, "Die Horazische Ode" [1923], in *Vom Geist des Römertums* (Stuttgart: Teubner, 1960), 188. See the excellent discussion in Lowell Edmunds, *Intertextuality and the Reading of Roman Poetry* (Baltimore: Johns Hopkins University Press, 2001).

23. "Delicati" = "alluring" with a connotation of effeminacy. "Modes" are different rhythms or meters.

24. Kenneth Quinn, *Catullus: An Interpretation* (London: Batsford, 1972), 235, 280. On the contrary, C. J. Fordyce maintains, "The lines are 'To Calvus,' but Calvus did not need to be told what he was doing the night before; Catullus is writing for other readers." *Catullus: A Commentary* (Oxford: Oxford University Press, 1961), 215.

25. Paul Veyne, *L'Élégie érotique romaine* (Paris: Seuil, 1983), 196. David Wray, *Catullus and the Poetics of Roman Manhood* (Cambridge: Cambridge University Press, 2001), 107. In sum, "the poem was not written to be a private letter. In spite of the direct address to Licinius and the use of the vocative, the poem is addressed to an audience which is wider than one friend. The form of the poem is similar to poems 31 and 67, both of which are addressed to a specific recipient, but the recipient is an island in one case and a door in the other. It is evident that Catullus felt no hesitation in addressing a poem to a specific recipient even though it is written for a larger audience." William Scott, "Catullus and Calvus," *Classical Philology* 64 (1969): 172.

26. For instance, this poem "has been read as a narrative of the same transformation of superficial urbanity into profound seriousness that criticism has itself performed on Catullus." William Fitzgerald, *Catullan Provocations* (Berkeley: University of California Press, 1995), 110.

27. Giselle Mathieu-Castellani, "A qui s'adresse le message amoureux?" in *L'Offrande lyrique,* ed. Jean-Nicolas Illouz (Paris, Hermann, 2009), 57–76. Veyne, *L'Élégie,* 211. C. S. Lewis, *English Literature in the Sixteenth Century* (Oxford: Oxford University Press, 1954), 491.

28. Allen Grossman, *The Sighted Singer* (Baltimore: Johns Hopkins University Press, 1992), 13.

29. Baudelaire, *Oeuvres complètes,* ed. Claude Pichois (Paris: Gallimard, 1976), vol. 2, 164.

30. Quintilian, *Institutio Oratorio* IV, 1, 63–70, vol. 2 (Cambridge, MA: Harvard University Press, 1980), 41–45. Lausberg's *Handbook of Literary Rhetoric* mentions "the opponent in court; absent persons, living or dead; things (fatherland, laws, wounds, etc.)," 38.

31. John Hollander, *Rhyme's Reason: A Guide to English Verse* (New Haven: Yale University Press, 1989), 48.

32. Barbara Johnson, "Apostrophe, Animation, Abortion," 185. In "Romantic Aversions: Apostrophe Reconsidered," *English Literary History* 59 (1991): 141–165, Douglas Neale accepts Quintilian's definition and criticizes me for treating invocations that open poems as apostrophes ("O wild West Wind" or "Thou still unravished bride of quietness"), though he admits that both poetic handbooks and eminent critics call such address apostrophic. If we imagine that poems are addressed to the reader or listener in default of other indications, then we can think of the opening address to an urn as a turn from the default addressee. But be that as it may, Neale fails to show that anything would be gained by systematically distinguishing address that begins the poem from address that occurs later (which thus could count as a turn)—as in Keats's "Ode to a Nightingale," where the "light-winged Dryad of the trees" is not addressed until line 5. For a judicious discussion, see Alpers, "Apostrophe," 3–4.

33. Bernard Lamy, *La Rhétorique, ou l'art de parler* [1715], ed. C. Noille-Clauzade (Paris: Champion, 1998), 233. Pierre Fontanier, *Les Figures du discours* [1821 & 1827], ed. Gérard Genette (Paris: Flammarion, 1968), 372.

34. Geoffrey Hartman, *Beyond Formalism* (New Haven: Yale University Press, 1959), 193.

35. Gregson Davis writes, "the explicit performative *dicente* has the self-fulfilling effect of ennobling the addressee," with the result that "the scene of the utterance becomes certified as an authentic (albeit Roman) locus of lyric creativity." *Polyhymnia,* 127–128.

36. William Fitzgerald offers a brilliant reading of the sacrifice of the kid in relation to *poetic* pleasure, which is radically different from the ordinary pleasure offered by a cool spring in summer. "Horace, Pleasure and the Text," *Arethusa* 22 (1081): 98–102.

37. Ibid., 99.

38. Alpers, "Apostrophe," 7.

39. William Blake, *Complete Works,* ed. Geoffrey Keynes (London: Oxford University Press, 1969), 175, 151.

40. Alpers, "Apostrophe," 5.

41. Percy Shelley, "A Defense of Poesy," *Shelley's Prose* (Albuquerque: University of New Mexico Press, 1954), 281. Wordsworth wrote that because of a childhood "sense of the indomitableness of the spirit within me . . . I was often unable to think of external things as having an external existence, & I communed with all that I saw as something not apart from but inherent in my own immaterial nature." *The Fenwick Notes of William Wordsworth,* ed. Jared Curtis (London: Bristol Classical Press, 1993), 61.

42. I am grateful to Simon Jarvis for his persuasive resistance to an anti-narrative reading of this ode.

43. I shamelessly modify Alice Fulton's already excellent apothegm, "Fiction is about what happens next. Poetry is about what happens now." *Feeling as a Foreign Language: The Good Strangeness of Poetry* (St. Paul, MN: Greywolf Press, 1999), 7.

44. Heinz Schlaffer, *Geistersprache.* For an alternative view, which takes enchantment and disenchantment to be intricately imbricated aspects of lyric, see Klas Molde, "Enchantment and Embarrassment in the Lyric" (PhD diss., Cornell University, 2015).

45. Thanks to Roger Gilbert for alerting me to this extremely pertinent example.

46. William Empson, *Some Versions of Pastoral* (New York: New Directions, 1960), 57.

47. James Longenbach, *The Virtues of Poetry* (Minneapolis, MN: Greywolf Press, 2013), 134.

48. Shakespeare, Sonnet 19.

49. Harold Bloom, *Shelley's Mythmaking* (New Haven: Yale University Press, 1959), 75.

50. Alphonse de Lamartine, *Œuvres poétiques* (Paris, Gallimard, 1963), 392.

51. Jean-Jacques Rousseau, "Monuments de l'histoire de ma vie," in *Œuvres autobiographiques,* ed. Michel Launay (Paris: Seuil, 1967), 74.

52. For a rich investigation of lyric potential, see Avery Slater, "Prepostrophe: Rethinking Modes of Lyric Address in Wislawa Szymborska's Poetry of the Non-Human," *Thinking Verse* 4:1 (2014): 140–159.

53. Friedrich Kittler, *Das Nahen der Götter vorbereiten* (Munich: Wilhelm Fink, 2011), 69. I am grateful to Klas Molde for this reference.

54. Theodor Adorno, "On Lyric Poetry and Society," in *Notes on Literature* (New York: Columbia University Press, 1991), vol. 1, 41. Jane Bennett, *Vibrant Matter: A Political Ecology of Things* (Durham, NC: Duke University Press, 2010), viii.

55. For example, Bruno Latour, *Reassessing the Social: An Introduction to Actor-Network Theory* (Oxford: Oxford University Press, 2005).

6. Lyric Structures

1. Alastair Fowler, *Kinds of Literature* (Cambridge, MA: Harvard University Press, 1982), 114.

2. Helen Vendler, "Appendix 5: Lyric Sub-genres," in *Poems, Poets, Poetry* (Boston: Bedford/St. Martins, 2002), 683–685. The *Companion to Poetic Genre,* ed. Erik Martiny (Oxford: Blackwell, 2012) offers some twenty-six possible lyric genres in the titles of its forty-three articles. In addition to genres defined by verse form, it lists Aubade, Alba, Elegy, Self-Elegy, Aisling (a vision poem in which a woman representing Ireland offers a prophecy!), Nocturne, Verse letter, Short Long poem, War poem, Bestiary poem, Pastoral, Garden poem, Topographic poem, and Ekphrastic poem. It makes no claim to systematic treatment.

3. See Alastair Fowler, *The Country House Poem* (Edinburgh: Edinburgh University Press, 1994); Roger Gilbert, *Walks in the World* (Princeton: Princeton University Press, 1991); and for the "lyric of inconsequence," Anne-Lise François, *Open Secrets: The Literature of Uncounted Experience* (Stanford: Stanford University Press, 2008).

4. Northrop Frye, *Anatomy of Criticism* (Princeton: Princeton University Press, 1957), 293. Subsequent references will be given parenthetically in the text.

5. Robert D. Denham, "Northrop Frye and Critical Method," fig. 22, "Thematic Conventions of the Lyric," 123. Available at fryeblog.blog.lib.mcmaster.ca /critical-method/theory-of-genres.html. I am much indebted to his fine discussion of Frye's schematism of lyric (pp. 122–127), and to his production of the visual representation used here. Frye's notebooks for the *Anatomy of Criticism* contain several earlier and simpler versions of this diagram, which is constructed by Denham to represent as faithfully as possible Frye's exposition in the text of the *Anatomy,* where there is no chart.

6. Denham notes that since Frye cites Hopkins's poetry as a typical example of this convention, he labels this cardinal point "inscape" and its opposite "outscape." Although *inscape* is related to epiphany, since it denotes the complex of characteristics that makes something unique, it does not in fact seem a good term for this point in the circle, which is inner-directed and oracular.

7. This seems an odd description of the poem of ennui. Baudelaire's *Spleen* poems, for example, paradigmatic for this mode, are quite remarkable in their introverted refusal to mention specific worldly situations or causes, as they evoke an inner space: "J'ai plus de souvenirs que si j'avais mille ans" ("I have more memories than if I were a thousand years old"). Or "Et de long corbillards, sans tambours ni musique, / Défilent lentement dans mon âme . . ." ("And long funeral processions, without drums or music, file slowly through my soul").

8. *Northrop Frye's Notebooks for the Anatomy of Criticism,* ed. Robert Denham, *Collected Works,* vol. 23, (Toronto: University of Toronto Press, 2007), 95–96, 100.

9. Northrop Frye, *The Well-Tempered Critic* (Bloomington: Indiana University Press, 1963), 94.

10. Fowler, *Kinds of Literature,* 246–249. In another ambitious attempt to map literature, Paul Hernadi puts lyric in a rhombus with meditative poetry at the top, quasi-dramatic monologues at the bottom, songlike poems on the left, and poems that enact vision through an objective correlative on the right. In the middle would be "meditative odes or hymns addressing a god or a human being other than the reader." *Beyond Genre* (Ithaca: Cornell University Press, 1972), 166–167.

11. Frye, *Notebooks,* 135. He posits for his discussion an opening sentence: "The word 'lyric' indicates thousands of beautiful poems in lit—oh hell—the lyric may be the paradise of poetry, but it is the Augean stables of poetics, and the most I can hope is that my suggestions may be of some use to the next interested person." Ibid., 185.

12. See Richard Bradford, *Silence and Sound* (Rutherford, NJ: Fairleigh Dickinson University Press, 1992) for a fine discussion of the historical dimensions of this issue.

13. There is a long but minor tradition of the shaped poem, from the Greeks to the moderns. See Jeremy Adler and Ulrich Ernst, *Text als Figur: Visuelle Poesie von der Antike bis zur Moderne* (Wolfenbüttel: Herzog August Bibliothek, 1987); and, more conveniently, discussion in John Hollander, "The Poem in the Eye," in *Vision and Resonance* (New Haven: Yale University Press, 1985).

14. Max Jacob, "Le Coq et la perle": "Comme un bateau est le poète âgé, / Ainsi qu'un dahlia, le poème étagé. / Dahlia! Dahlia! que Dalila lia!" A (useless) translation would be: "The aged poet is like a boat, the layered poem like a dahlia. Dahlia! Dahlia! that Delilah tied."

15. Mary Louise Pratt, *Towards a Speech Act Theory of Literary Discourse* (Bloomington: Indiana University Press, 1977), 38–78. She adopts Grice's theory for a discussion of narrative, but it is even more pertinent to lyric.

16. Roland Greene, *Post-Petrarchism* (Princeton: Princeton University Press, 1991), 14.

17. Randall Jarrell, *Poetry and the Age* (New York: Knopf, 1953), 16.

18. John Crowe Ransom, *The World's Body* (Baton Rouge: Louisiana State University Press, 1938), 254–255.

19. See Elizabeth Howe, *Stages of the Self: Dramatic Monologues of Laforgue, Valery, and Mallarmé* (Athens: Ohio University Press, 1990), for a comparison of the two traditions.

20. Robert Langbaum, *The Poetry of Experience: The Dramatic Monologue in Modern Literary Tradition* (New York: Random House, 1957), 187–188.

21. David West, ed. and trans., *Horace Odes I: Carpe Diem* (Oxford: Oxford University Press, 1995), 42–44. Gregson Davis disagrees, seeing this as a

convivial poetic performance, not a fictional speech act. *Polyhymnia: The Rhetoric of Horatian Lyric Discourse* (Berkeley: University of California Press, 1991), 150–153.

22. Leo Spitzer, *Etudes du style* (Paris: Gallimard, 1980), 198–216, speaks of a "present of evocation."

23. Ralph Rader, "The Dramatic Monologue and Related Lyric Forms," *Critical Inquiry* 3 (1976): 133.

24. By "literary ballads" I mean simply ballads by recognized authors. Keats's stanzas rhyme normally but consist of three four-beat lines and a fourth two-beat line. Goethe's four-beat lines rhyme aabb.

25. *The Norton Anthology of Poetry,* ed. Alexander Allison et al. (New York: Norton, 1975). I count as in the past tense a poem without present tense or future tense verbs, except in subordinated positions. Vendler's *Poems, Poets, Poetry* provides an anthology with 194 poems in the present against 43 in past tenses, with another 11 moving from past to present.

26. Barbara Herrnstein Smith, *Poetic Closure* (Chicago: University of Chicago Press, 1968), 253.

27. Sharon Cameron, *Lyric Time: Dickinson and the Limits of Genre* (Baltimore: Johns Hopkins University Press, 1979), 204.

28. Suzanne Langer, *Feeling and Form* (New York: Scribner, 1953), 260. Strangely, John Crowe Ransom claims, "The tense of poetry is the past. More accurately, it is the pluperfect—the apodosis of a contrary-to-fact condition." *The World's Body* (New York: Scribner, 1938), 250. His argument is that lyric is nostalgic, either regretting what has been lost or re-creating a past experience. In his discussion, though, tense seems to be metaphorical, since the apodosis of a contrary-to-fact condition is not in fact in the pluperfect but the conditional perfect: "If you had not left [protasis], I *would have loved* you [apodosis]." Perhaps he has confused protasis and apodosis. At any rate, his claim is not fundamentally at odds with mine, since poems of nostalgia characteristically foreground the present in which the lack is felt, and poems that re-create the past may evoke it in the present.

29. See Langer, *Feeling and Form,* 269–277, for an excellent discussion of this poem and of the present tense in ballads, though I question her stress on the timelessness of the present and her conclusion that in general settings are given in the present and the events in the past.

30. Greene, *Post-Petrarchism,* 23, 49.

31. Wolfgang Kayser, *Das Sprachliches Kunstverk* (Bern: Franke, 1959), 339.

32. These are the opening lines of Shakespeare's Sonnet 129, Baudelaire's "Corrrespondances," and Emily Dickinson's Poem 254.

33. Rodney Huddleston and Geoffrey Pullum, *Cambridge Grammar of the English Language* (Cambridge: Cambridge University Press, 2002), 117, 119, 128.

34. Ibid., 129–130.

35. Langer, *Feeling and Form,* 268.

36. George T. Wright, "The Lyric Present: Simple Present Verbs in English Poems," *PMLA* 89 (1974): 563–566.

7. Lyric and Society

1. John Crowe Ransom, *The World's Body* (Baton Rouge: Louisiana State University Press, 1938), 131. Theodor W. Adorno, *Notes on Literature* (New York: Columbia University Press, 1991), vol. 1, 39. Jacques Rancière, *La Politique des Poètes* (Paris: Albin Michel, 1992), 9.

2. For similar denials of the appropriateness or the ability of the lyre to sing of war, see Odes 2.12 and 4.2.). Michele Lowrie analyzes Horace's ways of converting epic narrative and political thematics to lyric in *Horace's Narrative Odes* (Oxford: Oxford University Press, 1997).

3. See Christopher Nealon, *The Matter of Capital: Poetry and Crisis in the American Century* (Cambridge, MA: Harvard University Press, 2011).

4. G. W. F. Hegel, *Aesthetics* (Oxford: Oxford University Press, 1973), 976–977, 1006.

5. Robert Kaufman, "Adorno's Social Lyric and Literary Criticism Today," in *The Cambridge Companion to Adorno*, ed. Tom Huhn (Cambridge: Cambridge University Press, 2004): 354–375.

6. Benedict Anderson, *Imagined Communities* (London: Verso, 1991).

7. Walter Benjamin, "Some Motifs in Baudelaire," *The Writer of Modern Life* (Cambridge, MA: Harvard University Press, 2006), 171. For Bennett, see Jahan Ramazani, *Poetry and Its Others* (Chicago: University of Chicago Press, 2014), 75–79; and for postcolonial poetry generally, *The Hybrid Muse* (Chicago: University of Chicago Press, 2001). Daniel Tiffany, *Infidel Poetics* (Chicago: University of Chicago Press, 2009), and *My Silver Planet: A Secret History of Poetry and Kitsch* (Baltimore: Johns Hopkins University Press, 2014).

8. Leslie Kurke, "Archaic Greek Poetry," in *Cambridge Companion to Archaic Greece,* ed. H. A. Shapiro (Cambridge: Cambridge University Press, 2007), 158; Jeffrey Walker, *Rhetoric and Poetics in Antiquity* (Oxford: Oxford University Press, 2000), 16, 9.

9. Hesiod, "Theogony," 81–103, in *The Homeric Hymns and Homerica,* trans. Hugh G. Evelyn-White (Cambridge, MA: Harvard University Press, 1914), 85. Plutarch, "Life of Lycurgus," in *Plutarch's Lives,* trans. Bernadotte Perrin (London: Heinemann, 1914), vol. 1, 213–215.

10. Marcel Detienne, *The Masters of Truth in Archaic Greece* (New York: Zone Books, 1996). Pindar, seventh Isthmian Ode, lines 17–19.

11. On repeatable apothegms, see Mark Payne, "On Being Vatic," *American Journal of Philology* 127 (2006): 165. Plato, "Protagoras," in *Laches, Protagoras, Meno, Euthydemus,* ed. W. Lamb (London: Heinemann, 1924), 183–184, 93. Simon Goldhill, *The Poet's Voice: Essays on Poetics and Greek Literature* (Cambridge: Cambridge University Press, 1991), 168.

12. Plato, *The Laws,* trans. R. G. Bury (Cambridge, MA: Harvard University Press, 1926), vol. 2, 77, vol. 1, 245.

13. Ibid., vol. 1, 245–249.

14. Plato, *The Republic*, trans. Paul Shorey (Cambridge, MA: Harvard University Press, 1935), vol. 2, 465.

15. Gregory Nagy, *Pindar's Homer: The Lyric Possession of an Ancient Poet* (Baltimore: Johns Hopkins University Press, 1990), 114.

16. Gregory Nagy, "Theognis of Megara: A Poet's Vision of His City," in *Theognis of Megara: Poetry and the Polis,* ed. T. Figuera and G. Nagy (Baltimore: Johns Hopkins University Press, 1985), 27.

17. Daniel Javitch, *Poetry and Courtliness in Renaissance England* (Princeton: Princeton University Press, 1978), and William Kennedy, *The Site of Petrarchism: Early Modern National Sentiment in Italy, France, and England* (Baltimore: Johns Hopkins University Press, 2005).

18. See Nancy Armstrong, *Desire and Domestic Fiction* (Oxford: Oxford University Press, 1987).

19. Jacques Rancière, *Le Partage du sensible* (Paris: La Fabrique, 2000).

20. Petrarch, *Canzionere,* 71. Ullrich Langer, "The Lyrical Singular: Petrarch, Ronsard," Lecture, Cornell University, April 2013.

21. Roland Greene, "The Lyric," *Cambridge History of Literary Criticism,* vol. 3: *The Renaissance,* ed. Glyn P. Norton (Cambridge: Cambridge University Press, 1999), 222.

22. Wordsworth's memorable formulation in "Scorn not the Sonnet" is "with this key / Shakespeare unlocked his heart."

23. Helen Vendler, *The Art of Shakespeare's Sonnets* (Cambridge, MA: Harvard University Press, 1997), 47, 76. Christopher Martin, *Policy in Love: Lyric and Public in Ovid, Petrarch and Shakespeare* (Pittsburgh: Duquesne University Press, 1994), 5. On the Renaissance sonnet, see Walter Cohen, *A History of European Literature* (Oxford: Oxford University Press, 2016), ch. 8.

24. These are the opening lines of sonnets 129, 121, 116, and 94.

25. Sandra Bermann, *The Sonnet over Time* (Chapel Hill: University of North Carolina Press, 1988), 56–57.

26. Joel Fineman, *Shakespeare's Perjured Eye: The Invention of Poetic Subjectivity in the Sonnets* (Berkeley: University of California Press, 1986), 25.

27. Mary Lewis Shaw, *Cambridge Introduction to French Poetry* (Cambridge: Cambridge University Press, 2003), 111. Du Bellay's sonnet is listed as the fifth most frequently consulted poem on a major site for French poetry, "Poésie française: Les grandes classiques," www.poesie.webnet.fr/home/index.html.

28. John Stuart Mill, "Thoughts on Poetry and Its Varieties," in *Autobiography and Literary Essays,* ed. J. M. Robson and Jack Stillinger (Toronto: University of Toronto Press, 1981), 348.

29. William Wordsworth, "Preface" to *Lyrical Ballads,* in *The Prose Works of William Wordsworth,* ed. W. J. B. Owen and Jane Worthington Smyser (Oxford: Oxford University Press, 1974), vol. 2, 124.

30. Jacques Rancière, *The Flesh of Words: The Politics of Writing* (Stanford: Stanford University Press, 2004), 10, 9. Wordsworth, notoriously, passed from enthusiasm for the French Revolution ("Bliss was it in that dawn to be alive, / But to be young was very heaven!"), to sober conservatism, but his political opinions are not at issue here.

31. Jacques Rancière, *Politics of Literature* (Cambridge: Polity, 2011), 3, 4, 10.

32. Rancière, *The Flesh of Words*, 13, 19.

33. Ibid., 12–13, 15, 17.

34. Ibid., 19–20.

35. Wordsworth, "Preface," 120, 128.

36. Thomas Pfau, *Wordsworth's Profession* (Stanford: Stanford University Press, 1997), 249–250.

37. Ibid., 210–211, 228.

38. Ibid., 229.

39. Ibid., 123.

40. Wordsworth, *"The Ruined Cottage" and the "Pedlar"* (Ithaca, Cornell University Press, 1979), 374.

41. Pfau, *Wordsworth's Profession*, 11.

42. Marjorie Levinson, "Insight and Oversight: Reading 'Tintern Abbey,'" in *Wordsworth's Great Period Poems* (Cambridge: Cambridge University Press, 1990), 14–57. David Miall counters the claim of suppressing the social by investigating the nature of actual scene on the river a few miles above the Abbey. "Locating Wordsworth: 'Tintern Abbey' and the Community with Nature," *Romanticism on the Net* 20 (November 2000). Available at www.erudit.org/revue/ron/2000/v/n20/005949ar.html.

43. Levinson, "Insight," 2.

44. Ibid., 37, 46, 3. Levinson, "Revisionist Reading: An Account of the Practice," *Studies in the Literary Imagination*, 30 (1997): 123.

45. Theodor W. Adorno, "On Lyric Poetry and Society," in *Notes on Literature* (New York: Columbia University Press, 1991), vol. 1, 40. Subsequent references to this essay will be given parenthetically in the text.

46. Max Horkheimer, "Art and Mass Culture," in *Critical Theory: Selected Essays* (New York: Herder and Herder, 1972), 275.

47. In music and art, avant-garde creators compel Adorno's attention, but not in lyric. For a fine discussion, see Paul Fleming, "The Secret Adorno," *Qui parle?* 15 (2004): 97–114.

48. Adorno, *Aesthetic Theory*, trans. Robert Hullot-Kentor (Minneapolis: University of Minnesota Press, 1997), 123–124. *Ästhetische Theorie (Gesammelte Schriften*, vol. 7) (Frankfurt: Suhrkamp, 1970), 188. The German for the second quotation is: "Der Gestus, der darauf deutet, als wäre es anders gar nicht möglich, verklagt, wie es ist, durch Selbstverständlichkeit, die lückenlose Immanenz des Ritus hält Gericht über diesen. Nur durch Enthaltung vom Urteil urteilt Kunst. . . . Die Form, welche die Verse zum Nachhall eines mythischen Spruchs fügt, hebt deren Gesinnung auf. Echo versöhnt."

Hullot-Kentor translates "hebt deren Gesinnung auf" as "negates its fateful-ness" but it might better be taken to mean, as I have translated above, that there is a dialectical sublation *(aufheben)* of the poem's attitude, conviction, or way of thinking.

49. In a brilliant reading of Adorno, Sianne Ngai claims that the category of *cuteness,* which involves a protectively sentimental attitude toward the weak or diminutive (a consumerist aestheticizing of powerlessness), helps us to understand Adorno's *Aesthetic Theory,* with its strange focus on a poem like "Mausfallen-Sprüchlein" as a central example of critique. "If cuteness is a lighthearted aesthetic," she writes—alluding to the title of one of Adorno's essays—"an aesthetic of ineffectuality par excellence, one might say that there is, astonishingly, no better theorist of this minor taste concept than Adorno himself, seemingly the dourest defender of high modernism for the left." "The Cuteness of the Avant-Garde," *Critical Inquiry* 31 (2005): 840. See also Ngai, *Our Aesthetic Categories* (Cambridge, MA: Harvard University Press, 2012), 100–109. It is true, I think, that the mousetrap poem is cute, and that its power of critique for Adorno must be tied to the sense that it is harmless, powerless, despite its appearance of celebrating the slaughter of animals. But for Ngai categories such as the cute are valuable precisely for their ability to help explain the "remarkable smoothness" with which supposedly resistant art has integrated itself in consumer culture. Can the cute today judge by failing to judge?

50. Jacques Derrida, "Che cos'è la poesia?" in *A Derrida Reader,* ed. Peggy Kamuf (New York: Columbia University Press, 1991), 223, 233.

51. *The Letters of Robert Frost to Louis Untermeyer,* ed. Louis Untermeyer (New York: Holt, Rinehart, 1963), 47.

52. Thanks to Lytle Shaw for suggesting this connection.

53. W. H. Auden, "Forward," in *W. H. Auden: A Bibliography, 1924–1969,* ed. B. C. Bloomfield and Edward Mendelson, 2nd ed. (Charlottesville: University of Virginia Press, 1972), viii. Later he called it "the most dishonest" poem he had ever written. John Fuller, *W. H. Auden: A Commentary* (Princeton: Princeton University Press, 1998), 292–293. In context, I would note, this line does not really seem a lie: it is true that we will all die anyway, but the implication here is that only by loving one another will we survive collectively, and this is how I believe readers take it.

54. See Stephen Burt, "'September 1, 1939' Revisited, or, Poetry, Politics, and the Idea of the Public," *American Literary History* 15 (2003): 534.

Conclusion

1. Robert von Hallberg, *Lyric Powers* (Chicago: University of Chicago Press, 2008), 10.

2. Northrop Frye, *Anatomy of Criticism* (Princeton: Princeton University Press, 1957), 278–279.

3. Northrop Frye, "Charms and Riddles," in *Spiritus Mundi: Essays on Literature, Myth, and Society* (Bloomington: Indiana University Press, 1976), 126, 135.

4. Klas Molde, "Lyric Enchantment and Embarrassment" (PhD diss., Cornell University, 2015). He astutely offers a qualification: it is, at least, "indissociable from *some relation* to enchantment, however thin or negative this relation may be, and whatever capacious conception of enchantment this claim may require."

5. Von Hallberg, *Lyric Powers,* 4.

6. Susan Stewart, *Poetry and the Fate of the Senses* (Chicago: University of Chicago Press, 2002), 104.

Index